PREFACE

You now have the new, upgraded version of Turner Shakespeare's "Julius Caesar" in your hand.

Existing books on Shakespeare devote scores of pages on chapters which are of no consequence, especially from the examination point of view. Moreover, the answers of various aspects of each play are nothing more than an accumulation of paragraphs of criticism from various English scholars. Since two or more questions are clubbed together, and critical excerpts are joined by a few sentences, the students often do not get an authentic answer to any single question.

We need a cogent philosophy based on an inviolable sense of integrity if we, as students of Shakespeare, are to do complete justice to our existence. It is this inviolable, unimpeachable integrity that students will find throughout this book.

The book in your hand is so designed that it is as readily understood by school as by graduate and post-graduate students. Despite the simplicity, neither the lyrical quality of Shakespeare nor his comprehensive and profound understanding of human emotions is compromised. The book is thus of as much utility to serious scholars as to teachers and professors.

An attempt has been made to remove all shortfalls that are glaringly evident in other books on Shakespeare. This book contains:

(a) Answers to questions selected from question papers of universities and schools throughout India.

(b) Exhaustive notes explaining Shakespearean English and Latin, Greek and Biblical references.

(c) Paraphrase of the main text.

(d) Story and scene-wise summary of the play, along with critical comments.

(e) Reference to context (Annotations) selected from question papers of schools and colleges.

I hope you will find this book valuable for a better understanding of Shakespeare and for clearing your examinations with better marks.

Dr. Pravin S. R. Bhatia

Scene II: Forum / Brutus speaks to the
mob / Antony's oration /
The mob mad

Shakespeare's

Scene III: Cinna the poet-episode.

ACT IV

Scene I: Antony / Octavius & Lepidus meet

JULIUS CAESAR

& list out the people who should
die. y Antony & Octavius discuss
about / Lepidus's character.

Scene II: Camp @ Sardis / Brutus, Lucilius

EDITED BY
W. TURNER M.A. (Edinburgh)

Titinius & Pindarus opens the
scene / Cassius comes to Sardis

Scene III. Inside Brutus's tent clash between
Cassius & Brutus / All solved &
Cassius departs with Lucilius &
M_____ after marching plan
to building is confirmed for

S. CHAND & COMPANY LTD.

RAM NAGAR, NEW DELHI-110,055

the next day / Caesar's spirit.

S. CHAND & COMPANY LTD.
(An ISO 9002 Company)

Head Office : 7361, RAM NAGAR, NEW DELHI - 110 055
Phones : 23672080-81-82; Fax : 91-11-23677446
Shop at: **schandgroup.com**
E-mail: **schand@vsnl.com**

Branches :

No. 6, Ahuja Chambers, 1st Cross, Kumara Krupa Road, **Bangalore**-560 001. Ph : 2268048
152, Anna Salai, **Chennai**-600 002. Ph : 8460026
S.C.O. 6, 7 & 8, Sector 9D, **Chandigarh**-160017, Ph-749376, 749377
Pan Bazar, **Guwahati**-781 001. Ph : 2522155
Sultan Bazar, **Hyderabad**-500 195. Ph : 24651135, 24744815
Mai Hiran Gate, **Jalandhar** - 144008 Ph : 2401630
613-7, M.G. Road, Ernakulam, **Kochi**-682 035. Ph : 381740
285/J, Bipin Bihari Ganguli Street, **Kolkata**-700 012. Ph : 22367459, 22373914
Mahabeer Market, 25 Gwynne Road, Aminabad, **Lucknow**-226 018. Ph : 2226801, 2284815
Blackie House, 103/5, Walchand Hirachand Marg , Opp. G.P.O.,
Mumbai-400 001. Ph : 22690881, 22610885
3, Gandhi Sagar East, **Nagpur**-440 002. Ph : 2723901
104, Citicentre Ashok, Govind Mitra Road, **Patna**-800 004. Ph : 2671366

Published with New Improved Get-up 2001
Reprint with New Edition 2003
Reprint 2003

ISBN : 81-219-0939-2

PRINTED IN INDIA

*By Rajendra Ravindra Printers (Pvt.) Ltd., Ram Nagar, New Delhi-110 055
and published by S. Chand & Company Ltd.,
7361, Ram Nagar, New Delhi-110 055*

CONTENTS

CHAPTER 1

SHAKESPEARE AND HIS AGE

Sixteenth Century Europe was dominated by Kings

Europe in the sixteenth century was dominated by Kings. The Church of Rome had moulded the Middle Ages, which came to an end with the Reformation of Henry VIII (1529 – 39). Elizabeth I faced a short, difficult period, but she finally ensured that the monarch, and not the Church of England would mould the destinies of people. Elizabeth I was supreme largely because of the nation's desire for security at home.

The role of aristocracy

Yet, the Tudors could not have governed effectively without the help of a new kind of aristocracy that had emerged out of the new social churning.

The Age of Shakespeare and the Elizabethan Age

The period between 1528 to 1625 is termed as "The Elizabethan Age." Other critics call it "The age of Shakespeare", although Shakespeare was born in 1564. The era conveys the full idea of the beginning of Renaissance and its close. It began in 1558, when Elizabeth I became Queen and ended in 1625 when James I died. The Renaissance in England was thus bound up with the consolidation of the Tudor regime.

Renaissance and humanism

The term Renaissance means "rebirth". It ended the darkness of the middle ages and brought about the mental and spiritual rebirth which marked the beginning of the modern world. It brought about a revival of learning. There was re-discovery of antiquity which resulted in a new culture of humanism. The interest shifted from human sins and penance to human joys and rewards. The balance shifted to some extent from God to man. It created the new ideal of human perfection through superimposition of intellect upon philosophy. The Renaissance also brought a new spirit of inquiry, even into the control of the church over human destinies. The attention shifted from Rome to England, and from the Pope to the Crown. The effect of Reformation upon poetry is clearly evident in Spenser's works. This era saw a spirit of nationalism in England. Devout Christians shifted their allegiance from the Church of Rome to the security of national interest.

The effect of incredible discoveries

The Renaissance was given enormous (momentum) impetus by some incredible discoveries. In the last decade of the fifteenth century, Columbus discovered America, and Vasco da Gama went round the Cape of Good Hope. From then

1

onwards more and more ships began to cross the Atlantic Ocean. The world became bigger and better. This had great influence on English literature.

The invention of the printing press

The Renaissance also saw the invention of the printing press. This brought about great enthusiasm and impetus to learning. Education shifted away from the hands of the Church and became more secular.

Renaissance and vitality of language

What made the Renaissance age outstanding was its range of interests and vitality of language. The Elizabethan public was more trained in listening than in reading, and more accustomed to group life than to privacy. English language during this period became supreme in expressing sensation and the outward, demonstrative aspects of feeling. This meant a natural inclination towards drama. A tradition of entertainment in the form of pageantry became a celebration of communal events. This age also saw the rise of capitalism. This capitalism had opposing effects on society. It strengthened the monarch against Catholicism due to the printing press, but it also increased the gulf between the rich and the poor.

Renaissance challenged Aristotle's authority on learning

We must understand that before the advent of the Renaissance, higher education was largely based on Aristotle. Sir Thomas Aquinas reconciled Aristotle with medieval Christianity. The Renaissance challenged Aristotle's authority. The thrust was now in favour of more productive forms of scientific learning. The "new philosophy", written by Donne, "calls all in doubt". This sense of unrest was further depicted by Marlowe, Raleigh and Bacon.

Influence of Renaissance on Shakespeare

There can be no doubt that Shakespeare's greatness was enhanced due to the remarkable age in which he wrote. Spenser and Sidney had already mastered the verse, and Marlowe and the University Wits had excelled in the theatrical management of character and situation. This age saw literature becoming an instrument of reason. The theatre was the focal point of closest contact between humanism and popular taste. This period saw an ardent revival of the study of Greek. This brought about a distinct finesse to the earlier coarseness of English literature as well as language. Greek and Latin words were readily included into English usage. Classical literature brought a new dimension to mythology.

English translations of other literary works

The Renaissance was a period of great originality, but it had its rise in hundreds of ancient translations. Sir Thomas North translated Plutarch's "Lives" from French and John Elorio translated Montaigne's "Essais". Arthur Golding translated Ovid's "Metamorphoses", John Hartington translated

Ariosto's "Orlando Furioso" and Richard Carew translated Tasso's "Gerusalemme Liberata". These translations broadened the horizons of understanding and brought a pleasant suppleness to the English language. These also resulted in abundance of literary output. This literary output had new romantic elements. The quest was for the remote, the wonderful, and the beautiful. The familiar and the mundane were sidelined. This impetus to the new culture was provided primarily by Italy. Italianism was most evident in the stories and lively dramatic tales of Boccacio, Cinthio, Bandello and others.

English literary writers did not adhere to strict rules

Despite the influence of foreign literature, English literary writers did not adhere to their strict rules. This was apparent in the use of language and versification. There was no established grammar to fix any sterotype syntax. The tyrannical rules of grammar and versification were mostly overlooked as new styles and manners came into existence. There was admiration and respect for ancient precedents and traditional rules but there was no mindless acceptance of these rules.

Development of poetry was lesser than drama

Poetry too developed during this period, though its production was not as extensive as drama. Spenser's "Shepherd's Calendar" is still considered as the harbinger of great Elizabethan poetry. Spenser described poetry as "no arte, but a divine gift and heavenly instinct not to be gotten by labour and learning, but adorned with both :and poured into the witte by a certain enthusiasmos and celestial inspiration." This philosophy is closer to Plato's concept of art. It seemed to have penetrated more deeply than elsewhere into the spirit of English poetry.

Surge in lyrical poetry and blank verse

The adventurous spirit of the age was most evident in its dramatic poetry. Blank verse replaced the heroic couplet and Shakespeare gave enormous fluidity to the stiff end-stopped verse of Gorboduc. The temper of the age was lyrical and this age saw a surge of lyrical poetry. Its use began with Wyatt and Surrey and continued in the dramas of that age. The sonnet was an interesting extension of the lyric. Both the "Italian or Petrarchan form" and the "English or Shakespearean type" of sonnets flourished during this age.

Surge in descriptive and narrative poetry

This period also saw great enthusiasm for descriptive and narrative poetry. It began with Sackville's "Induction to the Myrroure of Magistrates", continued with Marlowe's "Hero and Leander "and Shakespeare's "Venus and Adonis" and "The Rape of Lucerce"and it culminated in Spenser's sumptuous allegorical poetry. These poems were distinguished by strong descriptive power, freshness of fancy, and sometimes by positive richness of style.

Surge in religious, satirical and didactic poetry

This period also saw the upsurge of religious, satirical and didactic poetry. It began with Gascoigne's "Steele Glas" and was followed by Donne's "Satires" and Hall's "Satires"

Breakthroughs in the essay, the novel and in literary criticism

The development of prose was somewhat sluggish during the Elizabethan age. The introduction of the printing press saw greater stress towards prose. This period saw some breakthroughs in the essay, the novel and in literary criticism. Some famous novels during this period were Sidney's "Arcadia", Lyly's "Euphuses", Bacon's "New Atlantis" and Nash's "The Unfortunate Traveller". Literary criticism was made famous by Sidney's "Apology for Poetry" and Daniel's "A Defence of Rhyme". The style of the prose of this period was dull and slow in the beginning. Though it made some development with the lapse of time, yet, it could not be considered modern.

This age was most remembered for its drama :

The Elizabethan age was most remembered for rapid advances made in the development of drama. This development began with the work of the University Wits—Peele, Greene, Lodge, Kyd and Marlowe. They added exuberance and vitality to scholarly tone of earlier drama. This spirit of exuberance was elevated to dizzy heights by Shakespeare between 1595 and 1615. This period saw the following types of drama:

(a) **Comedy.** The treatment of comedies was mostly romantic. The settings were imaginary as well as imaginative. There was considerable fancy. Despite this flight of fancy the plays were related to real life. Decker provided realism to comedy. Jonson's satirical realism was largely centered around the comedy of "humours." Comedy reached its most delicious elevation in the hands of Shakespeare.

(b) **Tragedy.** In dramatic history, the art of tragedy was fully developed by Shakespeare.

(c) **The revenge play.** The revenge play of Kyd was carried on by Chapman, and continued by Shakespeare (Hamlet), Beaumont and Fletcher (Maid's Tragedy). It was difficult to distinguish between revenge play and horror-drama.

(d) **Romantic tragi-comedy.** Beaumont and Fleteher (A King and No King) wrote these plays. The latter probably influenced Shakespeare in his last three plays "Cypmbeline", "Pericles" and "The Winter's Tale".

(e) **The chronicle drama was created by the University Wits.** Peele wrote Edward I, Marlowe gave us Edward II and Greene wrote James IV. Shakespeare was inspired by the University Wits and wrote plays of this genre.

(f) **The masque.** This type of play was written by Jonson, Fletcher and Shakespeare (The Tempest).

Famous poets of the Elizabethan age

The famous poets of the Elizabethan age were Sir Thomas Wyatt (1503 – 42), Henry Howard, Earl of Surrey (1516 – 47), Thomas Sackville (1536 – 1608) and George Gascoigne (1525 – 77). The most worthwhile poet of he age was, however, Edmund Spenser (1552 – 99). His famous poems were "The Shepherd's Calendar" (1579),"The Faerie Queene" (1589), "Prothalomion and Epithalamion" (1594),"The Amoretti" (1594) and "The Four Hymns" (1598). Spenser was the child of Renaissance and Reformation. This was most evident in his poems. Spenser may have been influenced by Taso, Plato and Ariosto, but his outlook in his poems was very modern. Other poets who wrote during this era were Sir Philip Sidney (1554 – 86), Christopher Marlowe (1564-93), Shakespeare (1584 – 1613), Ben Jonson and John Donne, who was famous for metaphysical poetry.

Renaissance's development in Europe and England

The Renaissance followed the middle ages. It began in Italy in the late fourteenth century and spread to other countries during the fifteenth and sixteenth century. The Renaissance affected every form of art, including painting, sculpture, architecture and literature. The Renaissance reached England late in the sixteenth century. It flowered only during the Elizabethan (1558 – 1603) and Jacobean Ages. John Milton (1608 – 74) was the last of the great Renaissance poets.

Infuence of the Mysteries and the Miracle Plays

The drama in England had its roots in the Mysteries and the Miracle Plays during the Middle Ages. Elizabethan drama was largely influenced by these plays. The first Miracle in England was "Ludus de Sancta" which was performed in Dunstable about the year 1110. For the next four centuries the Miracle Plays gained popularity in England. The Morality Plays superceded the Miracle Plays around the end of fifteenth century. It was not till 1556 that a true English play, comprising of a plot, acts and scenes was available to the English public.

Influence due to the revival of Latin literature

The revival of Latin literature had a decided influence upon English drama. The influence of Latin literature also restricted English drama due to the senseless adherance to the classical unities of time, place and action. These unities were flaunted by Shakespeare, despite considerable opposition from the University Wits. Sidney upheld the classic in his "Defense of Poesie". Finally, native drama prevalied, primarily because popular taste demanded it.

The establishment of theatres

The establishment of theatres was the beginning of regular drama. Lord Leicester's actors were given royal permit in 1574 "to give plays anywhere throughout our realm of England". By the time another thirty years had lapsed, at least seven regular theatres, and a dozen inn yards were established in the city or in the suburbs. The stage was primitive, and female parts were played by boy actors, because the law forbade women acting on stage.

Qualities of dramatists just prior to Shakespeare

The dramatists just prior to Shakespeare had some very noteworthy qualities. These qualities were :

(a) All of them were actors as well as dramatists.
(b) They started as actors, elevated to revising old plays, before becoming independent writers.
(c) They often worked together, as Shakespeare did probably with Marlowe and Fletcher.

Elizabethan theatres were crude and elementary

The initial regular theatres of the Elizabethan age were crude and elementary. A change of scene was conveyed through words. Shakespeare's dramatic language was considerably influenced by this need to convey the action of the scene through words. Elizabethan audience loved brisk action and violent stage effects. Their stage had an abundance of thunder and lightning, wrestling bouts and sword fights. The Fool was also a popular figure. The Elizabethans loved genial humour and droll philosophy. This was provided by the Fool. His songs further added to his charm. The favourite instruments of the stage were the lute, the fiddle and the viol de gamboys. The fool's song was accompanied by the pipe and the tabor.

CHAPTER 2

THE LIFE AND WORKS OF SHAKESPEARE

Shakespeare's birth

Shakespeare was born at Stratford-on-Avon in Warwickshire on 23rd April 1564. His mother Mary Arden descended from nobility and his father John was a prosperous businessman of the village. John and Mary had four sons and four daughters. William, the third child and the first son was christened on 26th April 1564. The only member of the group to survive the dramatist was his younger sister, Joan.

Shakespeare's father was a man of modest means

It is largely believed that John Shakespeare neglected his business in his inordinate zeal for public life. He lost heavily in business, and was in all probability a man of modest means.

Shakespeare's marriage

Shakespeare married Ann Hathaway in November 1582. Their first child, Susanah, was born in May 1583. In February 1585, Shakespeare and Ann had twins, Hamnet and Judith.

Shakespeare's initiation into drama

Some historians believe that Shakespeare was an ignorant youth who was driven from his careless rustic existence to a very different career in London. The same historians tell us that Shakespeare began by rewriting the plays of others, among them those of Robert Greene. This transformation from a village rustic to a literary figure has been left unexplained and appears highly improbable. Why the works of a writer like Greene, who boasted of a degree from both universities, should have been turned over to an illiterate new-comer, is hardly comprehensible ? There are some others who indicate a different and more natural course of events. Those who accept Beeston's version that Shakespeare was a schoolmaster would find it easier to understand his progress as a dramatist.

Shakespeare's arrival in London

Though no fixed date can be given for Shakespeare's arrival in London, it is normally accepted that he reached there in 1584. In any case, by 1594 he had to his credit the quantum of work which could have been possible only through a considerable number of years.

Shakespeare was trained as an actor

Shakespeare elevated to new, inconceivable heights. Some critics believe he was a born genius, while others believe he was a creation of his environment. There is no doubt that he was guided by public sentiment. He was trained, first as an actor, and then as a reviser of plays, before he started writing plays independently.

Shakespeare wrote 37 plays

Shakespeare wrote 37 plays. Out of these, there were 17 comedies, 8 tragedies and 12 histories. There has been a desire to group Shakespeare's plays into slots. This is a difficult exercise because Shakespeare mixed comedy and tragedy, and his historical plays could also have elements of comedy or tragedy.

Dowden's classification of Shakespeare's plays

The life of Shakespeare is mostly accepted to have four distinct phases. Edward Dowden broke them as follows :

(a) First period between 1584 and 1594 was named by Dowden **"In the Workshop"**, primarily because Shakespeare was still learning his craft.

(b) Second period between 1594 to 1599 was named **"In the World"** because Shakespeare was making rapid advances in the world of prosperity.

(c) Third period between 1599 and 1608 was named **"Out of Depths"** because Shakespeare probed deep into his sensibilities and created four great tragedies. This was also a period of inner turmoil.

(d) Fourth period between 1608 to 1613 was named **"On the Heights"** because this period saw Shakespeare ascending a pure and serene elevation from the earlier years of inner turmoil.

Classification of Shakespeare's comedies

Shakespeare's plays can also be divided as comedies, tragedies, histories, problem plays and romances. Shakespeare's comedies were romantic because they flaunted the rules of classical comedy, and they were written according to the dictates of his fancy. He mingled the tragic and the comic, the serious and the happy. These made his plays more realistic. Shakespeare's comedies can be classified as follows :

(a) They early boisterous comedies, written between 1584 and 1592.

(b) Joyous or sunny comedies, written between 1592 and 1594.

(c) Dark comedies, written between 1599 and 1608 .

(d) The later comedies or dark romances, written between 1608 and 1613.

Shakespeare's problem plays

The problem plays written by Shakespeare include :

(a) "Julius Caesar", because it had a series of conflicts in human motives. These conflicts appealed to the imagination. They were also extraordinary.

(b) "Hamlet", whose conflict was conveyed in the famous phrase "To be or not to be". This phrase evoked numerous interpretations.

(c) "Troilus and Cressida", which was sometimes called a satire, sometimes a comedy, sometimes a history and sometimes a tragedy. It was a reflection of the fading splendour of the Elizabethan age.

(d) "All's Well That End's Well" was partly a serious and partly a farcical comedy. It conveyed the intellectual blindness brought about by prejudices.

(e) "Measure for Measure" dealt with sexual licentiousness and state cruelty.

Classification of Shakespeare's tragedies

Shakespeare's tragedies may be divided as follows :

(a) His early tragedies(1584—1599). These include "Titus, Adronicus" and "Romeo and Juliet".

(b) His great tragedies (1599—1613). These include "Othello", "King Lear", "Macbeth" and "Hamlet" as well as "Julius Caesar", "Timon of Athens", "Antony and Cleopatra" and "Coriolanus". The last four are also categorised as Roman histories.

Dramatic Romances

Most critics, including the editors of the folio of 1623, divided Shakespeare's plays into comedies, tragedies and histories; but his last four plays "Pericles", "Cymbeline", "The Winter's Tale" and "The Tempest" cannot be put into any of these classification. They have tragic incidents but their ending is happy. This necessitated the evolution of a new term – "Dramatic Romances" – to fully express the characteristics of these plays.

Grouping of Shakespeare's plays in order of composition

Shakespeare's plays can be grouped in the approximate order of their composition as given in the diagram.

PERIOD	COMEDIES	HISTORIES	TRAGEDIES
	COMEDY OF ERRORS	1,2,3 HENRY VI	TITUS ADRONICUS
	TAMING OF THE SHREW	RICHARD III	
1584-1592 IN THE WORKSHOP	TWO GENTL-EMEN OF VERONA	KING JOHN	
	LOVE'S LABOUR'S LOST	VENUS AND ADONIS (Poem)	

		RAPE OF LUCERCE (Poem)	
	MIDSUMMER NIGHT'S DREAM	RICHARD II	ROMEO AND JULIET
	THE MERCHANT OF VENICE	1. HENRY IV	
1594 - 1599 LIFE IN THE WORLD	MERRY WIVES OF WINDSOR	2. HENRY IV	
	MUCH ADO ABOUT NOTHING	HENRY V	
	AS YOU LIKE IT		
	TWELFTH NIGHT		JULIUS CAESAR
	TROILUS AND CRESSIDA		HAMLET
1599 - 1608 OUT OF DEPTHS	MEASURE FOR MEASURE		OTHELLO
	ALL'S WELL THAT END'S WELL		TIMON OF ATHENS
			KING LEAR
			MACBETH
			ANTONY AND CLEOPATRA
			CORIOLANUS

	PERICLES— PRINCE OF TYRE	HENRY VIII	
1608 - 1613 ON THE HEIGHTS	CYMBELINE		
	THE WINTER'S TALE		
	THE TEMPEST		

Shakespeare's profundity defies classification

The grouping of histories, comedies and tragedies is more for the sake of convenience rather than a fool-proof division of his art. Shakespeare was too profound, his each work too complex to be fitted into a particular group. Critics grouped his plays as tragi-comedies and comic-tragedies, their preference based on whether the play was inherently tragic with a residue of comedy or the reverse.

Growth of Shakespeare as a dramatist

Some critics believe that Shakespeare wrote his earlier plays like "Titus Adronicus" in collaboration, and that the first play entirely written by him was "Love's Labour's Lost". It is remarkable that the earlier and the latest plays, this and the "Tempest", are apparently the most original in plot. Shakespeare's penchant for drama is evident in "Love's Labour's Lost". Shakespeare's period of apprenticeship lasted till he wrote the "Two Gentlemen of Verona" in 1592. Once Shakespeare went past this period most of the crudities and the doggerel disappeared. He began to use blank verse more and more in place of rhyme. Most historians date Shakespeare's plays as per the use of blank verse and rhyme. Shakespeare became a master of characterisation and plot. This advancement was more visible in "Romeo and Juliet", his earlier tragedy, and in "The Merchant of Venice" Shakespeare was an exceptional poet, but at no stage did he permit his poetic and lyrical faculty to dominate his drama. Shakespeare borrowed for his English Histories mainly from Holinshed's "Chronicles". He used this source in a very unique and effective manner. He took his subjects in a moral order, beginning with the weakest and the worst kings, and ending with his ideal of kingship in Henry V, which was written in 1599.

Shakespeare was at his best in his tragedies

Shakespeare abandoned English history and gave three masterpieces in comedy , "Much Ado About Nothing", "As You Like It", and "Twelfth Night", Shakespeare was at his playful best in these comedies as he turned

nature as his ally. After these three comedies Shakespeare shifted his attention
to his Roman histories. He wrote "Juluis Caesar" in 1601, followed by "Antony
and Cleopatra" and "Coriolanus". He borrowed his sources from Plutarch for
his Roman histories. From 1602 began the period of the great tragedies,
"Hamlet", "Othello", "King Lear" and "Macbeth" and the dark comedies,
"Measure for Measure" and "Troilus and Cressida". It is unanimously accepted
by critics that tragedies were Shakespeare's greatest plays. Even amongst
these Shakespeare perhaps was at the height of his dramatic ability in "King
Lear", where he blended his language and metre to heighten the dramatic
effect of the play.

Shakespeare's last plays

For the small group of last plays, "Pericles", "Cymbeline", "The
Winter's Tale" and "The Tempest" the name "romances" has been suggested.
These plays have scenes of pardon and reconciliation. Whether these in part
explain the poet's approaching retirement to Stratford or not, the calmer and
serener outlook to life is very much an extension of the Shakespearean magic.

CHAPTER 3

SHAKESPEARE'S MIND AND ART

Shakespeare's universality

It is widely accepted that Shakespeare's supreme gift was his universality. He was not of an age but for all times, because his plots and characters were true to the eternal aspects of human life and not limited to any society. It is also widely accepted that Shakespeare was too great to be identified with his own characters. Shakespeare effectively hid himself behind his creation. He had a delicacy of understanding. Very little escaped his penetrative mind. He conveyed complex ideas with geniality and simplicity. Despite depiction of vulgarity and a rather broad humour, it is also universally accepted that he had profound respect for human worth. There were times when he doubted humanity's ability to counter evil, but he regained his faith in man quickly.

Dowden's classification loosely depicts Shakespeare's art

Shakespeare did evolve his mind and his art as a dramatist. This prompted some critics to divide Shakespeare's art into distinct periods. The most effective division was undoubtedly by Dowden. His picturesque licence divided Shakespeare's career into four parts, "In the Workshop", "In the World", "Out of Depths" and "On the Heights". These four stages do loosely depict Shakespeare's dramatic progress as much as they depict the natural course of a pilgrim's process. That Shakespeare himself emerged from darkness to attain that bright, solemn vision achieved by sages is neither a surety nor a necessity. It is criminal to classify a genius, and Shakespeare's most primitive work was still a masterpiece in its own right. Shakespeare's plays were created by a distinct philosophy about life and art. He did not superimpose his personality on his plays. He did not, for instance, have the artistic selfishness of Goethe. He wrote with peaceful humanism. He understood and sympathised with all that surrounded him, but he never seemed to lose control when surrounded by conflicting emotions. Coleridge was wrong when he labelled Hamlet as the perplexed and brooding Shakespeare and Prospero as the royal and calm Shakespeare. Shakespeare's sensibilities were too large to be limited to any one of his creations.

Shakespeare's penetrative sensibility

A man torn by the problems of evils, the injustice of universal laws, the betrayal of innocence, the triumphs of villainy, may write burning verse, the lyrics of a Shelley, the epic of a Byron, but Shakespearean tragedies could not be written by a defeated spirit. They are too royally designed, too

13

masterfully controlled, guided, rounded and finished to be considered the creation of a suffering man. Shakespeare saw and understood too much, could pierce the heart with too many passions, could fathom the real rhythm of life, without being tied to the rack of any power. There was no moral philosophy or conduct of life that he did not touch upon, and no mystery that he did not probe. He excelled in the perfect naturalness of dialogue. In all his impassioned dialogues, each reply is a mere rebound of the previous speech. Every natural interruption, lack of restraint due to tempestuous passion, hasty interrogative, ardent reiteration to evade a question, scornful repetition of hostility are as alive in Shakespeare's dialogue as in life itself.

No distinct Shakespearean philosophy exists

A lot of critics and historians have tried to establish a distinct Shakespearean philosophy. There is no doubt that he was endowed with supreme wisdom. Most people are tempted to think that his thoughts constituted a distinct body of doctrine. In truth, no Shakespearean philosophy exists. Shakespeare's genius was an end product of his extraordinary pliability which let him convey the most divergent, the most striking, and the most ingenious arguments in his plays. His naturalism made him convey life as he saw it. He depicted whatever he considered remarkable or striking. He chose artistically rather than intellectually. He showed frigidity and sexual passion, love and hatred, wisdom and stupidity with equal passion. He left it to his readers to arrive at their own judgement. He was so successful because he had no desire to preach his audience. He did not belong to any creed or party. He offered no ready-made solutions to the problems faced by humanity. He knew life was complicated and unexpected business, and that our fortunes did not always answer to our hopes, or to our deserving. However, his final message was not one of despair. He had enormous faith in man, and he knew that man would one day assert himself over the conflicting vicissitudes of existence.

He wrote on diverse topics

Shakespeare wrote on diverse topics. His main concern appeared to be the upliftment of society. He was, as Ben Jonson put it "not of an age, but for all time". He could communicate with all other minds, without any particular bias. As a poet he was gifted with imagination, fancy, observation, analysis and the divine gift of song. This contributed to his unique success as a dramatist. He had greater absolute vision, transcendental imagination and creative power than any writer known.

He asserted himself through style and versification

Despite his desire to hide behind his plays, Shakespeare's personality asserted itself in his plays through his language, style and versification. He had all the faults and virtues of his age. Yet, his style was unmistakably unique and his very own. His dramatic skills alone were sufficient to make him immortal, but he was also a great poet. This was most evident in the lyrical quality of the songs in his plays. He fused the lyrical and dramatic with exquisite finesse in his plays. This elevated the level of his plays to a more exalted height, without diluting the precise proportions of their constituent elements. His myriad images were exalted, his metaphors were triumphantly wedded to his words. They created an extremely sonorous symphony. He used blank verse in plays, but shifted to rhyme for his songs, where he managed to inspire hearts without compromising with probability.

He was alert, noble and energetic

Shakespeare was indefinably alert and noble. He was also prodigiously energetic. Age could not wither, nor custom stale his charm. He was different things to different people. He appealed to the wit as well as the buffoon, to the courtier as well as the "groundlings of the pit". He delineated the Fool with a distinct philosophy. The Fool advanced Shakespeare's own standpoint as a comic dramatist; the idea that the deepest and greatest things in life may be hidden from the wise and the prudent and be revealed to children and fools; that however much the stupid and the simple may be overwhelmed by confusion and ignominy that pervades in the world, they are allowed the right to appeal to a higher court; that what matters is not wealth and rank, but native and unassuming humanity. Shakespeare believed life's purpose was for our good. He accepted love, patience and forgiveness as virtues, and worthy of endeavour. He obviously agreed with Hamlet that "What a piece of work is man... How like a God!"

His character-interest was independent of performance

Some critics believe that character-interest in Shakespeare's plays was independent of performance. They also accept that Shakespeare was careless in the construction of plot. This may be somewhat of an exaggeration but it carries an undeniable truth. Shakespeare's characters were termed as "ideal realities" by Coleridge. Lamb thought that they were objects of meditation, where their intellectual activity and aspiring spirit inspired us more than their actual actions.

His tragic characters were better than his comic characters

Not a single literary writer has come even remotely close to the quality and range of Shakespeare's characters. His tragic characters were greater than those in his comedies. It could hardly have been otherwise. His character of comedy were as a rule, normal. They were straight-forward and likable. They had normal human virtues and vices. Shakespeare's tragic characters, however, were unusual, complex and even abnormal. Hamlet was the most complex character delineated by Shakespeare. He was so complex that no two critics can agree what Shakespeare had in mind while delineating him.

His humour was broad, sunny and varied

Shakespeare's humour was broad and varied. As per Meredith it was "as ten thousand beeves grazing on a sunny hillside." His humour was an extension of his deep knowledge of nature. It was sunny due to his profound sympathy of mankind. His many-sided humour did not permit him to pledge himself to any one view of life. As per Samuel Johnson, "In tragedy he is always struggling after some occasion to be comic but in comedy he seems to repose, or to luxuriate as in a mode congenial to his nature... His tragedy seems to be skill, his comedy to be instinct". He abounded in kindly mirth. His humour was dramatic. He could mingle humour with beautly, or with pathos, or with thought. He had no bitterness in his laughter. It was unadulterated joy and it was full of humanity. Shakespeare did lack moderation in his use of wit. Johnson regretted that his irrepressible impetuosity could not be checked. This led Shakespeare into a muddle from which he could not extricate himself. Johnson comments about his inordinate use of quibble thus. "A quibble is to Shakespeare, what luminous vapours are to the traveller. He follows it at all adventures; it is sure to lead him out of his way, and sure to engulf him in the mire... A quibble, poor and barren as it is, gave him such delight that he was content to purchase it, by the sacrifice of reason, propriety and truth. A quibble was to him the fatal Cleopatra for which he lost the world and was content to lose it".

He flaunted the classical unities of time and place

Some critics object to his technique of combining tragic and comic elements, because it flaunted the classical unities of Greek drama. He chose this because he found both joy and sorrow in life. Samuel Johnson comments, "He had no regard to distinction of time or place, but gives to one age or nation without scruple, the customs, institutions, and opinions of another at the expense not only of likelihood, but of possibility".

Shakespeare's concept of love

Shakespeare thought of love in terms of the sun, and moon and the stars, night skies and vast seas, of spring and summer. He saw engagement in love as a game, a quest, a war, a sickness, a willing servitude, and the fulfillment of human beings. To him love was a kind of wealth. It was a merchandise. Juliet bought "a mansion of a love". Romeo wished to seek "adventure for such merchandise". The two loved as a commercial enterprise. The Princess in "Love's Labour's Lost" refused to grant her love immediately, and to "make a world-without-end" bargain. Troilus considered himself a "merchant" and "Cressida a pearl". In Shakespeare's plays, giving in love is, however, more important than getting. The acceptance of "love's truth" depends on the imagination of the audience. Even the sustained theme of appearance versus reality depends on the imagination of the audience. "The Merchant of Venice" stressed the point of outer versus inner beauty concept of love. "All that glisters is not gold", and what the eyes perceive might be a falsity. Shakespeare believed in love at first sight, as was evident in all his comedies, but he wanted modulation in love, as was evident in "Romeo and Juliet". There was plenty of wooing in his plays. Love also depended on the lover's ability to seek true beauty. Ideal love to Shakespeare meant mutual sharing, generosity, truth and order. A Shakespearean comedy was a story of love which culminated in marriage. It was a play where almost all characters were in love. This resulted in a surfeit of marriages at the end. The love depicted by Shakespeare was everlasting. It uplifted and inspired the lover and the loved.

Shakespeare's delineation of women

George Bernard Shaw believed that "in Shakespeare it is women who always take the initiative". Women are vastly superior to men in terms of moral and intellectual resources. They have greater pluck and wit than men. Those critics who believe that Shakespeare's women characters act not on thought but on instinct consider Shakespeare's character-delineation in a limited way. Portia and Cleopatra were bold and rational women, though Rosalind and Celia in "As You Like it" may appear to be inspired by instincts rather than by thoughts and action. William Hazlitt thought that Shakespeare's "women were... exquisite logicians; for there is nothing so logical as passion. They knew their own minds exactly; and only followed up a favourite purpose, which they had sworn to with their tongues, and which was engraven on their hearts, into its untoward consequences. They were the prettiest little set of martyrs and confessors on record."

Use of soliloquy as a perfect stage device

Shakespeare used the soliloquy as a perfect stage device. He employed it :

(a) As a device for telling the story.

(b) As a means for analysing the psychology of a character.

(c) For creating a humorous effect.

(d) For creating a tragic effect.

The dramatic purpose of a soliloquy

The soliloquies revealed the most intimate thoughts of his characters. They were integral to his plays, mainly because they contributed to action as well as to characterisation, and were never mere lyrical ornamentations. The purpose of a soliloquy is self-revelation, specially of contemplative persons. It is a device to probe the hidden recesses of a person's nature. It sometimes provides information. Sometimes, specially in case of villains, it serves as an explanation. With Shakespeare it gave information regarding the secret spring as well as outward course of the plot. Shakespeare used the soliloquy extensively in his tragedies. The most complex and exquisite soliloquies undoubtedly belonged to "Hamlet".

Division of his plays as per use of metre

Shakespeare's use of metre is an important parameter for historians to fix the sequence of his plays. Metrically, Shakespeare's plays can be divided into four periods. These are :

(a) **Vanity of Rhyme (1584 – 1594).** This was a period of Shakespeare's weakness for rhyme. He wrote more by sound than by sense. It was a desire to make his writing decorative.

(b) **Balance of Power (1594 – 1600).** A mature and balanced handling of style and thought were evident in this phase. It had less of rhyme and more of prose. The lines ran on more than before. Double endings too were more on the increase.

(c) **Discordant weight of thought (1600 – 1606).** This is the period of the great tragedies and the bitter comedies. There is major deviation in blank verse. Thought outweighs expression. There is a rise in dramatic force, and poetry is integrated to the play. The lines are split up. Speeches are cut short in the middle of lines, there is frequent evidence of short broken lines. Shakespeare is almost inarticulate. His imagery is clouded and his verse is spasmodic. Prose descends to the level of everyday use.

(d) **Of weak endings (1606 – 1613).** Shakespeare uses the metre with careless freedom. He luxuriates in weak endings. His verse is now on occassions as flat as prose.

Shakespeare's use of blank verse

Shakespeare's plays had about two thirds of blank verse, less than one tenth of rhymed verse, and less than a quarter of prose. The basis of blank verse is the iambic pentameter. Shakespeare elevated the blank verse from the monotonous use made by his predecessors with skilful and adventurous changes. His blank verse changed in character and movement as his thoughts became more profound. He varied it to suit the purpose of his tragedies, comedies and histories.

Shakespeare's use of prose

Shakespeare used prose when he wished to lower the dramatic effect without wanting to make it appear poetic. He used it when he wanted to convey the impression of people talking together. A prime example of creative use of prose was in "As You Like It". Touchstone never spoke even once in rhyme. His alteration between prose and verse suggested change of moods or circumstances. Shakespeare also used prose :

(a) For his comic characters, like the clowns of his comedies.

(b) For peasants, servants, soldiers, and other characters of humble background.

(c) For conversation in scenes of "low type", such as the grave-diggers' scene in "Hamlet".

(d) For letters, proclamations and documents.

(e) For depiction of mental imbalance. Hamlet, Ophelia and King Lear used prose in their insanity.

Shakespeare flaunted the Aristotelian unities

The Aristotelian unities of time and place were consistently flaunted by Shakespeare. He only adhered to unity of action. "The Tempest" and "The Comedy of Errors" were the only two plays where Shakespeare observed all the unities of classical drama. Shakespeare ignored the unities, despite immense criticism from his contemporaries, because he did not find them conducive to his style of writing.

Shakespeare's comedies were romantic

Shakespeare's comedies were considered romantic for many reasons. He flaunted the rules of classical comedy, and he wrote according to the dictates of his fancy. He mingled the tragic and the comic, the serious and the joyous. This made his plays appear more realistic. The main characteristics of a Shakespearean comedy were as follows :

(a) It was romantic because it flaunted the unities, and also because it was an escape from the sordidness of everyday life.

(b) It had a world of romance, where realism was introduced in very subtle terms.

(c) It was poetic and imaginative, but it was not fanciful or unrealistic.

(d) It was a story of love which culminated in marriage.

(e) It was a story in which love came virtually to every character of the play.

(f) Its love was everlasting.

(g) It had an abundance of music, dance and merry making.

(h) The fool was an intrinsic part of his comedy. He was at the same time a butt, a critic, a satirist and a wit.

(i) The course of love did not run smooth, but it always triumphed in the end.

(j) The God of Shakespeare's comedy was benevolent and helpful to lovers.

(k) The fate of the tragedies, existed in a milder from in his comedy as fortune. It was sympathetic.

(l) His comedy had superfluity, improbability and absurdity. These added to the charm of the play.

(m) It did not adhere to the unity of time and place, barring "The Tempest" and "The Comedy of Errors".

(n) The characters were gentle, kind, merry and humorous.

(o) Women dominated the action in his comedy and men had suppressed voices. The heroines generated an abundance of sunshine.

(p) Shakespeare's humour was totally devoid of bitterness or cruelty. His satire was rare, and only limited to satire of manners.

Shakespeare's histories

Shakespeare depicted the horrors of civil war in his histories. He gave us the picture of an ideal monarch at the head of a united nation in Henry V. His plays on English history depicted six kings. He began portraying kingly weaknesses and ended portraying kingly strengths. These eight plays on English history contained one single drama. He conveyed that retribution inevitably caught up with selfish kings. Shakespeare's political philosophy was one of social stability, in the form of a hierarchy of rank or degree, crowned by the monarch. Skakespeare believed that the king must be wise, of strong character, and have a firm policy.

Shakespeare's response to tragedy was intellectual

The main concern of Shakespeare's tragedy was with truth and with the pleasure that knowledge invariably provides. Plato had used the word catharsis to mean purification and sublimation. Accepting this meaning, Aristotle believed that tragedy, first by arousing pity and fear, ultimately sublimated and raised the spectator to a state of understanding. Aristotle believed that pity and fear distorted our vision of truth. Tragedy took us through various rational responses, culminating in intellectual purification. Plato's approach to tragedy was emotional. Aristotle sought an intellectual response to tragedy, and that response applied consistently to Shakespeare.

Bradley's concept of Shakespearean tragedy

As per A.C. Bradley, "A Shakespearean tragedy..... is a story of exceptional calamity leading to the death of a man of high estate." Bradley himself accepted that Shakespearean tragedy was clearly much more than this. The tragic hero was a man of exceptional quality. His fall was a direct consequence of a fatal flaw, or an excess of some character or trait (known as "harmartia"). His flaw led to his downfall, and because of his status, to the downfall of others around him. Since the fall was in excess of the flaw, it aroused emotions of pity and fear in the audience to such an extent that they were purged off these emotions (known as "catharsis").

Dramatic Romances

Shakespeare last four plays, "Pericles," "Cymbeline," "The Winter's Tale", and "The Tempest" could not be included by the editors of the Folio of 1623, as comedies, tragedies or histories, because they did not fit into any of these classifications. They had tragic incidents with happy endings. This necessitated an evolution of a new term – "Dramatic Romances" – in order to provide a distinct slot for these four plays. The atmosphere of these plays indicated the development of a new art in Shakespeare. The turmoil seen in Shakespearean tragedies was not evident in these plays. Some critics accused Shakespeare of being pessimistic till he wrote these plays. In the Romances, Shakespeare seemed to be in a state of perfect peace of mind. His God was just and benevolent, and he was convinced that justice would ultimately prevail. He introduced genial emotions like reconciliation, forgiveness, kindness and tolerance in these plays. His comedies had sunshine, but in the Romances the new found sunshine and joy was wrung out of experience. He no more agonised over evil. He accepted it with fortitude. He advocated forgiveness, gentle atonement, tying together of human bonds and reuniting of parted kindred. Enemies and wrongs were pardoned. Repentance was gentle and painless. Shakespeare created an atmosphere where love could flourish between enemies and friends. The style of these plays was an extension of the style acquired by him in his tragedies. The thought was rapid, the expression was fast and fluent, sometimes even at the expense of logic.

CHAPTER 4

THE STORY OF THE PLAY

The period is 44 B.C. in Rome. It is a period of political uncertainty and strife. Caesar has just returned after defeating Pompey's sons. There is double celebration due to the feast of Lupercal (February 15). The ignorant people forget their woes and cheer Caesar. This worries the free-born patricians. They are convinced Caesar has become inordinately ambitious, and that he will soon be crowned king. Two tribunes, Flavius and Marullus, openly criticise Caesar infront of a huge crowd. They further show their disrespect by removing the trophies won by Caesar from the statutes existing in the city.

Cassius, is the most bitter critic of Caesar. He decides, along with Casca, Cinna and a few others to plot Caesar's downfall. They decide that it will be impossible to counter Caesar's might without the help of Marcus Brutus. He is the most honourable man in Rome. Their intrigue will have an air of respectability if Brutus joins them.

Soon the traditional foot race begins. Amidst hectic activity, a soothsayer approaches Caesar and tells him to, "Beware the Ides of March". Caesar is annoyed by the Soothsayer and he angrily dismisses him. Cassius is left free with Brutus. He arouses Brutus' fear about Caesar's ambition.

Caesar leaves the festivity in a disturbed state of mind. As he leaves, he tells Mark Antony to be wary of Cassius. After Caesar leaves, Brutus and Cassius talk with Casca, who tells them that Caesar was offered the crown of Rome thrice. Casca makes it appear as if Caesar wanted the crown but refused it in order to deceive the public about his ambition. He tells Brutus and Cassius that Caesar went into an epileptic fit when he heard the cheering of the crowd.

Brutus loves Caesar dearly, but he loves Rome even more. He decides to sacrifice Caesar for the good of Rome. He, however, refuses to kill Antony, despite ardent pleas from the other conspirators. He wants to be a sacrificer and not a butcher. He must not kill without a reason.

A month later, it is the eve of the Ides of March. A terrible storm blows in Rome. It portends that something unnatural will happen. Cicero meets Casca. The latter narrates a series of disturbing and unnatural events. Cicero soon leaves, and a badly shaken Casca is joined by Cassius, who thinks that the storm is a warning of impending trouble if Caesar were to become king. Cinna joins the two and receives instructions from Cassius to throw an inflammatory letter into Brutus' window, in a manner that the latter receives it by chance. It would be from one of the citizens, pleading him to do something to prevent Caesar from fulfilling his inordinate ambition. The three depart after deciding to meet later at Pompey's Porch, where Decius Brutus, Trebonius, and Metellus Cimber await them.

Brutus receives the letter thrown by Cinna. The letter finally makes up his mind to join the conspirators against Caesar. He leaves the next morning with Caius Ligarius to join the other conspirators in their prearranged plan to accompany Caesar to the Capitol.

Portia, Brutus' wife and Calphurnia, Caesar's wife are both in turmoil. They both have forebodings of impending disaster. Calphurnia requests Caesar not to step out of the house. Caesar's priests too advice him to stay indoors. They too portend disaster as a consequence of the sacrifices and religious rituals made by them. Caesar is about to relent when Decius Brutus intervenes. He gives a new and more favourable interpretation to Calphurnia's dream the previous night. Caesar decides to ignore the warnings of his priests and his wife, and leaves for the Capitol. He is accompanied by Mark Antony, Senator Publius, and all the conspirators, except Cassius.

As Caesar approaches the Capitol he is warned by Artemidorus and a soothsayer. Caesar angrily dismisses them. Once they all reach the Capitol, the conspirators manage to take Mark Antony away from Caesar. The conspirators then surround Caesar. Metellus Cimber presents a petition to Caesar. He begs Caesar to revoke the banishment order of his brother. Other conspirators, including Brutus, request Caesar to revoke his order of banishment. Caesar refuses to revoke the order. The conspirators then stab Caesar. Brutus delivers the final fatal blow on him.

Mark Antony had fled on seeing Caesar's assassination. He, however, returns to the Capitol. He pretends to seek the approval of the conspirators in order to remain next to Caesar's body. The conspirators leave him alone with Caesar's body. Antony pledges to avenge Caesar's murder. He seeks Brutus' permission to address the citizens of Rome. Cassius is wary of Antony, but Brutus overrules his objection and permits Antony to speak to the crowd. It is Brutus who speaks to them first. He tells the crowd that he loved Caesar, but he loved Rome more. Since Caesar had become ambitious, he had to kill him. It was the only way to prevent the citizens of Rome becoming his slaves. He then requests the crowd to listen what Mark Antony has to say. Antony arrives at the rostrum and displays "sweet Caesar's wounds". The crowd sees the wounds and is roused into anger. Antony then begins to speak. He tells the crowd about Caesar's virtues, and the generous bequests that he had made in favour of the citizens of Rome. The crowd becomes fully incensed. It cries for vengeance. The conspirators are forced to flee from Rome. Antony joins hands with Octavius Caesar and Lepidus in order to overthrow the conspirators. This new triumvirate decides to oppose the military threat of the conspirators.

The triumvirate decides who all must die. Among them is the son of Antony's sister. Antony readily agrees that he will have to die. The three decide to reduce Caesar's legacies in order to raise money for the forthcoming battle. Antony and Octavius then agree to join their forces and set out in pursuit of the conspirators, who have encamped in Sardis.

In the camp of the conspirators, Brutus learns that his wife, Portia has committed suicide. She swallowed burning coals after she could not bear the separation from her husband. She had learnt about the might of the triumvirate and this made her extremely scared about her husband's safety. Brutus accepts his wife's death with stoic resignation, despite growing apprehension. Cassius is a source of worry for him because he has considerably reduced the supply of funds for Brutus' army. Brutus comes to an uneasy compromise with Cassius over funds. After bitter differences over tactics, it is decided to implement Brutus' plan and advance to Philippi and meet the army of the triumvirate there. The same night Brutus is visited by Caesar's ghost, who tells him that the two will again meet at Philippi.

The two armies meet for battle on the plains of Philippi. Both armies seem to be plagued with inner dissensions. The decision to meet the enemy at the plains of Philippi instead of letting it come to the heights of Sardis is to soon become a costly blunder.

At Philippi, Brutus sends Messala to Cassius with a plea to move at once against the army of Octavius. Cassius cannot comply because his army has been forced to retreat by Antony's troops. Brutus accuses Cassius' troops for looting Octavius' troops, after victory over them, instead of coming to the rescue of his troops.

Later, in battle, Cassius becomes so confused that his mind starts sending dangerous signals. He mistakenly believes that his messenger, Titinius, has fallen into the hands of the enemy, which means that they have lost the battle. Cassius asks Pindarus to stab him. Titinius returns with Messala. He stabs himself, when he finds Cassius dead. Messala conveys this tragedy to Brutus, who leaves to engage the enemy, after bidding a sad farewell to Cato, Strato, Volumnius and Lucilius.

Brutus inspires his men for one last battle with the enemy. Lucilius is captured by Antony's troops. They mistake him for Brutus until Antony recognises him. Brutus 'army is defeated. Brutus tells his friends, Clitus, Dardanius and Volumnius to help him commit suicide. Strato finally agrees to hold his sword while Brutus falls upon it and dies.

Antony enters with Octavius, Messala and Lucilius, and finds Strato holding Brutus' body. Antony declares that Brutus was "the noblest Roman of them all". Octavius orders an honourable burial for Brutus, before they leave to share the joys of victory.

CHAPTER 5

ACT-WISE, SCENE-WISE SUMMARY

ACT I : SCENE I

Julius Caesar celebrates his triumphant return to Rome after defeating Pompey's sons. The trophies won by him are hung on the statues of Rome. The year is 44 BC. There is added festivity due to the feast of Lupercalia (February 15 as per the English calendar). The citizens of Rome are out on the streets in large numbers. The crowds cheer Caesar's defeat. They believe it is the end of one of the most destructive civil wars that tore the Roman world apart. Rome had celebrated victories over foreign powers in the past. This is the first time it was celebrating victory over one of their own citizens. This divides Rome among those who support Caesar and those who are opposed to him.

Two tribunes, Flavius and Marullus enter. They have the power of a magistrate and hence are legally very sacred to the people of Rome. They rebuke a number of craftsmen for absenting themselves from work and aimlessly coming out on the streets of Rome to celebrate the death of one of their own. The Roman citizens enjoy feasts of any kind. For them Caesar's return is another opportunity to make merry. They ignore the chiding of the two tribunes, who are opposed to Caesar and plot to murder him. They are extremely bitter of the manner in which some of the craftsmen cheered Pompey's triumphal procession when he returned as a hero not so long ago. Now, they cheer his death, and the two tribunes are extremely bitter at their flippant nature.

Flavius and Marullus then decide to remove all the trophies won by Caesar from the statues on which they had been displayed. They also remove other decorations like wreaths and neck-garlands.

Commentary

The opening scene of a Shakespearean tragedy is of crucial importance. It establishes the central theme that is to dominate throughout the play. The present scene discloses the impending assasination of Caesar. Some members of Rome's nobility are scared of Caesar's inordinate ambition. They think he wants to become king. It is their aim to retain senate rule. The conflict in the play is provided by Caesar's alleged dictatorship and the establishment of rule by majority by those opposed to him. The scene also portrays that the civil strife is far from over after the death of Pompey's son. The present feast is the lull before the storm.

There is no doubt that Caesar is popular and strong; yet some members of the nobility are prepared to put their own lives at stake and challenge the might of Caesar. The two tribunes come out on the streets of Rome in order to incite the commoners against Caesar. They are horrified that Caesar can generate so much passion after killing some of their own.

It is obvious that the patricians have not won the sympathy of the crowd. It keeps quiet when the two tribunes order them. However, some members of the crowd indulge in private repartee as soon as the tribunes are out of hearing range.

The nobility may worry about Caesar's power but they themselves treat the commoners with contempt. This irony is not lost on the audience. The contempt of the tribunes reflects the hypocrisy which powerful men indulge in. They do not wish to give power to the people. They only wish to usurp it themselves.

The opening scene also brings into sharp focus the fickleness of the common people. They had once cheered Pompey; they are now prepared to cheer the death of his sons. He was once a hero; he has now vanished from the collective sensibilities of the Roman citizens. This fickleness of the mob will remain the undercurrent by which two opposing sides gain advantage over one another.

ACT I : SCENE II

A triumphant Caesar enters Rome. He tells his wife Calphurnia to stand by the side of Mark Antony, who is to run the traditional foot race of the Lupercal. Antony had already been instructed by Caesar to touch Calphurnia while running. Romans believed that barren women conceived if they were touched by one of the runners of Lupercal. Calphurnia had not conceived for a long time and Caesar had hoped that she would become pregnant if touched by Mark Antony.

A soothsayer approaches Caesar and tells him to "Beware of the Ides of March". Caesar pays no attention to the soothsayer, and the procession continues. Two conspirators, Brutus and Cassius, drop out of the procession. They admit to each other that they would hate to be present when Caesar is made King. There is rumour that Caesar will be offered the crown of Rome. Cassius tries to probe Brutus' feelings about Caesar. When he realises that Brutus is not very well disposed towards Caesar, Cassius discloses his own resentment at the thought of how powerful Caesar has become. Brutus tells Cassius that he loves Caesar but he hates the kind of inordinate power that he has acquired for himself. Cassius ceases this opportunity and tells Brutus about Caesar's physical and mental weaknesses and the comparative strength of Brutus. He is convinced that Brutus is the best candidate to lead a fight against tyranny. Cassius compares himself and Brutus with Caesar and declares that Caesar is not extraordinary. He is convinced that their own lowered esteem has made Caesar so powerful. Brutus fails to comment on Cassius' bitter remarks but the fact that he listens so patiently reveals he is not fully opposed to his views.

The two hear loud shouts from the direction of the forum. These loud shouts are repeated once again. Cassius becomes more bitter against Caesar after the shouts, while Brutus is a picture of concentration.

The games of the Lupercal come to an end. An angry Caesar returns with his procession. There is fear on the face of Calphurnia and an inner seething rage on the face of Cicero. Suddenly Caesar's eyes fall on Cassius. He tells Mark Antony that Cassius worries him. He is too thin and discontented. Such men must be constantly suspected. Caesar is not afraid of Cassius, but he is constantly weary about his motives. Antony is convinced that Cassius is not powerful enough to cause any harm.

Brutus tells Casca to remain behind with him. Casca tells Brutus that Mark Antony had offered a crown-like coronet on three occasions to Caesar. On each occasion Caesar had set it aside. Casca is convinced that Caesar set it aside reluctantly in order to show the citizens of Rome that he did not wish to become king. The crowd applauded enthusiastically in approval. Then Caesar fell on the ground in an epileptic fit. Casca is contemptuous of the sweaty, foul smelling mob. Cassius wants to know where his political sympathies lie. Casca refuses to commit himself. He says that Cicero was also amused by the events concerning Caesar. He was, however, scared to openly comment against Caesar. He spoke to his supporters and friends in Greek. They understood what he was saying, and smiled.

Brutus leaves, after promising to think about what Cassius has said. He also promises to meet Cassius the next day. Cassius, left alone, in a solilosquy, reveals his concern over winning Brutus' sympathy. He decides to forge a few letters and drop them at places where Brutus can receive them. These letters will be written on behalf of eminent citizens of Rome. They will implore Brutus to save them from Caesar's tyranny.

Commentary

This, and the previous scene, are examples of how Shakespeare converted his play into acts and scenes in order to cater to the primitive nature of the Elizabethan stage. Flavius and Marullus leave from one side of the stage in Scene I and Caesar enters from the other in Scene-II.

This may be Caesar's first appearance on stage, and not all events may have been explained in the play itself. This need not worry us too much because the Elizabethan audience was completely aware of Roman history, perhaps because they were themselves on the verge of creating an empire. They must have considered Caesar as a monumental figure, which means that Shakespeare did not have to sing paeans in the greatness of Caesar. It also means that he could concentrate on the conspirators without making them lose their sublimity. The conflict of the play could not have been intense had Shakespeare depicted them only as stupidly jealous men. In many ways, the conflict is as much about democracy and dictatorship, and about tyranny and freedom, as it is about conflict between Caesar and the conspirators. Shakespeare retains Caesar's greatness and shifts his attention to the lack of understanding by the conspirators about Caesar's true greatness. Shakespeare provides sublimity to the conspirators by giving sufficient hints about Caesar's innermost desire to become king. This motive never surfaces in the entire play. Shakespeare's greatness lies in managing to give his hero a negative emotion without making him lose his sublimity.

Throughout the scene, Shakespeare establishes the power Ceasar has on the citizens of Rome. Antony underlines this power when he says, "When Caesar says 'Do this', it is performed". Caesar is depicted as someone who is consciously arrogant, fearless and one who inspires fear. He contemptuously disregards the soothsayer as somebody who is an ineffectual dreamer. Shakespeare knows how seriously the superstitious audience of his time accepted omens and auguries. He uses them as powerful dramatic devices to increase the anticipation of the audience.

This scene also displays dramatic irony. This irony may be unconscious, as when Cassius calls Caesar "immortal" at the very moment when he has plans to kill him. It may also be conscious where the characters interpret one thing but the audience is aware of a deeper significance. The friend who warns Caesar is his future assassin. This face is known to the audience but not to Caesar. Caesar's arrogant dismissal may be an extension of his own courage, but the audience knows that it will bring about his downfall.

It is worthy of mention that the soothsayer's warning is actually given to Caesar by Brutus. Brutus' first line in the play has a distinct ironic touch to it. It also reveals his character. He is a stoic and he lacks the "quick-spirit" of Mark Antony. Shakespeare delineates him as graceful and cold, dispassionate but not without undercurrents of resentment and disdain.

It is obvious that Brutus is "with himself at war". Caesar is a personal friend, but his growing ambition is a painful aberration to Brutus. Cassius takes advantage of Brutus' confusion to try and win him over in a plot to assassinate Caesar. For nearly one hundred lines Cassius does all the talking, in a masterful display of insinuation and persuasion. He begins cautiously, with restrained praise of Brutus. Brutus is a stoic. He believes that man must neither react to pain nor to pleasure. Cassius is aware of this but he is also aware that no man rises above the level of pleasure that praise provides to him. After the initial praise Cassius circumvents around the subject of Rome and Caesar. He does not bring up the subject of assassination till Brutus talks about his fears that Caesar may become king, as he hears shouts form the crowd. Shakespeare uses the shouts as a brilliant dramatic device. It brings Brutus' subconscious fears about Caesar's inordinate ambition to the surface. Brutus may love Caesar, but he would not let a foolish mob give Caesar the kind of powers that will make him a despotic dictator. Cassius is clever enough to wait till Brutus talks about the danger that would befall on Rome if Caesar were to become king. Cassius is too cunning to press home his advantage even when Brutus conveys his fears. He talks about honour instead. He knows this is of crucial importance to Brutus. Cassius links the idea with freedom instead of intellectual truth. He wants Caesar murdered and Brutus may join in the plot in the name of honour, freedom and the welfare of the citizens of Rome. Cassius talks about the time when he rescued Caesar from the River Tiber. This seemingly senseless story drives home two points. It reduces Caesar's godlike superiority and makes him appear as ordinary as any human being. Cassius also mentions Aeneas, Rome's great ancestor. Brutus is immediately reminded of the traditional republican freedom that Aeneas stood for when he fought against the royalist Tarquins. Brutus is sufficiently incited to fury. He yells, "why man, he doth bestride the narrow world like a Colossus."

Cassius takes this as a cue to attack Caesar openly. Now his appeal to justice and morality are accompanied by personal jealousy and violent resentment. He even calls Caesar "a sick girl" while they find themselves peeping into "dishonourable graves". Now it becomes evident that Cassius does not merely want to strip Caesar of his power; he wants it for himself.

Brutus is non-commital throughout the scene. He initially wonders what Cassius wants from him. Shakespeare wishes to delineate Brutus as an outwardly honourable man who does not have the depth to understand the kind of political intrigue that Cassius can mount. Cassius is delineated as a consummate manipulator who incites men into terrible deeds without letting any accusation fall on him. Shakespeare deliberately keeps Brutus unaware of what Cassius has in mind. Shakespeare keeps the phrases and sentences brief and the rhythm short and choppy, suggesting intrigue and confusion. Cassius indulges in long, powerful phrases, once his confidence grows. Brutus' language and tone are those of a man who is in great turmoil.

Caesar returns on stage with his procession. His remark to Mark Antony about Cassius' "lean and hungry looks" is a subtle suggestion of where Shakespeare's sympathies lie, and how he wishes to unfold his plot. Caesar's suspicion about Cassius is soon driven home when the wily manipulator incites the simple and honourable Brutus. Caesar knows such men are dangerous. However, he is so convinced about his own power that he decides to do nothing about what his mind clearly thinks to be a threat.

Casca speaks in prose when he reports about Caesar to Brutus and Cassius. Casca is a static character, and Shakespeare makes all his static characters speak in prose. Casca is sour and blunt. He is the cynical realist with irritating speech and manner, who can convey his disgust better in prose than in blank verse. Shakespeare also uses prose to break the monotony which blank verse (or iambic pentameter) can create if used for long on stage. Shakespeare introduces sixty lines of prose after 200 lines of blank verse.

Casca is delineated to show that Caesar has become a demagogue. Caesar refuses the crown with definite hypocrisy. He presents himself to the citizens of Rome as a heroic actor who plays to their sentiments. Casca is critical of both the hypocritical Caesar and the foolishly gullible public. Casca provides an unflattering portrant of a mob. This is of crucial importance because Shakespeare will use their fickleness and brutality to telling effect in Act II, Scenes 2 and 3. Casca ends his damning condemnation of Caesar when he casually mentions that Flavius and Marullus, "for pulling scarfs off Caesar's images, are put to silence". Caesar's image of a brutal demagogue is fully entrenched in the minds of the audience.

Shakespeare is full of subtle grace in depiction of the characters of his plays and in the development of his themes. Casca's character becomes a device by which Brutus' simplicity and Cassius' astute understanding of characters is delineated. Brutus believes Casca was "quick" when he was young, but he has now become "blunt". Cassius believes that Casca has changed only in form, suggesting that the change is a mere pretence. Later, it will be Cassius who sees the threat of Antony at Caesar's funeral. Brutus overrules Cassius and lets Antony speak at Caesar's funeral. Antony manages to turn the tables on Brutus and Cassius, and a hostile crowd forces the conspirators to flee from Rome. Cassius symbolises pragmatism, while Brutus symbolises an unbending and misplaced sense of integrity.

Shakespeare gives the first soliloquy to Caesar because he is the kind of man who is constantly indulging in intrigue and deception. A soliloquy is a stage device where the inner thoughts of an actor are conveyed to the audience. A play has its limitations because its dialogue must strictly adhere to the circumstances and the characters of the moment. A soliloquy is uttered by a character when he is alone on stage. Another stage device to convey the inner thoughts of an actor is an "aside". A soliloquy is used when an actor is alone on stage, while an aside is used when other actors are also present. A soliloquy also provides a general comment on the progression of the play. Cassius' soliloquy serves both these purposes. He reveals that he is a vindictive and cold-blooded schemer. His villainy advances the dramatic action of the play, though the audience does not know how it will be really brought about. The soliloquy also tells the audience about how the conspircy is taking place.

Shakespeare's delineation of character needs to emphasised. Caesar is delineated through a few bold strokes and through what others utter about him. Brutus and Cassuis are delineated at greater length. They are both brooding characters who do not fully understand the nature of things that surround them. Cassius may talk about the freedom to the people but all he wants is power. Brutus may talk about integrity and honour but he does not have the intellectual integrity to seek first-hand information whether Caesar is infact inordinately corrupt or not. He also does not know of any non-violent means for stopping Caesar. As the play unfolds, we are made aware that Caesar would have power if he could; he would live with his need if the cost of acquiring it is unacceptable.

Shakespeare delineates Caesar as a vain and superstitious man; but even here he brings about a certain valour, perhaps because he is a public figure and be must limit his superstitions to what the public would accept. He would thus reject the soothsayer as a dreamer, because it interferes with his public duties, but he would let his wife be touched by a runner of Lupercal, because it adheres to the public perception.

Cassius knows that it is wise to win Brutus over. Brutus is known for his integrity and honour. This would camouflage Cassius' own desire for power. Moreover, Caesar is a powerful man. Cassius needs the troops of many nobles in order to counter the kind of military might that Caesar can mount in case of an attack.

ACT I : SCENE III

A fearful storm brews in Rome. A terror-stricken Casca has his sword drawn to meet the menace that surrounds him. He is met by Cicero. Casca narrates to him the supernatural phenomena which have occurred. He talks about the rain of fire, the quaking of the earth, a common slave remaining unscathed despite his hand being "inflamed like twenty torches joined". He talks of a lion gazing aimlessly at the Capitol, about the walking dead, and about an owl who hooted at noon in the market place. Casca is terrified because all these portend ill. Cicero is unimpressed though he agrees that times have changed. He is more interested to know if Caesar will be at the Capitol next day to meet the Senate. Casca confirms that Caesar will be there. He then hurriedly leaves to seek shelter for himself.

He is replaced by Cassius, who had heard Casca's voice. His terror prompts Cassius to enlist him in the conspiracy. He tells Casca that he had gone through the storm with bare breast, challenging the thunder to strike him. Casca is terrified to learn that Cassius had challenged the Gods. Cassius tells Casca that the storm already reveals the Gods are angry over the state of affairs in Rome. Casca can do no more than utter Caesar's name in terror. Cassius knows it is time to strike. He makes a passionate speech to incite Casca. He tells Casca that he would rather kill himself than let Caesar be king. Casca is sufficiently moved to pledge his undying support to the conspiracy to kill Caesar.

These two are soon joined by Cinna, who is already part of the conspiracy. He is terrified due to the fearful night. Cassius tells Cinna to drop the forged letters through Brutus' window so that he can find them unexpectedly. He tells Cinna to meet them later at Pompey's Porch. Casca accepts Brutus as the leader because he is very upright and honourable. It will give a colour of patriotism to their conspiracy.

Commentary

The prime reason for this scene is to compress historical facts and reduce the chronological time of history. This helps in giving unity to the play. Historically, the feast of Lupcrcal and the Ides of March are seperated by a month. Shakespeare runs these two days together.

Elizabethan plays were mostly conducted during the day. Despite this fact Shakespeare wrote many night scenes in his plays. The crude and primitive nature of Elizabethan theatre was not equipped to depict night on stage. Fortunately, the Elizabethan audience was not unduly worried about projection of reality on stage. They were more concerned with what they heard. That is perhaps the reason why Shakespeare uses the kind of language which would create a mental atmosphere of the backdrop of the play. Shakespeare had the ability to create electricity through his language. He could also generate the most terrifying of thunder and lightning. Night was of crucial importance to Shakespeare because all the evil deeds are done at night. In this scene, the darkness of the night is a physical manifestation of the terribly violent emotions that lurk in the basement of the sensibilities of the conspirators. The storm continues through the next scene with Brutus and in the scene after that with Caesar. It becomes a link between the two. The significance of the storm is not lost on us. The Elizabethan audience considered human beings and nature interchangeable. The disorders in society would brew violent storms and unnatural events in the collective psyche of the Elizabethan audience. Whether this was readily accepted by the more advanced and logical Romans is not of any consequence. Shakespeare wrote for his Elizabethan audience. He was prepared to give Roman history an Elizabethan colouring, in order to appeal to his audience.

Shakespeare communicates the storm by the effect it has on a character. A terrified Casca runs on stage with his sword drawn. The stupidity behind the act may amuse modern audience, but the audience during Shakespeare's time would have been sufficiently impressed. In King Lear, it is the old King who enacts the storm. Casca may not have the sublimity and the grandeur of Lear, since he is a minor character, but he conveys the terror of the storm reasonably well. The storm has different effects on different people. Cicero is unmoved by it, though it terrifies Casca. Cinna's terror is within acceptable limits, where the physical discomfort of the storm is the only thing which troubles him. To Cassius, it is an opportunity to incite others to do terrible deeds. Casca speaks in blank verse in the scene, though he had spoken in prose the last time we met him. Shakespeare gives him blank verse in order to elevate the terror of the storm and the unnatural occurrences. Casca had been tough and unrelenting in the previous scene. His abject surrender to what is essentially a harmless physical occurrence gives us an impression that nature has colluded with men to shower terror on other men. The storm provides a supernatural quality to the conspiracy; it also forebodes terrible days for Rome.

The imagery used by Shakespeare is such that it conveys the unnatural and terrifying events that are taking shape in Rome. The storm rains fire on earth instead of merely bursting into lightning in the sky. This is followed by a human hand being set ablazed "like twenty torches joined". A lion comes unafraid and unhindered to the Capitol. These are unnatural and violent events. They depict terror and desolation. When we are told that an owl hooted at noon, our impression of the world standing on its head becomes complete. The Elizabethan audience traditionally considered an owl as a bad omen. It is significant that Shakespeare superimposes an Elizabethan superstition on a Roman play.

Shakespeare uses music as a powerful image to advance the movement of his play. In Scene 2 we are told that "Cassius hears no music". We are not surprised that he welcomes the storm in this scene. He is the kind of character who will shun music and accept the storm. The latter suits his violent and conniving nature.

Cassius had ended the previous scene foreseeing the possibility of "worse days". This scene, as an extension of his terrible remark, begins with thunder and lightning. It sends the self-controlled Casca of the previous scene into inexplicable terror. Shakespeare balances Casca's superstitious terror with Cicero's rationality. We must not, however, forget that Casca appears more in tune with the darkened undercurrents of conspiracy than Cicero. Shakespeare is aware his audience already knows that Caesar would be killed in the end. He lets logical consistency take a back seat to dramatic consistency by using the storm and the portents of ill omen to advance the movement of the conspiracy. It can only flourish against a backdrop where no sane person can venture outdoors. It can succeed against a powerful man like Caesar only if it is carried out in extraordinary secrecy. Caesar is extremely powerful and he is liked by a large number of Romans. The chances of the conspirators getting caught are huge. Shakespeare has to create the kind of precise backdrop against which the conspiracy can remain a secret.

The storm and other evil omens are presented with precision. It represents Brutus' inner turmoil. Cassius links it with Caesar's misrule, while the audience equates it with the dangers that are faced by Caesar. The "hundred ghastly women" are the Roman citizens, who will decide the final direction that Rome is to take after Caesar's assassination.

Casca reveals that the next day the senate intends to crown Caesar king of all the Roman dominions "save here in Italy". This should mean that the conspirators need not have a burning cause against Caesar because they will not have to endure a king directly. However, Caesar's attitude as the head of the Roman government, and the silencing of Marullus and Flavius emphasises that he is a potential threat to personal liberty of the citizens of Rome.

ACT II : SCENE I

Brutus' raging mind is unable to let him sleep. He has still to make up his mind about the conspiracy against Caesar. He calls his slave-boy and orders him to light a candle in the study. Lucius returns with the news that he has placed a candle in the study. He also gives a letter to Brutus. He had found it when he was searching the window for a candle. It is the anonymous letter which Cassius had written to incite Brutus to join the conspiracy. Brutus had already found several such letters earlier. He reads the letter, and then analyses his reasons for joining the conspiracy to murder Caesar. He realises that he has no personal reasons to murder Caesar; yet the citizens of Rome must be protected from the oppression of a tyrannical king. Brutus wants to kill Caesar for what he might become one day. Caesar cannot possibly have greater powers than he has at the moment of Brutus' contemplation, but he fails to recognise this fact.

Cassius arrives at Brutus' door with five other conspirators, Casca, Decius, Cinna, Metellus and Trebonius. Cassius brings Brutus up to date with the progress of events while others discuss the time of sunrise.

Brutus clasps the hands of the conspirators, but refuses to take an oath. They are all working for the good of the country and no oath is required among brothers. Brutus takes charge of the conspiracy, with able support from Cassius, because he wants Brutus at all costs. Burtus' integrity fails to see why. Cassius wants an oath to be taken. By sunrise one of the conspirators will have betrayed their confidence to Artemidorus, who will unsuccessfully try to pass on the information to Caesar. The conspirators would have been exposed had fate not intervened in their the favour. Cassius wants Cicero to be included in the conspiracy. All other conspirators agree. Brutus makes his second blunder by vetoing the inclusion of Cicero. Brutus believes that Cicero will have nothing to do with an enterprise which has not been initiated by him. The other conspirators accept Brutus' veto because they regard him highly. Much later it would turn out that how badly the conspirators need the masterful oratorial skills of Cicero, when Mark Antony so easily incites the citizens of Rome against the conspirators and forces them to flee from Rome.

Brutus, perhaps makes his biggest blunder by vetoing Cassius' desire to kill Mark Antony along with Caesar. Cassius sees the threat that Antony can be to the conspirators. Brutus wants that the conspirators be called "purgers, not murderers". He also wrongfully believes that Mark Antony will be no threat without Caesar. Later events would prove Buruts wrong when Antony would challenge and win against them.

Cassius is not sure that Caesar will attend the senate meeting. Decius promises to lure him to the Senate. Brutus decides that they must all meet at the Senate at the eighth hour. Metellus wants Cassius Ligarius to be included in the conspiracy. Brutus tells Metellus to get Ligarius to him and promises to persuade him to join the conspiracy. The conspirators leave Brutus' house at three o'clock. They decide to meet at Caesar's house.

Brutus, left alone, is joined by Portia. She is sad for not being taken into confidence. She is also worried about Brutus, because of late he has been moody, aloof and sleepless. She invokes her right as a wife to know the secrets of his mind. She tells him that she is Cato's daughter. Her father was the giant of Roman public life. Moreover, she is his wife. She reveals to Brutus a voluntary wound that she had made on her thigh, in order to prove that she can bear her husband's secrets. Brutus is deeply touched. He promises to share his secrets with her.

They are disturbed by the arrival of Ligarius. His head is in bandage. He has been ill, but he has risen form his sick bed in order to have a word with Brutus. Brutus tells him that the enterprise he has in mind is of great importance. Ligarius has a hint of what it may be. He removes his bandages as Brutus tells him to follow him, obviously with an intent of telling him everything.

Commentary

Brutus begins the scene by describing the darkness that surrounds him. The terrible storm of the previous scene is still raging in Rome. That and the ensuing darkne·s is given subtle but crucially symbolic significance. The darkness reflects the darkness that exists in Brutus' mind. When the conspirators arrive at Brutus' house, night and darkness acquire sinister and evil connotations; so do everything the conspirators say or do.

Brutus seeks light from Lucius. His name is derived from the Latin word Lucere, which means "to light". He thus symbolises the kind of mental illumination that Brutus needs. It is significant that Brutus asks Lucius to put a candle in the study and he never reaches it. He is interrupted by the conspirators, who collectively symbolise ill-will and destruction. Lucius may be a minor character, but he shows the kind of tranquillity that Brutus does not possess. Shakespeare often links sleep with peace. Brutus is totally bereft of sleep. He recognises Lucius' innocent sleep and his own guilty wakefulness. Lucius has the "honey-heavy dew of slumber", while he is plagued by "busy care". Brutus' gentle dealing of Lucius and Portia reveal an essentially kind man. He is plagued by darkness so much probably because he is not used to it as much as some of the conspirators.

Sufficient stress must be placed on Brutus' soliloquy at the beginning of the play. Shakespeare's brilliance creates his confusion in a manner which suits his dramatic purpose just sufficiently. The dramatist does not let Brutus become aware of his confusion. Shakespeare's tragic heroes are all certain on the surface. Their confusion and doubts exist at a sub-conscious level. Brutus too is certain of what he must do. He begins the soliloquy with the ominous sounding, "It must be by his death". He had already arrived at a terrible decision. He now superimposes reasons on his decision in order to justify it. Brutus clears his conscience when he says that he has no "personal cause" for killing Caesar. He has to die in order to prevent him from misusing his power. It is significant that Brutus admits of having no reason for thinking that Caesar would misuse his power. He uses conventional phrases like a "bright day" bringing forth "the adder" to incite "young ambition's ladder" as excuses to convince himself. They are not extensions of logical evaluation. Brutus admits that he has to "fashion" a "quarrel" that has no "colour". He also accepts the need to twist his opinion of Caesar in order to inspire himself to act. He decides to compare Caesar to " a serpent's egg". As Brutus convinces himself about his decision we become more uncertain about the quality of his thoughts.

As Lucius leaves to bring in the conspirators, Brutus talks about how he has compromised himself. He once again reiterates about his integrity and we accept it, because he is superficially so honest. He knows that they must meet in the darkness of the night because conspiracy's "visage" is so "monstrous" that it must hide in "smiles and affability". Once Brutus meets the conspirators he condemns himself to this hypocritical combination of monstrosity hidden behind a facade of fake smiles.

Brutus and Cassius withdraw to one corner. In their absence the other conspirators indulge in irrelevant talk about the direction from which the sun will rise. Despite its trivial nature the anticipation of the sun heightens our curiosity about the terrible deed that would be done during the forthcoming day.

Brutus obviously makes three huge blunders after he assumes leadership. His blunders reveal his character. He understands people at face value and his honour and integrity are not sufficient to help him provide leadership on complex issues. Brutus is a simple and sincere man, but his sincerity becomes an impediment in his path to recognise the true nature of men and political action. In contrast, Cassius is complex and shrewd. He understands how men think. He instinctively knows how to counter them. Cassius backs Cicero because he is calm in a calamity. Brutus wonders why such a self-contained man would back something which has been organised by others. Cicero symbolises intelligent statesmanship. The conspirators need his "good opinion" in order to "commend" their deeds. Cassius wants Antony to be killed with Caesar because he instinctively understands the threat he can cause to the conspirators. Brutus thinks he will be totally ineffectual without Caesar. Brutus makes the mistake of underestimating a possible threat. He thinks a man who is given to "sports, to wildness, and much company"cannot be of great threat. Brutus' uprighteousness and physical bravery does not make him see threats unless they are palpably visible. He also oversimplifies characters. This oversimplification of Antony will return, quite literally, to haunt him in Act IV, Scene 3. Cassius gets it right when he considers Antony a threat due to his "ingrafted love" for Caesar.

Despite his moral justification about being part of the conspiracy, there is no doubt that Brutus is surrounded by uncertainty and guilt. He talks of religious sacrifice in order to justify the assassination. He wishes to "carve" Caesar in a way which is "fit for the gods", and not as "a carcass fit for hounds". Brutus tries his utmost not to face the bloody nature of his deed. It is ironic that he uses metaphors of hunting. Antony will later describe the dead Caesar as a "brave hart" who has been surrounded by "hunters" and "bloody butchers".

Does Shakespeare condemn Brutus and accept Cassius? To frame such a question is to suggest a complete lack of understanding of Shakespeare. Both Brutus and Cassius are characters who are independent of Shakespeare's own point of view. He is too much of a dramatist to let his personal views surface in a character. Brutus and Cassius are both flawed individuals in some respect and worthwhile in some others. The mere fact that they conspire to kill Caesar with misplaced or misunderstood motives reveals that Shakespeare does not wish his audience to admire either of them. He gives them good qualities in order to make them worthy of a great tragedy.

Portia and Lucius represent the normal aspects of what should have been sources of joy and peace to Brutus. They are in sharp contrast to the dark nature of the conspiracy, the struggles of conscience, and the creepy violence of the sinister plot of assassination.

The play deals with struggle for power. It is hardly surprising that the play is so dominated by men, discussion and bloodshed. Brutus is mostly depicted in his role as a public figure. He is surrounded by men and by affairs of state. Portia, his wife, is provided depth and humanity to what may otherwise have been a unidimensional character.

Portia's character is simple due to a theatrical need. Female parts were played by boys on Elizabethan stage. It was necessary to keep female characters simple so that they did not become a source of laughter when their part was played by a boy. A boy-actor could not be expected to convey the subtle shades of complexities present in a female character. It is true that Lady Macbeth and Cleopatra are complex characters, but even they are simple in comparison to Hamlet or Othello.

Portia's love reminds us how contented Brutus must have been before he plunged into the dark recesses of conspiracy. It adds a distinct amount of pathos to the destructive course that Brutus chooses to follow. When Portia dies, we realise how misplaced thoughts and actions can bring about destruction of those we care. Brutus destroys whatever he strongly cares for. Republican freedom falls to the domination of the triumvirate and Portia has to commit suicide.

Portia reminds Brutus that she is Cato's daughter. Cato the Elder was a perpetual symbol of Roman strength and courage. Shakespeare takes this information from Plutarch, his original source for the play. He wishes to exemplify the sort of stern self-discipline associated with Cato, especially when Portia inflicts a voluntary wound on herself to convince her ability to keep a secret. This has direct reference in Plutarch. Shakespeare only fleetingly refers to the wound because his prime concern is to drive home the tenderness of Portia.

The scene ends with the Ligarius episode. Ligarius' remarkable recovery from his illness needs special mention. Does Brutus have healing qualities or does his nobility inspire enthusiasm which may be destructive ? We must accept that Ligarius' inexplicable enthusiasm is his personal reaction to a man whom he considers worthy. Nothing more need to be attached to it. Shakespeare underscores the destructive nature of such misplaced enthusiasm when Ligarius is prepared to follow Brutus "To do I know not what".

Shakespeare portrays Brutus as a public man of affairs in the Roman Government and a private man who is compassionate for the commoners and extremely fond of his wife and his domestic life. His tragedy arises from the fact that his tenderness and humanity are not extended to Caesar. He is unable to bring about rational evaluation to what he sets out to do. He has no reason to believe that Caesar will become a tyrant. In fact every evidence proves to the contrary. He comes to drastic conclusions because of his fear regarding what power can do to men, little realising that his action will transfer power from a trusted friend to a few self-seeking individuals. He may not be craving for power himself but there is nothing in his agreement to suggest that he can prevent power from being usurped by the conspirators.

Brutus seems to be a man who is easily influenced by others. Cassius' impassioned speech in Act I, Scene II and a few anonymous letters are sufficient to influence him into a thoughtless crime. Honour and integrity demand an inviolable understanding of life. Brutus does not inspire any confidence to convince us that he understands life. His honour and integrity are thus only superficial. They are without profound understanding of existence. He thinks honour demands that he should be above the desire to acquire power. It does not occur to him that he may be helping others to acquire power, It never concerns him to think how the death of an individual would change everything.

Cassius had asked Brutus in the previous scene, "Can you see your face?". He offers to be the mirror to reflect his true worth. The anonymous letter urges Brutus to "awake and see thyself". Cassius blames the Roman nobles for allowing Rome to be ruled by one man. He reminds Brutus of his ancestors who drove the Tarquins from Rome. The anonymous letter re-stresses these references. Shakespeare wishes to emphasise that a lie becomes a truth if it is repeated often enough. Brutus falls into this trap. All he can say is that he cannot look "quite through the deeds of men".

ACT II : SCENE II

We had experienced the charm of Brutus' domestic bliss in the previous scene. Shakespeare now takes us to Caesar's house. Caesar is awakened by the storm. He finds Calphurnia crying out in her sleep that Caesar has been murdered. Caesar orders a servant to tell the priests to present sacrifices and let him know what they portend for the future. Calphurnia, by now awake, pleads with Caesar not to leave home. She has just heard from someone on watch about the happenings on the streets of Rome, as well as in the sky. It is her basic habit not to be scared, but she is now frightened for her husband. Caesar tells Calphurnia not to be unduly worried because no one can avoid what the gods propose. Caesar tells Calphurnia that he will go because these predictions are as much valid for the world as for him.

The servant enters and informs Caesar that the omens are not favourable as per the priests. A sacrificed beast did not have a heart, therefore, Caesar must not step out of the house. Caesar dismisses these omens as well. He tells the servant that the Gods do this to put cowardice to shame. A man who is afraid is as terrible as the beast without the heart who has been recently sacrificed. A desperate Calphurnia kneels in front of Caesar. She tells her husband to let Mark Antony go and inform the senate that Caesar is not well. A visibly moved Caesar lifts Calphurnia and agrees to heed her advice.

Just as Caesar makes up his decision, the tender couple is joined by Decius. Caesar tells him to take a message to the senators that he will not be present. Decius wants a reason why Caesar does not wish to go. Caesar tells him that it is sufficient that it is his will which makes him decide not to go. However, he tells Decius about Calphurnia's dream and her ardent please to her husband not to leave home. Calphurnia had seen a hundred spurts of blood gushing out of Caesar's statue. Many Romans were gleefully bathing in his blood. The clever Decius tells Caesar that the dream has been wrongly interpreted. The dream does not portend something evil. Infact, it means that Caesar shall revive the commonwealth. The bathing of Romans in Caesar's blood indicates that Rome shall renew its strength from him and that great men shall get their nourishment and inspiration from him. Caesar is convinced that it is an excellent interpretation of Calphurnia's dream. Decius drives home his advantage by telling Caesar that the senate has decided to give him the crown today. Their minds may change if Caesar refuses to go. He will become a source of ridicule to all the senators. They may not wait till Caesar's wife has a better dream. Caesar chastises Calphurnia for her foolish fears. He is himself ashamed for succumbing to them. Caesar decides to leave for the senate.

Publius is admitted inside along with some of the other conspirators. Caesar welcomes the conspirators graciously for showing their courtesy of accompanying him to the senate.

Commentary

A raging storm had continued in the previous scene as Brutus and Ligarius had left the stage. It continues in this scene in the house of Caesar as well. The storm symbolizes violence. The violent intention of the conspirators looms as a dark cloud over Caesar's head. This dramatic device intrinsically links the intentions of the conspirators with Caesar's safety.

The previous as well this scene are also linked in another way. We had seen the tender domesticity of Brutus's house in the previous scene. We now see the tender domesticity of Caesar's house. Portia had been worried due to her husband's unnaturally brooding disposition. Calphurnia is terrified due to her dreams. Both want the safety of their husbands and the continued tranquillity of their homes. Shakespeare brings in the wives to give a tender touch to two essentially public-figures. Without this tenderness, both Caesar and Brutus may have appeared heartlessly unidimensional. The tenderness of the two wives makes the tragedy truly horrifying. Two public figures dying on the battlefield, fighting for a piece of land would hardly move any audience, but the tragedy erupts out of the fact that death causes enormous misery to innocent people. We feel there is a terrible distortion of the world moral order. Both men discard the pleas of their wives. Shakespeare always presents a moment in his play when his tragic hero could have prevented his fall. The tragedy erupts when he chooses to ignore the substantial evidence that is available to him and walks on the path of destruction. Brutus would not have joined the conspirators had he shared his secret with Portia. Caesar would not have died had he listened to the fears of the priests and his wife. Dreams and omens may be dismissed by modern sensibilities, but there is sufficient evidence that Caesar believed in them. There is no point going through the prolonged ritual of sacrifices and then ignoring the warnings of the priests.

Shakespeare dwells on these chaotic omens to drive home the point that Caesar's murder is not merely an individual act of violence. The Elizabethans believed that the king was the God's deputy on earth. To have him murdered without divine will would have irritated the audience. The storm identifies the terrible destruction that is brought about when a king dies. The Elizabethan audience would have been terrified with such a thought.

Shakespeare delineates Caesar with great skill. He is able to combine conflicting traits in a man into one magnificent blend, and yet retain the sharpness of those individual traits. Caesar, the public figure and the hero of many public battles, is unaware of fear. Caesar, the private man, the husband of loving Calphurnia is given to sacrifices and omens. Subconsciously, he may be scared, but his stature is such that he cannot afford to display it publicly. There is somewhat of a primitive Roman in Caesar as he indulges in all those sacrifices of animals. Men in power are known to invoke the gods to help them remain in power. All powerful men need divine help because public opinion can be an extremely fickle thing.

When Calphurnia tells about her fear to Caesar, he pacifies her. We are immediately aware that Caesar is not only the Colossus that "bestrides the narrow world", but he is also a man who is moved by the distress of his wife. Caesar, the private man, reverts to his public posture with the arrival of Decius. He is once again the monumental public hero that the world has known. He is ashamed that his domestic weakness has been exposed. The most powerful man on earth seeks the help of humbug priests and a terrified wife. Caesar can find no other escape route than to take refuge in pride. It may be a terrible response, but it adequately reveals Caesar's embarrassment. Caesar psyches himself into a position to be weakened to implied threats due to the superiority that he surrounds himself in. Decius seizes this opportunity with both hands. He had promised the conspirators to manipulate Caesar and to bring him to the senate. He now sets out to play on Caesar's misplaced superiority and convince him to venture forth to the senate. There are two things which Caesar's sort of pride cannot stand. One is ridicule, and we note how Decius had said in line 70 about his fear "Lest I be laught at". The "I" can be easily replaced with "you" and Caesar may himself be a source of ridicule to others. The other is contempt. Decius understands this and suggests the ridiculous situations where Caesar is dependent on his wife's dreams, and the even more ridiculous thought that he is scared. It is inevitable that Caesar is trapped into ignoring the warnings and venturing forth to the senate.

Shakespeare focuses first on Caesar's vanity and superstition, and then on Caesar's sense of inviolability. The latter is most evident when Caesar says that by facing things he removes their danger. This is an extremely ironical statement, because the audience is aware that Caesar would soon be killed. Caesar is both rational and fatalistic when he tells Calphurnia that it is absurd to fear something as inevitable as death, but he soon wishes to know the results of the sacrifices made by the priests. He is told that the results do not augur well for him, but he rejects their warning. He tries to steel his courage by saying that he is fearless and more terrible than imagined danger. There is sufficient hint here that the conspirators may have reasons to fear his misplaced sense of power. Caesar refuses to be afraid but is prepared to use Calphurnia's fear as an excuse for remaining at home. He gives an impression as if he is doing her a favour by making her fear as an excuse for his action. Decius understands this and draws Caesar out of his domisticity. Caesar may show fear in his private chambers but he must show absolute fearlessness in public. This deception makes him an easy prey to Decius' cunning manipulation. He tells Caesar that the senators would ridicule his misplaced fear. Decius then plays on Caesar's vanity and greed. He reinterprets Calphurnia's dream in a manner that it would flatter any vain man. Caesar must have been flattered with the thought of being the cause of rejuvenation of Rome. Decius does not stop merely at flattering Caesar's vanity. He now plays on Caesar's greed. He talks about the possibility of Caesar being presented the crown by the senators. Caesar may not admit it openly but his desire to be king is strong. It is all that he needs to discard his fears and go to the Capitol.

The play has plenty of worthy men being duped by lesser men. Brutus is duped with consummate ease by Cassius. Here Decius dupes Caesar. Later Antony would dupe Brutus to his downfall. In many ways Shakespeare delineates Brutus and Caesar as simple men who are particularly vulnerable to deception. However, their vulnerability, is not only due to their simplicity. They have some alarmingly horrifying flaws. Brutus is a terrible judge of character. He arrives at conclusions irrationally, and then tries to superimpose logic on them; and he thinks death of a man is sufficient impetus to give the citizens of Rome their freedom. He never tells us why those who replace Caesar would let the citizens have freedom. If power corrupts then it can corrupt Caesar as well as a group of men who would replace him. Caesar is superstitious, vain and ambitious. He is also very uncomfortable with his flaws. He is subcosciously aware of the flaws in his character but he does not have the ability to consistently rise above them.

The scene ends with a cynical aside by Trebonius, while Brutus agonises over his sorrow for being forced to wear a false face. Brutus continues to experience the kind of inner struggle that has been a part of his existence from the beginning of the play. This struggle will be part of him till the very end. The play may not have been a tragedy if Brutus had come to grips with his inner struggle and arrived at an inviolable solution.

ACT II : SCENE III

As Caesar sets forth for the Capitol, we find ourselves on a street near the Capitol. Artemidorus, a teacher of rhetoric, reads from a ˙ paper which warns Caesar of the dangers that lie ahead. He names Brutus, Cassius, Casca, Cinna, Trebonius, Metellus Cimber, Decius Brutus and Caius Ligarius as the conspirators who wish to kill him.

Artemidorus decides to stand at a vantage point on the street and wait for Caesar, so that he can hand over the paper to him. His heart is sad, but he hopes that Caesar may yet escape the designs of the conspirators. He is sure that Caesar would live if he reads the paper.

Commentary

This and the next scene provide the time that must lapse for Caesar to reach the Capitol after leaving his house. The three characters who appear in these two scenes—Artemidorus in this scene and Portia and the soothsayer in the next—all know or suspect that Caesar is in trouble. They communicate their fears to the audience.

Until now we had heard the version of the conspirators regarding Caesar's flaws. Now we hear the voice of the Romans who are not opposed to Caesar. There is nothing to suggest that Artemidorus is anything but honest. We must thus accept him at face value when he talks of Caesar's "virtues" and thinks that the conspirators are "traitors". This view prevents us from being influenced by the exaggerated hatred of the conspirators. Caesar may have his flaws but he also has "virtues". However, it would be foolish to oversimplify his character.

Artemidorus wishes to remind Caesar that he is not immortal, so he must be watchful. This is a repetition of Calphurnia's warning in the previous scene. It reconfirms our opinion about human frailty, no matter what Caesar may think about himself.

ACT II : SCENE IV

In Brutus' house, Portia sends Lucius on an errand to the Senate House. Lucius does not know what job he has to perform. Portia is uncertain what to tell him. She wants to do the right thing without revealing Brutus' secret. She tells Lucius to go to the Senate and see whether his master appears well. She is suddenly startled by a noise which she believes is coming from the Capitol. Lucius cannot hear any noise.

The two are interrupted by a soothsayer. Portia asks him what news he has. She wants to know if he has been at the Capitol, then the time, then whether Caesar has gone to the Capitol or not. The soothsayer tells Portia that it is the ninth hour and that Caesar has not yet gone to the Capitol. She asks the soothsayer if he has a favour to ask from Caesar. The soothsayer says that he has a favour to ask from Caesar which very nearly concerns his personal interest. Portia is alarmed at the thought that the secret may be out. When she learns that the soothsayer does not know about the conspiracy, but merely fears one, she almost faints with relief. She is worried that Lucius may have heard her when she said that Brutus has a suit for Caesar which he will not grant. She once again grows faint with fear. She tells Lucius to go to Brutus, give her best wishes to him and then return to her.

Commentary

The suspense of the impending disaster is conveyed through Portia's agitation. We are told that Caesar has not reached the Capitol as yet. This further increases our suspense. We know that Brutus has not confided in Portia about the conspiracy. However, Shakespeare is obviously not interested in logical development of events. His prime concern is the development of the theme of the play and the creation of dramatic tension. This tension is enhanced first through Portia's fears and then through the apprehension whether or not Caesar will be warned either by Artemidorus or by the soothsayer. We know that it is the Ides of March, and also that the plans of the conspirators are known to some persons who are not part of the conspiracy.

Portia's prayer that "heavens speed thee in thine enterprise!" shows that she is not against Brutus killing Caesar. She is only concerned that her husband's secret should not be revealed to other people. She never questions the morality of the assassination..

ACT III : SCENE I

Caesar arrives at the Capitol with Antony, Lepidus and the conspirators. The soothsayer approaches Caesar. Caesar reminds him that the "Ides of March are come". The soothsayer answers, "Aye, Caesar, but not gone." Artemidorus then comes forward and urges Caesar to read his suit written on a paper because it concerns him the most. Caesar tells Artemidorus that what touches him personally shall be looked into last of all. Artemidorus urges Caesar not to delay reading the paper. Caesar angrily wonders if he is a man. Cassius tells Artemidorus to present his petition at the Capitol and not on the street. Caesar leaves without reading the paper.

Popilius, the senator, gives the conspirators a start by whispering to Caesar that he wishes him luck. Cassius is fearful that their conspiracy has been discovered. He tells Casca that he will kill himself if their secret becomes public. Brutus tells him to get hold of himself because Caesar's face shows no hint of suspicion. Cassius is relieved. He points out to Brutus that Trebonius is taking Mark Antony away from Caesar as planned by the conspirators. Decius wonders where Metellus Cimber is, since he must present his petition to Caesar at once. Brutus tells Decius that he is ready to address Caesar. They must close in and help him. Metellus Cimber, with exaggerated humility, kneels to present a feather to Caesar, who thinks that he wants to urge him to cancel the banishment of his brother. Caesar is disgusted at his un-Roman show of humility. He tells Metellus to rise. His brother was banished from the country by a fair judicial order. He would spurn him like a dog if he bent to flatter him. He reminds Metellus that Caesar does not ever do any wrong and cannot be convinced to reverse his order without a proper cause. Metellus asks Brutus, Cassius and Casca to come forward and plead on his behalf. As per plan they move closer to Caesar, but they are refused with even greater rudeness. Then Casca, in seeming desperation, strikes the first dagger-blow at the back of Caesar's neck. He bungles his aim through excitement, but the others press in and repeatedly stab Caesar, who ceases to resist when he sees Brutus too delivering the blow of his sword.

Caesar dies, but the conspirators do not have a plan what to do next. Cinna and Cassius let out hysterical cries about liberty and freedom. Brutus tries to address the senators, who seem to be tumbling over one another in order to get outside and away. He only manages to reassure the aged Publius. Trebonius reports that an amazed Antony has fled to his house.

Mark Antony's servant soon comes on the scene with a gesture of respect from his master. Antony only wishes to be told why Caesar deserved this fate. Brutus tells the servant to send his master. He promises upon his honour that Antony will not be harmed. The servant leaves to convey the message to Antony. Brutus wants to have Antony on their side but Cassius is not sure how he may react.

Antony appears with painful lamentations for the mighty Caesar. He tells the conspirators that if they intend to kill him there can be no place or time more fit than here and now. Brutus tells Antony that his heart is full of brotherly love for him. Cassius too reassures Antony. Brutus promises to explain in detail why Caesar was killed once the people have been quietened. Cassius cannot find any blame in Antony for praising Caesar. He wishes to know on what terms does he wish to be with them. Antony tells Cassius that he wants to be friends with them. He is in a delicate position and they may think of him as a coward or a flatterer. Antony then goes into an eulogy on Caesar and ends with a subtle comparison between Caesar and a deer driven to bay and pulled down by a pack of dogs.

Antony seeks permission to speak at Caesar's funeral. Cassius is alarmed. Brutus overrules Cassuis and makes his fourth blunder. Brutus poses conditions for Antony. He tells Antony that.:

(a) He must speak before Antony.

(b) Antony must not blame the conspirators.

(c) He may speak all the good he can of Caesar.

(d) He must tell the crowd that he is speaking with the permission of the conspirators.

(e) He must speak from the same platform as Brutus.

Antony accepts these conditions, and the conspirators leave the scene. Antony, left alone, with Caesar's body, pays homage to the great leader. He gives us sufficient hint of what he would do later in the Forum. He asks Caesar's body to forgive him for appearing to approve the bloody deed of the conspirators.

A servant of Octavius Caesar enters and informs Antony that his master is only twenty miles outside Rome. Antony sends the servant back with the message that Rome is not safe for him. He must stay where he is. He delays the servant long enough to hear his speech and inform his master accordingly. The two then remove Caesar's body.

Commentary

This is also known as the assassination scene. It is the central moment of the play. It is the climax of the intrigues and actions that have occurred till now in the play. It also provides the impetus for the second half of the play. The scene is full of theatrical violence. Due to this reason alone it deserves to be visualised carefully.

Shakespeare builds tension at a furious pace from the very beginning of this scene. Caesar is offered a verbal warning by the soothsayer and a written one from Artemidorus. They are unable to create any impression on Caesar due to the deft manner in which Decius and Cassius distract Caesar. The suspense reaches its highest point when Popilius Lena wishes Cassius success in his enterprise. This is the signal for the conspirators to strike. All this action occurs in the first twenty-four lines of the scene. When Trebonius manages to take Antony away from Caesar, the conspirators have the freedom to assassinate Caesar.

Some literary critics disagree about the central moment of the play. Some believe that the action of the play shifts only when Caesar is killed; some believe it occurs when Antony re-enters the Capitol, planning revenge; still others believe that it occurs when Brutus gives permission to Antony to speak at Caesar's funeral. Despite these differences, there is no doubt that Caesar's death is the major event in the play.

Caesar's speeches are uttered in utmost arrogance as the conspirators close in on him. He projects himself as the kind of man who does not change once he gives an order. He also links his justice with divine will. He is the "Northern Star", the conspirators are flatterers who are given to "Low-crooked curtsies"; they are dogs whom Caesar kicks aside. As Caesar elaborates on his own greatness, the conspirators surround him in mock humility. Metellus is already on his knees. Cassius falls as "low as to thy foot". Cinna and Decius chant in chorus, "Ceaesar, great Caesar". This fawning is as superfluous as Caesar's pride. It is evident on stage with telling effect, especially when it is offset against Caesar's arrogance. The audience feels a sense of hypocrisy and betrayal. This is further emphasized when Casca delivers the first blow on Caesar. It is significant that he strikes Caesar from behind. This is a deliberate attempt by the dramatist to show the lowness of the assassination despite the self-proclaimed righteousness of their cause. Caesar's hopeless resignation when he sees Brutus among the conspirators is particularly effective on stage. We feel two things at the same time—pity for Caesar, and sorrow for Brutus who had to kill his friend for his principles.

There is complete chaos after the assassination. The conspirators try to calm the frightened spectators by telling them that they have acted to end Caesar's tyranny, and to restore freedom to the citizens of Rome. Brutus stands absolutely firm in the midst of this. He announces that the conspirators take responsibility for what they have done. Cassius is a pragmatic man, who is constantly eliminating threats. He checks on the whereabouts of Antony. The conspirators are full of suggestions, but they do not seem to have a plan of action. Brutus actually accepts that future events would develop as a matter of chance. Much later we will be forced to compare the lack of direction among the conspirators with the wonderful planning of Antony and Octavius Caesar.

The conspirators wash their hands in Caesar's blood because Brutus prompts them to do so. He wanted the assasination to look like a sacrificial killing, and washing of hands in blood was considered a proper ritual of sacrifice. This rather grotesque ritual is carried out in order to make the conspirators look like "purgers" instead of murderers. The modern audience may believe this to be a silly act, but primitive Roman citizens would have been adequately moved on seeing such a thing. Despite his integrity, Brutus is not sure of his act; and because he is not sure, he wants to change the opinions of others through what is at best an act of deception. Shakespeare added this ritual because the Elizabethan audience was very pleased with blood on stage. There is another ironical statement made by Shakespeare when he literally shows the conspirators in blood upto their elbows. Dramatically, this would show the conspirators in terrible light, after having committed a horrendous act. As stated earlier, the Elizabethan stage was very primitive and Shakespeare had to make some very profound statements through very meagre resources. This ironical understanding of the conspirators would become even more cynical when they shout "Peace, freedom, and liberty !"

The arrival of Antony changes the movement and the direction of the action. From now on he will be the nemesis of the conspirators. The conspirators will be on the run till they are finally hounded and killed. This central moment in the play will also change the way in which different characters treat each other. Till now, there was a huge difference between Brutus and Cassius. The latter was politically cunning, hard-headed and a realist, whose actions were defined by the ends they would achieve. Brutus on the other hand was an idealist in a rather ineffectual way. His integrity had a hollowness which was bound to make him suffer in the complex world of public life. Brutus' moral concern for the good of Rome is shown in sharp contrast to his ability to convert this concern into reality. Cassius, till now was a foil to Brutus. The latter stood out as a shining star because of the flaws in the former. Once Antony comes into center stage, it is he who becomes the foil to Brutus instead of Cassius. The contrast is most evident in their speeches to the citizens of Rome in order to explain Caesar's death.

Antony sends his servant to the conspirators in order to make sure that his life is not in danger. It is obvious that the servant has been carefully prepared to utter what could not be misconstrued by the conspiratiors. It is significant that the servant speaks with servile flattery. Antony knows the unpredictable nature of people who can kill a man like Caesar. He also knows that their extraordinary pride can be won over through flattery.

Antony enters almost immediately. Whatever he says is carefully planned to dupe the conspirators into believing that he is a simpleton, who does not have the capacity to counter the menace mounted by the conspirators. Cassius is constantly suspicious of Antony. However, Antony is aware that it is Brutus who is the leader of the conpirators and he will accept at face value whatever is seen by his eyes. That is the reason why Antony directs his performance to Brutus. He clearly understands that Brutus thrives on honour and integrity. He would have to be somehow reminded that he killed a friend who was truly worthy of support. Antony begins with undiluted praise and grief of Caesar over his dead body. Brutus is hugely impressed by this sense of loyalty because it is the outer manifestation of an inner love for a dear friend. It must not be construed that Antony is hypocritical, though his performances over Caesar's body is designed to move Brutus and to excite the mob.

Antony knows how the mob would react when he shows grief for a lost friend. He does exactly what Brutus might have done in the same position. He offers himself as a victim to be killed and placed by the side of the body of his friend and ruler. Once Antony is prepared to die, the conspirators are culled into believing that his existence cannot harm them in anyway. The only person who is still suspicious is Cassius. He epitomises political intrigue and he instinctively recognizes a manipulator when he sees one. That is why he does not extend his grief and loyalty to Antony; he simply offers to share the political power and material wealth arising out of Caesar's death. Antony only wishes to convince Brutus. No matter how tempting the offer may be, he is shrewd enough to reject it. After winning Brutus's support Antony enlarges his role a little bit by shaking every assassins hand. This is deliberate deception from a man who is seething within himself over the heinous crime by people whom he considers no more than murderous hounds. It is not without cause than Antony calls them "Gentlemen". He does this to buy time to excite the Roman citizens and to acquire his military forces in order to do battle with the conspirators.

Antony carries out two extremely practical tasks in order to advance his intention of avenging Caesar's death. He requests that he be told why

Caesar deserved to die. He also seeks the permission of the conspirators to
speak at Caesar's funeral. As later events would reveal, these two actions are
crucial for Antony's plan.

Cassius takes Brutus aside in order to convince him not to grant
Antony's wishes. Cassius is as cunning as a fox, and he immediately sees
through the opaque density of Antony's intrigue. Brutus, on the other hand,
is an upright man. He believes a person once he is given assurance of his
good conduct. It is ironical that Brutus' naive integrity gives him the right to
be a leader over the complex political intrigue that Cassius can muster.

Antony's violent outburst, after the conspirators leave him alone on
stage, is a fair indication of the kind of turmoil that is brewing inside him. He
had used words with great care in front of the conspirators. Once they leave,
we experience unadulterated grief, and a burning desire to avenge Caesar's
death. Now the conspirators are "butchers", though they had been earlier
addressed as "gentlemen". Antony conjures Caesar's spirit to come "hot from
hell" and "ranging for revenge". Antony's invocation of Caesar's spirit is not
merely to refer to the stage convention of the revenger or to cater to the need
of the Elizabethan audience. It also tells us of the presence of two Caesars —
the mortal body of Caesar which the conspirators have destroyed and his
spirit which will haunt the rest of the play. Antony predicts "domestic fury
and fierce civil strife" because Caesar's spirit will pervade through Rome.
Shakespeare had managed intense dramatic pressure till Caesar's death. The
pressure vanishes once the conspirators succeed. Antony's speech, where he
invokes Caesar's spirit, reintroduces this pressure.

ACT III : SCENE II

Brutus and Cassius appear at the Forum amidst a throng of citizens.
The forum is full of excited men who are agitated after the death of their
beloved Caesar. They angrily demand the reason for his death. Brutus decides
to control half the mob, while Cassius controls the other half. Brutus addresses
his half of the crowd, in a logical but unappealing manner. His style is laconic
and spartan. People listen to him because they know he is upright. He tells
them that he loved Caesar, but he loves Rome and the freedom of its citizens
even more. He had to kill Caesar because he had become ambitious and
wanted to make the Roman citizens his slaves.

The citizens are convinced with Brutus' speech. They want Brutus to
be crowned King. They decide to honour him by carrying him home in a
procession. Brutus tells them to stay and hear what Mark Antony has to say.

Antony addresses a crowd which has been swayed by Brutus. The crowd shouts that Caesar was a tyrant. Antony assures the crowd that he has "come to bury Caesar, not to praise him". He tells the crowd that he will try to be as logical as Brutus. He accepts that Brutus spoke with honourable intentions when he called Caesar ambitious. If Caesar was ambitious then he truly deserved to die. He then reminds them that Caesar had filled the state with ransom received from freeing captives. Caesar wept whenever the poor cried. Does that amount to ambition ? Yet Brutus says that he was ambitious, and Brutus is an honourable man. He reminds the crowd how Caesar had refused the crown thrice during the feast of Lupercal. Did he refuse the crown due to ambition ? Yet Brutus says he was ambitious, and surely he is an honourable man. Antony tells the crowd that he does not wish to disprove Brutus. He only wishes to speak what he knows. He reminds the crowd that they all loved Caesar for very good reasons. He wonders what prevents them from mourning for him ? He wonders if men have lost their power to think. After saying this Antony seeks the crowd's permission to pause. His heart is in the coffin with Caesar's body. He must wait till it returns to him. As Antony takes a theatrical pause, the crowd is slowly swayed in his direction. Antony knows now he has them. It only remains for him to excite them to anger.

Antony incites the crowd in a systematic manner. He uses every device known to oratory—irony, passion, flattery, ridicule and finally material reward. He shows the crowd Caesar's will, but he refuses to read it to them just yet. He flatters the crowd, who demands to hear what is written in the will. Antony descends from the platform and shows the blood-soaked body of Caesar to the crowd. He connects the assassins to the various holes in Caesar's cloak. It may be an unscrupulous act of purposeful incitement, but it is sufficient to rouse the crowd to anger.

Once the mob absorbs the fact that the conspirators had indulged in mutiny, Antony tells those present to protect their interest and show gratitude to their greatest benefactor. He then decides that it is time to read Caesar's will. He tells the crowd that Caesar has left seventy-five drachmas for every citizen of Rome. He has left all his famous gardens across the Tiber for public use. The crowd is sufficiently incensed to become a senseless mob. They seize benches, chairs and anything wooden and place them one on top of the other in a pyre. They place Caesar's body on it. They snatch torches from the pile and rush to set fire to the houses of the assassins.

Antony is thoroughly satisfied with what he sees. He decides it is time for the words uttered by him to take affect. He knows mischief is at work. He decides to let it take whatever course it desires.

A servant arrives and tells Antony that Octavius Caesar has already arrived in Rome. He is in Caesar's house along with Lepidus. Antony is pleased that Octavius Caesar has arrived at the most opportune moment for him. He decides to visit Octavius Caesar. The servant informs Antony that Brutus and Cassius were fleeing like mad men from the gates of Rome. Antony feels that they may have learnt how he stirred the passions of the people of Rome.

Commentary

Chronologically, the scene at the Forum immediately follows the scene in the Capiol. It is, perhaps, one of the most dramatic scenes written by Shakespeare. Antony surfaces as a master in oration and manipulation of the crowd. He is able to incite the Roman citizens so much that they become a senselessly destructive mob. They had praised Brutus just minutes ago for killing Caesar and liberating them; now they want to burn the houses of the conspirators. This masterful scene brings into sharp contrast Brutus and Antony. Brutus defends the assassination while Antony attacks it. Brutus thrives on logic, while Antony uses emotions. Shakespeare understood mob psychology. He knew that reason inspires man in his individual capacity. He succumbs to emotions every time he huddles into a group. Antony's speech is all the more masterful because it works within the limitations made by Brutus. If anything , Antony uses these limitations to his advantage.

Antony's power as a verbal persuader is important to the play as a whole. Julius Caesar is a political play. It deals with the manner in which men achieve power, and how they convince society that their actions are worthy. It deals with the stupidity of an average citizen who can be swayed to extreme views. It deals with the lack of rationale in society and the individuals who form part of it. It is surprising how often people are swayed by self-seeking politicians into giving them inordinate powers. A large part of the first half of the play is concerned with pursuasion. Since pursuasion mostly means the superimposition of one's will over others, a lot of irrationality comes into play if the pursuader succeeds in advancing lies. We have to make a choice in this play whether Caesar and Antony or Brutus and Cassius choose the path of truth. Shakespeare, as is his wont, does not provide us with a simplistic view to things. He gives some remarkably good qualities to all four men; he also provides them with some extremely bad ones. The reader of Julius Caesar has to make an option between which out of these two views appear plausible. Most of us can make a choice between good and bad. Our problem arises when we have to choose between emotions and logic and between prejudices and intellectual truth. Caesar may be burning with greed but he knows that the sensible thing is to suppress it and to rule Rome compassionately. His will is a direct reflection of how rationality can win over greed. Caesar is portayed as having sufficient desire to become king, He is heroic because he wins over this inordinate desire. Cassius, on the other hand, is a perfect picture of sacrifice, but we all know that the master manipulator has an eye on the power that will come to him once Caesar is out of the way. Brutus is not power-hungry. He genuinely wants the good of the Roman citizens. There is, however, a huge difference between a desire to do good and to actually achieve it. Brutus kills Caesar without any evidence. He thinks that power will corrupt Caesar. This may be a fair summation of what absolute power can do to men. Yet, it cannot justify brutal death of a trusting friend. Shakespeare had to let Brutus lose in order to maintain an inviolable moral order in his play. Antony becomes the physical manifestation through which Shakespeare can restore this moral order.

The funeral speech, what the Romans called "laudatio funebris" was a common custom is ancient Rome. Plutarch had mentioned this in his account though he had not provided details of how it was to be achieved. Shakespeare uses this brief mention by Plutarch and converts it into a huge dramatic contrast, specially through the speeches of Brutus and Antony. Everything about the two speakers—their characters, their political ideologies and their thought-process—is evident in what they say.

Brutus speaks in prose. It is suited to his calm, logical and factual utterances. In sharp contrast, Antony speaks in poetry. Brutus begins his speech as if he is trying to attract the attention of his class. We will later learn that his speech is infact, a lesson in learning, delivered by a teacher. He constructs words with controlled care. He uses parallel constructions. He talks about "loved-weep", "valiant-honour", etc. It is a rational manner in which a logical person would speak. Brutus delivers his lecture as if he is making a mathematical demonstration. He pauses for a reply as a reflection of his superb confidence in his own truth. Brutus makes two crucial errors due to his two best qualities that we ought to admire so much. It never occurs to him that a right when carried to extremes becomes a wrong. His honour and integrity are valuable traits among people who understand them; but they can be dangerously useless commodities in front of a senseless and unthinking mob. Brutus makes the error of believing that since his cause his just, all he needs is to present facts to the people. He is confident that justice and truth prevail in the world, once the facts are made available. This is so contrary to the manner in which the world reacts, that we can at best consider Brutus to be naïve. His second mistake is to believe that people huddled into a crowd will listen to logic. When two or more people form a group, the first thing that normally rushes out of the window is logic. Groups are formed when

individuals find themselves incapable of handling life. They obviously want
to extract an inordinate amount of advantage for themselves from the group.
Since every member wants this unfair advantage, it is inevitable that a group
becomes a chaotic entity. Brutus' dangerous lack of insight into the practical
realities of mob-mentalily is further revealed in his complete misunderstanding
of the reaction to his speech. It is obvious that the crowd hasn't understood
him. It mindlessly shouts "Let him be Caesar", which means that the crowd
can replace one with the other without due justification. It never occurs to
Brutus that if he can sway the crowd to mindless acceptance then so can
Antony.

Granville-Barker comments thus about Antony's speech, "The
cheapening of the truth, the appeals to passion, the perfect carillon of flattery,
cajoling, mockery and pathos, swinging to a magnificent tune, all serve to
make it a model of what popular oratory should be. In a school of demagogues
its critical analysis might well be an item on every examination paper."

Antony succeeds because he backs truth, and because his emotions
are so genuine. He ardently loves Caesar, he has no personal ambition and he
genuinely wants the good of the people. He uses these emotions to inspire the
mob, to rise against the conspirators. Antony knows that he does not have the
strength to counter the collective might of the conspirators. He needs the
crowd on his side in order to win against them. We may assume that even
Brutus understands the need to sway public opinion, but it is Antony who
truly understands how to achieve it.

Antony deliberately takes a pro-Brutus stand. He tells the crowd that
he does not wish to praise Caesar. He calls Brutus noble. He concedes that
Caesar may have been ambitious. We know that he uses it as a double-edged
sword when he says "If it were so". This means that Antony wishes to use the
accusations of the conspirators and turn them to his advantage. He is not in
too much of a hurry to sway the crowd to his side. He knows that Brutus is an
honourable man. He uses the word honourable as a repeated refrain in order
to convince the crowd that Brutus has not acted honourably. He uses the
word honourable eight times—each time with increased bitterness and
sarcasm, and finally in open contempt. An actor, playing Antony must begin
uttering the word with warmth and slowly add bitterness and sarcasm to it.
Most actors make the mistake of uttering the word "honourable" with sarcasm,
the very first time. This loses the effectiveness of Antony's gradual tempo.

Antony talks about Caesar's ambition and then reminds the mob how
he had filled the "general coffers" and wept for the poor. He reminds them
how Caesar had refused the crown thrice. He then tells the mob that "men

have lost their reason". He tells the crowd that "there is much reason" in what he says. It is an obviously ironic reference to Brutus' reasoning. Once he has the crowd's attention, Antony shifts from reason to rhetoric. He moves the crowd to rise in "mutiny and rage" against the conspirators, in order to "wrong the dead..... and you". This subtle hint unmistakably links the crowd to the dead Caesar. It makes the crowd and Caesar's cause direct enemies of the conspirators and their cause. Once this is achieved Antony finds no reason to indulge in innuendos. He now introduces something as tangible as Caesar's will; but even now, Antony, the master manipulator, decides to tease and torment the crowd. He shows Caesar's will and does not read it, despite the chanting of the crowd. Instead, he comes down from the forum and shows Caesar's dead body. The crowd is further roused to anger. Antony points at every hole in Caesar's body and links it with a conspirator who made the hole. The crowd reaches a boil. He tells the crowd that he has revealed the "blood treason" of the conspirators. He wishes he had the skills to move "The stones of Rome to rise in mutiny". A fully incensed crowd decides to find the conspirators. Antony calls them back. It is obvious that he holds the mob in amused contempt when he tells the people, "you got to do you know not what". The crowd has forgotten Caesar's will. Antony knows that the crowd needs to have some material benefits in order to act. He tells them that Caesar has bequeathed "walks, arbors, orchards" and to "every several man, seventy-five drachmas". Antony knows it is time to let the mob lose on the conspirators.

As the mob runs off, Antony says in an aside, "Now let it work. Mischief, thou art afoot/Take thou then what course thou wilt"! Antony does not merely let the mob take change. He fully understands that a mob can only create destruction. He knows that he must pick up the rubble and convert it into something constructive if Rome is to survive.

ACT III : SCENE III

Cinna, the poet is on his way to attend Caesar's funeral. He is stopped by an angry crowd who asks him to tell them his name and where he is going. He tells them that his name is Cinna and that his destination is Caesar's funeral. The crowd mistakes him for the conspirator Cinna. He pleads to the crowd that he is Cinna, the poet and not Cinna, the conspirator. The crowd decides to kill him anyway because of his "bad verses." They capture Cinna and then leave with an intention to burn the houses of Brutus, Cassius, Decius, Casca and Ligarius.

Commentary

This scene is a physical manifestation of what a crowd can do when it is angry. Shakespeare wishes to stress the totally illogical nature in which a crowd responds when it is excited. The scene also confirms the complete success that Antony has achieved in rousing the mob against the conspirators. It now lusts for blood, in its irrational thirst for revenge. It is prepared to kill innocent people. It would not mind killing Cinna, the conspirator, but Cinna, the poet would also do to satiate its thirst for blood. We must contrast this angry mob with the delightfully well behaved and pleasant individuals of the first scene of the play. Shakespeare drives home the point that it takes very little spark to incite a peaceful crowd and relegate it into an angry mob. This transformation of peaceful individuals into a murderous mob is also the prime concern of Antony. In a way Antony behaves as does any self seeking politician. To that extent he must be condemned, but we may pardon him because he has no choice but to use the mob to counter the threat posed by the conspirators.

This scene advances some other important themes of the play. Cinna had revealed his dreams and the numerous portents that preceded Caesar's death. These carry a foreshadowing of further violence and personal tragedy. Brutus wanted to remove a tyrant, little realising that Antony has turned the tables on him by making the mob become tyrannical.

ACT IV : SCENE I

In actual history, the events of the scene occurred more than a year after the events of the previous scene. Shakespeare compresses it for the convenience of stage management.

The conspirators have fled from Rome, which is now ruled by the triumvirate comprising of Antony. Octavius Caesar and Lepidus. They make a list of people who must not be protected by law. In other words, it means that they can be killed by anyone. The list includes Lepidus' brother and Antony's nephew. Both agree to include their names in a shameless bargaining of lives.

Lepidus is obviously the juniormost triumvir. Antony makes him fetch Caesar's will so that some of his legacy is distributed among the poor. While he is away, Antony tells Octavius Caesar that Lepidus does not deserve to be one of them. Octavius tells Antony that Lepidus is a wonderful soldier, and that he was a close friend of Julius Caesar. Antony is not impressed. He decides to use Lepidus as a tool and then discard him when he is no more useful.

Antony tells Octavius that Brutus and Cassius are raising an army. They must at once engage them in battle. He decides it is time for their alliances to unite. Octavius agrees that it is time to call a meeting between them. He is scared that their position is dangerous, since they are surrounded by enemies and there are infinite number of mischief makers in their midst.

Commentary

This scene is peacefully quiet, in sharp contrast to the violence of the previous scene. Antony is once again shown as a master manipulator. The triumvirs have acquired power. They now plan to maintain it. In many ways their desire to retain power is similar to what the conspirators had wanted for themselves.

Antony is shown to be even more brutal than the conspirators. The conspirators had atleast spared Mark Antony. He is, however, not prepared to spare anyone who may be remotely a threat to him. The shameless bargaining that the triumvirs indulge in over the lives of their own kith and kin reveals the terrible nature of power. It can only be retained by preventing others from acquiring power and this is only possible by resorting to violence.

Antony had used the mob to serve his purpose. He is now prepared to use Lepidus. Lepidus is a magnificent solider. He is required to counter the threat of the conspirators. He will, however, be ruthlessly discarded after his use is over. Antony appears as bad as Cassius. Atleast, Cassius could be controlled by the misplaced integrity of Brutus. Antony is unmoved by the calming influence of Octavius Caesar.

Octavius is a man of independent ideas. He is prepared to disagree with Antony. He, however, has the intelligence not to indulge in needless arguments with a man who has convinced himself about his own power. This does not mean that Octavius Caesar is any better. He is as power hungry as Antony. He is prepared to destroy the enemies that surround him.

ACT IV : SCENE II

In the camp of the conspirators, Brutus and Cassius organise their armies which have been recruited separately in the various Roman provinces and kingdoms of Asia Minor. They decide to join forces at Sardis on their way to meet the forces of Antony and Octavius, who are advancing across Macedonia. The crisis in the Roman empire has reached a stage where only a showdown can resolve it.

Brutus orders his army to halt, as he sees Lucilius returning with a message from Cassius' army. He has a letter and is accompanied by Pindarus, a servant of Cassius. Brutus reads the letter and then makes the unpardonable mistake of criticising Cassius in front of his own servant. The servant has the grace to support his master in front of Brutus, who adds another mistake by asking Lucilius, how he was treated by Cassius. He then criticises Cassius in front of Lucilius.

They are soon joined by Cassius, who does not even wait to exchange greetings. He is very angry and accuses Brutus of doing him wrong. Brutus is surprised. He tells Cassius that he cannot wrong a brother. He invites Cassius into his tent so that they are not seen fighting in front of their two armies. The two order that their armies be taken to a safe distance and that no man be permitted into their tent till they have finished their conference.

Commentary

We have already seen how Octavius and Antony plan to fight the conspirators. Now, we see a sharp division between Brutus and Cassius. From this point onward, until the end of the play, Brutus and Cassius are the only conspirators who figure in the action. Their decline in fortunes is contrasted by the rise in the fortunes of Antony and Octavius. The martial sounds and crisp commands convey the scene of a big military camp. Brutus has failed as a political man. It is to be seen if he can succeed as a commander of men in the field of battle.

The difference between Brutus and Cassius seems to be of a serious nature. It could threaten their friendship, and the morale of their armies. Brutus shows hints of stoicism when he decides to be unaffected by the decline of friendship between him and Cassius. When Cassius enters, however, he is anything but calm. Fortunately the two decide to sort out their differences in the privacy of their tents.

Plutarch had made only a passing reference to the fight between Cassius and Brutus. Shakespeare portrays it in detail. This has invited conflicting criticism. Rymer talks about "two-drunken Hectors huffing and swaggering for a two-penny reckoning". Bradley considers the incidence dramatically irrelevant. Most critics, however, consider the scene necessary to the development of the play.

ACT IV : SCENE III

This scene is known as the quarrel scene. It is arguably one of the most famous single scenes written by Shakespeare. The emotions in the scene range between cold fury and a reassertion of warm friendship, and finally, to cool calculations for the tactical battle at hand.

Cassius is angry that Brutus has punished a friend for taking bribe in Sardis, despite his request to leave him alone. Brutus tells Cassius that the guilty must be punished. Caesar was also punished so that justice might prevail. Brutus accuses Cassius for wrongly accumulating money from the people of the country. He also accuses him of refusing to send him some of that very money to pay his troops. Cassius makes violent threats; Brutus is unmoved by them; Cassius breaks down in misery because Brutus has lost all affection for him. Brutus is finally moved; and he and Cassius reunite in friendship. Brutus tells Cassius that Portia is dead. She had committed suicide by swallowing burning coals. Cassius is amazed by Brutus' self-control. The two then decide to plan future action along with their generals. Cassius and Brutus drink together and are joined by Titinius and Messala. We learn that Octavius and Antony are marching with their armies towards Philippi. They have already "put to death an hundred senators" including Cicero. Brutus proposes that they march towards Philippi to meet the enemy at once. Cassius thinks it would be better to wait for the enemy to counter them. This would ensure that the enemy is tired while their soldiers remain fresh. Brutus overrules Cassius. Cassius wants to intervene once again, but he keeps quiet when he sees that Brutus is very adamant.

After the guests have departed, Brutus asks Lucius to ask some of his men to sleep with him in his tent. Varro and Claudius enter and offer to keep watch, but Brutus tells them to go to sleep as well. He then asks Lucius to play some music. Lucius sings briefly and then falls asleep. Brutus decides to read a book, but he is interrupted by Caesar's ghost. Brutus wants to know if the ghost is "some God, some angel, or some devil". The ghost tells Brutus that it is "thy evil spirit," and that they will meet again at Philippi. Brutus awakens Lucius, Varro and Claudius. He accuses them of crying out in their sleep. They tell him that they did not cry out in their sleep. He asks them if they saw anything. They confirm that they did not. Brutus decides to convey to Cassius that they must move their armies early in the morning, ahead of schedule.

Commentary

There is no doubt that Brutus is still at war with himself. This is evident in his bitter and long argument with Cassius in the privacy of his tent. Despite this inner turmoil, Brutus never doubts the course of action he has undertaken. He still flinches at anything that is dishonest. That is why he is so angry with Cassius, who has been acquiring wealth in an unfair manner from the people of Rome. Some people see hypocrisy on the part of Brutus, when he accuses Cassius for not sending money to him. He had accused Caesar of acquiring money by unfair means and he wants to have the same money for his army. Much need not be ascribed to Brutus' demands. He needs money to raise his army and not all money in Cassius' possession may have been acquired through dishonest means.

The lack of understanding between the two men is most evident when Cassius claims that he is a better soldier than Brutus. Cassius wishes to stress his greater experience in military service. Brutus thinks that Cassius is suggesting he is a better soldier in battle, and by extension, a better leader in general. This difference in understanding, results in needless arguments over trivial things, especially when one remembers the massive task they have in hand.

Shakespeare delineates Brutus as a person who is at times incapable of logical evaluation. His idealism has a misplaced naivete which makes him appear a school bully. In this scene at least, he does not even display the stoic calm that he claims to practice. The only time he shows it admirably is when he absorbs the news of his wife's death.

Brutus' naivete is most evident in the utter disdain with which he handles Cassius. At one point he calls him a "useless man". He is a general and a senior politician. He should be indulging in staid statesmanship; instead he indulges in the kind of callous behaviour which would put a school bully to shame.

It is fortunate that Brutus and Cassius reconcile after needless letting out of steam. Shakespeare does manage to elevate Brutus when he depicts his stoic resignation to Portia's death. We are acutely aware of Brutus' love for Portia. Despite his stoic resignation, we can presume that his irrational behaviour in front of Cassius is partly due to stress.

After the visiting soldiers have left Brutus' tent we are again face to face with a delicate moment. Shakespeare provides sufficient stage directions to add to the languid details of this moment. Lucius sleeps after singing a few lines. Lucius had symbolised calm and peace at the beginning of the play. He displays this tranquillity once again. In sharp contrast, Brutus is unable to sleep on both occasions. He seems to have lost his peace forever once he joins the conspiracy. The innocent boy is a constant reminder of what Brutus has lost by joining a misplaced cause. Brutus' compassionate treatment of Lucius, Varro and Claudius reveals how humane and sensitive he can be at times. Once we understand this scene we can somewhat explain why Brutus makes those terrible blunders throughout the play. He turns to literature and music when he is alone; he is forced to do battle when he has to face the world. He is familiar to scholarship, but he is totally unsynchronised with the terrible realities of the rash and heartless world of politics and war. Brutus argues with Cassius so bitterly because his principles have been compromised. He had killed Caesar to prevent injustice. He had spared others like Antony because this would have amounted to injustice. In sharp contrast, Antony and Octavius assassinate a hundred senators who may have been a threat to their authority. Brutus suffers because his greatest private virtues become his biggest public enemies. His idealism has no place in a battlefield, because war is the most irrational way of solving any problem.

Music provides relief from the strain of dialogue and action. It also adds to the overall emotional atmosphere of the scene. The song provides melancholy and nostalgia, which underscore this moment of calm.

Shakespeare introduces Caesar's ghost at a very appropriate moment. Brutus may have acquired partial peace, but the fact that Caesar's assassination has failed to achieve any of his noble aims, continues to haunt him. The ghost's entrance is signified by the candle that burns ill. The Elizabethan audience believed that a ghost appeared with a gust of wind. It is also an effective stage device. Brutus had to be interrupted by something, in order to make him look up from his book. The gust of wind achieves that. It also becomes an adequate forerunner to the arrival of the ghost. During Shakespeare's time there was no provision for light and sound affect to show the arrival of an apparition. The Elizabethan audience simply accepted the presence of a ghost when a man appeared wearing a special garment, which was called "a robe for to go invisible". The audience accepted him as invisible even when he was present on stage.

Is the ghost a reality, or is he merely a creation of Brutus' tired mind ? In either case it is a frightening reminder of Caesar, whose presence is felt continually in the second half of the play. The conspirators had hoped to resurrect Rome by killing Caesar. Ironically, Caesar proves to be more powerful dead than alive. The irony is further driven home to us when we remember that Brutus had wanted to only destroy "Caesar's spirit" (II. I. 169) and not "dismember" him. However, he manages to destroy Caesar's body and not his spirit.

The play "Julius Caesar" uses omens and supernatural occurrences more than any other play of Shakespeare. These are introduced to suggest to the audience a sense of impending disaster. This is precisely what the ghost of Caesar conveys as he tells Brutus that he will see him once again on the plains of Philippi. The ghost tells Brutus that it is "thy evil spirit". There is thus no suggestion that it is Caesar's spirit. It is more reasonable to accept it as the evil genius which some classical writers allotted to every man. European tradition necessitated that the spirit be made into the ghost of the murdered Caesar. The Elizabethan audience would have empathised with Caesar's ghost more than an evil spirit. Shakespeare made this change from Plutarch to suit his audience, but in his carelessness, allowed the dialogue to remain unchanged.

ACT V : SCENE I

On the plains of Philippi, Octavius, Antony and their forces await the arrival of Brutus and Caesar. A messenger arrives with the message that the enemy is approaching. Antony wants Octavius to take the left side of the field, but he insists upon taking the right and Antony taking the left.

Brutus and Cassius enter with their followers, and soon, opposing generals confront one another in a parley. The two sides insult each other. Antony calls Brutus a hypocrite for killing Caesar. He also calls other conspirators cowards for the manner in which they killed Caesar. Cassius accuses Antony of using deceit in his meeting with the conspirators following the assassination. He tells Brutus that there is no reason why they must tolerate Antony's uncouth language. They would not have had to endure all this if they had killed Antony along with Caesar. Octavius suggests that they end their talking and begin fighting. He announces that he will not put his sword back in its sheath. until he has avenged Caesar's death. Brutus denies being a traitor. Cassius calls Octavius a "peevish schoolboy" and Antony a "masker and a reveller". Antony responds and says that Cassius is "Old Cassius still". Octavius challenges Brutus and Cassius to fight at once or whenever they have courage to face him. He then leaves with Antony and their armies.

Commentary

We had been told in the previous scene that Brutus and Cassius will confront their enemy on the plains of Philippi. Now Octavius and Antony witness the arrival of Brutus and Cassius. The parley that occurs between them is designed to show the contrast between the leaders. Antony and Octavius are supremely confident about their victory; Brutus and Cassius, in sharp contrast, are filled with doubt. Even when the generals were in parley, Brutus wanted conciliation. This is evident when he tells Octavius, "Good words are better than bad strokes". However, neither Antony nor Octavius are in any mood for a peaceful settlement. It is significant that Antony calls Brutus a hypocrite. This is bound to hurt Brutus, who prides himself in being a man of integrity and honour. Brutus had hoped that the assasination of Caesar would be a ritual of sacrifice to the Gods. This hope is totally belied when he realises that he is considered a cowardly butcher. Antony cleverly manipulates the situation where Brutus has to defend the assasination of one man to a person who has murdered a hundred senators. Cassius accuses Antony of deception. This falls lightly on Antony's ears. He is now the general of a mighty army, and he is supremely confident of his victory. He has no need to remember the moment when he had to grovel in front of the conspirators after Caesar's assasination. Cassius had accused Antony of stealing the buzzing of the bees. Antony tells him that he has the sting of a Hybla bee. The parley ends when Octavius and Antony challenge Brutus and Cassius to fight whenever they dare.

When Antony says "Old Cassius still" he refers to Cassius' well known cynicism and caustic wit. Cassius is fully aware that Antony is not merely a reveller. He is also a dangerous enemy. His needless remark shows that he has lost some of the effectiveness of his caustic wit. He indulges in baseless accusations. We remember that he had once manipulated Caesar extremely effectively; then he became dependent on Brutus, which limited his ability to manipulate others. Once friendship flourished between the two, Cassius deferred to Brutus. In this scene he is an odd mixture of emotions and despair. He is oddly aware that the battle has to begin on his birthday and it may end his life. He is also reluctant to venture everything on the result of one battle. He is not sure that he will win in this battle. Eagles were the symbols of the Roman legions, but the eagles that had accompanied his army from Sardis had left and had been replaced by "raven crows". Cassius is convinced that his army would become prey to birds that are traditional harbingers of death. He had once accused Caesar of being superstitious; now he is inflicted with the same disease. All he can tell Messala is that he will face all dangers bravely. Yet, when he and Brutus converse, they do so as if it will be their last.

Brutus, despite his stoic indifference to pain, is also ready for inevitable defeat. He decides to choose personal honour over consistency of philosophy. He will take his own life rather than permit the enemy to parade him on the streets of Rome. We know he thinks that his cause is a hopeless one when he wishes to end the war one way or the other.

There are differences between Antony and Octavius as well. This is evident rather early in the play when Octavius challenges Antony and reverses his order on which side of the field each must take. According to Plutarch there was a disagreement between Brutus and Cassius as to who should lead the right wing of the army. It is evident that Shakespeare made use of this incident, but transferred it to the opposite camp, in order to bring out the character of Octavius. He is depicted as a headstrong boy. In comparison, Antony shows enormous maturity when he does not challenge Octavius, for what is essentially an immature demand. However, Octavius' challenge has a profound reason. Shakespeare had read Plutanch and known that Octavius and Antony would later struggle for supremacy, where Octavius will emerge victorious. This phase of the story will provide Shakespeare with the plot for his next play "Antony and Cleopatra". Thus Shakespeare had Octavius' potential power in mind when he gave the youngster a mind of his own. The mind may as yet appear immature but it at least demands attention.

The parley between leaders of the opposing armies may appear stupid to modern sensibilities, but it was pretty common with Shakespeare. He introduced it because the battle itself can be given only a restricted representation on stage. The parley is a very affective way of showing the mental disposition of opposing leaders. Antony's seering anger and Octavius' utter contempt are contrasted by Brutus' desire to reconcile and Cassius' inability to muster his famous caustic wit.

Both Cassius and Brutus make reference to philosophy. Cassius' epicurean view held that human beings must live sensibly in a controlled and restrained manner. It is a view that cannot include any kind of superstition. Brutus' stoicism preached acceptance of suffering with out any pain. Shakespeare makes it very clear that both men abandon their principles. Cassius is illogically superstitious and Brutus indulges in exaggerated pain.

ACT V : SCENE II

It is still the beginning of the battle of Philippi. Brutus sends Messala with a message to Cassius that he must engage the enemy forces without delay. He believes that Octavius' army is vulnerable because it is low on morale.

Commentary

We are given first glimpse of battle. Brutus has an upper hand. He believes that it is possible for him to win with some help from Cassius. He has broken the will of Octavius' forces, and all he must do is to prevent Antony from strengthening him. That is the reason why he wants Cassius to engage Antony's forces. Brutus decides to act on behalf of Cassius as well as his own. Plutarch had given a detailed version of the folly behind Brutus' thought. His action does not take into consideration the consequence if the two armies do not act in complete cohesion. If Brutus were to attack before Cassius can act, it would expose Cassius' flank to encirclement by Antony. The next scene would fully expose this flaw.

ACT V : SCENE III

Cassius sees his men retreating. Brutus' forces, having driven back Octavius' forces advance in order to seek maximum advantage. This leaves Antony's army free to surround Cassius' troops. Cassius sends Titinius to ride towards the soldiers seen in the distance, in order to find out who they are. To make things doubly sure he sends Pindarus to mount the hill and watch Titinius. Pindarus returns and tells Cassius that he had seen Titinius surrounded by soldiers who were shouting with joy. Cassius mistakenly believes that Titinius has been taken prisoner. He arrives at a decision that he must kill himself. He tells Pindarus to keep his oath of obedience and stab him. Pindarus does as ordered. Cassius dies, saying, "Caesar, thou art revenged, Even with the sword that killed thee."

It becomes obvious that Cassius had made a mistake. Titinius had not been captured. He had infact been hailed by Brutus' troops when he arrived in their midst. He soon returns with Messala to comfort Cassius with the news that Octavius' men have been overthrown by Brutus. The two find Cassius dead. Titinius kills himself with the same sword with which Cassius had committed suicide. Messala goes to report the tragedy to Brutus.

Brutus comes to where Cassius' dead body is lying. He is accompanied by Messala, Young Cato, Strato, Volumnius and Lucilius. Brutus pays a sad farewell to Cassius, and calls him "the last of all the Romans". He then leaves with the others to engage the enemy once again.

Commentary

We now realise the tactical blunder committed by Brutus in the previous scene. His premature attack permits Antony to encircle Cassius. It is also easily obvious that Brutus' men do not have their master's upright integrity. They indulge in looting after their victory over Octavius' army. Their looting means that they are not ready to do battle when Cassius is surrounded by Antony's men. This makes Cassius' position very vulnerable because Brutus' tactics would have only worked if there had been complete synchronisation between his and Cassius' armies.

Shakespeare could not possibly have stimulated a battle on the primitive Elizabethan stage. He does the next best thing by letting Pindarus report the action occurring on the surrounding battlefield to Cassius and to the audience. It is Cassius' mistaken judgement of Pindarus which leads to his suicide. Pindarus reports that Titinius is captured by the enemy. Cassius sends Pindarus because his own eyesight is "thick". On stage Pindarus would climb to the upper level. This would represent a point "higher on that hill".

Brutus had been extremely sure of his victory in the previous scene. We quickly learn how illusory his hope has been. Cassius is defeated by Antony but Brutus wins against Octavius. The problem arises when Brutus cannot come to Cassius' help. It is ironic that the upright Brutus' men indulge in looting instead of coming to Cassius' rescue. It is even more ironic that the same Cassius, who had lived his entire life through pragmatic realities, is now duped into believing what a servant's limited intelligence can convey. Shakespeare brings about a huge transformation in both Brutus and Cassius. In a way he lets us know that most of us can uphold our philosophy only till the going is smooth. We discard our values when we succumb to the pressure of the moment. Shakespeare shows another side of Cassius, in order to dramatically advance his play. Until Caesar was killed, there was sharp dramatic contrast between the unscrupulous Cassius and the upright Brutus. Once Caesar is killed the conflict is largely between Antony and the conspirators. There is no inconsistency in the presentation of Cassius. He was the hunter in the first half of the play; he becomes the hunted in the second half. Cassius had predicted that he will have to commit suicide, and now when he kills himself he can only sadly remark that Caesar's murderer has become his avenger.

Shakespeare concentrates the two battles of Philippi into one. This leads to a minor error. Titinius had mentioned about the setting sun, but later Brutus talks about another encounter with the enemy at three o'clock in the closing part of the scene.

Ferguson talks about the pathos in the deaths of Cassius and Titinius thus : "Brutus, however, hopes to live and triumph. The play approaches its climax as does a symphony. The rhythm quickens momentarily, offering a tentative hope of a return to a happier theme. Then chord after chord leads to the tragic close."

ACT IV : SCENE IV

On the battlefield, amidst intense fighting, Brutus tells Young Cato, Lucilius, and others to stand upright and be brave. He leaves, and Young Cato shouts his name and loyalty to Rome. Soon Antony's soldiers enter. In the ensuing fight, Cato is killed, and Lucilius is taken prisoner, because the enemy mistakes him for Brutus. He is then left under guard, as one of the soldiers runs to bring Antony to him. Soon Antony arrives and asks for Brutus. Lucilius tells him that Brutus is alive and will never be taken prisoner. Antony tells the guard to keep a close watch on Lucilius. He then sends his soldiers to search for Brutus and to report to him in Octavius' tent.

Commentary

There was no clear winner in the first battle at Philippi, because Brutus had defeated Octavius but Cassius had to commit suicide. In this scene, Brutus tries desperately to keep the morale of his men high, but fails. Young Cato dies, uttering his hatred for tyranny, suggesting that the triumvirate has become even more tyrannical than Caesar. Once Cato is killed and Lucilius is taken prisoner, the defeat of the republican armies becomes inevitable. Antony is brimming with so much confidence that he leaves the outcome of battle to his soldiers, as he himself retreats to Octavius' tent.

Shakespeare stresses on Lucilius' loyalty. He impersonates Brutus in order to give his commander time to regroup or to escape. Even in the jaws of defeat, Lucilius is never in doubt that Brutus will act in an upright manner. It is a fair reflection of how an admiring friend accepts Brutus' entire existence. Antony orders for Lucilius' protection because he knows how rare it is to find loyalty. He is investing in men like Lucilius for the future when he will govern Rome along with Octavius.

ACT V : SCENE V

Brutus enters along with Dardanius, Clitus, Strato, and Volumnius. It is obvious that they are on the run after having lost the battle. Brutus first requests Clitus and then Dardanius to kill him. They both refuse to do his bidding. Brutus tells Volumnius that Caesar's ghost had once again paid him a visit; he knows that it is time for him to die. Volumnius does not agree with Brutus, who tells him that in any case they are totally cornered by the enemy. He asks Volumnius to hold his sword while he runs into it. Volumnius refuses to do this, because it is not a task that a friend must perform. Clitus tells Brutus to escape because the place is too dangerous. Brutus is too tired to run. He knows it is the moment of glorious death. He bids farewell to Volumnius, Strato and his countrymen.

Clitus, Dardanius and Volumnius flee when Brutus tells them that he will soon follow. He then requests Strato to hold his sword while he runs upon it. He tells Strato to turn the other way so that he cannot see him die. Strato agrees; Brutus runs over the sword and dies.

Amid the ringing of alarms, Octavius, Antony, Messala, Lucilius and others enter. They find Strato along with Brutus' body. Octavius offers service to all those who had served Brutus. Antony delivers a brief oration over Brutus' body. He calls Bruuts "the noblest Roman of them all...". All other conspirators attacked Caesar because they were jealous of him; only Brutus killed him for the good of Rome. Octavius promises a proper funeral for Brutus. He orders his men to stop the battle. Once this is done, he realises he can call his friends to join him in celebrating their victory.

Commentary

The sounding of the alarms adds to the urgency of an already desperate situation for Brutus and his army. Brutus, like Cassius, believes that the cycle of his life is complete. He decides to kill himself, but Clitus, Dardanius and Volumnius refuse to kill him because they honour him very much. Brutus may be in a predicament, but their love for him must be very satisfying to his tired bones. Brutus reconciles his defeat by forcing himself to believe that no man has ever been untrue to him. This is, of course, not true, because Cassius had obviously used him at the beginning of the play. He was also used by Antony, who promised to be his friend, but took advantage of his naivete. Brutus is convinced Antony and Octavius will be gracious in victory because he has maintained his integrity and honour. To the very end, Brutus believes that he was justified in killing Caesar.

Octavius decides to take those who were loyal to Brutus into the new political establishment, and Antony praises the noble Brutus. This is consistent with the basic characters of the two victorious leaders. Both of them try to strengthen themselves in order to gain superiority. We know the death of Brutus is only the beginning of another power struggle between Antony and Octavius.

Brutus wanted to still the spirit of Caesar, without killing Caesar the man. Antony uses Caesar's death to seek revenge and to use the opportunity to his advantage. Brutus reveals that the ghost of Caesar had visited him once again, and his final words are "Caesar, now be still; I kill'd not thee with half so good a will." The spirit of Caesar becomes still because it now resides in Antony. It is noticeable that both Antony and Octavius make no mention of Caesar as they celebrate their victory, and concentrate on establishing a new order.

CHAPTER 6

SOME USEFUL INFORMATION

Ques 1 : What is the date when the book "Julius Caesar" was published and composed?

Ans. : Julius Caesar was first published in 1623 in Folio edition. There is no evidence that it had been issued previously in Quarto. The play was written in the year 1601.

Ques 2 : Name the plays on Roman history written by Shakespeare.

Ans. : Shakespeare wrote four plays on Roman history : Julius Caesar, Antony and Cleopatra, Coriolanus and Timon of Athens.

Ques. 3. Which play of Shakespeare does "Julius Caesar" resemble?

Ans. : Julius Caesar most intimately resembles "Hamlet", since both are tragedies of reflection.

Ques. 4 : Where does the play begin and why ?

Ans. : The play begins on the streets of Rome. This was a common practice with Shakespeare. "Romeo and Juliet" opens with a street fight and "Coriolanus" with a mob. Moreover, "Julius Caesar" is intimately linked with the influence of the mob on the governance of a state.

Ques 5 : What is the crowd doing at the opening of the play?

Ans : The crowd is rejoicing Caesar's triumph over Pompey's two sons at Munda in Spain in September 45 BC.

Ques 6: What do Flavius and Marullus tell the crowd?

Ans : Flavius and Marullus rebuke the crowd for their fickleness. It had honoured Pompey recently and it is now rejoicing the death of his two sons.

Ques 7 : Who is the runner, and what does Caesar want from him on the occasion at the Feast of Lupercalia.

Ans : Antony is one of the runners of the course of the religious Feast of Lupercalia. Caesar asks Antony to touch his wife while running so that she would be cured of the curse of infertility. The Romans believed that barren women were cured if one of the runners touched them during the Feast of Lupercalia.

Ques 8 : What prophecy is made to Caesar during the Feast of Lupercalia ? Who makes this prophecy to him?

Ans : Caesar is told by a soothsayer to beware of the Ides of March, which was the 15th day of the month in March as per the Roman calendar.

Ques 9 : How does Caesar respond to the soothsayer?

Ans : Caesar dismisses him as a dreamer.

Ques 10 : How does Cassius manage to win Brutus to the conspiracy of murdering Caesar?

Ans : Cassius incites Brutus by touching upon his love for the Roman citizens, on his honour and on his hatred for tyranny.

Ques 11 : How many times is the crown offered to Caesar by Antony? What is Caesar's response?

Ans : Antony offers the crown thrice to Caesar. He refuses to accept it everytime.

Ques 12 : What is Caesar's illness?

Ans : He is deaf in one ear. He is also prone to epileptic fits.

Ques 13 : Who utters these lines and why ?

"…. they are portentous things

Unto the climate that they point upon"

Ans : These lines are spoken by Casca in reference to the thunderstorm.

Ques 14 : Why does Shakespeare use prodigies, omens and portents in "Julius Caesar" ?

Ans : Shakespeare uses them to add to the supernatural dread of the play and thus create a fitting backdrop to the impending catastrophe of the human world.

Ques 15 : Who speaks the words: "O, he sits high in all people's hearts?"

Ans : These words are spoken by Casca in reference to Brutus.

Ques 16 : Why does Brutus decide to kill Caesar?

Ans : He thinks Caesar might become a tyrant after he is crowned King . He thus kills him for the good of the Roman citizens

Ques 17 : Who utters these words ? Whom are these words uttered to and why?

"O, Rome, I make thee promise,

If the redress will follow, thou receivest

Thy full petition at the hand of Brutus!"

Ans : The above words are spoken by Brutus, in reaction to a letter thrown through his window and brought to him by Lucius.

Ques 18 : What does Calphurnia ask Caesar to do on the morning of the Ides of March and why?

Ans : Calphurnia, Caesar's wife, asks his husband not to set forth from the house because she had dreamt the previous night that he would be murdered on that day.

Ques 19 : Who persuades Caesar to go to the Senate House on the Ides of March? How does he manage to do it ?

Ans : Decius Brutus persuades Caesar to go the Senate House. He manages to persuade him by interpreting Calphurnia's dream in a favourable manner. He tells Caesar that the Senate would laugh at his lack of courage. He also reminds him that the Senate may offer the crown to him on that day.

Ques 20 : Who offers a piece of paper to Caesar as he approaches the Capitol on the morning of the Ides of March ?

Ans : The piece of paper is presented to Caesar by Artemidorus. The paper is a petition warning Caesar of the conspirators.

Ques 21 : Who stabs Caesar first ?

Ans : Caesar is first stabbed by Casca.

Ques 22 : What is Caesar's reaction when Brutus stabs him?

Ans : He cries, "Et tu Brute ! — Then fall, Caesar !"

Ques 23 : What does Antony do soon after Caesar is murderred?

Ans : Antony flees to his house.

Ques 24 : What conditions are imposed on Antony for allowing him to speak on Caesar's funeral?

Ans : Antony is told that he must not blame the conspirators, he must tell the mob that he is speaking with the permission of the conspirators and that he must speak from the same platform from which Brutus is scheduled to deliver his speech.

Ques 25 : How does the crowd react to Brutus' speech?

Ans : The crowd is convinced that Caesar was a tyrant and that Brutus was as noble as Caesar.

Ques 26 : How does the crowd react to Antony's speech?

Ans : The crowd completely changes its mind and believes that the conspirators are criminals. They are so incensed that they want to set the houses of the conspirators on fire.

Ques 27 : Who is killed by the mob in place Cinna, the conspirator?

Ans : Cinna, the poet is killed by the mob in place of Cinna, the conspirator.

Ques 28 : What is the outcome of the quarrel between Brutus and Cassius before the commencement of the battle of Philippi?

Ans : They both reconcile in the end.

Ques 29 : Why and how does Cassius kill himself ?

Ans : Cassius kills himself because Pindarus wrongly tells him that Titinius has been taken prisoner by the enemy. He asks Pindarus to stab him with the same sword that killed Caesar.

Ques 30 : What does Brutus do when he is finally defeated?

Ans : He commits suicide by running over his sword held by Strato.

Ques 31 : Who utters the word "This was the noblest Roman of them all"?

Ans : These words are uttered by Antony over Brutus' dead body.

CHAPTER 7

REFERENCE TO CONTEXT

(ANNOTATIONS)

1

These growing feathers pluck'd from Caesar's wing

Will make him fly an ordinary pitch;

Who else would soar above the view of men,

And keep us all in servile fearfulness.   [I.i.77-80]

The above lines are spoken by Flavius to Marullus in Shakespeare's play "Julius Caesar". Both these men are tribunes in the government of Rome. Flavius, like some other officials in the Senate, is jealous of Caesar's growing popularity and power. He is convinced that Caesar's ambition, if not checked in time, would make him a tyrant and threaten the freedom and liberty of every Roman citizen. The two tribunes, first try to disperse the crowd from the streets of Rome, and then decide to remove all the banners and decorations hanging on the statues of Caesar.

The metaphor in these lines is of a hawk. It is taken from the sport of falconry. Flavius compares Caesar to a hawk because he has begun to soar high in the air. His new honours are compared to the growing feathers of a bird. Just as a bird cannot fly if the feathers are plucked, Caesar will also be deprived of his ambition if popular support is taken away from him. In other words, it will prevent Caesar from soaring to the heights of power that he has begun to enjoy. He would then not look down upon lesser mortals with disdain and keep them all in fearful servility.

2

If it be aught toward the general good,

Set honour in one eye, and death i' the other,

And I will look on both indifferently;

For let the gods so speed me as I love

The name of honour more than I fear death.   [I.ii.85-89]

The above lines are spoken by Brutus to Cassius in the play Julius Caesar written by Shakespeare. Cassius is extremely ambitious man. He is jealous of Caesar's popularity and greatness. After winning many officials to his side in a conspiracy to kill Caesar, he knows it is crucial to win over the honourable and noble Brutus. Brutus is afraid that the people of Rome may make Caesar king. Cassius asks Brutus if such a thing worries him. Brutus admits that he does not like Caesar being made king. He asks Cassius what he wishes to tell him. If it is anything in the interest of the public, and if it is a choice between death and honour, he will make his choice calmly. He swears to Caesar, as he wishes the gods to help him, that this love for honour is greater than his fear for death.

One of the themes of Julius Caesar is honour blinded by barren idealism. Brutus symbolises such honour. This makes him susceptible to manipulation by the clever Cassius. Brutus' honour has no rational code and moral process of thought. Shakespeare exposes the danger of practicing virtuous emotions without any profound understanding of life.

3

> I, as Aeneas, our great ancestor,
> Did from the flames of Troy upon his shoulder
> The old Anchises bear, so from the waves of Tiber
> Did I the tired Caesar. And this man
> Is now become a god; and Cassius is
> A wretched creature, and must bend his body,
> If Caesar carelessly but nod on him.   [I.ii.112-118]

The above lines are spoken by Cassius to Brutus in Shakespeare's play "Julius Caesar". Cassius is extremely jealous of Caesar. He tells Brutus that Caesar is an ordinary person, without any great quality. Cassius tells Brutus that he is greater and stronger than Caesar. He narrates the incident when Caesar had asked for his help when he was once downing in the River Tiber. Once their ancestor, Aeneas had rescued his old father from the old Anchises bear and the burning town of Troy upon his shoulders. In the same manner did he carry the tired Caesar from the waves of the Tiber. And now the same feeble Caesar is regarded as God, whereas, he, Cassius is treated no better than a wretched creature, who has to bow everytime Caesar even nods in his directions.

The incident of Aeneas and the Trojan War is described by Virgil in the epic Aeneid. Anchises was the father of Aeneas. He was too old and weak, and was trapped in the burning city of Troy. Aeneas rescued his father from the burning city by carrying him on his shoulders. Cassius calls Aeneas his ancestor because as per belief, Rea Silvia, the mother of Romulus, who was the founder of Rome, was a descendant of Silvius, who was the son of Aeneas and Lavinia.

4

> Why, man, he doth bestride the narrow world
> Like a Colossus, and we petty men
> Walk under his huge legs, and peep about
> To find ourselves dishonourable graves.   [I.ii.135-138]

The above lines are uttered by Cassius to Brutus in Shakespeare's play "Julius Caesar". Cassius tells Brutus that Caesar has become a tyrant. Despite being feeble and weak, Caesar has gained immense popularity. This is evident from the shouts of the crowd during the Feast of Lupercal.

Cassius knows that Caesar stands over their narrow world as the Colossus (statue at Rhodes) bestrides the harbour. They, miserable men, walk far below him, and can look for nothing but dishonourable death.

The most celebrated of the Colossal statues of antiquity was the bronze statue of Apollo, the sun god. It was one of the seven wonders of the world. It was one hundred feet high. It was made by Chares, a sculptor from Rhodes, between 292 and 280 BC. It was destroyed by an earthquake in 224 BC. As per legend its legs spanned the harbour of Rhodes.

5

> Age, thou art sham'd!
> Rome, thou hast lost the breed of noble bloods!
> When went there by an age, since the great flood,
> But it was fam'd with more than with one man?   [I.ii150-153]

The above lines are uttered by Cassius to Brutus in Shakespeare's play "Julius Caesar". Cassius is extremely critical about the servile spirit of the age in which the Romans are born . He thinks it is a shame to his age that Rome has lost the race of noble souls she once produced. He wonders whether there was any age in Rome, since the flood of Adam, which was not made famous by more than a single man ? When was an age in Rome so barren as to be dependent on the greatness of one single man ?

Cassius consistently plays on Brutus' republican philosophy in order to belittle Caesar. He cannot find anything concrete against Caesar, but his hatred and ambition is such that he would not be satisfied until Caesar is dead. He wants Brutus on his side because he wants his terrible deed to appear honourable.

6

> Such men as he be never at heart's ease
> Whiles they behold a greater than themselves;

> And therefore are they very dangerous.
>
> I rather tell thee what is to be fear'd
>
> Than what I fear; for always I am Caesar   [I.ii. 209-213]

The above lines are uttered by Julius Caesar to Mark Antony in the play"Julius Caesar" written by Shakespeare. Caesar is convinced that Cassius must not be trusted because he is a dangerous man. Antony thinks that Cassius is loyal and well-disposed towards the regime. Caesar, however, believes that Cassius can never be at ease with himself because he is a lean and hungry-looking man. He is constantly in deep thought, he reads too much, and he appears to be a calculating and shrewd man. Such men as he are never quiet at ease in their hearts when they see someone who is greater than them. Therefore, they are very dangerous. Caesar tells Antony that he is merely pointing out what should be feared and not what scares him. He shall always remain Caesar, who knows no fear.

The above lines show that Caesar is an astute judge of character. It also shows his inability to use his insight to his advantage because he is vane and arrogant. It is surprising that Antony makes a mistake about assessing a character . Fortunately this will be the last mistake that he will make in the play.

7

> Well, Brutus, thou art noble; yet, I see,
> Thy honourable metal may be wrought
> From that it is dispos'd : therefore 'tis meet
> That noble minds keep over with their likes;
> For who so firm that cannot be seduc'd?
> Caesar doth bear me hard, but he loves Brutus :
> If I were Brutus now, and he were Cassius,
> He should not honour me.   [I.ii.312-319]

The above lines are uttered by Cassius in a soliloquy in the play "Julius Caesar" written by Shakespeare. Cassius plans to murder Caesar. He tells Brutus that Caesar must be killed because he has become too ambitious. Brutus promises to see him at his house the next day, and then leaves. Left alone on stage, Cassius, in a soliloquy, admits that Brutus is noble.. Yet, he sees that Brutus' honourable nature can be bent from its natural direction, and inclined towards dishonourable actions . In a statement of profound irony, he admits that noble minds should always keep company of noble minds, because no one can be so determined that he cannot be led astray. Cassius admits that Caesar dislikes him, but he loves Brutus. If he were Brutus, right now, and Brutus were Cassius, he would not influence him against Caesar.

Nobility and honour are two words which are constantly linked with Brutus throughout the play. Shakespeare exposes the dangers of misplaced honour and nobility when he ends Brutus' life in tragedy.

8

I have seen tempests, when the scolding winds
Have riv'd the knotty oaks; and I have seen
The ambitious ocean swell and rage and foam,
To be exalted with the threatening clouds :
But never till to-night, never till now
Did I go through a tempest dropping fire.
Either there is civil strife in heaven;
Or else the world, too saucy with the gods,
Incenses them to send destruction.   [I.iii.5-13]

The above lines are spoken by Casca to Cicero in the play "Julius Caesar" written by Shakespeare. A terrible storm is brewing in Rome.. It terrifies Casca. He tells Cicero that he had seen storms where the angry winds splitted the hard, knotted oak trees. He had seen the rising ocean swell and roar and froth as if it was trying to rise upto the height of the clouds, in order to bring down rain and thunder. However, he had never till that night experienced a tempest which dropped fire. He is convinced that either a civil war has begun in heaven, or else the world, behaving too rudely in front of the gods, has provoked them to send down destruction.

The strife in the skys is a violent manifestation of the terrible conspiracy against Caesar. It was a common device used by Shakespeare. He used the supernatural to convey the chaos in the world moral order. There is civil war in Rome. The Gods seem determined to punish men for their insolence.

Nature symbolises the forces of good as well as the turmoil that exists in the hearts of the conspirators.

9

Therein, ye gods, you make the weak most strong ;
Therein, ye gods, you tyrants do defeat:
Nor stony tower, nor walls of beaten brass,
Nor airless dungeon, nor strong links of iron,
Can be retentive to the strength of spirit;
But life, being weary of those worldly bars,
Never lacks power to dismiss itself.   [I.iii.91-97]

The above lines are uttered by Cassius in the play "Julius Caesar" written by Shakespeare. Casca is fear-stricken due to the terrible storm. He roams on the streets in terror and is met by Cassius. He tells Cassius that the senate intends to make Caesar king. Cassius tells Casca that would be the most unfortunate day in the history of Rome. He will have no option but to kill himself rather than commit himself to slavery. Cassius invokes the gods and tells them that it is in this manner that they make weak men strong. By doing this they give them the power of self destruction. This preserves even the weakest human being and frustrates the designs of the cruelest tyrant. No tower of stone, no wall of hammered brass, no airless prison-cell and no strong iron chain can enclose a powerful human spirit. For life, when it tires of these worldly limitations, never lacks power to set itself free.

Cassius wishes to kill Caesar because he is jealous of his massive power. Here he talks about another motive to kill Caesar – freedon from tyranny. Overall, however, we may accept this as no more than a public face of Cassius, who cannot possibly convey his most intimate secret in front of Casca.

10

Poor man! I know he would not be a wolf,

But that he sees the Romans are but sheep :

He were no lion, were not Romans hinds.

Those that with haste will make a mighty fire

Begin it with weak straws : what trash is Rome,

What rubbish, and what offal, when it serves

For the base matter to illuminate

So vile a thing as Caesar!   [I.iii.104-111]

The above lines are uttered by Cassius to Casca in the play "Julius Caesar" written by Shakespeare. Casca too agrees with Cassius that the gods have given them the power of self-destruction. They would use it if Caesar becomes king.

Cassius believes that Caesar would not remain a wolf and a tyrant if the Romans did not behave as meekly as sheep. Caesar would not appear to be a lion if the Romans did not behave like female deer, incapable of understanding what is good for them. Those who are in a hurry to ignite a mighty fire make use of weak straws, which burn easily. This is to suggest that Romans are weak straws whom Caesar ignites to kindle his own glory. Romans are absolute trash, rubbish and chips of wood, since they serve to illuminate a degraded and wicked person like Caesar.

Cassius is encouraged by Casca's response. He is convinced that Caesar would not be a tyrant if men were ready to free themselves from his yoke.

11

O, he sits high in all the people's hearts:

And that which would appear offence in us,

His countenance, like richest alchemy,

Will change to virtue and to worthiness.   **[I.iii.157-160]**

The above lines are spoken by Casca to Cassius and Cinna in the play "Julius Caesar" written by Shakespeare. Casca wants Brutus to be included in their conspiracy to kill Caesar. Brutus is held in high esteem by the Romans. Therefore, his inclusion would be very useful for the conspiracy. Casca knows that Brutus has a high place in the hearts of all Romans, and a thing which appears bad in them, will, by his presence, as if by magical transformation, change into virtue and merit.

Shakespeare advances the theme of truth versus pretence to truth in these lines. Casca is not interested in truth. He is only interested in making a murder appear as an act of liberation in the eyes of the people of Rome. Casca thus also advances the truth about the lack of intellectual worth in human beings when they huddle into a group.

12

Between the acting of a dreadful thing

And the first motion, all the interim is

Like a phantasma or a hideous dream :

The Genius and the mortal instruments

Are then in council; and the state of man,

Like a little kingdom, suffers then

The nature of an insurrection.   **[II.i.63-69]**

The above lines are spoken by Brutus in a soliloquy in the play "Julius Caesar" written by Shakespeare. Brutus' mind is in tremendous turmoil. He cannot understand the cause of the conflict in his mind, specially after he has decided to join the conspiracy to murder Caesar. Cassius has incited Brutus into murdering Caesar. The actual assassination is to take place the next morning. It is late in the night. Brutus does not have any sleep in his eye. He admits that the interval between the performance of a dreadful act and the first conception of it is like a nightmare or a horrible dream. During this interim period, the guardian spirit, allowed to a man at birth to guide him to virtuous action, and his bodily faculties are at conflict with one another. Brutus compares his conflict to a kingdom, which is paralysed when different constituents are in a state of constant agitation. It is at this crucial junction that the guardian spirit protects man from doing anything dreadful.

Shakespeare advances the theme of virtue and vice through the comparison between what our sensory perceptions want and what is virtuous. The need of the body is a mere sensation. This may be dangerous or evil. It's worth can only be evaluated through contemplation or rational thought.

13

No, not on oath: if not the face of men,
The sufferance of our souls, the time's abuse, —
If these be motives weak, break off betimes,
And every man hence to his idle bed;   [II.i.114-117]

The above lines are spoken by Brutus to Cassius in the play "Julius Caesar" written by Shakespeare. Cassius wants every conspirator to be bound by an oath. Brutus overrules Cassius. He believes that no oath is necessary if they are all firm in their purpose. If the sad faces of men, the sufferings of their souls, the evils of their time – if all these are not motives enough to bind them, then he would rather break this discussion of killing Caesar. Each conspirator would still have time to leave and get back to his empty bed.

Shakespeare wishes to tell us the futility behind every oath. If a motive to do something is not strong enough then it is impossible to see how an oath can work. It would either be broken or it will be followed without inspiration – an entity which is so crucial for the success of any enterprise. Some critics believe that Brutus idealises the situation of the conspirators at every turn. This may be true, but it may not be a negative trait which critics make out to be. In a way it may be desirable. In case of Brutus, however, there is no scope for churning out something worthwhile, simply because his desire to assassinate Caesar itself is without worthwhile evaluation.

14

Let's kill him boldly, but not wrathfully;
Let's carve him as a dish fit for the gods,
Not hew him as a carcase fit for hounds :
And let our hearts, as subtle masters do,
Stir up their servants to an act of rage
And after seem to chide 'em.   [II.i.172-177]

The above lines are spoken by Brutus to Cassius in the play "Julius Caesar" written by Shakespeare. Cassius is wary of Mark Antony. He wants him to be assassinated along with Caesar. Brutus overrules him. He wants the conspirators to kill Caesar boldly, but not savagely. They must slay Caesar as if they are making a sacrificial offering to the gods, and not like a dead body that is being cut into pieces in order to feed the hounds. Let their hearts, like some crafty masters, stir up their servants (their hands) to undertake an act of anger, only to rebuke them for it after the act has been committed.

Brutus makes a series of blunders in the play. He refuses to bind the conspirators in an oath. This would become crucial when Antony completely turns the tables on the conspirators. It is ironical that Cassius, despite his sharp insight and vision, has to succumb to Brutus' follies. It is obvious that the dramatist wishes to tell us how misplaced sense of honour and virtue can be as harmful as evil itself.

15

Never fear that: if he be so resolv'd
I can o'ersway him; for he loves to hear
That unicorns may be betray'd with trees,
And bears with glasses, elephants with holes,
Lions with toils, and men with flatterers:
But when I tell him he hates flatterers,
He says he does,— being then most flattered   [II.i.202-208]

The above lines are spoken by Decius to Cassius in the play "Julius Caesar" written by Shakespeare. The conspirators have decided to murder Caesar during the meeting of the senate in the Capitol the next day. Cassius is not sure that Caesar would arrive there. He is a superstitious man and the portents of the terrible night that they are all experiencing may prevent him from venturing out the next day.

Decius tells Cassius not to have any fear about that. He can persuade Caesar to change his mind, in case he decides to stay indoors due to fear or superstition. Cassius loves to hear how unicorns may be trapped by making them to charge a tree; or bears may be captured by fooling them with mirrors, or elephants by holes dug in the ground, or men can be trapped by flattery. But, when he tells Caesar that he hates flattery, he admits that he does, though it is at that very moment he is most flattered.

Shakespeare exposes the hypocrisy about flattery and how powerful men are influenced by it. Even Caesar, who is the mightiest creature in the world, is not above flattery. He may wish to believe that he is above flattery, but this false belief itself makes him a victim of flattery.

16

Cowards die many times before their deaths;
The valiant never taste of death but once.
Of all the wonders that I yet have heard,
It seems to me most strange that men should fear;
Seeing that death, a necessary end,
Will come when it will come.   [II.ii.32-37]

The above lines are spoken by Caesar in the play "Julius Caesar" written by Shakespeare. These famous lines are spoken in response to Calphurnia's request to Caesar not to go out of the house. She has a premonition that Caesar's life will be in danger. Caesar's priests also suggest that the time is not auspicious for Caesar to venture out.

Caesar tells Calphurnia that cowards die many times before their actual death, due to their fear of death. The brave only experience death once. He tells his wife that of the many wonderful things in life it seems most strange to him that men should be afraid of death, despite the obvious fact that no one can evade it. Caesar says that death is not only inevitable, but it is also a necessary end. It will come only at a time when it is destined, neither before its time nor after.

Caesar stresses on three important aspects of existence. First, the absence of death is not life, because human beings can deteriorate the quality of their existence by constantly worrying about death. Secondly, that death is necessary, because there can be no construction without destruction. Old age must move away so that new blood can take charge of the world. Thirdly, that death and it's time is predestined by a force higher than what is within the understanding of man.

17

Danger knows full well
That Caesar is more dangerous than he :
We are two lions litter'd in one day,
And I the elder and more terrible:
And Caesar shall go forth :   **[II.ii.44-48]**

The above lines are spoken by Caesar to Calphurnia in the play "Julius Caesar" written by Shakespeare. Calphurnia has portents that Caesar's life is in danger. She requests her husband not to venture out of the house. Caesar proclaims that he is not afraid of death. A servant comes in and informs that the priests do not want him to step out because their sacrificial offerings to the gods do not portend well for Caesar. Caesar thinks the gods are putting men to shame for their cowardice. He says that he is more dangerous than danger itself. He and danger are twins, and that he was the one born earlier. He is also the more dangerous of the two. He shall therefore venture out.

Shakespeare focusses first on Caesar's vanity and superstition and then on his sense of inviolability which is most evident when he says that he is more dangerous than danger itself. This statement gives a double twist of irony. The audience is aware of the conspiracy and it also knows that the assassination attempt will succeed. Shakespeare gives enough hints that the plotters may have good reason to fear his growing power and ambition.

18

Here wast thou bay'd brave hart,
Here didst thou fall; and here thy hunters stand,
Sign'd by thy spoil, and crimson'd in the lathe.

O world, thou wast the forest to this hart;
And this, indeed, O world, the heart of thee—
How like a deer, strucken by many princes,
Dost thou here lie! [III.i.204-210]

The above lines are spoken by Antony in the play "Julius Caesar" written by Shakespeare. Antony flees to his house as soon as Caesar is murdered. He returns only after Brutus assures him of his safety. When he returns he sees Caesar's dead body. He is filled with grief and horror. Antony points out to the place where Caesar fell. He then points out to the murderers and says that here stand Caesar's hunters marked with his blood, which they have shared between them. The allusion he refers to is the killing of an animal and its division between the hounds which killed him. This was known as "spoil". The place is besmeared with the blood that flowed from Caesar's wounds, and it is dyed in that blood. Antony says that the world, was Caesar's natural realm. He roamed in this world as freely as a heart or a stag roams in a forest. This stag had inspired the entire world. The same stag now lies dead like a deer struck down by many princely hunters.

Antony's lamentation at Caesar's body is partly genuine; partly it hides the real motive. He laments on Caesar's body in order to hide his actual desire to expose the conspirators and to turn the tables on them. He mentions the conspirators as princes and Caesar as an animal hunted down by them. This would please the conspirators because hunting was a royal pastime and was closely linked with valour. Moreover, the description of Caesar as an animal is designed to tally with Brutus' thought. He had always wanted to sacrifice Caesar to the gods instead of being a heartless butcher. It may be true that Brutus is as hearless as other conspirators, but Antony needs to keep the pretence in order to fool the murderers.

19

And Caesar's spirit, ranging from revenge,
With Ate by his hole come hot from hell;
Shall in these confines with a monarch's voice
Cry "Havoc" and let slip the dogs of war;
That this foul deed shall smell above the earth.
With carrion men, groaning for burial. [III.i.270-275]

The above lines are spoken by Mark Antony in the play "Julius Caesar" written by Shakespeare. Standing before Caesar's dead body alone, Antony makes a prophecy. He says that Caesar's spirit will roam throughout the world like a beast of prey. Caesar's spirit will be in the company of Ate, the goddess of mischief, who as per legend leads men blindly into rash deeds. The goddess will come in response to the call of Caesar's spirit, which will assume the authority of a monarch in death, though bereft of all powers when alive. It will create havoc among the enemy and let slip the dogs of war (viz. famine, death, fire etc.). Antony alludes to hunting, in which the unleashing of grey hounds was given the technical name of "let slip". The foul deed shall spread an evil smell over the earth along with the rotting bodies of men, which will cry for immediate burial.

Antony alludes to a civil war which will cause so much death and destruction that it would appear as if the gods have descended on earth in order to punish people for killing someone as noble and great as Caesar. The civil war would be so bloody that there would not be sufficient place and time to bury the dead. He also refers to Ate, who as per classical mythology, was the goddess of vengeance and mischief. She was hurled down by Zeus from Mount Olympus, because she had lured him into acting rashly. Ate was regarded to have the power of nemesis, which resulted in retributive punishment rather than mischief.

20

Friends, Romans, countrymen, lend me your ears;
I come to bury Caesar, not to praise him.
The evil that men do lives after them;
The good is of interred with their bones;
So let it be with Caesar.   [III.ii.79-83]

The above lines are spoken by Mark Antony to the Roman citizens in the play "Julius Caesar" written by Shakespeare. Antony manipulates the conspirators so that he can talk to the citizens of Rome. He asks his friends, the citizens of Rome and his countrymen to listen to what he has to say. He has come to bury Caesar, not to praise him. The evil that men do lives long after they are dead, but the good deeds are often forgotten. He agrees that is the manner in which the world exists, so let Caesar also be treated in the same manner.

Antony's speech is a masterful display in mob psychology. Brutus' speech prior to him was based on logic. Antony, in contrast; knows that the crowd is incapable of acting reasonably. He relies specifically on that very inability as he manipulates their emotions, concentrating increasingly on their mounting passion. By the time he finishes his speech the citizens of Rome have been collectively converted into a violent mob. This is the impetus that Antony needs to seek revenge against the murderers of Caesar.

21

For Brutus, as you know, was Caesar's angel :
Judge, O you gods, how dearly Caesar lov'd him !

This was the most unkindest cut of all;

For when the noble Caesar saw him stab,

Ingratitude, more strong that traitors' arms,

Quite vanquished him: [III.ii.185-190]

The above lines are spoken by Mark Antony in the play "Julius Caesar" written by Shakespeare. Slowly, but surely, Antony wins over the people of Rome. He exposes the conspirators as murderers and establishes Caesar's greatness completely. He tells the crowd that Brutus was Caesar's good angel, and his second self. He invokes the gods to judge how dearly Caesar loved him. He then shows the crowd the hole in Caesar's body which was made by Brutus. He says this was the most cruel blow of all. Caesar's blood gushed out profusely, as if to make sure that it was indeed Brutus who stabbed him. When Caesar was convinced that Brutus had in fact stabbed him along with the other murderers, he was so pained over Brutus' ingratitude, that he stopped resisting. It was this sense of ingratitude which defeated him, because it was stronger then all the arms of the traitors.

Shakespeare uses the double superlative "most unkindest cut of all" to telling affect. The image of a friend betrayed is depicted with a potent blend of horror and sorrow. Antony manipulates the crowd with skill and dexterity. It was hostile when he began his funeral speech. It becomes his ally and strength by the time he ends it.

22

There is a tide in the affairs of men,

Which, taken the flood, leads on to fortune;

Omitted, all the voyage of their life

Is bound in shallows and in miseries. [IV.iii.218-221]

The above lines are spoken by Brutus to Cassius in the play "Julius Caesar" written by Shakespeare. Brutus and Cassius discuss the strategy they must adopt to counter the enemy. Cassius wants the enemy to come to them at Sardis so that it is tired while their forces remain fresh. Brutus wants to advance to Philippi and engage the enemy there. He believes the time is ripe to engage the enemy.

Brutus suggests that favourable opportunities are like tides or waves. Just like the greatest advantage is achieved only from a tide which is at its highest, if a ship is to have a successful journey, so is the case of life. Misery and failure result in case opportunities are not seized at the right moment. Brutus is convinced that their army is at its peak strength and efficiency, and its efficiency can only go down with time. Cassius is an epicure. He believes that men have power over their destiny. Brutus is a stoic. He insists on the role of providence over men.

23

O setting sun,

As in thy red rays thou dost sink to night,

So in his red blood Cassius' day is set,—

The sun of Rome is set! Our day is gone;

Clouds, dews, and dangers come: our deeds are done!

Mistrust of my success hath done this deed. [V.iii.60-65]

The above lines are spoken by Titinius to Messala in the play "Julius Caesar" written by Shakespeare. Titinius arrives with Messala in order to inform Cassius about Brutus' victory over Octavius, but he finds that Cassius is dead. He gives vent to his sorrow and shock over the death of a friend.

Titinius compares Cassius to the setting sun due to which he emanates red rays. Just as the sun sinks in the evening among red rays, so does Cassius, the sun of Rome, die amidst the red colour of his blood. With the setting of the sun of Rome, their deeds have ended. His lack of confidence over the victory of his friends led him to suicide.

Titinius' lament over his friend's death is a cry against hopelessness and the terrible state that the forces of the conspirators are in. It is ironic that Cassius, who had so consistently demonstrated clear foresight suffers from weak eyesight to an extent that he commits suicide because of a false report by a man he chooses to be an observer for him in battle. However, his act of suicide is consistent with his often repeated desire to either live as a free man or die.

24

This was the noblest Roman of them all :

All the conspirators, save only he,

Did that they did in envy of great Caesar;

He only, in a general honest thought.

And common good to all, made one of them.

His life was gentle, and the elements

So mix'd in him, that Nature might stand up

And say to all the world, "This was a man !"   [V.v.68-75]

The above lines are spoken by Mark Antony in the play "Julius Caesar" written by Shakespeare. Brutus commits suicide by running over his own sword held by Strato. This is the way in which the avenging army finds thim. Octavius orders that Brutus be given a ceremonial funeral, while Antony pays tribute to the dead Brutus. He says that Brutus was the most noble Roman among all the conspirators. Apart from him, every other conspirator killed the great Caesar out of hatred and jealousy. Brutus was the only man who killed Caesar due to an honest thought that it was for the good of the citizens of Rome. Brutus' life was noble, and his qualities were very well-balanced. The "elements" mentioned here are fire, air, water and earth. As per medieval physiology they were transformed in the body into the corresponding "humour"—choler, blood, melancholy and phlegm. They formed a man's physical and mental faculties, since they were mixed or "tempered" in different measures. In an ideal human being they were present in equal proportions. In Brutus these elements were so well proportioned that even nature may stand up and declare that this was an ideal man.

Antony's praise for his adversary is not inconsistent with the law of probability or his earlier utterances about Brutus. Antony recognises that Brutus was a noble and idealistic man. There is no irony or sarcasm in his utterances, though there may still be a distinct self-serving intent.

CHAPTER 8

QUESTIONS AND ANSWERS

Ques 1 : Comment on Shakespeare's conception of tragedy, with special reference to the play "Julius Caesar".

The meaning of the word tragic

Ans : We use the word "tragic" frequently in our daily lives to describe something that is very unfortunate. In literature, the same word has a richer and more profound meaning. It is not enough for a play (or a novel) to tell an unhappy story in order to be termed tragic. It must provoke in us a response of which sorrow is merely a part. In a Shakespearean tragedy certain features recur constantly to create this response.

Shakespeare's tragic hero

A Shakespearean tragedy has a hero, and in some cases a hero and a heroine (as in Romeo and Juliet), who is a man of admirable qualities. This is necessary so that we feel sorry at what happens to him, which we would not for a villain or someone who has negative qualities. A tragic hero must be such that his death causes in us regret that much good is lost. Shakespeare's hero is usually a man holding a high position in the state. Lear is a king, Hamlet is a prince, Julius Caesar is the head of Rome, Othello and Macbeth are generals, and so on. A tragedy surrounding an ordinary mortal rarely invokes the kind of strong emotions that kings and generals do. Moreover, Shakespeare delineates his tragic character in such a manner that we love him despite his flaw. We wish that he would somehow refrain from indulging in his fatal flaw.

Tragic fate should be both unlucky and deserved

We first meet the hero in happy circumstances. He is brought to ruin slowly through the course of the plot. The manner in which he dies needs special mention. A man who receives the punishment he deserves dies justly, not tragically. A tragic fate is one which is both unlucky and deserved, both unjust and just. In this the hero dies due to a combination of unfortunate circumstances as well as his own failure. We are not certain whether the man should or should not die.

A sense of inevitability once the fatal flaw is made

There is an increasing sense of inevitability about the final outcome once a Shakespearean hero makes his fatal mistake. We do feel an enormous loss when the outcome stares us in the face. Yet, despite everything, in an odd way we are relieved that the hero dies. Before he dies the hero has suffered so much that he has inviolably regained his initial sublimity and greatness. If

90

anything, he understands himself and the world that surrounds him better than he had ever done. Shakespeare leaves us in no doubt that his hero could not feel at home in the world that is available to him at the end of the play. This is precisely what brings relief in our minds despite the hero's terrible end.

The hero's downfall is brought about by his fatal flaw

Certain concepts drawn from Aristotle require a tragic hero of high standing, who must oppose some conflicting force, which may be either external or internal. The tragic hero should be dominated by a "hamartia" (a tragic flaw, or more appropriately, an excess of some trait in character like "hubris" or pride). His downfall is brought about by this hamartia. Due to his eminent status it is evident that his downfall would lead to enormous loss to many around him. The action of the tragedy must be accepted as real by the audience. It must raise the passions of those who see it, and its denouement or ending must bring a relief from this passion (catharsis).

The role of catharsis

The main concern of tragedy is with truth and the pleasure it gives is the pleasure of knowledge. Plato uses the word catharsis to mean purification or sublimation. Accepting this meaning, Aristotle seems to affirm that tragedy, first by arousing pity and fear, ultimately sublimates them and raises the spectator to a state of true understanding. Tragedy takes us through various emotional responses culminating in intellectual purification. Plato's approach to tragedy is emotional. Aristotle seeks an intellectual response to tragedy. It is this intellectual response which constantly applies to Shakespeare. Greek tragedy justifies the ways of the gods in a mystical, instead of an ethical sense. Shakespeare questions this error in his tragedies, simply because he finds this world more definitely theological than mysteriously cosmic.

Shakespearean tragedy cannot be typified into any slot

It must be very clearly understood that Shakespearean tragedy cannot be typified into any particular slot. Each tragedy is a new beginning, a fresh "raid on the inarticulate", for although there is development there is no repetition. There are even marked differences of manner, approach and intention in each of his tragedies.

Shakespeare's tragic vision is, to a large extent, Greek in design and execution. Bradley pointed out that a "Shakespearean tragedy may be called a story of exceptional calamity, of eventually one person—the hero, in high state, or at best two persons, the hero and the heroine, the latter coming into prominence in romantic tragedies like Romeo and Juliet".

Shakespeare combines comic and tragic elements

Shakespeare combines the comic and the tragic elements in the same play, mainly because this is evident in the real world around us. To depict only tragic or sad scenes would fill the audience with horror instead of arousing emotions of pity and fear in them. Moreover, the purpose of tragedy ought to be the elevation of the audience from darkness into illumination. This is possible if evil is offset by the goodness of virtue. The joy of virtue makes evil a worthless emotion.

Shakespeare succeeds due to his delicate understanding

Shakespare succeeds in his tragedies because he seems to have the kind of delicacy of understanding.which no other author in English literature seems to possess. He can create delightful possibilities with English language. He loves simplicity and straight-forwardness, and he advances everything with compassion. He never loses faith in the ability of man and he does not have the unintellectual pretensions that most writers seem to possess.

Shakespeare holds a mirror upto nature

What, finally, does Shakespeare tell us ? He does not wish to preach, yet, there is undoubtedly a central message. He shows things to us as they are, holding, as one of his characters says, a mirror up to Nature. He tells us that all human life is as uncertain as the weather and that life is vastly complicated and unexpected business. In this dark and bustling world there is no stouter shield that innocence and purity of heart. Our fortunes may not always answer to our hopes, or even to our desiring, yet innocence withstands the terror of existence better than anything else. He understands that there is a strong and unmistakable undercurrent of misery in this world and there are times when vice thrives and virtue fails.

Life's purpose is for our good

Despite the doubt and the despair, Shakespeare leaves us in no doubt that life's first purpose is for our good. He tells us that certain qualities and actions, for the most part, bring happiness, while others, surely fail. Among those which bring happiness include love, patience and forgiveness, while pride, ingratitude and cruelty can only bring sorrow.

Julius Caesar is not a tragedy in the conventional sense

Having established what a Shakespearean tragedy is all about let us see if this concept fits "Julius Caesar" or not. First, "Julius Caesar" is not a tragedy in the pure sense like "King Lear" or "Hamlet", concerned as it is with depicting history more than tragedy. Shakespeare has to do justice to historical facts while writing the tragedy. Despite this shortcoming; Shakespeare manages to give us an excellent tragedy, and within the parameters of his other tragedies. The hero of the play, Brutus, is a man of high status. The tragedy deals with the internal conflict that rages in the mind of the hero, instead of external conflicts like war, revolt etc., which were the subject of so many English historical plays. Brutus, upholds republicanism against Caesarian, which to him is synonymous to abject servitude for the people of Rome. Brutus obviously loves Caesar at the beginning of the play. It is left to Cassius to cleverly manipulate the prime emotion of Brutus and slowly poison his mind against Caesar. The ineffectual idealist is convinced with indecent haste that Caesar is after power. Brutus has no first hand information about this. In fact, there are moments when Caesar behaves quite selflessly, though there are also moments when we feel that Caesar may succumb to the temptations of absolute power. Yet, he does nothing to actually fill Brutus with fear. Brutus hates inordinate power and kingship. He does not, however, collect sufficient evidence to convince himself that Caesar wants to become king, or that he will usurp inordinate power.

Brutus' conflict is between respect for Caesar and love for Romans

Brutus' conflict is between friendship, born out of genuine respect for Caesar, and his intense love for public good and republicanism. The conflict ends when Brutus dies and republicanism falls. His death is a calamity for Rome, since the fall of republicanism means the rise of kingship and the horrors that are associated with it. Brutus may have been surrounded by some adverse emotions during the play, but true grandeur surrounds him when he dies. There is also terror and pity – pity for the common people of Rome and terror at what would happen to them.

Brutus' blind and ineffectual idealism

There is no doubt that Brutus' tragic flaw is his blind and ineffectual idealism. It is without a rational process of thought. He thinks that republicanism is the answer to all evils and that kingship is nothing but unmitigated vice. He does not tell us how this is true. Nor does he ponder to think why Caesar would want kingship against the wishes of the people of Rome. He indulges in no dialogue or intellectual introspection. He kills in a mental vacuum, merely incited by a misplaced formula that power corrupts and hence it would corrupt Caesar also at a future date. He kills without evidence, even without adequate cause, and he does not have a plan in place in case the people of Rome feel incited over Caesar's death. Murder and war are no answers to the woes of the people. The only answer lies in proper governance.

Shakespearean tragedies have an element of the supernatural

Shakespearean tragedies have a distinct element of the supernatural. This is evident in "Julius Caesar" as well, in the form of Caesar's ghost. It stands for retribution and nemesis, and for restoring the reign of higher principles of the ethical world. The ghost gives one message to the moral world – that good cannot come out of evil. Brutus, despite his ideals and lofty republicanism is nothing but a senseless murderer. He may have wanted to sacrifice Caesar to the gods, but we are acutely aware that no such sacrifice can be deemed ethical, specially by a man who is led more by his prejudices than by moral and intellectual worth.

Brutus dies after resublimating himself

Brutus dies due to this tragic flaw, but not before suffering at the hands of oppressive fortune. He kills Caesar without sufficient cause. His catharsis and resublimation begins as soon as he murders Caesar. He subconsciously takes actions that would hasten his death. He refuses to bind the conspirators in an oath, and the conspiracy is almost disclosed to Caesar. He lets Antony live, only to see him turn the tables on him. He meets the enemy in Philippi, thus tiring his troops, instead of letting the enemy come to him at Sardis. This means that the enemy is fresh and his own troops are tired when they actually engage in battle.

Brutus' stoicism does not inspire him

Brutus' stoicism is such that it cannot possibly inspire him to protect his own life. He accepts the suicide of his wife without any outward sign of suffering and he is enormously relieved when he himself embraces death. He yells out to Caesar's spirit to be still and let him rest in peace. Nemesis has been achieved, but not before the sublimation of the hero has occurred as well. He always lived with honour. Most of his honour is restored before he kills himself by running over his own sword.

Conclusion

Shakespeare leaves the message of the play to our own value judgement. Since a story of grandeur and of enormous suffering has been told it is inevitable that we draw our own conclusions. Brutus is an honourable man, but there comes a stage where his honour appears misplaced because it is without profound evaluation. Once he acts on something this misplaced, it is inevitable that he unleashes needless horror, which ruins the peace and tranquillity of Rome.

Ques 2 : Enumerate the principles of construction of Shakespeare's tragic plots. How are they brought out in "Julius Caesar"?

Division of Shakespearean tragedy

Ans : Normally, a Shakespearean tragedy can be divided into five parts as follows :

  (a) Exposition.

  (b) Rising action or complication due to conflict.

  (c) Crisis.

  (d) Resolution or falling action.

  (e) Catastrophe.

Exposition in Julius Caesar is available in the first two scenes

The first part sets forth or expounds the situation, or state of affairs. It is out of this that the conflict arises. In "Julius Caesar" the exposition is available to us in the first two scenes itself. Caesar's rising popularity leads to needless hilarity in the fickle people of Rome. However, it also fills some of his officers with jealousy, resentment and fear. The hostility towards Caesar results in conspiracy, led mainly by Cassius.

Conflict is evident in the mind of Brutus

Conflict is of crucial importance to Shakespearean tragedies. This conflict is also evident in "Julius Caesar", primarily in the mind of Brutus. The action of the play is rapid, and it swiftly leads to the crisis. The second act is devoted further to the conspiracy, and brings us to the brink of the crisis, which is ultimately reached in the third act. This stage is depicted by storms, hideous prodigies and supernatural happenings. The storm and the hideous prodigies are the external manifestation of the terrible conflict that exists in Brutus' mind. Brutus' conflict exists because he loves and admires Caesar, but he is horrified at the thought that he might become corrupt due to the inordinate power that surrounds him. Brutus knows that his love and admiration for Caesar are born out of his admirable qualities. He knows crime, especially murder of a trusted friend, is evil. However, he also believes that virtue can degenerate into vice, and that nothing is evil which is done to negate evil. He knows that kingship amounts to slavery for the citizens of Rome. The only thing that can rescue them from the tyranny of slavery is republicanism. He is prepared to kill his friends, and sacrifice him to the gods. He takes the fatal plunge towards doom—fatal because his decision is an end product of inadequate, even misplaced, information. He presumes that every human being becomes corrupt if he is surrounded by power. He does not pause to evaluate whether such power can corrupt Caesar as well or not. Neither does he have the understanding that Caesar's spirit is in complete synchronisation with the spirit of the times. Brutus' fault is that he does not have a foolproof plan once he kills Caesar. There is huge backlash when a man like Caesar is killed. Brutus is completely ill-equipped to cope with such a backlash. He can neither convince the people of Rome nor the members of the senate regarding the veracity of his act.

Brutus makes a series of blunders

Brutus, in fact, makes a series of blunders in his misplaced sense of truth. He does not bind the conspirators in an oath, he does not kill Antony, and he orders his army to proceed to Philippi, when it is so obviously clear that it should have stayed in Sardis. He uses his misplaced honour to bulldoze Cassius into submission. He never understands that he is not a man of action, which Cassius obviously is. Brutus flaunts every sane suggestion and thus sets the stage for a reaction to the crisis precipitated by him.

Antony keep's Caesar's spirit alive

This reaction is set in motion when Antony keeps Caesar's spirit alive in the funeral speech. This reaction, or falling action, causes enormous suffering and pain. Brutus may have once been respected by every citizen in Rome, but he has to now flee like a petty thief, as the violent mob searches to kill the conspirators and set their houses on fire. The agony does not end here. It merely begins a seemingly endless rot. Scores of friends of the conspirators die by way of proscription. Brutus' wife, Portia, has to kill herself by swallowing burning coals, and Brutus is haunted by Caesar's ghost. It is this ghost which incites Brutus into hasty action against the enemy forces. Cassius wants to bide his time. Worthwhile strategy suggests that Cassius is right, but Brutus is too indifferent about anything, to care about the consequences of his actions. He must exorcise Caesar's ghost at all costs. Brutus does not merely blunder at every step of the play. He actually incites his colleagues into suspicion and hatred. This is most evident in the senseless fight that Brutus and Cassius have in the heat of battle. If Cassius holds back it is because Brutus has an unimpeachable aura of integrity around him. He may lead men to certain death, but how does one counter a man who is not physically corrupt?

Brutus kills himself with the name of Caesar on his lips

Brutus runs over his own sword at the end of the play, but not before he requests Caesar's spirit to be "still now" that it has been avenged. Cassius had committed suicide a little earlier, and by the time the play ends every conspirator is dead. It is time that the moral and social order of the world is restored. Shakespeare unequivocally establishes that "no good can come out of evil". We had come to accept that only disaster can be the moral and intellectual culmination of the sequence of events of the play. We seem to feel that justice has been done finally, though we still feel that if Brutus had behaved in keeping with his unquestioned integrity, then so much needless bloodshed could easily have been prevented. It is the kind of loss that must be avoided at all costs.

The play has a remarkably even construction

Shakespeare manages a remarkably even construction of the play. He evolves the story in a systematic and symmetrical manner. The play has a single plot, and not a single scene in it can be considered superfluous or supererogatory to its plot. Every single element of action either directly springs from Caesar, or is subordinate to him. The play has basically two parts – Caesar murdered and Caesar avenged .Shakespeare manages to blend these two parts into a magnificent whole. The play, however, has a single motive – growing inevitability of monarchy as a natural offshoot of Caesarism, and the hopelessness of republicanism and democracy in Caesar's Rome. This one motive provides unity to the entire play. At the end it is Caesarism which asserts itself at the cost of republicanism.

Ques 3 : Who do you think is the hero of the play "Julius Caesar"? Give reasons for your answer.

OR

Comment on the statement that "Julius Caesar"may be regarded as a play without a hero.

Brutus, Antony, Cassius and Caesar are prominent men in the play

Ans : T.S. Dorsch once stated that "Caesar is the titular hero and Brutus the dramatic hero" of the play "Julius Caesar". There are four prominent men who call for our attention in the play–Brutus, Antony, Cassius and Caesar himself. Shakespeare manages to arouse in us some degree of admiration and sympathy for all four of them. He also reveals basic flaws in the characters of all four of them.

All Shakespearean tragedies are named after the hero

First of all it must be clearly brought out that all tragedies written by Shakespeare have been named after the hero of the play. For this reason alone, Caesar should become our obvious choice for the hero of the play. Moreover, he is the pivot around which the play revolves. Alive or dead he dominates the play.

There are critics who are against Caesar

There are critics, however, who think that Caesar is a tyrant and a bully. There are others who accept Brutus as a champion of virtue and freedom. Malone, and later Voltaire, went to the extent of saying that the play ought to have been called Marcus Brutus. A.C. Bradley says that "Julius Caesar is the dominating figure but Brutus is the hero".Fowler thinks that "the play Julius Caesar stands alone among Shakespearean tragedies in bearing the name of the man who was not the hero".

Most critics have great admiration for Brutus

Most critics have nothing but disgust for Caesar and great admiration for Brutus. Thus the majority vote of the critics must necessarily be moral;

which means that we should be able to accept this version in that inviolable manner which is a direct outcome of a profound integrity of thought – where no doubt exists and no question remains unanswered. No man can, however, be a Shakespearean hero and yet possess these qualities, because he must have a fatal flaw in order to qualify for it. Therefore, we must seek a lesser option of a man who possesses these positive qualities till he is overcome by his fatal flaw.

Antony and Cassius are not the prime motive force of the play

Having established the parameters for a genuine hero let us see if anyone really fits the bill of a hero in the play. We may safely discard Cassius and Antony, for both historical and other reasons. They are not the prime motive force of the play, and enough has already been written to reject their claims for being a hero. That leaves us with Caesar and Brutus. Caesar may have been a great hero in history, but in this play, his abilities are either not visible, or they are considerably diluted.

We see Caesar for a very small duration

Moreover, we see Caesar for such a less time that nothing much can be made of him. Since the play in any case is about Caesarism, and not Caesar, Shakespeare kills him early in the play. Caesar has physical deformities too— he is deaf in one ear, is epileptic, and despite his heroics in battle is not a very strong man. He is prone to flattery. He is ambitious. He is vain and arrogant, and he offers sacrifices in bizarre rituals, no matter what their validity may have been during his era in Rome. He has his good qualities too. He is a great soldier and leader of men. He is undoubtedly brave. He is a keen judge of character. He is generous and kind to his friends, and his victories are totally earned. He is revered because he has brought enormous glories and fortunes to Rome. His virtues and vices add up to a plus and make him a likable character. Yet there is nothing truly heroic in him.

Brutus' strengths and weakness

That brings us to Brutus – the obvious choice of the critics through the centuries for being called the hero of the play. He too has his good points. He is honourable. He is an idealist, in an ineffectual, but endearing sort of way. He admires and loves Caesar, but loves Rome more. He loves his wife and is true and loyal to his friends and colleagues. Moreover, he fits into Bradley's conception of a Shakespearean tragic hero, which is a man of high estate who suffers throughout the play due to a tragic flaw and then dies at the very end. Caesar does not suffer in the play due to any tragic flaw or due to any other cause. His ambition to be the king of Rome never materialises. Moreover, he never openly shows that he wants to be king. There is thus no conflict in his heart and he does not die as a direct consequence of any fatal flaw.

Brutus fits into Bradley's concept of a tragic hero

Brutus, on the other hand, fits the bill perfectly. He is a man of high estate, being a praetor or a magistrate in Rome. There is conflict in his mind between Caesarism and republican democracy, and between killing Caesar and letting him live. His tragedy emanates out of three things. First, he arrives at a horrible decision because he does not evaluate conflicting things well. Secondly, he carries his idealism and honour to extremes, and a right when carried to extremes becomes a wrong. Thirdly, he practices stoicism, and hence is indifferent to what might happen to him or to those around him. These make him violate the laws of preservation and existence. Once he acts as per his tragic flaw and kills Caesar, Brutus experiences nothing but suffering and pain, which finally ends in his suicide. He had wanted to kill Caesar's spirit and not the man. It is Caesar's spirit which haunts him till the very end.

Brutus faces nemesis and retribution

There is nemesis and retribution too. Caesar is avenged and Brutus sublimates himself in death, realising that he had not understood the spirit of the times. The spirit of the times wants the heroics of Caesar to inspire than merely let some grave men give it proper governance in a republican form of democracy. Common people do not understand the finer nuances of governance. What they understand is affluence. Caesar had provided it to them in abundance. They were not prepared to forgive a person who had taken so much away from them merely in the name of an abstract philosophy.

The entire play is wrought around Caesar

Thus, if we accept the logic provided till now, then Brutus easily becomes the hero of the play. Georege Bernard Shaw declared that Shakespeare wrote Caesar down for the technical purpose of writing Brutus up. Yet the entire play is wrought around Caesar — Caesar living upto Act III — and Caesar avenged from then to the end, the latter more powerful than the former. Dowden thinks that "Caesar is the inner inspiring cause of the whole drama – of the later scenes no less than of the earlier, for death really serves to intensify his power and is alone indispensable to it". Our vote would go to Brutus if we accept Bradley's arguments for the choice of the play's hero. Our choice would, however, be Caesar, if we accept what Dowden has to say.

Moral and intellectual evaluation of Brutus and Caesar

We have so far assessed the merits of Caesar and Brutus on the grounds laid down by others. Morally and intellectually, however, neither Caesar nor Brutus can be termed truly heroic. It matters little what Dowden, Bradley or the Greeks accepted as heroic. What matters is assessment as per inviolably profound parameters. Brutus murders a trusting friend in an ineffectual disgust at what may happen if Caesar is permitted to live. He thus kills on a mere conjecture and not due to any concrete evidence. He is a statesman. It is his job to negotiate changes in order to give better direction to Rome. Instead, he plunges it into a bloody civil war. Caesar is a hypocrite. He wants to be king but is afraid what others might think. He is superstitious, and this a dangerous trait in any head of state, because the first calamity in such a situation is rationality. He is also vain and arrogant. Even his impressive victories are more dependent on his magnificent army than on any personal skill. Moreover, bloodshed can never be considered heroic. It always means that human virtue and wisdom could not save the most important factor on earth – actual lives of human beings. Thus for intellectual and moral reasons the play does not seen to have a hero, though we cannot deny that our vote must go to Brutus if we are to accept the conventional parameters of Shakespearean tragedy.

Ques. 4 : Discuss "Julius Caesar" as a tragedy of internal conflict.

OR

"Shakespearean tragedies imply some clash of ideals". Discuss with special reference to "Julius Caesar".

A Shakespearean tragedy can be divided into five parts

Ans. :- A Shakespearean tragedy can be roughly divided into five parts. Bradley, however, divides it into three parts, because he condenses the five into three parts. The first of these three expounds the state of affairs of the play. The conflict itself, from its beginning to its end erupts from these states of affair. The conflict thus constitutes a major portion of the play. It is usually evident in the second, third and fourth acts of a tragedy. It may sometimes also occupy a portion of the first and the fifth acts. The final section of the tragedy shows the presence of the conflict in a catastrophe.

The division is mostly academic

The division is mostly for academic purpose only. In reality the three parts blend into each other in a manner that it becomes difficult to separate them. Into these three parts, we may also superimpose rising action and resolution. The exposition introduces us to the main characters involved and the world that surrounds them.

The conflict can vary

The conflict itself may vary, depending on whether we see it as a drama to be enacted on stage or merely something to be read. In theatre, the outward conflict, which influences the fortunes of the hero, is the aspect which catches our attention. Moreover, since plays vary so much from each other, no single way of regarding the conflict will answer precisely to the construction of all. Despite this limitation, we can still trace the method by which Shakespearean tragedy represents the rise and development of the conflict. Shakespeare begins with creating extreme agitation in the minds of his audience. He then manages to make this tension rise and fall throughout the play. He does this to ensure that his play does not become too oppressive and also that the audience does not lose the intensity of the conflict.

Shakespearean tragedy begins with conflict and ends in catastrophe

Shakespearean tragedy begins with conflict and invariably ends in catastrophe. This is the logical and moral culmination of the action. It also causes the death of the hero, and sometimes of the hero and the heroine. This conflict may be between two warring groups or two opposing principles. The conflict may be external, i.e. man against man. In Julius Caesar this conflict is between Brutus and Cassius on one side and Antony and Julius Caesar on the other. Caesar and Antony stand for Caesarism, which may have hints of extending it to monarchy and the divine right to rule. Brutus stands for republicanism and democracy. We may presume that Cassius too upholds republicanism, despite his personal greed and hatred.

The conflict may be internal

The conflict may also be internal, where the hero is at war with himself due to two opposing thoughts raging inside him. Brutus, for instance, is in turmoil due to his love for Caesar, which is in direct conflict with his love for the good of the people of Rome. Brutus loves Caesar and knows he is, or at least was, noble. The problem arises due to people's inordinate reverence for Caesar. Brutus is worried that Caesar may forget the principles of replublicanism and democracy, and may want to become king. Caesar symbolises personal gratuitousness and kingship. Brutus thinks that the common man can be free only in a republican democracy. He also believes that kingship results in servitude and extreme hardship for the common man. His conflict arises because Caesar is a great man and a friend. Brutus had admired him enormously. Moreover, there is nothing that Caesar has actually done which is alarming. In fact, he actually refuses to be king. Brutus is afraid that he may become despotic and corrupt at some future date. Despite all this, Brutus has reasons to be uncomfortable. Caesar is vain and arrogant. He is surrounded by the kind of power that can corrupt the most upright of men. The conflict is thus between what he sees and what he imagines may happen one day. He cannot let the people of Rome suffer. He is prepared to take any action in order to prevent such a thing. He comes to the conclusion that he must commit the worst kind of crime – murder, that too of a trusting and loyal friend – in order to prevent disaster. The conflict arises because he is an honourable man and fully realises that murder is a heinous crime.

The catastrophe is the death of the hero

Brutus makes up his mind to murder Caesar. He realises his error no sooner has he killed Caesar. The man was not corrupt, nor was he hungry for power. He loved the citizens of Rome and had bequeathed a large portion of his wealth to the citizens of Rome. The conflict begins with exposition, develops into rising action or complication and leads to terrible and far reaching consequences. The end result is of course the catastrophe, which is the death of the hero.

The conflict is psychological and metaphysical

The inner conflict is Brutus' mind is of two distinct kinds. These are as follows:

(a) There is psychological conflict between opposing ideals – personal love for Caesar, which is in direct conflict with his love for republicanism and love for the people of Rome.

(b) There is also a profoundly deep metaphysical conflict. This conflict is between a thinking man and a blind, unmotivated, malignant and senseless power called fate, destiny or nemesis.

Conflict between intellect and social convenience

Besides these two types of accepted conflicts, there is one conflict which has eluded most critics– that between intellect and social convenience. Social convenience suggests that Caesar may become despotic at an uncertain future date. This is based only on one premise that most people become corrupt when surrounded by power. The stress is on "most" because a few do not become corrupt as well. Moreover, Brutus is a magistrate of Rome. He knows justice demands that a person be given adequate choice to prove his innocence. It also demands that a magistrate applies his mind in intellectual, legal and moral manner before he convicts a person. No such thing happens in the play. Brutus convicts Caesar merely on the basis of his fears as to what might happen at a future date. There is no intellectual and moral introspection about available facts. We cannot possibly praise Brutus' actions. There would not be a single human being alive if man starts killing man only on the basis of negative emotions.

Brutus is intellectually blind

Brutus arrives at his terrible decision because he is intellectually and morally blind. No other conclusion is possible once Brutus commits himself to an unethical line of thought – that of condemning greatness because it may one day become corrupt. Brutus had known Caesar for a considerable period of time. He had easy access to him. He had the chance to talk to Caesar or to probe his mind without alarming him. Brutus does no such thing. He arrives at a judgement based on insufficient facts. His idealism may be an admirable thing, but it does not give him the authority to destroy a man who had brought enormous prosperity to Rome. His idealism is a sensation – a worthwhile thing in itself; but it becomes a nightmare because he does not superimpose adequate contemplation over it. The stress is on the word "adequate", because Brutus does give sufficient thought to the problem at hand. Brutus kills Caesar because he feels that even the remotest threat to his ideal of republicanism deserves to be eliminated. It never occurs to him that greatness ought to be preserved. It should be challenged only when it takes a downward plunge. Moreover, killing itself is the most anti-life thing on earth. A life, especially that of a loyal friend, should be preserved. It cannot be taken in the name of some misplaced ideology. Brutus may believe that Caesarism stands for concentration of power in one hand, but in reality it stands for bringing prosperity to Rome and its citizens through the heroics of a great leader. If it was public good that Brutus wanted then he should have let the public decide Caesar's future. Brutus does what most politicians and leaders do – kill or precipitate war to advance a personal prejudice or a dangerously half-baked philosophy. He gives external shape to his inner conflict. He kills Caesar when he cannot resolve the conflict in his own mind. Once he advances death it is inevitable that he surrounds himself in death as well. People reap what they sow within their own lifetime itself. There was no way that people would have let Brutus live after he killed their finest hope to prosperity – that of the towering presence of Caesar.

Ques. 15 : Discuss the appropriateness of the title of the play "Julius Caesar".

OR

The play "Julius Caesar" might more aptly be called after Brutus than Caesar. Discuss.

Brutus attracts many critics

Ans. : It was Brandes who said that "the play is called Julius Caesar, but it was not Caesar himself that attracted Shakespeare. The true hero of the play is Brutus. It is he who has aroused the poet's fullest interest." Voltaire believes that the play should more aptly be called Marcus Brutus because from the beginning to the end it is Brutus who is the prominent figure. Morton Luce suggests that the play has a claim to a double title : "The tragedy of the death of Caesar", and "The tragedy of the death of Brutus", since these two tragedies occupy roughly one half of the play.

Many critics consider Caesar a negative character

Caesar has a very small role in the play as compared to Brutus. Hazlitt believes that Caesar "makes several vapouring and rather pedantic speeches, and does nothing else". Hudson considers Caesar merely "a grand, strutting piece of puff paste... a glorious vapourer and braggart, full of lofty air and mock thunder". This view, with a few exceptions, has persisted to the present day. Dower Wilson considers Shakespeare's Caesar as a ruthless tyrant in the decline of his physical and moral powers. He considers him an "almost supernatural conqueror who out of lust for power ruined the Roman Republic". He thinks that Brutus nobly murdered Caesar. Caesar had illimitable ambition and ruthless, irresistible genius. He ruined his country and the mightiest commonwealth the world will ever see. He also considers Caesar a braggart and thrasonical. Wilson goes on to give a well worn-out list of Caesar's moral and physical deficiencies, and points out where Shakespeare has distorted Plutarch to give them prominence or increase them.

Did Shakespeare commit an error ?

Why then did Shakespeare call his play Julius Caesar? Did he commit an error by not naming the play around Marcus Brutus? Were the critics fair to call Caesar a braggart and a tyrant? If they were not, then why has there been such a preponderance of criticism against Caesar and so much acclaim for Brutus ?

It is unfair to undermine Shakespeare's genius

It is terribly unfair to undermine Shakespeare's genius and whatever he stood for in his dramatic vision, to think that he could have been contented to blindly follow Plutarch. He was a dramatist and it was his job to give an added dimension to history in order to suit his artistic purpose.

There is no need to unduly challenge the play's title

There is no need to unduly challenge the title of the play. Several points can be advanced to substantiate this thought. First, it is Shakespeare's play, and he alone has the right to give a title to his play. Secondly, Shakespeare was a man of undisputed genius. It would be unfair to his genius to think that he would not have given adequate thought to the title of a play. The truth is that Shakespeare chose the title with great care, and no other title could have fitted it better, specially keeping in mind the manner in which the facts are presented to us. So many critics have challenged Shakespeare because they have been needlessly besotted by Brutus' dangerously ineffectual idealism. It is true that Brutus does not succumb to greed and corruption, and that he loves the citizens of Rome more than anything else in the world. If we scrutinise closely it would be evident that Caesar also does not succumb to greed or corruption, and he loves the citizens of Rome as much as does Brutus. In fact, Brutus' qualities are meaningless because no temptation is available to him to prove otherwise. Caesar, on the other hand, is the mightiest of the mighty. He is offered the crown thrice by Antony, and he refuses it on all three occasions. He also bequeaths most of the wealth won by him to the citizens of Rome. Even the few faults, which can not be explained to modern sensibilities, may actually have been desirable in 44 BC Rome. His arrogance and vanity may have been an attempt to motivate his men to blindly rally behind him in order to fight for Rome.

Shakespeare does not depict Caesar as a hated character

Shakespeare does not follow Plutarch in depicting Caesar as a man universally hated in Rome, not merely by a few malcontents. Plutarch's Caesar was hated basically for his covetous design to be king, which first gave people just cause, and next his secret enemies honest colour, to bear him ill-will.

Caesar is respected and loved in Rome

Shakespeare delineates Caesar as a person who is enormously respected and loved in Rome. When he is killed the Roman citizens are "besides themselves with fear" (III. I. 100), and not delighted at the murder of a hateful ruler. It is true that Brutus manages to convince the people of Rome that Caesar was a tyrant, but this has more to do with the fickleness of a mob than any worthwhile merit in Brutus' arguments. This becomes amply evident in the ease with which Antony not only manages to win over the crowd in favour of Caesar but also manages to incite it to an extent where it is prepared to murder Brutus and the other conspirators.

Brutus considers Caesar as the foremost man of this world

Brutus himself considers Caesar as the "foremost man of all this world". There is no reason for us not to accept this truth in its entirety. This is implicit in the reverence that others have for Caesar throughout the play. Caesar makes his first appearance in the second scene of the first act. He is attended by the leading men of Rome and followed by a great crowd. We at once realise that he is a man of immense authority. Both Casca and Antony readily obey his every orders. Some commentators believe that he was superstitious because he wanted Calphurnia to be touched by Antony, who was one of the runners in the holy feast of Lupercalia. Superstition, per se, cannot condemn a man as bad, especially when it is so readily accepted. A leader of men has to abide by the wishes of the common men who surround him. Superstition has no insidious edge to it. Moreover, Caesar ignores every superstition when it matters the most – when it comes between him and the governance of Rome. He calls the soothsayer a "dreamer" when he tells him to beware of the Ides of March, and ignores Calphurnia's dreams and the warnings of the oracles of not setting out of the house. It may be argued that Caesar ignored the warnings due to ulterior motives, but the fact remains that he did ignore them.

Cassius' criticism is an extension of his resentment for Caesar

Cassius describes Caesar as a weak and ineffectual man. Most critics blindly accept his description. They forget that Cassius is an envious malcontent. Moreover, the weaknesses he portrays are human. To shiver in fever or to lose out to the furies of River Tiber do not make Caesar weak. They merely mean that he is human. They reveal how small Cassius is himself. Caesar had conquered every known enemy. He had made Rome prosperous. Cassius and Brutus had not achieved a fraction of what Caesar had achieved. Had they been so worried about the people of Rome, all they needed to do was match Caesar's brilliance and brought prosperity to Rome. Instead, they kill Caesar and plunge Rome into anarchy and chaos.

The relation between the mortal Caesar and his spirit

One thing must be readily accepted that Caesar attributes to himself the inviolability reserved for the divinely ordained ruler. Cassius, Brutus, and Caesar himself, each in their own manner, misconstrue the relation between Caesar's spirit, which gives us his magistracy and vocation, and the imperfect, vulnerable man, Caesar. Brutus considers Caesar's spirit as evil and wishes that he could kill it without killing the man. He will realise that his spirit cannot be killed; only the man is mortal.

Caesar is an arrogant man

One thing more must be readily accepted that Caesar is arrogant. Yet it is the kind of arrogance, which we have accepted, with considerable latitude, in leaders who have served us less well. Why then should Caesar be ostracised ? Brutus thinks that an ambitious man who has climbed to the top of the ladder scorns the lower steps – becomes a god and terrorises those who are below him. The problem is that Brutus' thoughts come in the realm of conjecture. One does not kill leaders on mere conjectures. Neither does one kill because a very great leader appears arrogant. Brutus himself admits that he is forcibly giving direction to his actions to tally with his irrational thoughts.

"So Caesar may;

Then, lest he may, prevent. And since the quarrel

Will bear no colour for the thing he is,

Fashion it thus; that what he is, augmented,

Would run to these and these extremities.   [II. I. 27-31].

Brutus kills Caesar on a whim

Brutus has never known Caesar to be governed by his feelings rather than his judgement, yet in his agony of indecision he is willing to "fashion it thus". He decides to kill a great man and a loyal friend on what is at best a conjecture or a whim. He auto-suggests himself into believing that what he is doing it for the good of the people of Rome. Brutus is not dishonest in thinking so. He is morally and intellectually blind.

Caesar's irrational inflexibility

Just before the assassination, Caesar's arrogance and pride are at their worst. We get increasingly inflated impression about his irrational inflexibility, as Metellus Cimber presents his petition. "Hence! wilt thou lift up Olympus?" he tells him. Immediately we feel there is monstrous pride which must fall. Yet, prepared as we are to accept this fall we realise that death is no way to bring it down, especially since pride is directed towards someone who wants to get a properly judicial judgement reversed. Moreover, no one barring the conspirators are hugely alarmed by his pride. A few of them who do see it remember it so fleetingly, that it is readily forgotten. We hear nothing but good for him after he is brutally killed. When Caesar utters his last words before dying, "Et tu, Brute?–Then fall, Caesar!" Brutus' treacherous act is completely driven home to us. The senseless bathing of the hands by the conspirators in Caesar's blood fills us with horror. We cannot ever consider this as a grand symbol of "Liberty, freedom, and enfranchisement !" as the conspirators wish us to believe.

Caesar is immensely respected

The interviews with Antony's servant and later with Antony tell us how much Caesar was respected. They are both under threat to their own lives if they praise Caesar, yet they do precisely that. Antony sees Caesar's body and immediately sets into motion his plan to avenge Caesar. He had been trembling with fear just moments ago, but even a dead Caesar's presence is enough to inspire and elevate him. Brutus manages to convince the fickle mob that Caesar was ambitious. Yet, Antony is able to win back the crowd with utmost ease. Brutus does not have the personality to win over Antony, leave alone the towering figure of Caesar. Antony justifiably describes the conspirators as "bluchers" and "bloody men", whose

That this foul deed shall smell above the earth

With carrion men, groaning for burial.   [III.ii.274 - 75.]

Caesar's spirit animates Antony

We soon see Caesar's spirit animating Antony, to outwit the naive Brutus and the shrewd Cassius. We also soon realise how wrong Brutus and Cassius were to think that Caesar was ambitious. He had given them no reason to believe in such a manner while he was alive. The reading out of his will by Antony proves that he was neither ambitious nor was he greedy. He had been the sole person responsible for bringing unprecedented wealth to Rome. He could have kept it for himself because he was powerful enough to do so. Instead he bequeathed the riches to the citizens of Rome.

The second half of the play is dominated by Caesar's spirit

The second half of the play is dominated by Caesar's spirit. He may have been murdered; the body after all, is mortal; but his spirit manifests itself in many ways. It is so evident that he is never long absent from the thoughts of even those who murdered him. Brutus had mentioned that they all stood "against the spirit of Çaesar", little realising how prophetic his words would turn out to be. It is this spirit which rises out from the base of Pomey's' statue to extract vengeance for bloody treason. Antony prophesies :

And Caesar's spirit, ranging for revenge,

With Ate by his hole come hot from hell,

Shall in these confines with a monarch's voice.

Cry "Havoc", and let slip the dogs of war.   [III. I. 270-273]

Brutus sees the power of Caesar's spirit in the death of Cassius:
O Julius Caesar, thou art mighty yet !

Thy spirit walks abroad, and turns our swords

In our own proper entrails.   [V. iii. 94-96]

Caesar's spirit dominates at Sardis and Philippi

This same Caesar's spirit dominates when Cassius and Brutus fight at Sardis. That same night Caesar's ghost visits Brutus. He will visit him again at Philippi. As per Dowden, the ghost "serves as a kind of visible symbol of the vast posthumous power of the dictator ". This power works through omens in order to despirit the conspirators and cloud their judgements. Both Brutus and Cassius die with Caesar's name on their lips. "Caesar, thou art revenged" says Cassius, and Brutus tells Caesar's spirit to be still, as he runs over his own sword. He dies a man who has painfully understoods the terrible flaw in his own action. This flaw had made him lose everything he held most dear— his wife, his friends, and most of all his cause. He realises his failure as he invokes Caesar not to torment him anymore. Caesar's murder is avenged. His body is dead, but his spirit has triumphed. Brutus' concept of republicanism is easily forgotten in the inspired warmth that Caesarism invokes. Both Brutus and Cassius die as ordinary murderers. It is left to Octavius to restore some honour for Brutus by giving him a funeral with full military honours.

Conclusion

Once we have established the truth there seems to be no scope for changing the title of the play to Marcus Brutus. It is Caesar who dominates the play, first when he is alive, and later as the spirit of his philisophy and whatever else he stood for. In comparison, Brutus is presented to us as an ineffectual idealist, an abject failure, a naïve politician, a disloyal friend and a destructive philosopher. He can kill based on a dangerously half-baked philosophy. He cannot inspire the people of Rome. No play can bear the name of such a man. There can only be one possible name for the play; and Shakespeare chose just that.

Ques. 6 : Discuss Shakespeare's use of the supernatural in his tragedies, with special reference to Julius Caesar.

Criticism against Shakespeare's use of the supernatural

Ans : Shakespeare has had his share of criticism in his use of the supernatural. Critics say that the ghost is seen only by one person in "Julius Caesar" and in "Macbeth". He is seen by a person whose mental turmoil at the time predisposes him to hallucinations. The apparition is thus nothing more than auto-suggestion, by a highly aggrieved person, who is under enormous strain. Gernivus, while discussing the supernatural element in Hamlet and Macbeth says :

"That they see ghosts is, with both Hamlet and Macbeth, the strongest proof of the power of the imaginative faculty. We need hardly tell our readers… that Shakespeare's spirit world signifies nothing but the physical embodiment of the images conjured up by a lively fancy, and thus their apparition only takes place with those who have this excitable imagination. The cool Gertrude sees not Hamlet's ghost, the cold sensible Lady Macbeth sees not that of Banquo".

Caesar's ghost is subjective

Brutus, on seeing Caesar's ghost says, "Now I have taken heart thou vanishest". Hudson, while commenting on this, says. "This strongly, though quietly, marks the ghost as subjective; as soon as Brutus recovers his firmness, his illusion is broken. The order of things is highly judicious here, in bringing the 'horrible vision' upon Brutus just after he had heard of Portia's shocking death. With that sorrow weighing upon him he might well see ghosts"

Shakespeare uses the supernatural to advance his dramatic purpose

Most critics write in this manner because they are convinced Shakespeare did not believe in ghosts. Yet, this line of thinking cannot explain every apparition in Shakespeare's plays. The ghost of Hamlet is seen by Marcellus, Bernard and even the extremely skeptical Horatio. None of them were under any stress, or had an excitable imagination. Moreover, the ghost does not merely appear and then vanish. It has a long conversation with Prince Hamlet. No theory of subjectivity can explain such a ghost. A simple thought would reveal that no such theory is required in any case. Shakespeare uses the supernatural as a dramatic device and nothing more. The ghost was an integral part of the original story from which Shakespeare borrows for his play. He retains it because it fits into his dramatic art. The ghost serves one very crucial purpose – it ensures Caesar's continued presence long after he is dead.

In Hamlet, the ghost is real

In Hamlet, the apparition is obviously meant to be "real" in the initial scenes. This means the ghost is external to, and independent of, the imagination of those people who see it. The ghost in this instance is truly a supernatural entity. In Macbeth we may dismiss it as something unreal, which is brought about by the hero's chaotic thoughts. Hence, it is not supernatural at all. Both interpretations are thus open to us while evaluating the use of the supernatural by Shakespeare in his tragedies. We must evaluate what to accept, depending on what a particular situation presents to us. It is unfair to explain every supernatural event in Shakespeare's tragedies as subjective or unreal. It is also difficult to establish whether or not Shakespeare believes in the supernatural. He has an "airy spirit" like Aerial, a monster like Caliban, and there are of course the witches (and their deity Hecate) in Macbeth. It is impossible to know what Shakespeare believes in, because he advances the supernatural only based on the situation or character at a particular point of time in the play.

The symbolic meaning of Caesar's ghost

Both the supernatural and the superstitious are important elements of "Julius Caesar". Both give the play a certain unmistakable tempo. The ghost of Caesar appears only on two occasions, and both times it is seen by Brutus – once at Sardis (V. iii), and then in the final scene of the plains at Philippi. In the play, the ghost is obviously not meant to be real. It is a subjective fantasy created by Brutus' imagination. It is thus not supernatural. Brutus sees the ghost the first time when he must have been sapped off his mental energy. He had heard the shocking news of Portia's death, followed by a long and violent argument with Cassius. He had consumed a bowl of wine, and he had difficulty in getting sleep. It is then, and only then, that he sees the ghost. He is the only one to see it, though there are others sleeping in his tent. The illusion is broken as soon as he recovers his poise.

The ghost is Brutus' evil spirit

The ghost stresses the continued influence of Caesar's towering personality. Apart from this it also serves another crucial purpose. Brutus, much earlier, had admitted his spiritual trumoil – his life has been "like a phantasma or a hideous dream" [II.i.65]. He is a man who constantly broods over good and evil. The ghost, not surprisingly, says that he is "thy evil spirit, Brutus". Brutus is a very disgruntled man by the time he reaches Sardis, because he realises that many things he once cherished have been untrue to him. Cassius is financially corrupt. Brutus realises that he killed Caesar but did not "come by" his "spirit". Brutus had made an unreal mental division of Caesar the man and Caesar the symbol of imperial power; so Caesar's disembodied "spirit", his ghost, which is Brutus' own creation, pursues him to death.

Shakespeare introduces the supernatural for his audience

Shakespeare introduces the supernatural because his Elizabethan audience wanted it, and loved it being presented on stage. In the play it may be only Brutus who sees the ghost, but on stage it would be presented to the entire audience. The introduction of the ghost would add to the mystery of the play. Thus, for Shakespeare, the supernatural is not merely a dramatic device. It actually adds to the intensity of his plays, specially his tragedies.

The supernatual does not merely include the ghost. It includes storms, prodigies, omens, and everything else that is not readily rationalised by the human mind. These two – the ghost and the rest – are distinct, but the distinction is one of degree and not of kind. Both presuppose credulity, irrational fear of the unknown and suspension of rational process of thought. The superstitious element in the supernatual is a lower order than ghosts, witches etc. Both, however, are the manifestation of an entity which is beyond the forces of nature. Both originate from some divine grace or anger.

Shakespeare's ingenious rearrangement of supernatural elements

Shakespeare's genius lies in the manner in which he borrows the element of supernatural from Plutarch. He rearranges his material magnificently, with deft strokes, and creates a distinct atmosphere in the play. He first places omens, portents and prodigies. They are an immediate prelude to Caesar's murder. He presents the first hint that Caesar may be murdered through the warning of the soothsayer in the festivity of Lupercalia. He then assembles all portents – the storm, the slave in fire, the lion, the hooting of the owl at daytime – all at one time. The storm is interpreted variedly by different people, as is Calphurnia's dream, which Decius so cleverly interprets to his own advantage. By the time the ghostt appears, the audience is well prepared for every supernatural occurence.

Does Shakespeare believe in the supernatural ?

Dealing with the supernatural elements in "Julius Caesar", A.D.Innes writes :

"It would be an error to base any argument as to Shakespeare's own belief is omens, spirits, and the like, or his use of them in the play. They are appropriate dramatically because they are part of the accepted narrative. Whether the things reported ever took place, or are really credible, is of no consequence : they are true, so to speak, as illustrations, whether true or not in fact. There is nothing in the tale as told in the play which the skeptics need complain of. In most of the signs and portents, from the appearance of the owl down to Cassius being slain with the very sword he slew Caesar, there is nothing incredible. Casca's assertions in I.iii, and Calphurnia's in II.ii are made in each case by a person in a state of superstitious alarm. All these intensify the feeling of doom; they affect us, so to speak, with the electricity in the atmosphere: but they do independently of the view   we may take of their explanation, and they convey no hint of what Shakespeare himself believed. It is characteristic of the great dramatist that he does never give us a clue to his own opinion on most subjects".

The discovery of the nature without and within

The storm scenes represent a distinct process of discovery – of the nature without and within. No summary can attempt to do them justice, and perhaps the best way of indicating what goes on in them is to revert to what has been said of Shakespeare's superb and daring technique. The affect is similar to that of a symphony in which themes are given out, developed, varied and combined. And since murder is planned of the greatest man on earth by none other than his greatest friend, the storm is vividly presented in all its power to cause harm. Shakespeare's use of the supernatural has a particular tone and texture. It increases our suspense and anxiety. The terrible storm on the night before the murder, is the physical manifestation of the terrible storm that is going on inside Brutus' mind. It reflects a mind which is on the brink of taking a disastrous decision. It would destroy Rome more than any physical storm. The ghost mentioned earlier is the external manifestation of Brutus' painful awareness that he had gone terribly wrong.

Ques. 7 : Enumerate Shakespeare's use of omens, portents, and other superstitions in drama. Comment on whether they are to be distinguished from the supernatural in the play "Julius Caesar".

Ans. :

The meaning of supernatural

The supernatural includes anything that is not according to the usual course of nature. It also means to include the miraculous and the spiritual. It is obvious from the definition that both the superstitious and the supernatural are to be included as part and parcel of the supernatural. In "Julius Caesar, superstitions exists in the following scenes :

(a) In I, ii, where Caesar instructs Calphurnia to stand in Antony's path during the festival run of Lupercalia. This is followed by the soothsayer's warning to beware of the Ides of March.

(b) In II. i, where the storm creates superstitious terror in some of the characters of the play.

(c) In II. ii , where Calphurnia is terrified by the dream she had the previous night and Caesar's request to the priests to tell him the outcome of the sacrifices of animals made by them.

(d) In III. i, when the soothsayer returns to once again warn Caesar.

(e) The numerous portents, prodigies and omens depicted throughout the play, but more predominantly, in the first half of the play.

The reason for introducing the supernatural

We know for a fact that Romans during Caesar's time were superstitious. So were the Elizabethans during Shakespeare's time. The supernatural was also an established dramatic device on Elizabethan stage. Shakespeare thus introduced the supernatural and the superstitious to cater for the needs of his audience. He used them with enormous dexterity in order to heighten the anxiety of his audience, and also to reveal the rage brewing inside the minds of his characters, especially the hero. The storm, for instance, is unmistakably accepted as the external manifestation of Brutus' chaotic mind, as he tries to decide the sanctity of murdering Caesar. Other prodigies and omens heighten our anxiety for Caesar's well-being. Calphurnia's dream is the result of a woman who is frail at the best of times. It may also be accepted as an intuitive warning to any threat that a loving wife experiences for a dear husband. The soothsayer and the augurers, all portend that something terrible is about to happen. It is impossible to believe that an animal sacrificed by the augurers did not have a heart. Men are known to exaggerate when they are on the edge. There has been a terrible storm, and the augurers have been asked to carry out an irrational ritual. They cannot possibly take a chance with Caesar's life. The situation is such that it is bound to create turmoil in anyone's mind. There are other improbable incidents as well. Most of them are narrated by a stupidly agitated Casca (I. iii). He talks of tempests and angry winds which have torn tough oak trees. He saw a tempest, which dropped fire; a common slave's hand in flames; a lion roaming angrily in the Capitol; an owl at mid-day hooting in market–place. It is significant that Cicero, to whom Casca narrates these incidents, is quite bemused with the narration.

All the scenes are not improbable

All the above incidents are not completely improbable. They add sinsiter meaning to the events due to the improbable manner in which Shakespeare presents them to us. We may as well dismiss the soothsayer as a dreamer if we were to evaluate him in isolation, but we cannot ignore him in the play.

Superstition should be included as a part of the supernatural

Both dramatically as well as otherwise it is desirable to include superstition as part and parcel of the supernatural. Both heighten the intensity of the play and are preludes to terrible things. In "Julius Caesar" Shakespeare reverses the natural order of things. It is not easy to explain this phenomenon as per the accepted laws of natural science. The disturbances in the physical world symbolise the chaos in man's moral world. It is not without reason that Casca sees all the prodigies. The dramatist delineates him as a typical Roman, who is normally in a constant state of excitability. The thunderstorm and the prodigies affect people differently. Brutus and Cicero are indifferent to the strom. Cassius considers it as a warning, while Casca attaches sinister meanings to it. He constantly tries to incite others to be as terrified about the prodigies as he is.

Brutus' and Cassius' philosophies disintegrate under stress

These prodigies naturally culminate in the appearance of Caesar's ghost. Brutus was not affected by the supernatural till he killed Caesar. He is surrounded by terrible thoughts once he carries out that heinous crime. He is also not helped by the company he keeps. Most of the conspirators like Casca are perpetual doomsdayers. They can terrify any human being. Even Cassius, who sticks to his ideals of epicurism til the very end, does not remain unaffected by it. He searches for mysterious, even sinister, reasons for the desertion of the eagles, as his army advances from Sardis to Philippi, He is troubled that the eagles are replaced by ravens and crows, which were known to bring misfortune. Superstition is an inherent part of the play's atmosphere. It is a phenomenon belonging to a plain lower than supernaturalism, though it has the same ascription of nature's ability to cause destruction.

Symbolic meaning of the darkness of the play

A Shakespearean tragedy has a distinct atmosphere. The prodigies, the storms and the ghost, all add to this special atmosphere. The darkness of the night, as Brutus broods over his terrible thoughts about killing Caesar, symbolise the pall of gloom that is to fall on Rome. The storm externalises the storm raging in Brutus'mind. It also preempts the chaotic world of post-Caesar Rome.

Darkness is broken by light and colour

The atmoshhere, however, is not that of unending black. It is replaced by bright daylight. This is symbolised by Antony's heroic rising, which begins the avenging of Caesar's death.

Inclusion of the unnatural

"Julius Caesar" has both the supernatural and the unnatural. This is common to all Shakespearean tragedies. The hooting owl, the prowling lion, the departure of the eagles, Calphurnia's weird dreams, the horrid rituals of the augurers, all add to the darkness of the night. Casca sums up the prodigies and the unnatural happenings thus:

"A common slave — you know him well by sight —

Held up his left hand, which did flame and burn

Like twenty torches join'd; and yet his hand,

Not sensible of fire, remain'd unscorch'd.

Besides — I ha' not since put up my sword —

Against the Capitol I met a lion,

Who glar'd upon me, and went surly by,

Without annoying me : and there were drawn

Upon a heap, a hundred ghastly women,

Transformed with their fear, who swore they saw

Men, all in fire, walk up and down the streets.

And yesterday the bird of night did sit

Even at noonday, upon the market-place,

Hooting and shrieking".   (I. iii. 14-28)

And when Casca replies thus to the disbelieving Cassius

"But wherefore did you so much tempt the heavens?

It is the part of men to fear and tremble,

When the most mighty gods by tokens send

Such dreadful heralds to astonish us."   (I. iii. 51-54)

he sums up Shakespeare's views about them. The fear is within us. We discard it through rational process of thought, or retain it if we succumb to our irrational fears. The choice thus is clearly ours.

Casca's supernatural prophecy reveals Brutus' capricious environment

The supernatural prophecy not only gives us this option, it is also a dramatic device to reveal the nature of Brutus' capricious environment. The deception in these devilishly supernatural incidents conveys Brutus' betrayal of self. This has a two-fold effect. It increases the suspense of the play. It also exposes the weird and violent world of treason and crime. The prodigies and omens are manifestations of the general vice rampant in the world. Man can either overcome this crime and retain his goodness, or he can succumb to vice and become bad, as does Brutus.

Ques 8 : Discuss the significance of the storm that precedes the murder of Caesar.

Ans. :

Shakespeare enlarges the storm mentioned by Plutarch

Plutarch had written about the storm that preceded Caesar's murder. He had talked about many strange sights visible on that night. Shakespeare accepts this and enlarges it considerably to suit his dramatic purpose.

There is thunder and lightning

The third scene of the first act opens with thunder and lightning, "when all the sway of earth/Shakes like a thing unfirm.?" The scene opens with the cowering figure of Casca, whose fear of the violent storm, and the prodigies consequent to it, is thrown into relief by the philosophic, scornful and calm Cicero.

"Indeed, it is a strange-disposed time :

But men may construe things after their fashion,

Clean from the purpose of the things themselves." (I. iii. 33-35)

The storm's symbolic meaning

Cassius, despite his ardent belief in epicurism, is still worked into a state of frenzy by the terrible violence of the heavens. He rashly dares them to do the worst with him. It is interesting that Cassius links Caesar with the portents of the night. He believes Caesar is "prodigious grown" and a tyrant. The storm is thus symbolic of the malice that Cassius has for Caesar, as much as it is symbolic of Brutus' mental turmoil over the terrible thoughts that occupy his mind. Over and above this, the storm also serves another purpose. The Elizabethan audience sees it as an omen of Caesar's inevitable death. They would not need Calphurnia's later warning to give real shape to their fears.

"When beggar die, there are no comets seen;

The heavens themselves blaze forth the death of princes."

[II. ii. 30-31]

The storm means different things to different people

Act I, Scene i is depicted on stage as heightened excitement because it must reveal the terrible face of the hideous conspiracy. The storm means different things to different people. Brutus and Cicero are indifferent to the storm. Cassius considers it a forewarning. To Casca, it has a terrifying and sinister meaning. He actively tries to incite people into accepting the terror that he attaches to the storm. Though Brutus is not outwardly affected by it, some of Casca's shameful outbursts do seem to affect him as well. Much later in the play, after he has committed the terrible deed of killing Caesar, he is actually subjected to hallucinations.

A Shakespearean tragedy has a distinct atmosphere

A Shakespearean tragedy has a distinct atmosphere. The storm and the prodigies add terror and darkness to the atmosphere. This darkness symbolises the pall of gloom that is to fall on Rome. It also symbolises the lack of illumination in the moral world. Once mankind reverses the world moral order and treads on the path of vice, there can be nothing but chaos. The people of Rome will have to face this chaos if the world moral order is not reversed.

The darkness is broken by light and colour

Darkness, even blackness, looms over the tragedy of "Julius Caesar." This darkness unleashes terrible fears. The atmosphere, however, is not that of unending black, groping darkness. There are flashes of light and colour that break out ever so often. The brilliant light of the thunderstorm, men set aflame, a common-slave's hand burning like a torch, all break the darkness with immense violence. The colour of blood, "which drizzled" upon the Capitol, and visible in Calphurnia's terrible dream, adds as much to the atmosphere of the play, as it lessens its darkness.

The imagery awakens the dread of the supernatural

The imagery of the storm is vivid, violent, and vitriolic throughtout the play. The whelping lioness, the yawning graves yielding up their dead, dying men groaning, an owl hooting, the terrifying presence of a ghost, men set aflame – all add to the terrifying imagery of the play. It is not without reason that the thunderstorm precedes the murder of Caesar. All this is designed to awaken in us the dread of the supernatural.

Depiction of a particular kind of evil

Shakespeare brings forth a particular kind of evil in his tragedies. Macbeth depicts the evil that erupts out of lust for undeserved or unearned power. Julius Caesar conveys how dangerous even seemingly virtuous ideas can be if they are without rational and pro-life evaluation. Shakespeare depicts this evil poetically as well as dramatically in his tragedies. His tragedies are not a result of abstract thoughts. Their action is earthy and real. They reveal evil in terms of direct human experience. The play's rationality demands from us an equally rational and profound response. We have to superimpose adequate contemplation over our sensations, if we are to fully understand the meaning of the play.

Shakespeare's creativity blends with the gloom of the hero

Unlike "Macbeth" the atmosphere is not completely dank and dark in "Julius Caesar". The storm exists only for a short duration of time. There can be no denying the fact that Shakespeare blends his poetic creativity with the murderous instincts and gloom of the hero. Yet, Brutus does not once believe that the storm can cause any harm to the moral world.

Caesar is not unduly affected by the storm

The storm, however, triggers those terrible dreams in Calphurnia, who entreats her husband not to step out of the house. Caesar himself is not unduly upset either by the storm or by the prodigies. He says that "these predictions. Are to the world in general as to Caesar", and that:

"Cowards die many a times before the deaths;

The valiant never taste of death but once.

Of all the wonders that I yet have heard,

It seems to me most strange that men should fear;

Seeing that death, a necessary end,

Will come when it will come."   [II. ii. 32-37]

The storm conveys the role of destiny in Caesar's death

The storm conveys to us the role of destiny in Caesar's death. Shakespeare manages to let his audience repeatedly think that the elements have conspired with fate to destroy Caesar. The storm brewing in the political world of Rome is not known to Caesar. Neither is he aware of the storm that brews in Brutus' mind; but this storm would ultimately destroy both of them.

Ques. 9: What is the dramatic significance of introducing the ghost in "Julius Caesar"? Give a detailed answer.

Ans. :

Plutarch had mentioned about Brutus' supernatural spirit

Plutarch had mentioned about the appearance of Brutus' supernatural spirit, in his "Lives of Caesar and Brutus."

Shakespeare advances Plutarch's thought

Shakespeare obviously borrows this from the original source. Plutarch had, however, kept the subject ambiguous. He had called the ghost Brutus' "ill angel" or "evil spirit". Shakespeare enlarges Plutarch's evil spirit into the ghost of Caesar. The conversation between Brutus and the ghost advances this thought.

Brutus : How ill this taper burns! — Ha! who comes here?

I think it is the weakness of mine eyes

That shapes the monstrous apparition.

It comes upon me — Art thou anything ?

Art thou some god, some angel, or some devil,

That mak'st my blood cold, and my hair to stare

Speak to me what thou art.

Ghost : Thy evil spirit, Brutus

Brutus: Why comest thou?

Ghost: To tell thee thou shalt see me at Philippi.

Brutus: Well; then I shall see thee again?

Ghost: Ay, at Philippi.

Brutus: Why, I will see thee at Philippi, then.   [IV. iii. 275-287]

Caesar's ghost is undoubtedly unreal

The ghost of Caesar is undoubtedly unreal. It is triggered off by Brutus' fragile imagination. The problem whether Caesar's ghost is meant to be real (i.e. an external, objective phenomenon) or it is a product of Brutus' imagination (a subjective fantasy, and thus not supernatural at all) has long since been solved. There are some other plays written by Shakespeare where the ghost is obviously meant to be real, but in "Julius Caesar" it is not. Brutus has just learnt that Portia is dead, he has had a long and violent argument with Cassius, he has consumed a bowl of wine, and sleep is hard to come by. His nerves are obviously on the edge. He tries to relax, first with music, and later by reading, but fails. It is significant that he is the only one who sees the phantom and that too for a very short duration of time. The illusion is broken as soon as he recovers his poise. "Now that I have taken heart thou vanishest", says Brutus, and we immediately know that he had been hallucinating. It also suggests that the ghost is a subjective phenomenon.

The ghost is a prelude to Brutus' doom

The question that needs to be answered is why Shakespeare introduces the ghost. In all probability, he introduces it for the same reason for which he introduces the storm. The storm is a prelude to Caesar's doom. The ghost is a prelude to Brutus' doom. Moreover, it is a very clever dramatic device for stressing the continued presence of Caesar's influence despite his death. Shakespeare wants the audience to believe that the play is entirely about Julius Caesar – his murder in the first half of the play, and the avenging of his murder in the second half. He also wants to convey that Caesar may be dead but his spirit is alive and thriving.

The ghost symbolises Brutus' sublimation

The presence of the ghost is of much greater significance than merely conveying Caesar's continuous presence. Brutus admits about his inner turmoil when he says that his life has been "like a phatasma, or a hideous dream". (II. i. 65). Here is a man susceptible to delusions and nightmares because he broods over truth and falsity and arrives at hideously wrong conclusions. The ghost tells Brutus that it is his evil spirit. He can be nothing else to a man who kills a loyal and time-tested friend due to the first hint of falsity and hatred generated by an outsider. The evil spirit symbolises Brutus' catharsis or sublimation. By the time he arrives at Sardis he realises that most of the things he had considered valuable have wronged him. He murdered Caesar in order to get rid of his spirit. He got rid of the man instead, and not his spirit. He had believed in Cassius more than a trusted friend, only to find that he is indulging in bribery. The ghost visits him first at Sardis and then at Philippi. Dowden believes the ghost is a "visible symbol of the vast posthumous power of the dictator" It works as an omen and despirits the armies of the conspirators. It also clouds the judgement of Cassius and Brutus. They end up making fatal mistakes.

Caesar's ghost symbolises nemesis and restores Caesarism

The ghost is no more than Caesar's spirit "ranging for revenge". It is also the symbol of nemesis or retribution that haunts the murderers. Shakespeare had a rather delicate task on hand. He had to kill the conspirators in order to ensure poetic justice; yet, he also had to retain Brutus' sublimity despite his hideous crime. There is something very poignant about Caesar's ghost being the agent of nemesis. Shakespeare does not want the restoration of the world moral order. He wants to re-establish Caesarism. Nothing can achieve it better than Caesar's ghost.

The ghost adds to the play's atmosphere

A Shakespearean tragedy has a distinct tone and atmosphere. It is distinct and easily perceptible, but it is not easy to define. Caesar's ghost unmistakably adds to this atmosphere and tone. Nothing can convey Brutus' agonised soul better than the ghost. Its presence adds to the terror and mystery of the play. The ghost says that it is Brutus' evil self. Shakespeare manages to present the ghost when Brutus' confidence is at the lowest ebb. Even the timing is perfect. It is the dead of night and the taper has run thin. The ghost is symbolic of the dark recesses of Brutus' human mind.

The ghost symbolises Brutus' betrayal of self

The ghost makes a very worthwhile prophecy. It symbolises the capricious atmosphere that Brutus has submerged himself in. It is an atmosphere full of corruption and betrayal. It drains Brutus' mind and leaves him bafflingly devoid of rationality. He advances to Philippi when he should have stayed at Sardis. The arrival of the ghost prompts him even further. He decides to set forth for Philippi at once, as if lured by the gods to his inevitable doom. The ghost thus also symbolises Brutus' betrayal of self. He cannot see through Cassius, he cannot muster sufficient integrity of thought and kills a dear friend and a great leader, and he cannot find the right rhythm to motivate and lead his men. The ghost brings the terrible world of treason and betrayal to its logical conclusion.

The Elizabethan audience loved ghosts on stage

The Elizabethan audience loved ghosts being shown on stage. Shakespeare had no option but to cater for popular taste and give the audience what it wanted. Shakespeare's audience was not very sophisticated. Yet, it was definitely not barbaric as suggested by Jonson. Lale comments, "Shakespeare and his contemporaries bountifully illustrate the superstitious credulity which guided their contemporaries' conduct, moulded many of their social customs, and governed their interpretation of natural phenomena."

Ques. 10 : "Character is destiny". Illustrate this maxim with reference to the play 'Julius Caesar' ".

OR

"Fate or destiny plays a prominent role in the play 'Julius Caesar'". Discuss.

OR

"The play 'Julius Caesar' abounds in dramatic irony." Discuss.

OR

"Nemesis links together the principal incidents and connects them with what occurred in Roman history." Discuss.

Ans:

The definition of a Shakespearean tragedy

A Shakespearean tragedy is a story of exceptional calamity leading to the death of a man in high estate. It is, however, clearly much more than this. In his tragedies are seen a number of human beings placed in certain circumstances. Out of the cooperation of these characters arise certain actions. These actions in turn lead to other actions, until a series of interconnected deeds lead, by an apparently inevitable sequence, to a catastrophe. The effect of such a series, on imagination, is to make us regard the sufferings which accompany it, and the catastrophe in which it ends; not only for the persons concerned, but equally as something which is caused by them. This, at least, may be said of the hero, who invariably contributes to the disaster in which he perishes.

The link between character and action

The second aspect of tragedy differs greatly from the first, which accepts men primarily as agents, themselves the authors of their woe. Our fear and pity thus is altered according to this point, though it does not in any way diminish or cease to exist. The centre of Shakespearean tragedy lies in action issuing in character, or in character issuing in action.

The main elements of a Shakespearean tragedy

Though Shakespeare's main interest lies in character and the psychological interest that it generates, it would be a mistake to think that he ignores other aspects, for he is a dramatist to his finger-tips. The main elements that are found in his plays besides characteristic deeds, suffering and action are :

(a) Abnormal conditions of mind, like insanity, hallucinations and somnabulism.

(b) Introduction of the supernatural to add to the dread and gloom.

(c) Letting chance or accident have an appreciable influence at some point of the play's action.

Chance, fate and human actions

Chance or accident means the occurrence, other than the supernatural, which enters the dramatic sequence neither from the agency of a character, nor from the obviously surrounding circumstances. The central feeling we have due to these chance accidents is one of waste. It makes use accept the helplessness of man. Yet, by itself fate cannot cause harm. Shakespeare shows that man in some degree is the reason for his own undoing. There are other occasions in the tragedy when we are convinced that man is extremely unlucky. Caesar would not have died if he had listened to Calphurnia or the soothsayer, or had read Artemidorus' petition first. Brutus would not have become a murderer if he had been trained in the moral meaning of existence. He may have lived if he had killed Antony along with Caesar. He may have won the battle against the army of Antony and Octavius if he had listened to Cassius and let the enemy army come to him at Sardis, instead of marching his own army to Philippi.

Shakespeare's tragedies are totally devoid of fatalism

It is equally important to establish what we do not find in Shakespeare's plays in addition to what we do find in them. We find fate, accident and chance but we do not find any trace of fatalism. We do not see suffering predetermine independence of peoples thoughts, resolution and actions. Shakespeare never conveys that the gods are relentlessly working against the happiness of an individual or a family. Neither does he link crime to heredity.

The meaning of fate in Shakespeare's plays

What then is fate, which makes us believe that it is the ultimate power of the tragic world? It is a mythological expression for an entire system or order, of which individual traits form but a very small part. It is something, which is beyond any human understanding. It is not even certain that we ought to call it as "fate". The word "fate" may, in fact, imply something more. It includes a blank necessity, which is totally unconcerned about the rhythm of the human world or the need to differentiate between virtue and vice. Many readers may want to reject such an explanation. They may believe that this order shows characteristics of quite another kind, and that what it gives us is the name of fate, which makes us describe it as a moral order and a moral necessity.

There can be no tragedy without adverse human action

This leads us to one undeniable fact. No matter how much we may wish to think about fate, chance and accident, there can be no tragedy without adverse human action. The critical action is primarily wrong or bad. It varies only in degrees in each tragedy. The reaction to this adverse action results in catastrophe. This too varies only in degree in each tragedy. This catastrophe therefore brings about justice, since social and moral order demands punishment for evil actions. This is known as justice in place. This justice may appear terrible because a tragedy is a terrible story. That is why we do not reject it despite feeling fear and pity.

Shakespeare's tragedies do not have poetic justice

This justice need not always be poetic. Poetic justice means that actions are rewarded or punished in proportion of their merits or demerits; where the good is rewarded and the evil is punished; where the reward and punishment are equal to their goodness or crime. Shakespeare does not depict this poetic justice, simply because rewards and punishments do not follow a just pattern in real life. In the real world, a criminal may thrive and a virtuous man may be punished. It is not as if Shakespeare does not adhere to the moral rhythm

of existence. It only means that punishment or reward in his tragedies are not
visibly in keeping with the virtue or evil of the action in consideration.

The main source of convulsion is always evil

With Shakespeare, the main source of convulsion which produces
suffering and death is never good. Good contributes to the convulsion only
from its tragic implementation with its opposite in the same character. The
main source of this convulsion, on the contrary, is evil in its fullest sense in
most cases; and not a mere lack of perfection or an element of moral evil.
Romeo and Juliet die because of the senseless hatred which their two families
pursue. Guilt, ambition for inordinate power and dangerous malice influence
Macbeth's tragic actions. Even when this moral evil is not the obvious prime
source within the play, it lies behind it. "Julius Caesar" is the only tragedy in
which one is even tempted to find an exemption to this rule. The influence is
obvious. Evil disrupts the social moral order and this order cannot be friendly
to evil or indifferent to evil or virtue.

Destiny is the final arbiter of human affairs

Destiny, none-the-less, is the final arbiter of human affairs in every
tragedy written by Shakespeare. He is thus true to Greek concept of tragedy,
though he does not accept God as a cosmic and divine power. He finds the
existing world more definitely theological than mysteriously cosmic. Despite
this difference, Shakespeare does gradually notice a design in the suffering
of the world and the law of tragedy justifying it. He manages to bring out this
design in his tragedies.

Tradedy is brought about primarily by human flaw

Shakespeare never accepts tragedy as a result of a malevolent, all killing
God. He links tragedy to human flaws. He never advances the thought that
fate or accident arbitrarily cause pain to the virtuous and the innocent. Nor
does he believe that it is a random, isolated entity, which exists for its own
sake. He brings in fate as he does destiny and chance, in order to bring about
nemesis or retribution in his plays. This nemesis is never exact because
Shakespeare never depicts poetic justice in his plays. We are convinced that
both Lear and Brutus perpetrate terrible actions which deserve sufficient
punishment. Yet, our belief does not extend to death. Our belief and our pity
and fear for the tragic hero still forces us to acquire the final catastrophe that
Shakespeare works out for him. Shakespeare presents facts in such a manner
that we convince ourselves about the hero's tragic end. We somehow know
no other fate is possible for him. We also accept that he is better off dead than
alive. Brutus wishes to kill Caesar's spirit. All he can manage is to kill Caesar,
the man. He slowly comes to the conclusion that the human spirit is
unconquerable; only man is mortal. He also realises that he had been wrong

all along. He had killed a loyal and virtuous friend and backed a terrible schemer. Subconsciously, he may have also understood that a philosophy by itself means nothing unless it is backed by pro-life action. By the time this realisation reaches him, Brutus is a broken man. His wife and friends are dead. He has walked on the path of evil. He knows there is no retracing this path. He has no option but to kill himself. Brutus had lived by the rather vague concept of honour. Vague, because he seeks approval of others, while life demands that he should have worked out truth in its inviolable and unimpeachable form, before he committed himself to act. Brutus' philosophy is half-baked. His actions are tragically anti-life. If he loved republicanism and the people of Rome then he should have found ways to restore it, rather than indulging in senseless killing. If the people of Rome want Caesar to be made king then that is what they deserve. They were in any case much happier under Caesar than they ever are after Brutus thrusts Rome into an endless civil war. When a mountain falls, there is an inevitable earthquake. The same happens when Caesar dies. Brutus is totally ill equipped to prevent this earthquake from destroying the peace of Rome.

Intervention of fate

There is no denying the fact that fate does interneve in the play. The outcome of the play would have been different if Caesar had listened to Calphurnia or the soothsayer, or he had read Artemidorus' petition. The ending of the play would also have been different if Brutus had killed Antony. Despite this logic there is no way that the dramatist could have let Brutus win once he made the fatal error of killing Caesar. He had also to ensure that Brutus did not die innocent because then Shakespeare would have flouted every parameter of tragedy. No dramatist can do such a thing. Shakespeare arranges the action of the play in such a way that Brutus' death is largely a consequence of his terrible flaw. Fate or destiny merely adds to the tragic gloom that Brutus or the people of Rome have to face once Caesar is dead.

Ques. 11 : Write a note on Shakespeare's treatment of the mob.

OR

Give an account of Shakespeare's presentation of the Roman mob.

Ans. :

The mob is a merely a crowd at the beginning of the play

The mob is one of the main forces in the play. It is the underlying power that determines the outcome as it is worked on by the play's leading characters. That is the reason why Shakespeare introduces it in the very beginning itself. At first, the mob is merely a crowd – a happy collection of individuals with an odd hint of a real character like the cobbler. Despite the peaceful exterior, there are already ominous signs that it is fickle and prone to be swayed to emotional rhetoric and hero-worship. Throughout the following scene, the crowd is never far away from the minds of the leading characters of the play. The mob's presence is evident everytime Caesar is present. It rumbles threateningly in the background and gives point to Cassius's invective against Caesar. This is described sardonically by Casca. The crowd also works as a background to the anxieties of Portia and the soothsayer. It is finally transformed into a mindless and dangerous mob by Antony's inspiring speech.

The first movement of the play begins and closes with the crowd

The first movement of the play closes, as it begins, with the crowd. It's brutal arraignment of Cinna, the poet, is an ironic reversal of Marullus's arrogant questioning of the cobbler in the first scene, and their gay humour recurs in a warped and distorted form in the dark comedy of Cinna's murder.

Shakespeare gives an Elizabethan colouring to his mob

Shakespeare gives an Elizabethan colouring to his Roman mob. The mob cannot lay claim to correctness as a picture of Roman life and manners. The mob does not include the "Plebs" of Roman history. Shakespeare makes references to glasses (I. ii. 60) and striking clocks (II. ii. 114). This is unmistakably a characteristic of an English mob. The stage during Shakespeare's time had enormous limitations. Shakespeare could not have stretched realism too far and yet made his presentation on stage readily acceptable. Moreover, the Elizabethan era was one of creativity. The audience was more interested in creative endeavour than in the strict letter. Dramatists reset classical themes among romantic surroundings without worrying about the confusion of effect brought about by the amalgamation of the old and the new.

Shakespeare depicts the crowd differently from Plutarch

Shakespeare makes a conscientious effort to move away from Plutarch while depicting the mob. This is evident in the first scene itself. Plutarch had written that "the chiefest cause that made him mortally hated was the covetous desire he had to be called king; which first gave the people just cause, and next his secret enemies honest colour to bear him ill-will". In the opening scene in "Julius Caesar" we find the mob rejoicing, instead, in Caesar's triumph. The citizens are "besides themselves in fear"after Caesar is murdered. There is no evidence of delight at the death of a hated ruler. Brutus manages to convince the crowd that Caesar was a tyrant. Yet, this reveals nothing more than the fickle nature of the crowd, rather than any change in heart. It does not require much effort from Antony to convince it that the dead Caesar deserved the same love and respect that they had for him when he was alive.

Shakespeare depicts Caesar as the darling of the crowd

Critics believe that Caesar was a ruthless man because he did not hesitate celebrating a victory over his own countrymen. Yet, the celebration was a part of history. Shakespeare could not have removed it without altering a crucial rhythm of Roman history during that period of time. The celebrations suggest that Caesar was not hated, otherwise the crowd would have stayed away from it. Shakespeare uses it to show Caesar in glowing light. Unlike Plutarch, he delineates Caesar as a darling of the crowd. There is no denying the fact that the tribunes upbraid him, but that is inevitable, because they are followers of Pompey, whose defeat and death is being celebrated on the streets of Rome. The tribunes are also angry at the lack of gratitude towards Pompey by the fickle crowd. Marullus tells the crowd:

"Knew you not Pompey ? Many a time and oft.

Have you climb'd up to walls and battlements,

To towers and windows, yea, to chimney-tops,

Your infants in your arms, and there have sat

The livelong day, with patient expectation,

To see great Pompey pass the streets of Rome   [I. i 42-47]

It is his attempt to remind the crowd of its fickleness when they "strew flowers in his way/That comes in triumph over Pompey's blood"?

The crowd is fickle and irrational

Stanley Wood comments thus about the crowd : "The citizens and commoners are represented by Shakespeare as being a somewhat mean-spirited crowd, whose base metal is easily swayed this way and that. They are fickle and irrational, possessing little of that spirit of freedom that characterised their ancestors. Childish in love of shows and spectacles, their sympathies are readily moved and they are formidable only when their passions are aroused".

Shakespeare presents a universal truth regarding the mob

Wood utters a profound moral truth, and Shakespeare may have conveyed it as a universal concept worth remembering. The concept of collective versus individual depicts a moral process of thought. Every conceivable thought makes us arrive at the conclusion that collectivism harms, and is contrary to what constitutes life. Every great creation or creator must have its of his share of accolades. The problem is that a collective can give brickbats to the same creation one moment and accolades the next. It has to be morally established whether Caesar's triumph over Pompey is great or not, and whether Caesar himself deserves to be revered like a hero or not.

The crowd cannot vacillate between extreme reverence and terrible hatred for the same man or the same deed as they do in Rome.

A truly moral man does not need the backing of others

Only the weak and the useless need to backing of a crowd. A truly moral man is too busy living life to even contemplate seeking the approval of other men. Only the weak and the incompetent need to mobilise the crowd. There is no such thing as a collective brain, hence there can be no such thing as a collective thought. The crowd is not worried about republicanism or Caesarism. Its sole concern is affluence with least possible effort. It will make merry for the smallest cause, especially if it advances laziness. It is such a crowd that Brutus wishes to convince that his philosophy is a sound one. He fails miserably when Antony intervenes and incites the crowd. He understands the terrible ability of the crowd to cause harm. He uses only this to turn it into a massive force against the conspirators.

Shakespeare chooses greatness over common good

Shakespeare restores the world's moral order when he lets greatness prevail. Shakespeare's idea of a good government was gentle aristocracy. Republicanism and democracy may have considerable good points but it is also influenced by a multiple of zeroes. Both can fail if the people at the helm of affairs are corrupt or incompetent. Great men must provide leadership. They cannot be influenced by the whimsicality of a crowd; and yet provide proper governance.

The play displays the whimsicality of a crowd

This whimsicality of the crowd is bafflingly evident in "Julius Caesar". The crowd actually changes its mind and sides five times in the play. When Brutus delivers the speech, the crowd is completely behind Brutus. "Live, Brutus ! live, live" says one citizen. "Let him be Caesar", says another. "This Caesar was a tyrant", says yet another. Yet, it does not take Antony much effort to win them over. "They were villains, murderers", say a citizen about the conspirators. "Revenge! About! Seek! Burn! Fire! Kill! Slay! Let not a traitor live!" they say collectively after Antony's speech. The mob once favoured Pompey, then Caesar, then Brutus, then Antony, and finally Caesar again. Shakespeare thus is in no doubt, in stressing the danger that is intrinsically present in a collective. In unity there may lie strength, but this unity is invariably used to cause harm. Only individual brilliance constitutes life. It is this individual brilliance that can add life to the collective. The reverse, however, cannot be true. No matter how much we may wish to convince ourselves to the contrary, the truth is that the collective can only generate harm. Brutus reverses this relationship. He rejects Caesar's brilliance and inherent goodness, and thinks that the public can flourish merely by an inanimate theory of republicanism. He thinks ambition is bad, little realising that man cannot aspire to become great if he is not ambitious.

Shakespeare conveys that life's morality cannot be compromised

Shakespeare lets the crowd betray the person who puts his life at stake for it. The message Shakespeare wants to give is very clear – life is a moral concept, and its inviolability cannot be compromised. Brutus' tragic flaw is that his moral concept lacks inviolability. Its merits are open to question. That is why it is easily defeated on the parameter that differentiates right from wrong. It is for this very reason that Antony can counter his empty claims with the utmost of ease.

The senseless destructiveness of the crowd

The crowd may have been law-abiding in the initial scenes of the play, but it does not require much effort to incite it into becoming an angry mob. Shakespeare depicts one undeniable fact–that the collective can do no good. The way the crowd indulges in arson and looting after Antony's speech is symbolic of what every crowd invariably indulges in. The senselessness of the crowd is best evident in its arraignment of Cinna. The crowd rips him to pieces, first because he has the same name as one of the conspirators, and secondly for writing bad poetry.

Some critics wrongly accept the crowd as the real hero of the play

Some critics have let their imagination run wild and believe that the crowd in the real hero of the play. They think that Caesar, Brutus or Antony do not deserve to be the hero of the play. The mob decides whether Caesarism or republicanism is to prevail in Rome. Such a thought seems to be an outcome of a perverted psychology. It tantamounts to accepting that penicillin was invented by the mob since it wholeheartedly accepted it for centuries, and rejecting that Madane Curie, its real inventor, had anything to do with it. The crowd does not know a thing about the difference between republicanism and Caesarism. It is prepared to be swayed towards either of them without any rational cause. Moreover, the question that needs to be considered is not about republicanism or monarchy. What must hold our attention is what constitutes essential goodness, based on true moral values. The crowd reacts in moral blindness. Both republicanism and monarchy require a truly moral man in order to generate goodness. No mob can generate it. Only an individual or a group of individuals working in personal capacities can possibly generate goodness. A mob, which can be swayed to opposing views within a few minutes, cannot be said to have the right rhythm of existence.

The mob has the function of a classical chorus

The function of the mob in the play is in some respects similar to that of a classical chorus, though it lacks the tone and action of a chorus. It resembles the chorus only because it comments and provides a hint as to what will happen in the future. In some ways the crowd also symbolises the spirit of history which was then giving direction to Rome's destiny.

Shakespeare exposes uselessness in people

Many critics think that Shakespeare had no sympathy for the mob. This forces them to believe that Shakespeare is at variance with democracy. Critics also believe that Shakespeare had a crude attitude because he looked upon the common people with contempt instead of pity. These critics do not even deserve our attention because they are totally wrong. They find reference here because most people consider pity a virtue, whereas it is an insult to any human being. Pity must be reserved only for a person who is without hope. A moral view advances that no human being can be possibly without hope simply because he is the finest creation of god. Any human being who does not live up to his expectations must be exposed in order to provide a lesson to others. Shakespeare does just that in "Julius Caesar". It must be accepted that Shakespeare tries to consistently advance a moral view of life. A mob is inanimate, with no life of its own. Those who huddle together, devoid of any thought, have a singular meaning – they lack the capacity to exist alone and seek meaning in numbers instead. Such a thing, however, can never be achieved because life can only be lived alone. We have seen every conceivable form of collectivism – communism, Nazism, socialism, fascism – perish after causing enormous hardships to the individual. Shakespeare seems to understand the problem long before humanity experimented with it and suffered. Shakespeare, like scores of men of intellect over the centuries, wishes to tell us about the terrors hidden behind any collective.

Ques. 12 : Bring out the dramatic significance of the opening scene of the play "Julius Caesar".

OR

"The opening scene strikes the keynote of the drama". Discuss with special reference to "Julius Caesar".

Ans. :

The opening scene is meant to make a powerful impression

The opening scene in a Shakespeare play usually serves two functions. First, it must make an immediate and powerful appeal to the audience's attention. This was especially important in the Elizabethan theatre because of the informal, and sometimes rowdy, behaviour of the play-goers. In the first scene of "Julius Caesar", Shakespeare gets the attention of his audience and his readers the moment Flavius shouts at the commoners. Secondly, Shakespeare's first scene usually gives us some hint of the kind of situation, or theme, which is going to develop as the play goes on. For example Shakespeare's main concern in "Hamlet" is the dramatisation of the hero's lack of resolve. He opens the play with the tense, dramatic challenge and counter-challenge of some uneasy soldiers standing on guard. This immediately conveys to us the sense of confusion and uncertainty, which will spread and intensity as the play continues. In "Julius Caesar" we have two tribunes – Flavius and Marullus. They are not important characters; they are, infact, "put to silence" in the next scene, but they are dramatically significant because of what they say. They openly condemn Caesar in front of his plebeian admirers. This introduces us to the atmosphere of civil strife and chaos that is prevalent in Rome. The threat is yet vague and marginal, but it will become specific and strong as the conspiracy of Cassius comes to light in the next scene.

The opening scene provides a hint of the play's central theme

One thing must be stressed here. The tribunes are the official representatives of the people. They are shown as being violently against Caesar because he wants to become king and obtain absolute power in Rome. The people of Rome were traditionally in favour of a republican form of government, where the power was vested in people rather than in a single authority. It is this tradition that the tribunes are trying to uphold against the inordinate ambition of Caesar. This is the first hint of an uneasiness which will generate into full blown conspiracy when Cassius and Brutus decide to murder Caesar in order to prevent him from becoming king. The opening scene thus also provides us with a hint of the central theme of the play—a clash between republicanism and Caesarism.

The cobbler gets the better of the two tribunes

All drama depends on conflict of some kind, both throughout the play as a whole, and in individual scenes. The conflict in the opening scene is a verbal one between the cobbler and the tribunes. The tribunes have authority. This is reflected in their language ("You blocks, you stones, you worse than senseless things!"). Against this authoritarian rhetoric Shakespeare puts the verbal cleverness of the cobbler. This exasperates Flavius and Marullus, specially when he deliberately misunderstands what they say, and puns and plays on the meanings of the words they use. When reading a Shakespearean play we must always remember that the language is meant to be heard and not read, and the puns spoken on stage are more effective than they are on the printed page. As soon as the cobbler mentions "soles" he associates the word with "souls", the phrase, "with the awl" suggests "withal", By playing on the various meanings of the word, the cobbler is able to, no matter how fleetingly, get the better of two people who are obviously his social superiors. This would have pleased the commoners who surround him, as well as the groundlings of the Elizabethan stage, who presumably had lesser love for authority than does the cobbler.

The opening scene provides hints about the crowd's fickleness

Shakespeare makes another subtle but crucial point in the opening scene of "Julius Caesar". This prepares us for a crisis later in the play. The people have gathered to see Caesar and rejoice in his victory over Pompey and his sons. What we see is a traditional procession through the streets of Rome in honour of a returning hero. Marullus reminds the crowd of his fickleness, for it had once welcomed Pompey with "an universal shout," just as they now welcome the man "That comes in triumph over Pompey's blood". On the stage before us the holiday mood of the crowd changes at once. Flavius comments, "They vanish tongue-tied in their guiltiness". Shakespeare drives home the fickleness of the crowd and the ease with which it can be swayed. This quality of the crowd will reach its climax in Act III, Scene iii, when Antony's speech converts the crowd into a dangerous mob, which hounds the conspirators to their doom.

The festivities are for Caesar's victory over the sons of Pompey

The first Scene occurs on the streets of Rome. It is a working day but the commoners have gathered on the streets, ignoring the normal practice of not being away from work on a day other than a holiday. The crowd is celebrating Caesar's victory. He had defeated Gnaeus and Sextus, sons of Pompay the great, at Munda in Spain on 15th October, 45 BC. The actual celebration takes place on 15 February 44 BC, on the festival of Lupercal. Plutarch says that the celebration was resented by the crowd because it celebrated a victory over "the sons of the noblest man of Rome, whom fortune had overthrown". He also says that the crowd hated Caesar. "But the chiefest cause that made him mortally hated was the covetous desire he had to be called king, which gave the people just cause, and next his secret enemies honest colour, to bear him ill-will". Shakespeare alters all this. He makes the people rejoice Caesar's triumph. The crowd is boisterous and happy.

The opening scene reveals the forces which would produce the tragedy

The opening scene of a Shakespearean tragedy usually serves as a keynote of the play by revealing to us the forces which tend to produce the tragedy. It also provides sufficient information to enable the audience to anticipate the events that are to follow. The opening scene of "Julius Caesar" does all this and more. It is in the form of a prologue. It tells us in absolutely clear terms the state of affairs in Rome when the play opens. The play opens with a cheerful crowd. This is common in Shakespeare's tragedies. "Romeo and Juliet" opens with a street fight and "Coriolanus" with a crowd is commotion. Once the audience has had its effect on the audience, Shakespeare presents quiet speeches, which convey the cause of the excitement. Apart from the state of affairs in Rome, the opening scene also fixes the time of the action of the play. The feast of Lupercal was held on 15 February every year for purification of the walls of Rome. Its celebrants, the Luperci, were originally divided into two collegia, each under a magistrate. In 44 BC, a third collegium, the Juliani, was instituted in the honour of Julius Caesar, who appointed Antony as its magistrate. A great feature of the Lupercalia was the course run by the Luperci, around the city wall. They struck the crowd, specially women with leather thongs, which they carried with them. These thongs were made from the skin of the victims sacrificed. These were known as februa, and hence the ceremony was called februatio. The month of February got its name from here. This scene establishes that Caesar is superstitious because he asks Antony, one of the runners, to strike Calphurnia, so that she can bear a child for him.

The opening scene summarises recent events

The opening scene also summarises recent events. Caesar has defeated the sons of Pompey. He has brought enormous riches of Rome and he is greatly admired and loved by the citizens of Rome. Despite the outward show of rejoicing, there is an undercurrent of dissent. Caesar has become too powerful while Rome is used to republican democracy. This divides Rome into two groups–those who support Caesar and those who don't. Despite this divide, the average man on the street is not fully aware of the precise nature of things around him. He wants affluence without work. He is not unduly concerned which political philosophy will create it for him.

The opeining scene establishes the dominance of Caesar's spirit

"Julius Caesar" is a play about the dominance of Caesar's spirit. The opening scene manages to establish this dominance, as the commoners challenge the tribunes. They are prepared to clash with any authority that questions Caesar's might.

Ques. 13. : Describe in your own words the speeches of Brutus and Antony. List down the relative significance of both.

Ans. :

The speeches begin a few hours after Caesar is murdered

Caesar is assassinated on the morning of the Ides of March, BC 44, Mar 15 (Act III, Scene i). The speeches begin a few hours later (Act III, Scene ii). Both the speeches of Brutus and Antony occur in the second scene of the third act. Antony flees to the safety of his house as soon as Caesar is murdered. He returns only when Brutus assures him of his safety.

The speeches occur away from the scene of the murder

The speeches occur away from the Capitol, where Caesar was murdered. The crowd is stricken with grief and stunned into silence. Brutus tells the crowd that "ambition's debt is paid" (II. i. 83). Once he says this he sets into motion the trial for the cause of freedom. This is the first of many errors that Brutus would make. Cassius would have marched off the scene in triumph and ensured that the crowd went with him. Not so Brutus. Antony delivers his funeral speech because Brutus permits him to do so. He makes a list of meaningless restrictions on Antony. What is worse, he leaves Antony with the audience and moves away after his speech.

Brutus tells the crowd he killed Caesar for their freedom

Brutus' speech is replete with logic, but it is spoken to a crowd, which is so excited that there is no likelihood of logic motivating it. It is a mob, which can be dangerously spurred by misplaced emotions. Brutus enters the Forum and mounts the rostrum. He asks the citizens to calm down and listen to what he has to say, to bear in mind that he is honourable, and to use their reason in order to judge him. Brutus says that he loved Caesar more than any man present, and that when he killed Caesar, he did not love him less; he "loved Rome more". He asks the citizens what they would prefer to be – slaves, governed by a living Caesar or free men, freed by Caesar's death? He is sad for Caesar's death, because he was his dear friend. He celebrates Caesar's successes, and honours his bravery, but he had to kill him once he became tyrannical and ambitious. He is convinced that his act can only annoy those who are foolish or unpatriotic. He asks the crowd if anyone among then is offended. The citizens unanimously shout that they are not offended. Brutus tells them to refer to some documents which shall be placed in the Capitol. They would record Caesar's death.

The crowd wants Brutus to be made king

Brutus brings the crowd's attention to Antony, who enters with Caesar's body. Brutus tells the crowd that Antony was not part of the conspiracy. He concludes his speech by promising to kill himself when his own death will benefit the country. The crowd becomes emotionally unstable. It cries out that Brutus should be honoured and made dictator and king. Brutus calms them and instructs them to hear Antony. After that he leaves amidst acclamations that they will obey him, that Caesar was a tyrant, and that they will listen attentively to Antony.

Antony reminds the crowd of Caesar's generosity

Antony begins his oration with the famous words "Friends, Romans, countrymen, lend me your attention ; / I come to bury Caesar, not to praise him." He announces that he too will deliver a reasoned speech. He tells the crowd that Brutus thinks Caesar was ambitious. He accepts that Brutus is an honourable man. He tells the crowd that he speaks with the permission of "honourable" Brutus, but he questions if Caesar's well-known generosity in sharing the spoils of victory with the public and his compassion for the poor was consistent with condemnation of ambition. He reminds the crowd that Caesar had refused the crown thrice at the feast of Lupercal. He wonders if this can be considered an act of a dangerously ambitious man? The crowd ponders over what Antony has said, the wrong done to Caesar, Caesar's questionable ambition, and Antony's noble anguish.

Antony exposes his undiluted grief to the audience

Antony continues his oration without giving the crowd any break. He is agonised that not one citizen seems to feel humble enough to honour mighty Caesar. He announces that he would rather wrong Caesar, his own self, and even the citizens, rather than wrong "such honourable men" as Brutus and Cassius by asking the citizens to rise in revolt. Accomplished actor that he is, Antony allows the crowd to see him apparently overcome with grief for his friend. Such emotions are infectious. He knows what he must do to excite them to anger.

Antony shows the audience Caesar's will

Antony does not merely stop here. He displays a piece of parchment, which he claims is Caesar's will. He also lets the citizens know that they would profoundly mourn and search for momentos of their benefactor, Caesar, if they were to hear the contents of the will; but that he does not intend to read the will (he knows, of course, that the crowd will demand that he read it, which it instantly does.)

Antony delays the reading of Caesar's will

Antony lets the crowd wait for some more time before he reads the will to them. He tells the crowd about Caesar's generosity instead. He announces that the crowd will be incensed into anger if it learnt about Caesar's generosity. The crowd demands that he read Caesar's will. Antony expresses the fear that he has already said too much. He may have wronged "the honourable men. Whose daggers have stabb'd Caesar". The citizens shout that the conspirators are murderers. They once again demand that Antony read Caesar's will. Antony pretends to obey as ordered. He steps among them to stand beside the body of Caesar. He lifts Caesar's cloak and points to the wounds in it made by the knives of the conspirators. He refers to Brutus as Caesar's very dear friend and "angel", whose stab "was the most unkindest cut of all".

The citizens are moved to tears on seeing Caesar's bloody cloak

The citizens are moved to tears by the sight of the torn and bloody cloak. Antony commends them for it. He then removes the cloak and exposes the body itself. The crowd reacts with pity, which soon changes to anger. It disperses, uttering cries for revenge. Antony calls them back and tells the citizens that the honourable men who killed Caesar will no doubt provide sufficient reasons for their actions. In an example of supreme irony, Antony tells the crowd that he lacks Brutus' oratorial skills. He is nothing more that a "plain blunt man". If he had Brutus' ability to persuade, he would move the very "stones of Rome to rise and mutiny."

Antony reads Caesar's will only after the crowd is fully incensed

Antony had all through his speech told the crowd not to rise in revolt because he wanted to utter it only when it is completely incensed. Once he makes the suggestion, the mob rushes off wildly to search for the conspirators. Antony requests the mob one more time to return because he has still to read out Caesar's will. He says that Caesar left seventy-five drachmas (about three pounds in sterling) to every male Roman citizen. The crowd praises Caesar's nobility. Caesar also left them his woodlands, walks, and orchards on the Forum's side of the Tiber, and Antony inquires when they can expect another ruler like Caesar. The citizens shout "Never". They leave to cremate Caesar's body with due reverence, to burn the houses of the assassins, and to wreak general destruction. Antony can at last heave a sigh of relief and contentment. He muses, " Mischief, thou art afoot, Take thou what course thou wilt !".

The two speeches are the most powerful written in dramatic literature

The two speeches are the most powerful ever to be written by Shakespeare, or, for that matter, in all of dramatic literature. Antony's oration is a masterpiece of irony and crowd manipulation. He is able to persuade a crowd which is full of reverence for Brutus and hatred for Caesar. The two speeches amply illustrate the differences between Antony and Brutus : Brutus defends the assassination, and Antony attacks it; Brutus relies on reason, and Antony on the demagogue's appeal to emotions; Brutus fails to establish order, and Antony successfully creates a riotous mob and political chaos.

Brutus wrongly believes that the crowd will be moved by reason

Brutus asks the crowd to be patient and not to interrupt him until the end of his speech. He wants to provide them with information, not incite them into mutiny. He is convinced they will conclude that Caesar had to die if they were to be free and happy. He mistakenly believes that everyone respects reason as much as he, and that reason is the most powerful tool in the hand of an orator. He speaks in prose. The language suits his balanced statements. He tells them to believe him for his "honour". He states that Caesar was his friend, but he had to die if the republic was to be free. He readily accepts that Caesar had many good qualities, but is also convinced that Caesar's single, major flaw — his excessive ambition – outweighed all his virtues. There was no other way to curb Caesar's ambition than to kill him.

Brutus fails to absorb the crowd's whimsicality

Brutus talks about the documents filed by him in the Capitol, and the crowd calls for him to be crowned king. Here, especially, Brutus' lack of insight into human nature is obvious. It never occurs to him that the crowd is acting whimsically to the inordinate emotions whipped up by him in his speech. It is not acting as per his logic, as he so ardently hopes. He does not see the irony in their response to his discourse on the evils of tyranny by asking him to become the new tyrant. And when Antony enters with Caesar's body, Brutus should have realised that the people at the forum are not capable of accepting the responsibilities of self-rule. They want leadership so that they are free from the burden of thinking themselves.

Antony manipulates the emotions of the crowd

Antony, in sharp contrast, is aware that the citizens are incapable of thinking or acting rationally. His speech is designed to manipulate their emotions. Antony succeeds in slowly arousing their passions till they become a massive collective weapon of retribution against the conspirators. When Antony begins his speech, the crowd is clamouring so loudly for Brutus, that he cannot even make himself heard. He accepts that Brutus' prime reason for killing Caesar was his excessive ambition. He qualifies Brutus' claim of excessive ambition with the innocuous sounding phrase "if it were so". Once he creates doubt in the minds of the people, he directly attacks the argument that Caesar was ambitious, by referring to Caesar's generosity in sharing the spoils of war with them and showing compassion for the poor. He tells the crowd that "ambition should be made of sterner stuff". This is Antony's attempt to not only further arouse the sentiments of the crowd but also tie them to a Caesar who was himself not ashamed to display his emotions.

Antony distorts facts regarding Caesar's desire to be king

Antony reminds the crowd that Caesar had refused the crown presented by him three times. We all know Antony is hypocritical because Caesar had ardently coveted the crown. He had refused it because he did not wish to appear ambitious in the eyes of others and hoped that the people of Rome would force him to have it. Although Antony accuses the crowd of having lost its reason in its refusal to mourn Caesar, he is steadfastly alienating them from thinking rationally. He deliberately distorts facts. He mourns over Caesar's dead body in an emotional manner. All this is designed to stir the emotions of the crowd.

Antony uses every device known to oratory

Antony uses every device known to oratory — irony, passion, flattery, ridicule, and finally appeal to self-interest and material betterment. He displays a document, which he says is Caesar's will, which has made provisions for them; but he refuses to read it to them. The crowd wants it to be read at once. Antony flatters them instead. The crowd once again demands that he should read Caesar's will. Antony comes down from the platform, and shows them the bloody, mutilated body of Caesar. He points to the bloody mantle of the body and connects individual assassins with the various holes in the cloak. This is all pure acting, both regarding the identification of the cloak and the holes in it, because there is no way Antony could have known which hole was made by which assassin. But it is sufficient to incense the crowd. Antony tells the crowd he would rather wrong himself, and them, and even Caesar rather than wrong the honourable "conspirators". He calls them honourable men whose "daggers have stabb'd Caesar". He tells the crowd that if he had Brutus' power to persuade, he would bring them "to rise to mutiny". Now he knows that he has the crowd under his control. He can now manipulate them the way he wants. He had flattered them just a few minutes ago. He now uses sarcasm against them.

Antony reduces the crowd to an angry mob

Antony knows that by the time he is finished, they will be no longer a crowd; they will have become a mob, enraged to riot. He finally reads the will as if he is at their mercy. Once he reads the will he releases the mob to seek out the conspirators and destroy whatever order remains in Rome.

Brutus' speech is devoid of any histrionics

There is a need to compare the two speeches made by Brutus and Antony. Brutus' speech is bereft of any histrionics. He is comfortable in the knowledge that Roman citizens had honoured Pompey and were comfortable in his republican form of government. Caesar's ambition to become king horrified him. He thought that the Roman citizens would be horrified too.

When they respond to his horror, he is convinced that he has clinched the issue. That is why he finds no need to wait to hear what Antony has to say.

Brutus symbolises honour while Antony symbolises cunning

Brutus epitomises steadfast honour. Antony symbolises cunning resourcefulness and daring. Brutus appeals to the crowd's mind while Antony appeals to their emitions. Brutus is an intellectual man, totally unsuited to the cesspool of politics, while Antony is completely in harmony with it.

The speeches of the two men are a true reflection of their characters

The speeches of Brutus and Antony are a true reflection of the two men. Brutus is honest and straightforward. He cannot muster extremes of passion. He fails to excite the crowd because he is not equipped to match their lack of intellectual rhythm. A crowd wants only one thing – unearned or undeserved luxuries, freedom and wealth. Brutus tells them they are free to do what they want. The problem is that means they have to think and act. Antony wins because he takes away the painful option of being creative and functional. All he wants is that they become symbols of terror and destruction. He is satisfied only when he has relegated a peaceful crowd into a destructive mob.

Ques. 14 : Cassius is able to start Brutus but not regulate him" Discuss.

Ans. :

Cassius hands over the leadership to Brutus

Some critics think that Cassius should have been the leader of the conspiracy. Cassius resigns the leadership to Brutus as soon as he wins him over to his cause. The politician recedes into the background, giving way to the philosopher. There is distinct possibility that the ending of the play would have been very different if his ideas were adhered to by the conspirators.

Brutus and Cassius compliment each other

Brutus and Cassius, in many ways, compliment each other. Cassius is shrewd and enthusiastic, while Brutus is idealistic and peaceful. Both are intimately friends with other people—Cassius with Titinius and Brutus with Lucilius, but the two are not genuine friends. It is to Cassius' credit that he manages to curb his fire and keep the partnership in existence for such a long period of time. Yet, it is precisely this self-effacement which proves the undoing of both of them. Brutus loses some of his honour when he takes a hand in Cassius' undertaking, while Cassius, under the influence of a loftier mind, develops the better side of his nature. It is surprising that a man who is jealous of Caesar's greatness unequivocally admits and accepts his inferiority. Cassius is brave in a physical sort of way, though this is hidden behind his terrible hatred for Caesar. Most people believe that he is not the villain of the play (if there is one, it is Decius). He is shrewd and practical, and he has enormous understanding of people. He knows Anotny would be dangerous, and when he is vetoed by Brutus to have him murdered, he tries to pin him down to a definite statement of support or hostility, so that the conspirators know precisely how they stand with regard to him.

> Will you be prick'd in number of our friends;
> Or shall we on, and not depend on you ?   [III. i. 216 – 217]

He may be cruel and choleric, but he has the gift of making more number of friends that the calm, gentle and high - soul'd Brutus.

Cassius wants Brutus for the success of the conspiracy

The conspiracy to murder Caesar is a direct consequence of hatred and jealousy that Cassius has for Caesar's greatness and his growing popularity. Cassius manages to win over some officials to his side. However, Cassius is aware that he does not have the support of the masses. He realises that Brutus will have to be won over if his enterprise is to become successful.

Cassius choses Brutus for his honour and republicanism

Cassius choses Brutus with care. Brutus' ancestors had driven out the last of the kings from Rome and established a republican form of government. Brutus is honourable and noble. He loves Rome and its citizens, more than anything else on earth. Cassius knows that the conspiracy would appear honourable if Brutus joins him. Cassius plays on Brutus' passion for the people of Rome and for republicanism. Cassius warns Brutus that Caesar may one day become king of Rome. This thought horrifies Brutus. He realises that absolute power can corrupt anyone. It could lead to slavery and servitude for the people of Rome if Caesar is not checked. He realises that the only solution lies in killing Caesar.

Cassius' cleverness succumbs to Brutus' honour

Once Brutus joins the conspiracy he begins to regulate it according to his own thoughts. Cassius can only see helplessly as Brutus takes the upper hand. His moral stature is such that Cassius cannot argue even when he is right. Throughout the play we are made to believe that only Cassius has the ability to take a complex issue, such as the murder of Caesar, to its logical conclusion. He knows that it requires guile, insight and precision of action, if the conspirators are to succeed. Brutus cannot imagine indulging in any covert activity in order to achieve his purpose. He is simply not made that way, and would shun any person who would suggest that he resort to intrigue. Cassius thus has only two options – either to lose Brutus, or to let him lead the way in his own straightforward manner and hope that they would succeed. Cassius, for instance, knows that Antony is as dangerous as Caesar. That is why he wants him to be murdered along with Caesar, but Brutus would have nothing of it. First, because he thinks Antony would become insignificant once Caesar is dead. Secondly, because he wants to kill Caesar and sacrifice him to the gods, and not become a senseless butcher. Thirdly, because he wants to kill Caesarism and not any human being. It is another matter that Brutus is wrong on all three counts, What is important is that he remains on the fringes of violent withdrawal if someone disagrees with him. Moreover, his argument appears so pleasing and idealistic on face value, that any man who opposes it for the sake of expediency and end results would appear silly in comparison.

Brutus commits a series of fatal mistakes

Brutus commits a series of blunders throughout the play, as if he is fatally attracted to his inevitable doom. The worst mistake seems to be to let Antony speak at Caesar's funeral, because such a thing befits a friend. Cassius is shocked when Brutus agrees to such a thing. He takes Brutus aside and tells him :

You know not what you do. Do not consent
That Antony speaks in his funeral :
Know you how much the people may be mov'd
By that which he will utter ?   [III. i .233 – 236]

Brutus makes his next error when he enters into a public argument with Cassius. All he manages to do is demotivate his men. He aught to have quit if he found out Cassius was corrupt. A public chastisement of a corrupt man by a man who thinks he epitomises honour can hardly be explained, leave alone excused. Men of integrity do not rub shoulders with corrupt leaders. They kill them instead, so that the army does not suffer due to it. In many ways Brutus can do no more than get despirited himself when he learns about Cassius' corrupt practices. For Cassius' part, it seems petty that he accumulates bribes and yet hopes to free the people of Rome from the yoke of slavery. It is hardly surprising that he fails to regulate someone as upright as Brutus.

Brutus' blunder at Sardis

This string of errors continues in Sardis when Cassius wants their army to wait for the enemy but Brutus overrules him and marches to Philippi. Once again Cassius is correct. He wants his army to be fresh by waiting in Sardis. The armies of Brutus and Cassius are routed in Philippi and both of them have to commit suicide.

It is impossible to imagine that Cassius could have controlled Brutus

It is possible that the end result may have been different had Cassius regulated Brutus but it need not have been better. First of all it is difficult to

think how Cassius could possibly regulate Brutus. Cassius needs Brutus due
to his mass appeal and his integrity, but Brutus does not need him. Intellectual
men always lean towards their philosophy and virtue to show them direction.
Secondly, Cassius is a corrupt man. He wishes to kill Caesar to gratify his
own feeling of hatred, and not because of any good for the people of Rome.
Moreover, he is constantly using unfair means to accumulate money. It is
impossible to think how such a man can regulate someone as upright as Brutus.
Thirdly, both Cassius and Brutus kill Caesar in some sort of a mental vacuum,
and not for some real philosophy or threat. They kill Caesar but do not know
what to do once pressure is mounted on them. They do not have a contingent
plan in place. They hope that things would fall in place once Caesar is
eliminated. In fact, they should have catered for chaos. Such a thing is
inevitable when a great leader falls. Fourthly, death, that too violent death of
a great leader, invariably leads to unpredictable behaviour. It is almost
impossible to regulate events once they unfold so unfavourably. Fifthly, once
Brutus realises that he has killed Caesar and not his spirit, there is very little
evidence that he is interested in anything, including his own existence. It is
impossible to regulate such a man. Lastly, Cassius may be shrewd, but he
does not have the leadership qualities to lead someone as upright and
immovable as Brutus. He hands over the reins to Brutus because he knows it
is impossible to regulate him. On the few occasions that he tries he meets
with such an uncompromising man, Brutus behaves in such a forbidding
manner that Cassius has to retract quickly.

Ques. 15 : Give reasons why the conspirators failed.

Ans. :

Caesar is a man of heroic capabilities

Most critics have readily accepted that Caesar had a large number of
weaknesses. He was a tyrant, he was inordinately ambitious, he was physically
weak and he was prone to flattery. This, however, is not the truth. Though
Plutarch had depicted Caesar as a tyrant and a despot, Shakespeare made
him a true hero. He is a man of enormous authority. He is greatly admired
and loved. He has brought enormous wealth to Rome. He may want to become
king, but the crowd does not mind it. They want affluence. The type of
government that brings affluence is immaterial to them.

The people of Rome are hedonistic and amoral

It is such a man's victory that the crowd comes out to rejoice on the
streets of Rome. It is readily forgotten that the same crowd had rejoiced for
Pompey too, and it is the same Pompey's sons whom Caesar has killed is
battle. The crowd is perhaps amoral. In many ways it is hedonistic. It will

back anyone who will ensure material wealth.

Cassius chooses Brutus because he ardently cherishes freedom

It is under these circumstances that Cassius, one of the praetors in Rome, becomes bitterly envious of Caesar. This envy changes to so much hatred that he decides to kill Caesar. He is a man who thrives in a collective. He easily wins over some officials to back his cause. They are substantial in number, but they are ineffectual. Like any person who can thrive while huddled in a group, they have no individual standing or merit. Cassius is shrewd and intelligent in a negative and destructive sort of manner – like all politicians are all over the world. He knows the men he has accumulated have only negative emotions against Caesar to motivate them. He knows they would be seen with suspicion and disdain by the people of Rome. He realises that he needs a man of substantial standing. His choice falls on Brutus, who is a republican. Brutus hates kingship because it leads to slavery for the citizens of Rome. He is a man of impeccable honour and integrity. A man, who considers nothing more important than the freedom of the citizens, can be motivated to kill someone as ambitious as Caesar Cassius also realises that blind idealism, without an understanding of ground realities can make things go terribly wrong, but he has faith in his own ability to regulate Brutus.

Brutus loves Caesar dearly, but he loves Rome more

Brutus is Caesar's friend. He loves him dearly, but he loves Rome more. After considerable deliberation, he realises that Caesar must die if Rome is to be free. He will mourn for Caesar, but he will present him as a sacrifice to the gods so that Rome can prosper.

The conspirators succeed in killing Caesar but fail in their aims

The conspirators succeed in killing Caesar. This, however, cannot be considered success, since their personal aims never materialise. Brutus wanted to replace Caesarism with republicanism. He painfully realises that he has killed Caesar but not his spirit. The people of Rome reject republicanism, a concept so dear to Brutus.

The conspirators have no plan of action to be followed once Caesar is dead

Several reasons can be given to explain why the conspirators failed. One of them is the motive of the conspirators. Apart from Brutus, all of them kill Caesar out of envy and hatred for his greatness and power. Thus once they kill him, the conspirators do not have any plan for what is to be done. They do not have a contingency plan to be put in place if something goes terribly wrong. When it actually does, they have no option but to run away.

They had hoped to benefit from Caesar's death, but have to run to save their lives.

Brutus misunderstands the need of the people of Rome

Brutus joins the conspiracy to save the country from the terrible consequences of Caesarism. He believes it stands for tyranny, slavery and absence of freedom for the people of Rome. He is convinced that the people of Rome must want freedom and liberty over everything else. His speech after Caesar's death, to the people of Rome, suggests just this much. The people are swayed for some time. They are satisfied with Brutus' explanation; and they want him to be Caesar. Despite the upbeat mood, it is evident that Brutus has gone horribly wrong. He had wanted to establish republicanism. The people of Rome want kingship instead. They do not fully understand why Caesar was bad, but they are prepared to blindly believe it if Brutus says so.

Brutus does not understand the arbitrary nature of the crowd

There are dangerous warning signals, but Brutus ignores them. He cannot fully understand the arbitrary nature of the crowd, which can be swayed by any artful orator. He permits Antony to speak at Caesar's funeral. He makes an even bigger mistake when he does not even stay on the scene. This leaves Antony to manipulate the crowd as he wants.

Antony manages to arouse the crowd's anger against the conspirators

Antony does not talk of any profound political ideology. He only wants to tell the people of Rome how affluent they were under Caesar, how much he loved them and how he had refused to become king on three occasions. The crowd is swayed to Antony's way of seeing things. Antony, however, does not merely want them to see his point of view. He wants to incite them to the kind of anger where they become a destructive force against the conspirators. He uses every known trick to arouse their passions. He shows them Caesar's dead body and his blood-soaked mantle. He reads out Caesar's will after teasing them about it. He tells them that Caesar has left seventy-five drachmas to each citizen. He has also left all his private roads, groves of trees and newly-planted orchards and pleasure grounds for the citizens of Rome. The crowd is fully incensed. It does not understand freedom, but it does understand greed. It is prepared to destroy any person who killed such a generous and loving leader. Antony smiles and utters to himself "Now let it work. Mischief, thou art afoot", as the citizens go in search of the conspirators and kill them.

The conspirators lack unity of purpose

Another reason that can be given for the failure of the conspiracy is the lack of unity of purpose among the conspirators. Cassius is driven by hatred for Caesar and personal greed. Brutus is driven by a philosophy, which is out of tune with the times. Casca is brash and resentful while Cinna is a mere follower. The conspirators seem to be devoid of any discipline or direction. This is even more evident once Caesar dies. They do not know what to do once their feeling of hatred in satiated.

Caesar had made the citizens rich

The conspirators believe that every citizen wants liberty and freedom. He must thus necessarily hate Caesar who wants to become king. It never occurs to them that the citizens may support anyone who brings affluence for them. They would rather be affluent under a king than be poor with a right to self-governance. Shakespeare genuinely believed in the veracity of monarchy, especially the kind which changes people's lives for the better. That is why he gives Caesar so many worthwhile qualities, despite the fact that Plutarch had delineated him as a villain. Shakespeare's Caesar may not be truly heroic, but he is the darling of the crowed. Moreover, his victories have made Rome rich. The conspirators deprive the citizens of all this once they kill Caesar. There was no way to imagine that the conspirators would not have sooner or later faced the wrath of the citizens. That is why Antony needs so little effort to arouse their anger against the conspirators.

Morality demands that the conspirators should lose

Shakespeare always tries to establish moral order in his plays. The conspirators try to advance their point of view through deceit and violence whereas the world thrives on transparency and compassion. The conspirators are all politicians. Their job is to bring about change through diplomacy, statesmanship and negotiations. The conspirators advance their point of view through a heinous murder of a greatly admired and respected leader. Shakespeare could not have let his play end here. It would mean that he is actively backing violent means in order to bring about change. World moral order suggests that only compassion and truth can bring about real change. The conspiracy thus has to fail, if Shakespeare has to remain true to his dramatic, moral and intellectual concept of existence.

Ques. 16 :- State the reason why Brutus joins the conspiracy against Caesar. Compare his motives with those of Cassius.

Ans. :-

Brutus is a stoic who lives entirely by honour

Caesar's last cry, with its accusation of – and lament for – the betrayal of friendship, sums up the tragedy of Brutus. It immediately establishes that he is a tragic hero matching the definition of Aristotle. He has abundance of virtue and a single tragic flaw. This is the manner in which Plutarch also accepts Brutus. Brutus is a stoic. He is not affected by pleasure or pain. He is a philosopher and an idealist who will have his way at all costs. He is the kind of character who is rarely influenced by anything other than his own thoughts. Brutus lives by honour. His only duty is towards the citizens of Rome. His altruism is a flawed philosophy, as is his stoicism. Honour is a second-hander's emotion, since it is acquired only through others. It is arbitrary in nature because honour needs approval of a large number of people. The quality of people approving a man is of no consequence. This is at complete variance with the intellectual concept of existence. A man of intellect treads on the path of truth. He provides leadership to those who want to tread on the same path. He does not seek their approval. He walks on that path because anything else becomes a lie. Brutus seeks random approval instead.

Brutus joins the conpiracy due to his love for republicanism

Brutus joins the conspiracy because he loves republicanism and the people of Rome. He is convinced that only republicanism (which lays stress on self- governance) can provide freedom and liberty to Rome. Brutus loves Caesar, but he is also horrified about Caesar's motives. He knows power corrupts and absolute power corrupts absolutely. Caesar is as close to absolute power as any person can be in a republic. Moreover, Caesar has given sufficient hints that he wants to be king, despite the refusal of crown when offered by Antony. He is vain and arrogant, and he likes to be flattered. These are sufficient reasons for Brutus to be worried about Rome and its citizens.

Brutus is successfully instigated by Cassius

These may be sufficient reasons to cause him to worry, but they are obviously not sufficient to incite him to murder a person whom he admires and calls a friend. It requires someone as cunning and shrewd as Cassius to take him from the fringes of doubt and horror to actual violence. Cassius tells him nothing new. He just reminds him about what he already knows. He maintains sufficient pressure on him. He manipulates him so that he cannot think of saying no. Brutus may have remained disgruntled if Cassius had faltered even once. The fact that he does not falter makes the decision for Brutus. Despite Cassius' incitement, Brutus still has to "fashion it thus" in his mind." This means his mind does not have an inviolable solution to the problem. He has to stretch his imagination and the truth in order to convince himself to kill Caesar.

Brutus' nobility is at variance with his intellect

Brutus is in many ways a pathetic figure in the play, because his nobility and intellect are in direct variance with each other. His excellence is an extension of his lethargic mind. His honesty is humourless, edgeless and pedantic. It lacks the intellectual content which is the difference between joy and pain. Such a man is ill-equipped to take major decisions on behalf of the country, no matter how well-intentioned he may be. He is manipulated by Cassius because he carries his idealism as a thoughtless sense of uprighteousness. He joins the conspiracy because he cannot see behind the false façade of Cassius and he cannot remember the good Caesar has done for Rome.In addition, he forgets that no person kills greatness based on mere fear that such a man may become evil one day.

Brutus thinks Caesar will become a tyrant

The plot for the assassination is obviously formed against tyranny. It is evident that this train of thought is started by Brutus.

"There was a Brutus once that would have brooked

The eternal devil to keep his state in Rome

As easily as king"   [I.ii.158 - 60]

Brutus says he would "rather be a villager" than let Rome suffer under "these hard conditions". Cassius talks of suicide in order to shake off "tyranny." He sees the conspirators enshrined through ages. His complaint is against Caesarism. Brutus has nothing against Caesar personally, but he is horrified about the future of Rome and its citizens. Brutus does not consider Caesar dangerous. He thinks Caesar will become dangerous after he is made king. Cassius does not permit him to rest on his fears. He ensures that these fears are aroused to violent action.

Cassius is motivated by greed and envy

Cassius is a republican like Brutus, but unlike Brutus he is motivated by self-interest and envy against Caesar. His quick wit, pragmatism and opportunism make him a dangerous man. He does not believe in idealism. He only believes in realism, which includes shameless manipulation in order to achieve his aim. Cassius is a master at grabbing slender chances that provide themselves to him,. Brutus admits to him that he is "with himself at war." This is sufficient opportunity for Cassius. He begins cautiously, but becomes bolder as Brutus reveals that he is amenable to pressure.

Brutus' idealism is misplaced and dangerous

Most people think Brutus joins the conspiracy due to his idealism. This is a result of a misplaced understanding of idealism, Much good can be written about republicanism and kingship, and much can be written against them. Though our vote must go in favour of republicanism, we cannot approve violent death as a means of achieving it.Diplomacy, statesmanship and getting a favourable decision from the citizens are the only methods of bringing about change of a political nature. Caesar deserves to present his case in front of the citizens as much as Brutus, in order to establish what the citizens want. This, in any case, is the true essence of republicanism. More than anything, people need affluence and good governance. Brutus thrusts them into misery and anarchy by his brutal act. Such an act cannot be called idealistic. It is more an act of moral blindness. We cannot therefore think that Brutus' motives are good. If anything, we must condemn him. It is impossible to visualise how someone as shallow as Cassius could have succeeded in killing Caesar without the help of someone as powerful and liked as Brutus. It is Brutus' false sense of honour in the eyes of the people of Rome that provides the conspiracy impetus and cutting edge.

Shakespeare believes Brutus is wrong in joining the conspiracy

There are varied opinions as to whether Brutus is justified in joining the conspiracy or not. These is no doubt that Shakespeare believes Brutus is wrong in joining the conspiracy. He murders a trusting friend, he is influenced by misplaced emotions, and his solutions are terribly violent.Brutus indulges in considerable thought, but it is the kind of brooding that leads to terrible solutions. He indulges in thoughts which seem to be contrived. He pursues dangerously abstract realities at the cost of political truths which he does not fully comprehend. No matter how we see it, we cannot possibly condone Brutus or Cassius for murdering Caesar; nor can we think that one has a better cause for joining the conspiracy than the other. Murder is murder, whether it is done for self-interest or for misplaced idealism

Ques. 17 : How far is it correct to say that the character of Cassius serves as a foil to that of Brutus ?

OR

Compare and contrast the characters of Brutus and Cassius.

Ans. :

The biggest contrast is in their motives

The contrast in the characters of Cassius and Brutus is most apparent in their motives to join in the conspiracy to kill Caesar. Cassius starts the conspiracy because he is jealous of Caesar. This motive is evident at the very beginning of the play. Cassius speaks about the sharp difference between his own humble position and the exalted status of Caesar.

"And this man

Is now become a god; and Cassius is

A wretched creature, and must bend his body,

If Caesar carelessly but nod on him."   [I. ii. 115-118]

Cassius hopes that he can incite Brutus to similar levels of jealousy when he tells him.

"'Brutus' and 'Caesar' : what should be in that 'Caesar'?

Why should that name be sounded more than yours?"

[I. ii. 143-144]

When Cassius realises that Brutus has not been affected, he tries again, this time with a new motive. He talks about liberty and freedom, hoping that this would appeal to the honouarble Brutus.

"There was a Brutus once that would have brook'd

The eternal devil to keep his state in Rome

As easily as a king."   [I. ii. 158-160]

Cassius incites Brutus on vaguely understood words

Cassius labels Caesar a tyrant. He can say this because no one demands any proof. He can hide behind such vaguely understood words as republicanism, libery and freedom, specially to Brutus, who himself advances them as ambiguous threats to individual happiness. Cassius is, however, careful not to utter his personal hatred or interest in public. People appreciate protecting rights for others. They can never pardon self-interest.

Brutus has misplaced sense of his own superior thought

Cassius manages to influence Brutus because he has a misplaced sense of his own superior thought. He thinks his honour is sufficient reason to kill the greatest man on earth, not on the basis of any evidence, but due to fear for what might happen in the future. Throughout the play, Brutus gives an impression that he is violently impatient with any one who challenges his mind. Cassius uses this intellectual obstinacy in a manner that it becomes a ready tool to advance his own interest.

Brutus is a stoic while Cassius is an epicure

No matter how we see them, there is no doubt that Brutus and Cassius are a study in contrast. Cassius' character is an ideal foil to that of Brutus. Brutus is a renunciation-seeking stoic while Cassius is an opportunity-seeking epicure. Brutus is restrained, patient, grave and lonely while Cassius is talkative, theatrical, emotive and friendly. Brutus is straightforward and blunt to the point where he appears unpardonably foolish. Cassius is as cunning as a fox. Brutus kills Caesar so that he can save the citizens of Rome from slavery and tyranny. Cassius kills Caesar because he hates him. Brutus is an armchair philosopher, devoid of insight into human nature. Cassius, in contrast, is a shrewd manipulator; a practical realist, a crafty politician and an excellent judge of character. Brutus is a theoretical man who comes out of his anchorage only to find that he is miserably out of sorts with the world of practical affairs. Cassius is a man of the world. He is street smart in a manner that he will always be sought after but will never be admired.

Brutus and Cassius also have some similarities

Yet, after listing out the differences between Brutus and Cassius – massive and glaring as they are – we cannot but help seeing some similarities as well. It is impossible to see how the two could have carried out something as massive and terrible as Caesar's murder without having something in common. In their own ways both Brutus and Cassius are brave and fearless. Their suicide at the end of the play may appear wrong intellectually, but it is brave physically. It may appear as an escape but it requires absence of fear. Both prefer to commit suicide than face the ignominy of being led through Rome in chains. Both die with the name of Caesar on their lips. Both have a terrible flaw. Both are victims of negative human emotions. Cassius suffers from hatred and inferiority complex. He kills a man whom he cannot hope to equal. Brutus suffers from intellectual indifference. He simply does not care as long as his barren idealism is satiated. Both want an urgent fulfilment of their negative emotions. Cassius has disgust for Caesar and Brutus has disgust for any form of government other than republicanism. Both are not concerned about what the public wants. Both are prepared to kill in order to advance their own whim. Both suffer from under-confidence, because Brutus' over-confidence is nothing but under-confidence turned upside down. If anything, we must consider Brutus more guilty. He hides terrible emotions under the garb of honour, and hence, is more dangerous. Both are murderers, because both kill in a sly manner, a man who is universally acclaimed as great. Both men are politicians, but both play the role of terrorists when they kill Caesar. They should have resorted to diplomacy and statesmanship in order to advance their point of view. They should have gone to the people of Rome and told them what is at stake. They resort to senseless killing instead. Both kill not as brave soldiers, in a battle, facing an enemy, but as scared women, when Caesar in defenceless, both physically and figuratively, having just called them his friends.

Critics needlessly make virtue out of Brutus' vices

Critics have tried to make out a virtue of Brutus' qualities. The qualities he possesses are of little consequence in the play, or in life. He may not be a villain; neither for that matter is Cassius; but their enterprise and deeds are inhuman. They are against every ethic that a truly moral human being can think of. Gernivus and others have listed out the contrast in the characters of Brutus and Cassius. There is no point going into them. What matters is the kind of emotions the two advance in the play. Shakespeare constantly strives to give us a moral world in his plays. We must therefore, interpret his characters also in moral terms. His tragedies have a distinct kind of justice. It may not always to poetic and exact, but it is just sufficient to serve his purpose. It is also just sufficient to make the play appear tragic. Had justice in the play been in exact proportions to the crime and goodness of his characters, there would be no tragedy, for there would be no feeling of pity and awe. Thus if we are to establish or restore a moral world order, as Shakespeare's plays constantly intend to do, we have to accept that in moral terms both Brutus and Cassius are in the same league. Both indulge in an extreme act of violence to satiate their own whim. The differences between the two, endless as they may seen, are either superficial, or they do not advance the play as a moral entity if they are considered worthwhile.

Ques. 18 : "Brutus is a stoic by profession and in reality the reverse – acting deeds against his nature by the strong force of principle and will." Discuss.

Ans. :

A stoic is constantly seeking to control his passions

A stoic is a disciple of the school founded by philosopher Zeno, who died in the year 261 BC. He taught the principle of being indifferent to pleasure or pain. He attached great importance to the control of passions. It is this philosophy which Brutus believes he practises. Once we understand the true meaning of what he practises, it becomes easy for us to understand why Brutus fails so miserably in the play. Only a dead man can be indifferent to the pleasures and pains of life. It is impossible to visualise any man who is completely indifferent to pleasure and pain. It may be worthwhile to sublimate pain, but life's energies can only be built when a human being actively accumulates and rejoices in pleasures. Most philosophers shun pleasure because they do not provide it a worthwhile meaning or direction. They link it with hedonism or senseless acquisition or superficial pursuits. This amounts to pain, though most people call it pleasure. True pleasure is that demanding kind of joy which only the truly functional and creative can attain. It is true that even this needs to be given intellectual direction. A human being must rejoice when he gets pleasure but he must not indulge in pain when it eludes him.

Brutus is not a stoic at all

Brutus is in fact, not a stoic from the very beginning of the play. He indulges in too much pain for the citizens of Rome over their imagined fears. A true stoic would have been indifferent to their pleasures or pains. He would have let destiny take its own course. Brutus tries to change it, and that too in a violent and brutal manner. He indulges in brutal hostility due to fears that make him impatient. A true stoic would not indulge in fears, leave alone be pained by them. Brutus, most critics readily accept, is an honourable and idealistic man. This is totally untrue. An honourable man honours friendship. He does not kill a friend on the sly. An honourable man backs his own judgement. He does not change it at the first pressure put on him. Brutus had accepted Caesar as a friend. He must have evaluated his qualities before he arrived at the conclusion that Caesar was worthy of being his friend, He, however, changes his mind, without much reason, when a shameless manipulator like Cassius tells him that Caesar is a tyrant. Just this much information unleashes in him extreme fear, worry and pain, and he arrives at a terrible decision. He must indulge in covert hostility in order to kill the greatest man in Rome. A stoic would not have indulged in such extreme pain. He would not have indulged in pain at all. He would let it pass. At least he would have thought about the situation with equanimity. Brutus indulges in terrible brooding and extreme negativity.

Critics wrongly admire Brutus' idealism and stoicism

Critics praise Brutus' stoicism because they admire his other qualities. They think his honour and idealism are worthy qualities. In reality, his idealism is totally misplaced. Idealism must advance the person who practices it, and as an extension provide pleasure to those who surround him. It must also be inviolable and unimpeachable. Brutus' decisions provide endless pain to him and to those around him – Portia, Lucilius, Lucius, and finally Caesar. It is also not inviolable and unimpeachable. He loves Caesar as a friend, but kills him. He loves Portia, but is indifferent to her death. He thinks she is profound, but does not share his secrets with her. He backs republicanism because he loves nothing more than the freedom of the citizens of Rome, but he seriously undermines their liberty and affluence by killing Casear. Rome is pushed into a civil war and the people of Rome lose the one leader who had brought unprecedented riches for them. Thus it is impossible to see how Brutus is a true stoic or a real idealist.

Brutus is not honourable and honest

Brutus is not even honourable and honest. He hates deception, even in the conspiracy, but indulges in a still more hideous deceit.

"..... Seek none, conspiracy;

Hide it in smiles and affability :"   [II. i. 81-82].

He wants purity of motives, yet includes Legarius in the conspiracy because he has a grudge against Caesar. He hates Cassius for having an "itching palm", but does not mind using his ill-begotten wealth in order to pay his legions. He murders Caesar, but is afraid to accept it as such. He calls it a sacrifice to the gods in order to make it appear virtuous instead of evil. He publicly washes his hands in Caesar's blood like a violent brute and calls himself a liberator of men. He tells the people of Rome that he killed Caesar out-of a love for them, but does not tell them why killing was necessary. He tells them that Caesar was a tyrant, but he does not tell then which of his actions made him arrive at that conclusion. He wants to kill Caesar's spirit, but kills Caesar instead, only to realise that a spirit can never be killed. Only man is mortal. He has an active private life—a loving wife, a joyous marriage, loyal friends, social and official status. He ruins it all by pursuing a course on behalf of others, which he himself does not want, and those for whom he acts do not fully understand. He practises a correct philosophy wrongly. Republicanism is wonderful, but it is aimless if people do not want it. The people instinctively have the right rhythm. They would rather have a benevolent king like Caesar than have an ineffectual man like Cassuis or Brutus to lead a republic. Caesar had surrounded them in riches. Brutus and Cassius surround them in a painful civil war. He joins the conspiracy and then bulldozes others to accept one blunder after another. Everyone knows they are blunders, but Brutus' reputation prevents them from questioning him. He is honourable and upright. How can any one question such a man? Moreover, he constantly gives an impression that he can bring every one to the brink of disaster if his decision is challenged. He is an extremely poor judge of character but he insists on being the leader of the conspirators. He kills Caesar, but does not know what to do when the crowd turns hostile towards him.

Brutus fails because he does not understand things

Most critics believe that Brutus is a victim of circumstances, but this is not true. His failures are not thrust on him by providence. He makes all the errors because he does not understand things. He is an armchair philosopher but enters into the cesspool of politics. Once there, he contrives to have a rather fatal blend of idealism and politics. He kills Caesar but spares Antony after being warned that the latter could be as fatal to the cause as the former.

He lets Antony speak at Caesar's funeral, without bothering to hear what he says. He had seen the whimsical swaying of the crowd just minutes ago. He is not wise enough to know that the crowd can be swayed once again. He provides no rationale why Caesar had to be killed. He just says that Caesar was tyrannical and ambitious. The crowd accepts him blindly. He thinks he has sealed the issue. He never wonders why the crowd would not blindly accept Antony as well. The crowd understands affluence and greed. The type of governance which can provide luxury is of no consequence to them. Caesar brought them riches. He deserved to be king, provided he makes then rich. Brutus thrusts a needless war on them. He tells them they will be free if they have republicanism because they can then bring about self-rule. The crowd does not understand what self-rule means. They want affluence. They would prefer if they do not have to think or work for it.

Brutus has flawed values

Brutus is a victim of his own lack of values. His stoicism means that he does not seek pleasure. It must then be established what he seeks, and why does he live at all. If he lives for others then those who acquire pleasure due to his efforts must become useless in his estimation. Then where is the need to work for them if the end product is going to be their joy and happiness. Moreover, he is indifferent to his own pain. Why then can't he be indifferent to Caesar's tyranny, or to the agony of the citizens of Rome. A philosophy is worthwhile if it is equally relevant to everyone and if it advances some truth. What truth does Brutus' indifference to his own pleasure advance ?

Brutus is not even a true stoic

Brutus, in fact, is not even a true stoic, simply because only a dead man can practice it. Brutus loves his wife and the pleasure her company provides. He loves Lucius, wine and music. He is in pain when Caesar accumulates power. He is once again in pain when he hears that Caesar is being offered the crown; and he flees in fear when he is pursued by the citizens of Rome. Brutus loves the loyalty of friends. That is a pleasure. He would not let Cicero join the conspiracy, because he would not be easily amenable. That is a threat to pain. He challenges anyone who crosses his path. That is a serious attempt to avoid pain. Even his suicide is nothing but an attempt to avoid pain – the terror of being dragged in chains through Rome.

There is no reversal of philosophy in Brutus

There is thus no reversal of philosophy by application of principle and will. First, there is no worthwhile philosophy. Secondly, Brutus does not practice it, though his restraint may make it appear so. Thirdly, there is no principle or will. A principle is something which is inviolable. Everything that Brutus does raises doubts about it. He does not even possess a worthwhile will; unless deeds which include killing a trusing friend due to a misplaced philosophy can be called will.

Ques. 19 : "Brutus' action is the tragedy of error." Discuss

OR

Show how the action of the murder of Caesar was a crime as well as a political blunder.

Ans. :

Brutus is dispassionate from the very beginning

The first line that Brutus utters in the play is, as per Harley Granville–Barker "measured, dispassionate, tinged with disdain. It tells us sufficiently about Brutus himself. Shakespeare expands this quality of aloofness, brooding and lack of warmth in the next few lines. He is not "gamesome", nor does he have the "quick spirit" of Antony.

Brutus does not see through Cassius' sinister design

Brutus admits to Cassius at the very beginning that he is "with himself at war". This gives Cassius the opportunity to launch into his masterful piece of insinuation and persuasion. Cassius talks for almost one hundred lines. He is interrupted by Brutus on just few occasions. Brutus never sees through Cassius' design. He starts cautiously but Brutus' silence makes him brave enough to attack Caesar directly. He even calls Caesar "a sick girl" with a "feeble temper". Every one can see that Cassius is agitated, not because Caesar has power , but because he has been excluded from power–everyone, except Brutus.

Cassius wants Brutus' ineffectual idealism

Brutus is baffled by Cassius' onslaught. "What is it that you would impart to me ?" he asks Cassius, hinting his simplicity in matters of political intrigue. Cassius advances his argument as a seasoned manipulator who is working on an innocent subject. Such a man does not deserve to be part of a major political conspiracy. Then why does someone as shrewd as Cassius desperately wants him ? The reason for this is simple. Brutus' ineffectual idealism is appealing to the citizens of Rome. Cassius desperately wants someone to sway the crowd in favour of the conspirators after Caesar has been murdered.

Brutus displays ambiguity throughout the play

Brutus displays an ambiguous and confused state of mind throughout the play. This is most evident in his brooding on the night before the murder. His soliloquy reveals a mind which is not fully understood by the speaker himself.

Brutus brings nemesis on himself

Most critics believe that Brutus brings nemesis on himself by erring in his judgement. This may be accepted as partial truth, but it cannot be accepted as the primary cause of Brutus' decision. There is nothing in Brutus which can suggest that he is fit to arrive at fruitful decisions. He practices an impossible philosophy called stoicism. No one can exist by consistently rejecting joy or by thinking that both joy and pain deserve no thought. People think he is honourable, though no one wonders for whose benefit his honour works. He loves the people of Rome. His only contribution to their existence is the murder of Caesar. This pushes them into endless despair and chaos. He is considered idealistic, but one must question the quality of his idealism. He is a republican, and is prepared to thrust it down the throats of the citizens of Rome whether they like it or not. A man with such anti-life philosophy cannot be pardoned because he made an error of judgement. He must be condemned for following a fatal flaw. His love for Rome and its citizens would have been commendable if he had provided them with a true rhythm of life. He gives then misery and war instead. This is not a mere error. A man with a convoluted philosophy can only arrive at terrible decisions.

Brutus commits a terrible crime

Brutus commits a terrible crime. He kills a man of the stature of Caesar without due process of law. Brutus becomes the lawyer, judge and hangman rolled into one. He gives no opportunity to Caesar to defend himself, and he stabs him without challenging him to defend himself. He kills Caesar for the good of the people, without realising that they link their good unmistakably with Caesar.

Brutus does not merely commit an error of judgement

This is not a mere error of judgement. It is a totally flawed action. A politician uses diplomacy and statesmanship to win an intellectual point. A soldier challenges an opponent openly. He does not kill a friend on the sly, based on a half-baked thought.

Caesar's action cannot alarm any reasonable man

There is nothing is Caesar's action which would alarm any reasonable man. There are hints that he has ambitions to be king, but the truth is that he refuses the crown thrice. There is nothing wrong to be tempted, but it requires strength of character to stay within limits of probity. In the worst of scenarios, Caesar may actually have become king. Brutus should have used his political skills to prevent it, and his soldierly skills to negate it after it had happened. Brutus violates every tenet of cause and effect by killing Caesar merely on his own fears of what might happen in the future.

Both republicanism and monarchy have their advantages

Those who believe that Brutus commits a grievous error must realise that only a grievous error of judgement is possible from a man who follows a wrong philosophy, or a correct philosophy wrongly. Much can be written in favour of republicanism, but much good can be written for monarchy as well. Similarly, a lot of criticism can be directed against each. If kingship is despotic then republicanism is a multiple of zeroes. Moreover, republicanism can work only through representatives of the people. These representatives can become greedy and self-centred. Cassius is a fine example of such a thing. A dictator or a king can be generous and loving, as is Caesar. It is thus not merely the type of governance but the type of people who decide public good. Moreover, the citizens of Rome want a king – at least a king as benevolent and astute as Caesar. They know that he can give them affluence and joy. Brutus never asks them what they want. He is sure they would want republicanism if his mind says it is the best thing for them. A politician's job is to establish the will of the people and then initiate action. Brutus initiates action without bothering to know what the citizens want. In any case there is something terribly unappetising in the manner in which Brutus kills Caesar on the sly. Caesar's cry "Et tu, Brute ! – Then fall, Caesar" just before he dies is the final evaluation of betrayed friendship and fall from grace of a man who was considered the epitome of honour.

The reasons why Brutus fails ?

Brutus fails due to several reasons. He lacks practical wisdom. He lives mostly in abstractions. He does not know the will of the people. He condemns Caesar without knowing his true motives. He believes Rome will be free only if Caesar is dead. He wants to kill Caesar's spirit without dismembering him. When he cannot do so, he kills him. His inability to understand the political rhythm of Rome leads the nation to a civil war and endless strife. The citizens of Rome want kingship under someone as worthy as Caesar. Brutus thrusts republicanism on them under someone as cunning as Cassius. Brutus leads Rome to total confusion. He challenges Caesarism and wants to replace it with republicanism, but the confusion between the two is never resolved .

Ques. 20 : Comment on the theme of the play "Julius Caesar."

Ans. :-

Shakespeare advocates benevolent monarchy

Shakespeare's idea of a good government is perhaps a benevolent monarchy. He knows from history that rulers have their weaknesses; but history also teaches him that violent revolt against the established order normally brings untold suffering and defeats its own ends.

Brutus believes republicanism means freedom

Brutus believes that only republicanism can provide freedom and liberty to its citizens. He seeks to restore this freedom to the citizens of Rome, because they are incapable of preserving law and order by themselves. By itself republicanism is a worthwhile concept in theory. In practice, however, it works only when backed by several other imponderables. Any type of governance requires strong, upright and capable leaders. Republicanism under an incapable set of leaders can be as big a nightmare as kingship under a despotic ruler. Freedom and liberty are worthwhile concepts, but they cannot replace financial and material worth. These are of primary importance. Caesarism is prevalent in Rome because Caesar stands for financial and material benefits. Brutus' concept of republicanism fails because he does not cater for anything other than individual liberty. He wants the citizens to indulge in self-governance whereas they want someone to govern on their behalf.

Clash between republicanism and Caesarism

The obvious theme of Julius Caesar is the clash for supremacy between Caesarism and republicanism, and as an extension, between kingship and democracy.

Cassius plots Caesar's murder by alleging that he is a tyrant

The plot for assassination of Caesar is apparently formed against tyranny. Cassius starts the train of thought :

There was a Brutus once that would have brook'd.

The eternal devil to keep his state in Rome

As easily as a king.   [I. ii. 158-160]

Brutus then indirectly assents to the implied suggestions here:

Brutus had rather be a villager

Than to repute himself a son of Rome

Under these hard conditions at this time.

Is like to lay upon us.   [I. ii. 173-175]

Cassius is prepared to kill himself in order to shake off "tyranny". The cry after the assassination is "Liberty! Freedom! Tyranny is dead!" Cassius sees the conspirators enshrined through the ages:

So oft as that shall be,

So often shall the knot of us be call'd

The men that gave their country liberty.   [III. i.117-119]

Brutus asks the people whether they want freedom or slavery

In Brutus' speech after the assassination, the freedom is once again raised. He asks the people would they rather have Caesar "Living" and "die all slaves" than that "Caesar were dead to live all freemen?" He asks the people as to "who is there so base that would be a bondman?"

The theme of bondage versus freedom fades after Antony's speech

This theme of bondage versus freedom fades in the aftermath of Antony's speech. Therefore, freedom and liberty cannot be considered as central to the play.

Flavius is the first to openly resent Caesarism

Caesarism, however, is one of the major themes throughout the play. The first to sound the note of dissatisfaction with Caesarism is Flavius :

These growing feathers pluck'd from Caesar's wing

Will make him fly an ordinary pitch;

Who else would soar above the view of men,

And keep us all in servile fearfulness.   [I. i. 77-80]

Antony gives us the first hint of satisfaction with Caesarism. "When Caesar says 'Do this,' it is perform'd," he says, and we know immediately why some people may be alarmed by such servile flattery. One of Cassius' less sarcastic statements suggests his worry that Caesarism is about kingship and the despotic, absolute rule of one man.

When we went there by an age, since the great flood,

But it was fam'd with more than one man ?   [I.ii.152 - 153]

Brutus hates Caesar's desire to be king

Brutus has nothing personally against Caesar, but one possibility he takes exception to :

Crown him ? — that; —

And then, I grant, we put a sting in him.

That at his will he may do danger with.   [II. i.15-17]

Kingship is only one of the offshoots of Caesarism

It is obvious that kingship is only one of the offshoots of Caesarism, but it is the biggest threat as far as the conspirators are concerned. Casca has heard rumours that the senators mean to "establish Caesar as a king" of "every place save here in Italy". Cassius tells Casca that he would rather commit suicide than accept Caesar as King, and that "Cassius from bondage will deliver Cassius".

The conspirators fear Caesar's absolute powers

Thus the conspirators believe that Caesar will have absolute powers once be becomes king, though he would not have validity in Italy. Brutus admires Caesar and considers him his friend. He does not consider him dangerous, but he is convinced Caesar would become one once he becomes king. Brutus wants to eradicate Caesarism. He puts it as the discrimination he would like to make :

"O, that we, then, could come by Caesar's spirit,

And not dismember Caesar. "   [II. i. 169-170]

Caesar thinks he is invulnerable

Caesar himself never questions his own authority but frequently speaks of his invulnerability. He says "danger knows full well That Caesar is more dangerous than he". There are two occasions when he shows that his powers are absolute :

The cause is in my will, — I will not come;

That is enough to satisfy the senate.   [II. i. 71-72]

Know, Caesar doth not wrong, nor without cause.

Will he be satisfied.   [III.i. 47 - 48]

Yet in the number I do know but one

That unassailable holds on his rank.

Unshake'd of motion, and that I am he.   [III. i. 69-70]

Caesar's deeds never show that he is dangerous

Caesar provides a few hints that he could become autocratic, but these are to be understood as acceptable in a man who has reached an exalted position due to his own virtues. Not once does any of his deed show that he is dangerous. If anything, he manages to instil a new level of happiness in the citizens of Rome.

Brutus links Caesarism only with bondage but the crowd does not

Brutus, however, links Caesarism only with bondage. The last word on deliverance from bondge comes in his speech where he defends Caesar's assassination. The people themselves, running with the tide, just as they had been accused of by the tribunes at the beginning, seem to make no fine distinction between freedom and bondage. The crowd reacts to Brutus in the most unexpected manner. "Let him be Caesar." Brutus should have been alarmed by this outcry. He had wanted republicanism at all costs.. The people of Rome want kingship. It does not concern them whether Caesar or Brutus becomes their king. Brutus, instead of being alarmed, leaves the crowd alone with Antony, despite the warnings of Cassius. This inability to read the pulse of the nation has disastrous consequences for the conspirators as well as for Rome. Brutus should have stayed put and explained the advantages of republicanism. Mere freedom and liberty are not sufficient to inspire the citizens of any nation. They need food, clothing and housing. Caesar had given them all these to an exent where they had started to live luxuriously. Brutus should have explained to them how their lot would improve if they shift from the present form of government to republicanism.

Kingship and Caesarism

Brutus cannot make a distinction between kingship and Caesarism. It is left to the imagination of the commoners to sort out the difference between the two. It never occurs to Brutus that most common men do not think in a profound and precise manner. They choose leaders mainly so that they can lead them in areas beyond their understanding. Brutus takes away the affluence acquired by Caesar and asks the crowd to work for their own growth. His stress is on self-governance. The crowd becomes angry when Antony reveals to them how affluent they were under Caesar. The crowd wants maximum benefits with minimal, and preferably, nil, effort. Brutus tells them they must work for their affluence. Caesar accumulates riches for the people of Rome by the might of his sword. Brutus wants the citizens to make their endeavour and their skill as their true source of affluence. This is evident at the very beginning of the play where Flavius and Marullus chide the artisans for being away from their work in order to celebrate Caesar's victory.

The theme of tyranny

The idea of tyranny was one of the main causes why Caesar had to die. It is remarkable that the idea disappears after the assassination. When Brutus and Cassius confront Antony and Octavius, they quarrel with them peevishly but neither says anything about having stuck a righteous blow for freedom. They make no attempt to convince others with their line of thinking. Instead, the whole conflict becomes a personal one for Brutus and Cassius, as they both are painfully aware of oncoming death. When they die, both give credit to Caesar's spirit for seeking revenge against them. Neither of them declares that he has set in motion the cause of freedom. Brutus declares some vague generalisation on this issue :

I shall have glory by this losing day,

More than Octavius and Mark Antony

By this vile conquest shall attain unto.   [V. v. 36-39]

The conflict between Caesarism and republicansim is never resolved

We can safely say that the conflict between Caesarism and republicanism is never resolved by the dramatist for us, despite the fact that a clear definition is provided for both of them.

Ques 21 : Write a short note on the anachronisms in the play "Julius Caesar."

Ans. :

Shakespeare's interest is to recreate the spirit of the age

Shakespeare's prime interest in writing plays on Roman history is to recreate the spirit of the age which he is trying to portray and to bring to life the characters that played the leading role at that time. He achieves this with reasonable success, atleast to the extent he wishes to achieve. Shakespeare does not much care to be accurate in depicting the dresses, mannerisms, customs and usages of the time to which his play belongs. He makes his characters wear clothes which are more suitable to the Elizabethan age. He ascribes to them customs, which are unknown to their age, and makes then refer to things, which were not invented during the Roman era.

Glaring instances of anachronisms

The instances of anachronisms in "Julius Caesar" are pretty glaring. Some of these instances are :

(a) Caesar wears a doublet [I. ii. 262]. This is a common Elizabethan dress, but was definitely unknown to Roman's during Caesar's days.

(b) Both Casca and Brutus appear unbraced [I. ii. 49 and II. i. 262], a thing which was inconceivable in Roman dress.

(c) Broad-brinimed hats came into vogue in the fifteenth century, but were unknown to the conspirators, who wear them to hide their faces in the play.   [II. I. 73]

(d) Shakespeare makes Ligarius wear a handkerchief around his neck when he is ill [II. I.315]. This is undoubtedly an Elizabethan practice, but was unknown to the Romans.

Shakespeare is not a historical chronicler

Shakespeare's main aim is to dramatically portray historical reality. He is not a historical chronicler. He does not mind if Portia talks of marriage vows like a newly wedded Elizabethan bride. The Romans burned their dead. The Elizabethans buried them. Shakespeare uses both these forms in the play. Brutus orders a funeral for Cassius on the island of Thasos, but Octavius orders a burial for Brutus at the end of his play.

Mention of a clock, books and watchmen

There is a mention of a clock striking in the play [II. I 191], though it was invented only in the thirteenth century. A Roman poet uses rhyme, though historical facts reveal that this was not prevalent during Caesar's time; nor were books available with leaves that might be turned down, as done by Brutus. When Shakespeare mentions "horrid sights seen by the watch", he is definitely talking of London watchmen. There were no watchmen in Rome during Caesar's time.

Shakespeare's plays are meant to please his Elizabethan audience

Shakespeare presents political facts with reasonable accuracy, though we cannot say the same about the way in which he depicts Roman life and manners. This shortcoming is evident in every historical play written by Shakespeare, whether he is treating English, Roman or Celtic history (the last one is represented in Macbeth). In all these plays the social circumstances and customs have a distinct Elizabethan colouring. Such inaccuracies have a jarring influence on modern sensibilities. However, one thing must be clearly understood. A play is meant for a particular audience at a particular time. Correctness of local and historical colour may be crucial for a modern novel or play, but it would be unfair to expect it in an Elizabethan drama. Shakespearean theatre could not depict realism of even the most ordinary details. It had no scenery. It had crude equipment. Instructions had to be written with chalk on a blackboard in order to indicate the scene. The word Thames or Tiber was written on a blackboard, for instance, to indicate that the scene was set on the banks of river Thames or Tiber. Moreover, the Elizabethan audience was very partial so it's own customs, life and manners. It appreciated Elizabethan colouring on stage. This gave them a sense of national pride and it provided oneness with the play.

Shakespeare adds anachronisms deliberately

It is possible that Shakespeare may have deliberately superimposed anachronisms in his plays. It is difficult to label a master craftsman like

Shakespeare as merely lazy or reckless. He could control almost every element of his craft with perfection. It is difficult to see why he would become lazy so needlessly and senselessly.

The Elizabethan audience was creative and restless

It must be remembered that the Elizabethan era was both creative and restless. They had newly got insight into the classics. Elizabethan writers drew upon these new stories of inspiration and interest with the freedom and levity that considered life more important than the strict letter. Poets, thus, reset classical themes amidst romantic settings, not caring about the confused effect that the fusion of the old and the new had on the audience.

Shakespeare wrote for the Elizabethan stage

Shakespeare wrote essentially for an Elizabethan audience, and more importantly for the Elizabethan stage. He was interested in the dramatic and moral aspects of the play, and he could not upset the sensibilities of his audience by giving them the kind of setting that would irritate or confuse them. The Elizabethan audience loved the post-Renaissance setting of England. It was impatient to understand human values in great detail, but not at the expense of its customs and usage. Shakespeare would have confused, even annoyed, its audience by giving his plays authentic touches so unfamiliar to it.

Ques. 22: Critically examine the soliloquies of the play "Julius Caesar."

OR

How do the soliloquies of Brutus and Cassius unfold their inner nature?

Ans. :

The meaning of a soliloquy

A soliloquy is talking to oneself when no one else is present. In a play it is a speech made by a character in this manner. It is a dramatic device to convey to the audience the inner thoughts of a particular character. It thus lays bare the innermost soul of a character. Shakespeare makes use of a soliloquy frequently in his tragedies to expose the tormented soul of his hero. The most exquisite example of a soliloquy exposing torment of a hero is in "Hamlet". Shakespeare rarely uses a soliloquy in a comedy. He does not consider it appropriate to his dramatic purpose in a comedy. Plutarch, the main source for Shakespeare's play, does not make use of soliloquy.

There are two main soliloquies in "Julius Caesar." These are :

(a) The soliloquy of Cassius after he has made an attempt to incite Brutus against Caesar.   [I. ii. 302-304]

(b) The soliloquies of Brutus at midnight in his own orchard before Caesar's murder   [II. i. 10-35] and [II. i. 70-77]

Cassius' soliloquy reflects his character with precision

Cassius' soliloquy is a precise reflection of the man. His hatred for Caesar is an extention of his own inferiority complex. Caesar is a great man— atleast in the eyes of the citizens of Rome. Cassius is prepared to kill him in order to satisfy his envy and to get a part of his status and wealth after his death. Cassius has many friends. Every shrewd man needs the security of numbers in order to rise. Cassius is shrewd enough to realise that all his friends put together may not be sufficient to keep him out trouble after Caesar has been killed. He knows Brutus is just the right man to advance him. Brutus is honourable and liked by the citizens of Rome. He is also a committed republican. He believes that the citizens of Rome, whom he loves dearly, can only be free if they have the right to self-governance. Brutus knows that such a man could hate the idea of Caesar becoming the king of Rome and forcing a tyrannical monarchy on its citizens. Cassius also realises that Brutus is a weak man in many ways. His philosophy is abstract and somewhat removed from reality. He is hyper-sensitive about a second hander's emotion like honour, and a way of life which he considers idealistic but which is far removed from the truth. This is very obvious when Cassius utters:

Well, Brutus, thou art noble; yet, I see

Thy hounourable mettle may be wrought

From that it is dispos'd : therefore 'tis meet

That noble minds keep ever with their likes;

For who so firm that cannot be seduc'd ?   [I. ii. 310-14]

Cassius is a master contriver

Here is a master contriver who knows what he wants and how to get it. His approach towards Brutus is philosophical. He skirts around the real issue, absorbing Brutus' every word, and twisting it to his own advantage, in order to win him over. Both are victims of their own flaws – Brutus of his barren idealism and Cassius of his greed and contrivance. Cassius knows that an appeal for the public good would inspire Brutus.He knows that he must speak in abstractions and generalities about honour, tyranny and public good because Brutus is alien to specific realities. He realises that were he Brutus, he would not "humour" Cassius; but he knows that Brutus is Brutus, who can go to ridiculous, even dangerous, extremes, for the abstract ideal of public good. It is the same desire to confuse rather than inform which makes him decide to send letters in different handwritings and throw them through Brutus' window, suggesting that they have come from several citizens:

Writings all tending to the great opinion

That Rome holds of his name; wherein obscurely

Caesar's ambition shall be glanced at :   [I. ii. 322 – 24]

Brutus thrives on vague idealsim

The emphasis is on obscurity, because Brutus thrives on uttering abstractions. He has no time for realities throughout the play. He seeks honour, but only other men can provide such a thing. If he is on the path of truth then he does not need to seek the approval of others. If he is on the path of lies then appreciation from others becomes an aberration. If he is in doubt about what he is doing then he cannot be ideal, which most critics erroneously believe he is. Cassius understands that Brutus is not ideal, but his pretence to idealism has substantial acceptance among the commoners. It is this pretence to idealism that he wishes to use to satisfy his own greed and hatred.

Critics are divided about Brutus' soliloquy

Critics are divided about Brutus' soliloquy. Some accept him as a champion of freedom against tyranny. Others see him as a mistaken idealist who murders a trusting friend and a man who has the ability to bring sustained and prolonged prosperity to Rome. There are some hints that Brutus has become vain and autocratic, but there is little hint that he is actually tyrannical. Even Brutus admits that he has no cause to spurn or reject him.

.... and, for my part,

I know no personal cause to spurn at him [II. I. 10-11]; and later

I have not known when his affections sway'd.

More than his reason. [II. i. 19-21]

Brutus condemns Caesar for what he might become

In his soliloquy, as in his earlier reply to Cassius [I. ii. 174 – 175] he mentions only of probable future evils. He condemns Caesar not for what he is but for what he might become.

He would be crown'd

How that might change his nature, there's the question :

It is the bright sun that brings forth the adder,

And that craves wary walking. [II. i. 12 – 15]

Obscure inanities appeal to Brutus

This is the kind of obscure inanity that appeals to Brutus. It overlooks the fact that as a dictator, Caesar is already so powerful that a crown cannot add to it. It is thus, not Caesar that Brutus objects to. It is the concept of kingship that he objects to.

Brutus is at war with himself

Yet, it is not wise to be too harsh on Brutus. All that he stands for is in ruins. Caesar's "vile conquest" is hateful to him. Some of his "thrasonical" utterances must be put down to Shakespeare's technique of making his characters reveal their own qualities by direct reference to them. In Brutus, Shakespeare gives us a man "with himself at war", to use Brutus' own phrase. His conflict is between a friend he loves and a fear that he may one day become despotic and tyrannical. He may wish to pursue honour, but he engages himself in a dishonourable cause. He seeks principles but associates himself with unprincipled men. Brutus has never known Caesar to be governed by his feelings instead of his judgement, yet in his agony and indecision he is willing to "fashion it thus", in order to convince himself that Caesar must die. He is not prepared to accept that the greatest man on earth may have the ability to rise above ordinary emotions, and not let absolute power (if such a thing is ever possible) go to his head. He is prepared to brutally murder a trusting friend and the greatest man on earth on what is at best a completely hypothetical assumption. His motives may be lofty, but his reasoning is false, and his actions are destructive. Despite all this, among all the conspirators, he alone may have probably just passed off as a sacrificer and not as a butcher; but here too he fails us; for how can we pardon a destroyer of greatness ?

Brutus' soliloquy reveals his terrible error

Brutus' soliloquy is a wonderful exposition of a man who, with reasons that are very nearly right, reaches a conclusion that is entirely wrong. It is impossible not to sympathise with Brutus in his moments of agony and confusion; but it is difficult not to be angry at the final outcome. Brutus thinks prosperity would be in place once Caesar is dead. He does not visualise how this would happen and he has no contingency plan if things do not fall in place as visualised by him. He thinks Caesar to be a "serpent's egg" that must be killed before it is hatched. He realises that Caesar's murder is a "phantasma and a hideous dream." He forces himself to believe that the interim period between the "acting of a dreadful thing and the first motion" is the cause of his anguish. It never occurs to him that murder is the most dreadful thing of all.

Brutus'soliloquy is a device to reveal his confusion

Brutus' soliloquy is an example of Shakespeare's brilliance in revealing ambiguous or confused states of mind, where the confusion or ambiguity is not clearly realised by the speaker himself. The heroes of Shakespeare's tragedies often arrive at a terrible decision; the real terror behind the decision, however, is not fully understood by them. Shakespeare uses language, which reveals the superficial clarity, and the subconscious confusion of his heroes. Brutus is certain what course of action he has to take. He begins his soliloquy with a final decision: "It must be by his death", and then proceeds to justify to himself why he has arrived at such a conclusion. Shakespeare leaves us in no doubt that Brutus is confused, though his confusion is such that it can easily surround most of us. Brutus says that he has no "personal cause" for destroying Caesar. We immediately compare him to Cassius, whose hatred is made clear in Act I, Scene ii. Brutus is convinced that Caesar will abuse his power some day. He does not tell us why he has arrived at such a conclusion. Nor does he tell us why Caesar has to die. What is worse he admits to himself that he has no evidence that Caesar ever behaved unreasonably. The two remarks about "bright day" bringing forth "the adder", and "young ambition's ladder" both have the quality of conventional phrases: they are plausible excuses, not logical arguments. It is significant Brutus admits that the "quarrel" really has no "colour" – or excuse – as it stands. He is compelled to "fashion it" according to his own confused thinking. And he ends up unconsciously admitting that in order to be able to act he must, in a sense, distort his view of Caesar : "therefore think of him as a serpent's egg". We are more and more convinced about the uncertainty of his position, as Brutus forces himself into believing something that is not true.

Ques. 23 : Comment on the fact that "Julius Caesar" is more a tragedy than a historical play.

Ans. :

Shakespeare considers historical accuracy less important than his dramatic purpose

Shakespeare sacrifices historical accuracy to advance his dramatic purpose. He remains true to historical details if they do not interfere with his plays. Shakespeare depicts some historical facts with substantial accuracy in "Julius Caesar". More important among them are :

(a) The revelation that Caesar's covetous desire for the crown created a revulsion in the citizens of Rome.

(b) The reason for the conspiracy against Caesar was the animosity of some officials towards him as well as the misplaced devotion some of them had towards the ideals of ancient republicanism.

(c) The relation Brutus had with Caesar on one hand and with the conspirators on the other.

(d) The terrible consequences that the conspirators had to face after they killed Caesar.

(e) The relationship of the triumvirs with each other.

Shakespeare borrows from Plutarch

Shakespeare's main source for "Julius Caesar" is Plutarch's "Parallel Lives of Greeks and Romans." Shakespeare, however, does not borrow from Plutarch blindly. He is a poet and a dramatist, and his main purpose for writing plays is that they should be enacted on stage. It is here that Shakespeare enters into the spirit of Roman politics and gives it colouring to suit his purpose. The historian, however, has little to complain about.

Shakespeare sometimes compresses events

There are several instances when Shakespeare compresses the action, combining events, which are separated in reality by some interval of time. He uses this dramatic license in order to make sure that the play does not lose its dramatic effect or its tragic force.

Julius Caesar must be judged as a tragic play

"Julius Caesar" must be judged as a play – more importantly as a tragedy – and not as a document of historical facts. Shakespeare compresses action only because he wants to maintain the tragic intensity of the play. The play "Julius Caesar" has all the ingredients of a Shakespearean tragedy. Its chief protagonist, Brutus dies at the end of the play. He is a tragic hero in the conventional sense because:

(a) He is a man of high standing.

(b) He opposes a conflicting force, mostly internal, where his confusion leads him to the terrible decision that he must murder Caesar in order to save Rome and republicanism.

(c) Brutus has a tragic flaw (hamartia), which is his barren idealism. This makes him arrive at conclusions which he is not suited to carry out. His idealism and sense of honour are flaws only because they are excesses of a worthwhile trait directed to a wrong cause.

(d) Brutus' downfall (as well as of those around him) is a direct consequence of his tragic flaw.

(e) The action presented on stage is such that it is recognisable to the audience as real.

(f) The audience feels pity and awe due to the sufferings of the hero, and the conclusion of the action brings release from these emotions (catharsis)

(g) There is resublimation and regeneration of Brutus, as true wisdom dawns on him, just before dies.

Shakespeare depicts a tragic as well as a dramatic point of view

Shakespeare depicts a tragic as well as a dramatic point of view in "Julius Caesar". He improves upon the historical characters and makes them more suitable for his purpose. He does not accept Plutarch's Caesar blindly. He selects and adapts according to the emphasis he wants to give to his plot. Caesar may have been hated by the whole of Rome, but in the play only a few malcontents hate him. Even Brutus thinks he is "the foremost man of all this world." Shakespeare depicts him in this manner to suit his tragic purpose. The audience must feel tremendous loss after he is dead. The role of tragedy is to elevate the audience to higher levels of thought and existence. The audience would have felt pleasure after Caesar's death had he been a man devoid of virtues. They would not have felt pity and awe for a man whose absence meant such irreparable loss. The same holds true for Brutus. Plutarch had made him a man of virtue. Caesar makes him somewhat pompous and opinionated. His tragic flaw is an inevitable extension of his misplaced estimation of himself. He believes that his incomplete vision of existence would be sufficient to influence the citizens of Rome. Shakespeare's vision of the world is such that he cannot delineate outright villains or heroes. Even a shrewd contriver like Cassius has some good qualities. Mark Antony may have been a reveller and a drinker but these are of no consequence to the play. What matters is his loyalty to Caesar and his ability to understand the pulse of the crowd.

Characters and scenes increase the play's tragic intensity

Shakespeare creates characters and scenes with the sole purpose of increasing the tragic intensity of his play. His second purpose is to establish a world moral order. He cannot achieve it without bringing opposing emotions in conflict with one another. The sources of his plays, whether they are taken from history or elsewhere, merely serve as a backdrop against which Shakespeare achieves this. What we feel is tremendous waste, which could so easily have been avoided if some characters of the play had acted in a compassionate and wise manner. The play is a tragedy because this does not happen. We remember Brutus as a tragic hero and not as a historical figure. We remember Caesar as a man who brought affluence and prosperity to Rome and not as a despot and a tyrant that he may have been in history. More importantly, we remember "Julius Caesar" as a tragic play and not as a historical event. In any case it is so much better to see it this way. It brings us into greater illumination regarding the right rhythm in which the world exists.

Julius Caesar is a political problem play as well

It is also worthwhile to consider "Julius Caesar" as a political "problem play" in which each character presents his own approach to the problem of power. Shakespeare does not resolve the problem of republicanism versus kingship. He had himself preferred monarchy, but he leaves the choice of preference between the two to his readers.

CHAPTER 10

CHARACTERS OF THE PLAY

1
JULIUS CAESAR

The Julius Caesar of the play is at decline of his powers

The Julius Caesar of history (102 to 44 BC) was a brilliant military and political leader who influenced the course of world history. Shakespeare delineates him as a man who is at the end of a great existence. He is declining mentally as well as physically and he is convinced that he is a demi-god. He has physical weaknesses, the kind, which can be alarming in a head of state. He is deaf in one ear. He is afflicted with epilepsy, and if Cassius is to be believed his physical strength is waning. He is also superstitious because he is increasingly dependent on the predictions of fortune-tellers. He seems to have a cocky belief in his own invincibility. This idea creates resentment and worry in the aristocratic republicans, who want Rome to be a republic, so that they can share some power with Caesar. These republicans conspire to murder Caesar before he can manage to be elevated as king.

Caesar appears only in three scenes of the play

Shakespeare makes Caesar appear only in three scenes. This prompted a critic to suggest that Caesar is the titular hero of the play while Brutus is its dramatic hero. We learn a lot about Caesar from what others in the play tell us about him. Since all of them provide conflicting information about him, we have to form our own opinion. We can do this by differentiating between reliable and prejudiced judgement of the person who speaks about him. Hazlitt thinks Shakespeare has failed Caesar. He is surprised because Shakespeare is a master at delineating characters.

Shakespeare borrows Caesar's character from Plutarch

Most critics believe that Caesar is a glorious vapourer, a braggart, who is full of lofty airs and mock thunder. Dower Wilson considers Caesar a ruthless tyrant in the decline of his physical and moral powers. He thinks that Shakespeare accepts Caesar as an almost supernatural conqueror, who due to his greed and power is out to ruin the Roman republic, and is justifiably murdered by Brutus. He calls Caesar a "Ruthless, irresistible genius "and "a mostrous giant". He gives a well-worn out list of Caesar's moral and physical weaknesses and points out that in fact, Shakespeare distorts Plutarch to give pre-eminence to these weakness. This is great disservice to Shakespeare. There is no need – intellectually, moral or dramatically–to accept Plutarch blindly. He is merely a historical source for Shakespeare. History is different from literature because history depicts life as it is while literature depicts life as it may be or ought to be. This definition was provided by Aristotle. Wilson does not tell us why this definition is not relevant in literature and why reality has to be depicted blindly. Shakespeare accepts from Plutarch if it suits his purpose. He adds weakness which are not available in Plutarch's Caesar. For instance, he makes Caesar deaf and prone to epilepsy, traits which do not exist in Plutarch's Caesar. Shakespeare also gives his Caesar some good qualities. Plutarch's Caesar is hated by the people of Rome because of his covetous desire to be king, but in the play, the people of Rome love him. It does not take Antony much effort to win back the crowd after Brutus convinces it about the justification behind Caesar's murder.

He is a man of authority

Shakespeare depicts Caesar as a man of great authority. It is obvious that he is superstitious but this can be accepted as a weakness of the times.There are occasions when he ignores warnings from fortune-tellers.There is no clinching evidence that he is driven only by superstition. He dismisses the soothsayer as a dreamer and he actually ventures forth to the Capitol despite the pleadings of his wife and the warnings of his augurers.

Caesar's weakness are human while his strengths are superhuman

Cassius tells us about Caesar's physical weaknesses. He tells us that Caesar had once shivered in ague, and he once saved him from drowning in River Tiber. Cassius wants us to believe they are serious weaknesses. They, in fact, tell us much about the smallness of Cassius. He appears an envious malcontent than a true critic. Any human being can be defeated by fever or the massive currents of a river. Caesar's victories in battles are sufficient proof that he is physically strong.

Antony convinces the crowd that Caesar was not ambitious

Shakespeare was deeply concerned with kingship, and the King's divine right to rule. The citizens of Rome are shown to be undecided about choosing between republicanism and kingship. They choose Caesar because Antony convinces them that he had no ambitions to be king. They may have backed republicanism if they had a leader as worthy as Caesar.

Everyone misunderstands the relationship between Caesar and his spirit

Caesar himself, Cassius, and Brutus in the soliloquy in his garden, each in his own way misinterprets the relation between Caesar's spirit, which informs his magistracy and vocation, and the imperfect, vulnerable man

Caesar. Brutus believes that Caesar's spirit is evil, and wishes that he has a way to destroy it without killing the man. When he cannot find a way, he kills Caesar. He learns in the end that he has not been able to kill Caesar's spirit, because only the human body is mortal.

Caesar sublimates his desire to be king

Brutus kills Caesar for his ambition, without evaluating whether Caesar is ambitious or not, and whether ambition "per se" is bad or not. We realise that Caesar has a covetous desire to be king, but we also accept that his refusal of the crown is an effort to sublimate his own desire to the general desire of the citizens of Rome. There may be a certain wistful hope that he may one day become king; there may even be a desire to fool the public by refusing the crown; but we cannot ignore the fact that he actually does refuse the crown. His will is sufficient example that he loves the citizens of Rome. Ambition is not a bad trait. In fact it is positively desirable because it inspires us to rise to greater heights from our present level. Brutus wants Rome to have a republican from of government. Caesar wants to be king, but would rather be the head of a Roman republic if the citizens of Rome want it. Both want public good. Caesar brings back trophies, prisoners of war and riches. Brutus brings the nation to the brink of disaster through an unprecedented and avoidable civil war.

Caesar is a great judge of character

Caesar is a great judge of character. This itself amounts to something because it is a vital trait in any leader. His uncanny evaluation of Cassius is one of the most impressive passages in the play.

> Such men as he be never at heart's ease
>
> Whiles they behold a greater than themselves ;
>
> And therefore are they very dangerous.   [I. ii. 209-211].

This is Cassius stripped to the very soul, by the man he has been maligning. It is true that Caesar is extremely arrogant at times. Such arrogance may be pardoned in somebody as powerful and great as Caesar as a necessary excess. A head of state has to be arrogant at times in order to keep people at bay. When Caesar says that he is not afraid "for always I am Caesar" we may accept it in any one of the two ways: either as a silly utterance of a vain man or as a natural extension of a brave man who is not prepared to let fear come near him. Casca's utterances against Caesar are veiled in hostility. He has a "sour fashion" and is obviously an ineffectual malcontent. He flatters Caesar on his face and jeers at him behind his back. It is not without reason that Shakespeare makes him the only conspirator who stabs Caesar from the back. He does not have the courage to face a dying man as great as Caesar.

Brutus interprets Caesar wrongly

Brutus openly admits that he has no reason to spurn Caesar. He also admits that he has been influenced by Cassius against Caesar. He begins his argument in a soliloquy by thinking that "it must be by his death." Here is a man who has obviously reversed the cause and effect of things. He first pronounces his decision and then superimposes arguments to suit that decision. We immediately realise that Brutus is not to be trusted. His honour may make him appealing to the citizens of Rome, but this very same honour makes him an unrealistic and dangerous man. The fault does not lie in Caesar's character but in Brutus'own misplaced estimation of himself. Brutus kills Caesar because he is not sure what power would do to Caesar. It is not a stretched imagination which makes one wonder how blame can be put on anybody but Brutus. He thinks it is common knowledge that an ambitious man who has risen to the top scorns the lower steps and becomes a tyrant. "So Caesar may", presumes Brutus, totally unreasonably, about a person whom he has evaluated as his friend. It is Brutus' failure when he says:

And, since the quarrel

Will bear no colour for the things he is,

Fashion it thus;   [II. i. 28-30]

Brutus thus kills his "best lover" on a mere whim. Brutus is not dishonest; he is much worse; he is intellectually blind. His motives may be lofty, but his actions are terrible.

Caesar's superstition is not cowardice

Much has been written about Caesar's superstition. But it would be foolish to ignore the brave utterances he makes in the same breath with which he indulges in superstition. He may offer sacrifices but in the end he somehow gets it right. He makes some very worthwhile remarks, as he does about death.

Cowards die many times before their deaths;

The valiant never taste of death but once.   [II. ii. 32-33]

It is true that he is stupidly boastful when he says

Danger knows full well

That Caesar is more dangerous then he :

We are two lions litter'd in one day

And I the elder and more terrible: [II. ii. 44-46]

Caesar's boasting is designed to convey his fearlessness

This is the thrasonical Caeasar. A modern reader may find Caesar vain and stupidly arrogant, but an Elizabethan spectator, accustomed to the techniques of "direct self-explanation" in drama, would see in these words Shakespeare's handiest way of conveying Caesar's fearlessness. His arrogance may be less easier to explain, but it is, none -the-less, an extension of a fearless man. He is a brave soldier and there must have been need to psyche himself to remain totally devoid of fear. Soldiers do it all the time. Caesar is successful, perhaps because he has inspired himself to conquer fear.

Shakespeare deliberately lessens sympathy for Caesar nearing his end

Shakespeare lessens the sympathy we have for Caesar in the last seventy lines that lead to his murder. Shakespeare does this deliberately in order to heighten the dramatic conflict on the play. Caesar is so unabashedly arrogant here that we cease to admire him. Shakespeare restores our sympathy for Caesar when he says "Et tu, Brute ! — Then fall, Caesar!" Now Brutus becomes a symbol of treason and betrayal, though this is not revealed to him, and the theatrical episode where he and the other conspirators bathe their hands in Caesar's blood, leaves us with shame and disgust.

Antony restores Caesar's glory in the eyes of the citizens

It is left to Antony to restore Caesar's glory and respect in the eyes of the citizens of Rome. He uses every trick linked with oratory in order to incense the crowd against the conspirators. It is here that we see Caesar's spirit inspiring Antony to outwit the naivete of Brutus and the cunning of Cassius.

Caesar's spirit dominates the second half of the play

The second half of the play is dominated by Caesar's spirit. Caesar is never long absent from our thoughts, nor from those who killed him. Brutus had wanted to "stand up against the spirit of Caesar." It is this very spirit which rises from the base of Pompey's statue to seek revenge.

Antony's terrible prophecy

Antony gives a terrible dimension to Caesar's spirit in his prophecy over Caesar's body:

And Caesar's spirit, ranging for revenge,
With Ate by his side come hot from hell,
Shall in these confines with a monarch's voice
Cry "Havoc," and let ship the dogs of war;   [III. i. 270-74]

This prophecy is prevalent throughout the play from then on, and both Cassius and Brutus die with Caesar's name on their lips.

Caesar is the ruling spirit of the play

The play is called "Julius Caesar" because Caesar is the subject and ruling spirit of the play, but he is not the hero or the leading character of the play. He is of prime concern till he is alive, and his spirit holds our attention after he is dead.

2

MARCUS BRUTUS

Brutus is the dramatic hero of the play

Caesar is the titular hero of the play, while Brutus is its dramatic hero. Brutus is a complex character because Shakespeare delineates him with fascinating touches. Plutarch depicted him as a man of intellect, integrity, sound judgement and philosophical outlook. As per Plutarch he killed Caesar, because of his coveted desire to the king of Rome and because Cassius incited him to murder Caesar. It is obvious that Shakespeare had genuine reservations about such characterisation. A man of profound intellect and integrity does not become a murderer when incited by someone as dubious as Cassius. He keeps him pure of intention, but makes him less intelligent and likable.

Critics are misled by Brutus' exaggerated estimation of himself

Most critics are misled by Brutus' exaggerated estimation of himself. Macallum thinks Brutus attracts our chief sympathy and concern. There is no doubt that both Shakespeare and Plutarch had admiration for Brutus, but Shakespeare also gives him certain negative traits. He is easily misled and he is stupidly self-righteous. He is a statesman and his prime weapon for governance should have been discussion and diplomacy. He becomes a senseless murderer instead. He is led by the nose by Cassius and easily outwitted by Antony. At every moment of crisis, when fate demands from him a worthwhile decision, sees him thrusting himself and the conspirators into greater trouble. He is an ineffectual idealist, who is totally oblivious to reality.

Brutus is greatly respected

We establish Caesar's character mainly from what others tell about him, since we see so little of him. We learn much more about Brutus, both from him as well as from others. There is no doubt that every one who knows him respects him. Cassius calls him noble and Casca says that :

O, he sits high in all the people's hearts :

And that which would appear offence in us,

His countenance, like richest alchemy,

Will change to virtue and to worthiness.   [I. iii. 157-160]

Caius Ligarius calls him the "soul of Rome" and Caesar loves him dearly.

Brutus must be assessed as per the moral nature of his actions

Shakespeare normally wants to tell us about a person by making us hear what others say about him. We cannot judge Brutus like that. We must assess him as per his broodings and as per the difference between his theory and practice. He comes out less favourably once we apply all parameters on him.

Leadership comes naturally to him

Leadership comes naturally to Brutus. That is why he becomes the leader of the conspirators without any opposition. He assumes leadership because he has an exaggerated opinion of himself. He has built such an aura around himself that others also readily agree with his estimation of himself.

He makes a series of blunders as a leader

Assuming the role of leadership and being a leader are, however, two different things. He makes one blunder after the other as a leader. He refuses to bind the conspirators into an oath, and the conspiracy is almost betrayed before Caesar is killed. He refuses to kill Antony. He lets Antony speak from the same rostrum occupied by him to address the people of Rome after Caesar's death. He does this despite Cassius' earnest warnings and requests. Antony skilfully turns the tables on the conspirators. He incites the crowd to such an extent that they are prepared to kill them and burn their houses. Modern thinkers believe that Brutus prepares himself for retribution the moment he kills Caesar, and his every subsequent act is towards the achievement of this retribution. It is as if he wants the conspirators, including himself, to be caught and punished. The modern critics do not explain why Brutus murders Caesar, if he has to prepare himself for expiation of his sins. Their theory also does not take into account the attempts made by him to succeed till the very end of the play.

His selfless imagination renders him inactive

Shakespeare idealises Plutarch's Brutus. The chief sign of this is his set of scruples. His imagination is indeed so selfless, that it almost smothers his powers and renders him inactive. Shakespeare keeps him very conscious of a remote Roman grandeur. He expresses his author's idea of antiquity than his knowledge of life. He is a public man – so in fact are most of the characters of the play – and he must be evaluated as such. He must not be evaluated on the parameters that are valid for a private man. The irony is that Shakespeare's deepest interest is in Brutus the private man. And though he tries to find that man in Brutus he does not do so, because he has already submitted Brutus, like everybody else in the play, to the smoothing and simplifying process of a certain style.

Brutus' nobility muffles his intellignece

The blunders committed by Brutus are so large that they appear pathetic. They somehow do not achieve the dignity of tragic error, or of heroic fault, because Brutus' virtues are not positive enough. The mistakes of Brutus are the mistakes of a man whose nobility muffles his intelligence. His conquest of himself has dulled his wit. His excellence is not inconsistent with a certain lethargy of mind. He knows this well enough. He admits that he is "not gamesome" and lacks "that quick spirit that is in Antony." His honesty is absolute and disarming, but it is humourless and edgeless.

> There is no terror, Cassius, is your threats ;
>
> For I am arm'd so strong in honesty,
>
> That they pass by me as the idle wind,
>
> Which I respect not.   [IV. iii. 66-69]

Brutus may call this honesty; to others it may be boasting. Neither would he call his behaviour on hearing Portia's death as a piece of acting. He is a stoic, and it is befitting that he conducts himself elegantly and without undue pain. Most people would accept it as true manhood demonstrating itself for the benefit of other. Some may call him heartless and foolish. No one can deny that Brutus is good in an unapettising and humourless manner. Nobility has numbed him so much that he cannot see himself beyond his principles.

Brutus' principles bring unending misery

Yet, principles must bring joy for the practitioner and for those around him. His principles bring unending misery. He utters his principles with clarity, but his actions cannot be deemed worthy.

Brutus has flawed reasoning

Even his reasoning fails him when he convinces himself that Caesar should be murdered. He seems to be an inane juggler who makes up his mind first and then fits explanations to his decisions later. He indulges in pitiful phrases in his soliloquy. The fine man is a coarse thinker. The saint of self-denial has little self left to deny.

Brutus' reticence provides no intimacy

Shakespeare does as much as can be done with such a man, but what can be done is limited. Brutus is so reticent that no intimacy is possible with him. His blunders are difficult to excuse. Even his compassion to let Antony live comes in the realm of confusion, rather than out of any profound understanding. He is not mad, or haunted, or inspired. He is simply confused. He is such a negative man that it is impossible to know why he is confused. This makes Brutus so pathetic and uninspiring that it is impossible to think that there is anything heroic in him. H. Granville Barker comments, "A hero, let us be clear, is the character of which a dramatist, not morally, but artistically, most approves. Macbeth is a hero. Shakespeare's sympathy with Brutus does not imply approval of the murder of Caesar". H B Charlton admits that it "is indeed difficult to discount the muddle-headedness of Brutus, in spite of our national proclivity to condone the intellectual fuddles of a man whose heart intends good".

Brutus' messy fight with Cassius

Brutus is seen in terrible light during his quarrel with Cassius. He may have some merit in the main points of the issue, yet his demeanour is intolerable. He vacillates between being a haughty god, rebuking erring mortals, and a squabbling individual.

Brutus has many good qualities

Despite his flaws, Brutus has many good qualities. The problem with Brutus has been that critics have glorified him to the point of absurdity, without balancing their views with his flaws.

Brutus carries his uprighteousness as a sore wound

Brutus is a man who may receive our grudging respect, but it is impossible to love him. He is disagreeable. This is how we normally accept a man who carries his uprighteousness as a sore wound. Moreover, he is surrounded by a problem, which is beyond the scope of his limited resources. It is inevitable that he should arrive at the wrong decision. And once he kills Caesar, it is impossible to like him, leave alone consider him as virtuous. Shakespeare finally buries Brutus' crime in his virtues through Antony's tribute:

This was the noblest Roman of them all:

All the conspirators, save only he,

Did that they did in envy of great Caesar;

He only, in a general honest thought

And common good to all, made one of them.

His life was gentle, and the elements

So mix'd in him, that Nature might stand up

And say to all the world, "This was a man!"   [V. v. 68-75]

Brutus' tragedy lies in his betrayal of friendship

Caesar's last cry, with its accusation of, and lament for, the betrayal of friendship, is the sum total of the tragedy of Brutus. There is sufficient hint to make us believe that he is the tragic hero of the play. Yet, there are also sufficient hints to suggest that he is not heroic. Neither are his errors such that they can be called tragic. Brutus falls somewhat short of being called a tragic hero in the same class as Macbeth or Hamlet.

3
CAIUS CASSIUS

Cassius is an aristocrat and a republican

Cassius is an aristocrat and a republican in Rome. Like Brutus he hates tyranny, but unlike Brutus he is motivated more by self-interest and envy in plotting against Caesar. While Brutus is reflective, philosophical, idealistic, Cassius is contrastingly quick-witted, practical and opportunistic. Cassius is hugely aware of Brutus' shortcoming as a leader, but he uses the man's stature and influence to help the success of the conspiracy.

Cassius exists more on emotions than logic

Critics believe that Brutus would be better off to trust his emotions than his reasons, instead of allowing an unfavourable, abstract moral ideal to overcome his love for Caesar. This is why he has been compared unfavourably with Cassius as well as with Antony, who are primarily governed by their emotions. This approach is a terrible mistake, since it assumes that an arbitrary emotion is better than profound reason.

Cassius is an epicure in a philosophical way

In contrast to Brutus' stoicism, Cassius in an epicure. Epicurus (BC 342-270) was a Greek philosopher who founded the Epicurean school of philosophy. He taught that the end of life is either happiness or peace of mind resulting from virtue. He held that there was no god or higher power that could influence the lives of men. His followers thus freed themselves from supernatural fears because these hampered the enjoyment of the joys of existence. Cassius is a philosophical epicure, unlike Antony, who is an epicure in the popular sense. Cassius believes that one must show contempt for supernatural warnings and become a master of his own destiny.

His philosophy is rational but his practice is flawed

The philosophy seems to be profoundly rational, but the kind of practice that Cassius indulges in shows how even a slight convolution of an ideal can make it look terribly ugly. His epicurism is limited to opportunism and absence of moral scruple. He adapts his approach to the man he is addressing. He talks abouts omens to the superstitious Casca. He is philosophical with Brutus. He skirts the real issue, he poses questions in order to appeal to Brutus' brooding mind, and he throws back Brutus' words at him in order to create an unfair advantage for himself. He infects Brutus with his own hatred and he arouses Casca's "quick mettle" by a flambouyant display of his own recklessness. He makes theatrical gestures. On three occasions he readies himself for death. He even sees Caesar's death in terms of theatre. Words are meant to advance truth. Cassius' words hide or convolute it.

He hands over the leadership to Brutus

Cassius hands over the leadership of the conspiracy to Brutus, despite being more suited to lead it. He needs Brutus' unrighteousness and honour. He knows Brutus is not the kind of man who changes his values or his mind.

Plutarch says thus about him,"But Cassius being a choleric man, and hating Caesar privately more than he did the tyranny openly, he incensed Brutus against him". These words seem to be the basis on which Shakespeare builds Cassius' character. Plutarch says that Cassius "even from his cradle, could not abide any manner of tyrants." Plutarch depicts him as a cruel and choleric man, who wants to rule over others by fear. Cassius himself admits to have inherited a "rash humour" from his mother. Brutus accuses him of having "testy humour", "rash choler" and waspishness. Shakespeare dilutes his choler but depicts his envy and illwill towards Caesar.

Caesar thinks Cassius is dangerous

Caesar understands Cassius really well. He warns Antony to be cautious of him.

Yond Cassius has a lean and hungry look;
He thinks too much : such men are dangerous.   [I. ii. 194-195]

Cassius is not at ease with himself

Though Caesar boastfully announces that he is not afraid of him, yet he understands Cassius well. He is dangerous because "he loves no play", "he hears no music", he smiles rarely and that too as if he is mocking at his own smile. Caesar knows such men are not at ease with themselves when they see someone who is greater than them.

He is a courageous soldier and a loyal friend

Despite a long list of flaws there is no denying the fact that Cassius has some very worthwhile qualities as well. He attracts loyalty from others and he can genuinely show compassion to those he loves.

He is unstable

In the beginning of the play he is obsessed by his hatred for Caesar, and not in control of his feelings. In fact he is always inclined to be unstable.

He loses his nerve when Popilius Lena approaches Caesar at the senate house, and it is left to Brutus to assure him. After the assassination, his envy is replaced by an exaggerated enthusiasm for liberty. He even wavers from his epicurean beliefs when the omens despirit his soldier when they march from Sardis to Philippi. He takes his life in indecent haste, when he blindly accepts what Pindarus tells him. In his changeability as well as in his motive against Caesar, he is an admirable foil to the steadfast Brutus.

He becomes more likable after Caesar dies

Cassius becomes more likable after Caesar dies, as if he is liberated with the death of the person he hated so much. From now on he is as calm as Brutus and has greater far-sightedness than him. The quarrel he has with Brutus shows him in better light than Brutus. He makes the first move towards reconciliation, after having good-naturedly tolerated Brutus' vicious outburst. He is geiuunely sorry when he learns that Portia is dead, and he whole-heartedly joins Brutus in burying all their differences in a cup of wine.

My heart is thirsty for that noble pledge. —
Fill, Lucius, till the wine o'erswell the cup;
I cannot drink too much of Brutus' love. [IV. iii. 160-162]

Cassius is not the villain of the play

Cassius, thus, is not the villain of the play. His hatred for Caesar may be linked with self-advancement, but it is also linked with a worthy cause. Cassius has a gift of making more friends that the gentle Brutus. He has an uncanny ability to judge people, and he has a much better idea than Brutus on how to tackle friends and foes. He has farsightedness, though this does not extend to Brutus. It does not occur to him that Brutus is too obstinate and inflexible to succeed as a leader of an extremely complex conspiracy. He not only lets him be the leader but he also lets him overrule every worthwhile suggestion made by him.

He is an odd blend of good and bad

In Cassius there is an odd blend of the good and the bad, and of the weak and the strong. He is tactful, yet he bursts into a fiery temper. He is an epicure, but believes in omens once in a while. His hearing is sharp but his eyesight is poor. He is quick to recognise Casca by his voice but is unable to see at a distance, so that he trusts another's eyes at a critical juncture. This has disastrous consequences for him. He has a shrewd understanding of men, yet he is blind to his own sense of wrong. He accuses Brutus at least on three occasions for wronging him. He appears harsh and unattractive as compared to the gentle Brutus, despite the fact that he is more humane and affectionate than him.

His act of murder cannot be pardoned

Yet, all these evaluations are of no consequence. Life demands that truth be advanced gently and with compassion. Negative emotions can only bring destruction for the practitioner and for those on whom they are practiced. Cassius's envy and hatred lead him to murder and destroy his own peace of mind as well as that of Rome. He is a politician and a statesman. His difference with Caesar is a political one. He should have solved it through diplomacy and statesmanship. He should have taken his point of view to the citizens of Rome and understood their point of view. He indulges in cowardly murder instead. We cannot approve of Cassius, no matter how many good qualities he may have possessed.

4
MARK ANTONY (MARCUS ANTONIUS)

He is not a mere unmitigated self-seeker

Antony's character develops in the last three acts of the play. He is little more than "a limb of Caesar", as Brutus describes him, in the first two acts of the play. His enormous abilities as a soldier, statesman, motivator, organiser and orator make him the avenger of Caesar and a "triple pillar of the world", by the end of the play. Moulton believes Antony has "all the power that belongs to the intellectual and practical life." Yet, a large number of critics believe that he has only one aim in life, that of "unmitigated self-seeking". This, however, is not the truth. He is obviously a lot more than an unmitigated self-seeker.

He is a reveller

Antony's first appearance is as a runner in the feast of Lupercalia. It is obvious that he wants to please Caesar ("When Caesar says, 'Do this', it is performed"). He is a reveller, who enjoys the good things of life, and the feast of Lupercalia provides one such opportunity. It also provides him an opportunity to please Caesar.

He is not a senseless flatterer of Caesar

He utters only three more lines before the assassination. In two of them he thinks Caesar to be wrong in considering Cassius dangerous, since he is well disposed towards the regime. He is thus not a senseless and servile flatterer that most critics think he is. Nor is Caesar arrogant and despotic if he lets people like Antony oppose him.

He is a powerful orator and a quick-witted schemer

The story of Antony is continued in "Antony and Cleopatra", where the "peevish schoolboy" crushes the "masker and reveller." In "Julius Caesar" little is seen or suggested of Antony's military genius which made him Caesar's deputy. Neither is his self-indulgence, which finally led to his downfall, evident in this play. In "Julius Caesar" he is depicted mainly as a powerful orator and a quick-witted schemer. There is dash and fire in him which makes him very appealing. Brutus is deceived into believing he is harmless because he is constantly surrounded in music and merry making.

For he can do no more than Caesar's arm
When Caesar's head is off.   [II. i. 181-182]
Cassius, however, justifiably thinks otherwise
.... we shall find of him
A shrewd contriver ;   [II. i. 157-158]

He is a shrewd contriver

We learn other things about him, things which make him appear unimpressive. Brutus thinks that he is no more than a tool of Caesar, and will be totally worthless without him. Cassius calls him "a masker and a reveller" later on the plains of Philippi, but by then the words carry no meaning, and we can safely repeat what Antony utters in reply, "Old Cassius still!" Cassius is obviously jealous. He is "a shrewd contriver", but so is Cassius, and on available evidence Antony has got the better of him.

Antony openly shows loyalty for Caesar after his murder

Antony flees to the safety of his house as soon as Caesar is murdered. He later sends a servant to the assassins with a tactful message and a request for an interview. His plan is simple. He wants to set in motion his desire to seek revenge for Caesar's murder, but not before he has won over Brutus. His message does not hide his love for Caesar. He knows Brutus would respect such loyalty. His message also assures loyalty to the assassins if he is provided a satisfactory reason why Caesar deserved to die. He knows Brutus would show magnanimity if his supplication is worthwhile. Brutus is completely won over, to the extent that he even overrules Cassius' misgivings.

Antony tells the conspirators that he is ready to die

Antony arrives, and significantly sets his eyes on Caesar's body first, and on the assassins later. He tells the conspirators that he is ready to die. Brutus tells him that they love and respect him. Cassius is forced to offer him an equal share with the conspirators when new honours are distributed.

He requests the conspirators permission to praise Caesar publicly

From now on Antony is in total command. He feels his way with the conspirators exactly as he does later with the crowd. He praises Caesar and he praises the conspirators. One moment he shakes hands with the murderers and the next he turns aside to weep over Caesar's body. His request to be permitted to mourn Caesar in a public speech, "as becomes a friend", seems as guileless as his production of, and refusal to, read the will.

He makes a prophecy about Caesar's spirit seeking revenge

When he is left alone, Antony's pent up fury breaks out into a hideous prophecy, though the outcome of the issue is still uncertain. "A curse shall light upon the limbs of men" as "fierce civil strife" shall destroy all of Rome. And "Caesar's spirit , ranging for revenge" shall "let slip the dogs of war"

He is a picture of changing emotions

He is at his very best in the next scene as he rings in changes of humility, accusation, reminiscence, indignation, pathos, defiance, modesty, rebuke, until he reaches the climax : "Here was Caesar! When come another".

He uses every trick in oratory to incense the crowd

Antony uses every trick known in oratory to incense the crowd. When he knows that the crowd is on his side he uses his final weapon –undiluted greed–as he reads Caesar's will, but not before he has brought the crowd to a boil regarding the will. The crowd is converted into a hideous mob. Antony reveals the cunning which underlies his entire performance :

Now let it work. Mischief, thou art afoot,

Take thou what course thou wilt !   [III. iii. 265-266]

The mob's fury and violent lust for revenge fills him with fierce joy when he visualises the coming destruction :

Fortune is merry,

And in this mood will give us any thing.   [III. iii. 271-272]

Opinions of critics

There are critics who find Antony unstable and unscrupulous. Callum thinks he is a man of feeling and genius, but not of principle. He is resourceful, and daring, ambitious of honour and power, but unscrupulous in his methods and a voluptuary in life. There may be some truth in all this, but there is much to recommend Antony as well. He is loyal and intelligent, and above all, he does not murder people unthinkingly and in a cowardly manner.

In defence against criticism that he is hard-hearted

We may accept that his methods lack scruple, but do the men around him have any? What could he have done to punish the conspirators who kill Caesar in a cowardly manner? Cassius had inspired Brutus against Caesar. Antony incites the crowd to avenge Caesar's death. The conspirators kill to advance their own interests. Brutus kills in an intellectual vacuum. Antony may want power, but that is not a bad thing if it is deserved and within acceptable parameters. He refuses Cassius to share power with the conspirators. His prime concern is to avenge Caesar's death. His own interests are secondary. Critics also consider Antony callous and hard-hearted when he barters his nephew's life for that of Lepidus' brother during the proscription. It may easily be argued that some hard decisions had to be taken, and Antony may well be acting in a just and unsentimental manner. It is an ugly task, but it has to be performed if the state is to be cleansed of its bad elements, and if sanity is to be restored. Antony may have appropriated some money from Caesar's will, but he needs it for the battle against the conspirators.

Shakespeare does not consider him evil

It is safe to presume that Shakespeare does not consider Antony as evil. He gives Antony some very likable qualities. He is depicted as a man who can rise to great heights if he applies his mind to it.

5
OCTAVIUS CAESAR

He is Julius Caesar's legal heir

Octavius Caesar is one of the three triumvirs (along with Mark Antony and M. Aemilius Lepidus) after Caesar's death. He was Caesar's legal heir (grandson of his sister). He was a student in Apollonia when the assassination occurred. Receiving news of Caesar's death, he adopted his benefactor's name and hurried back to Rome. He was only twenty years old then.

He plays a small but significant role in the play

Octavius plays a small but significant role in the play. He appears only in the last two acts of the play. Antony calls him "young Octavius" and Cassius regards him as a "peevish schoolboy". Despite the unflattering epithets, he is a true successor of Julius Caesar. He may be young, but he carries himself with dignity and great intelligence.

He has an imperious will

Octavius Caesar is acutely conscious of his heritage and he possesses an indomitable will. He has the kind of character which may be termed brash by his detractors or positively assertive by those who support him. He is calm and serene. He says little when the triumvirs hold a conference; but he is precise in whatever he says. He fully develops in "Antony and Cleopatra", but we get sufficient hint which direction his personality is going. He has an imperious will and he does not hesitate to state his demands. He is aware of being the inheritor of Caesar's name, as well as being one of the triumvirs. He insists on the execution of Lepidus' brother as part of the proscription. He even challenges Antony on the fields of Philippi. "I do not cross you, but I will do so" is his firm but polite answer when Antony asks him why he chooses to challenge hin at a critical time. This shows how firm he can be. It also revelas his ability to become great once he throws off the yoke of Antony and asserts his own will.

He has leadership qualities

It is Octavius who puts an end to the senseless parley among generals on the plains of Philippi. He defies the conspirators and challenges them to fight. This may display brashness of youth, but it also displays leadership and sense of purpose. The hint that a new era is ushered into Rome is unmistakable.

He is restrained in his behaviour

He is restrained in his behaviour. He does not seem to have the purposeless enthusiasm that one associates with youth. He prefers to listen rather than talk. It is not silence born out of inhibitions or lack of confidence. It is an end product of peaceful and potent energy. Every word that Octavius utters is decisive. It is true that he brushes aside suggestions and expects people to obey him, but that is desirable in a person who is designated to head a state. An example of how he asserts himself, even in small matters, is evident when the triumvirs discuss the proscription.

Octavius : Your brother too must die, consent you, Lepidus ?

Lepidus : I do consent, —

Octavius : Prick him down, Antony.   [IV. i. 2-4]

He is a brave man

Octavius Caesar is a brave man, though he does not wear his courage on his sleeve like a few other characters do. He hides his courage behind a calm exterior. This is best evident in his brave declaration against the conspirators :

I draw a sword against the conspirators;

When think you that the sword goes up again?

Never, till Caesar's three and thirty wounds

Be well aveng'd; or till another Caesar

Have added slaughter to the sword of traitors.   [V. i 51-55]

He is portrayed as the future head of Rome

There is no denying the fact that Octavius is a natural leader. He seems to be at utmost ease at the helm of affairs and when he is imposing his will on others. He finds no need to consult Antony on every affair of the state. He even crosses him when he thinks it appropriate. He knows that he is the heir apparent to the great "Julius Caesar" and it is inevitable that his mantle shall fall on his shoulders one day.

6
CASCA

He fulfils a specific purpose in the beginning of the play

Casca's importance is in the beginning of the play. He fulfils an important dramatic purpose. He vanishes once he fulfils his purpose. Plutarch had written that Casca had participated in the Battle of Philippi, where he proved himself to be extremely cruel. Shakespeare ignores this aspect, because depicting cruelty for its own sake does not suit his dramatic purpose.

He is the first to stab Caesar

Casca's characterisation is of special interest to us, mainly because he is evolved entirely out of Shakespeare's mind. He is one of the conspirators who plot against Caesar. He is the first to stab Caesar and that too from behind. Shakespeare depicts him as a bluff, straight forward, somewhat crusty combat veteran, whose account of Caesar's behaviour at the feast of Lupercalia [I.ii] shows impatience with Caesar's pomposity, and with Cicero's learned manner. After Casca leaves, Cassius assures Brutus that though Casca has a "tardy form", he is actually more intelligent and can be relied upon in "any bold or noble enterprise"

He is terrified by the storm

Shakespeare uses him once again to narrate the prodigies that portend Caesar's death. He appears terrified by the terrible occurrences. Casca had been almost cynically self-controlled in the previous scene, but here he seems terrified. He stands out in sharp contrast to Cicero, whose intellect makes him skeptical enough to discard the thought that any supernatural wrath is descending from the heavens.

He is uneducated, rude and unrefined

Casca is uneducated, rude and unrefined. Brutus suggests, "what a blunt fellow is this grown to be". [I. ii 297-298] Cassius, however, thinks that his "rudeness is a sauce to his good wit". [I. ii. 302] It is possible that he pretends to be silly and assumes the garb to honesty in order to achieve his purpose. He is the only truly superstitious character in the play. The terrible storm scares him. He tells Cicero :

Either there is a civil strife in heaven;

Or else the world, too saucy with the gods,

Incenses them to send destruction.   [I. iii. 11-13]

He does not have a mind of his own

Casca does not seem to have a mind or a will of his own. He can be prevailed upon rather easily by Cassius, mainly because he holds him in awe primarily due to his superior intellect. Cassius chooses Casca to strike the blow, simply because he is convinced Casca will obey his orders blindly. It is obvious that he is a coward. He strikes Caesar from the back.

Whilst damned Casca, like a cur, behind

Struck Caesar on the neck.   [V.i. 43 - 44]

His character is inconsistent and without direction

Casca's character is inconsistent and without direction. His sole motive seems to be to flatter those who are above him. He flatters Caesar and obeys his every command, but ridicules him behind his back. He attaches sinister motives to people's actions. He had seen Caesar refuse the crown three times. He first jokes about the crown, because it was nothing more than a coronet, and then suggests that Caesar was merely pretending to refuse it, and to his "thinking, would fain have had it". He thinks that Caesar fainted because the effort of refusing the crown "almost choked" him. Casca twists details because he is convinced those hearing him would not want rationale or proof, mainly because he utters what others wish to hear. All in all, Casca is a terrible example of the kind of mischief that sycophants can create.

7

M. AEMILIUS LEPIDUS

He is part of the Triumvirate

Lepidus joins Antony and Octavius to form the second Triumvirate to rule the Roman empire, following the assassination of Caesar. He was a wealthy Roman general before he joined the Triumvirate.

He is a weak man

Lepidus is depicted, both in history and in the play, as a weak man. Shakespeare gives him no new dimension apart from what Plutarch writes about him, thinking that what he has is enough to suit his purpose. He is really a subordinate of both Octavius and Antony, thought the "dramatis personae" describe him as one of the triumvirs. His weak character stands out like a sore thumb in comparison to the other two.

He is a mere tool who is finally sent into retirement

Lepidus is seen in "Antony and Cleopatra "as well, where he is depicted as a good-natured simpleton who is made to run from one end to the other by Octavius and Antony. Lepidus tries to maintain peace with the other two, but he is no more than a mere tool. He is finally sent to live in retirement when Octavius tires of him.

He appears only in one scene

In "Julius Caesar", he appears only is one scene, when the three triumvirs decide who all must die in the proscription after the conspiracy. Antony sends Lepidus off to fetch Caesar's will so that some of Caesar's legacy can be distributed to the poor. Antony calls him" a slight unmerited man" who is fit only "to be sent on errands". He wonders if it is fitting that the world is to be divided between three rulers, out of which he is one of them. Octavius reminds Antony that Lepidus is a "tried and valiant soldier". Antony says so is his horse. He thinks Lepidus is :

A barren-spirited fellow; one that feeds

On objects, orts and imitations,

Which, out of use and staled by other men,

Begin his fashion; do not talk of him

But as a property.   [IV. i. 36-40]

Antony treets him poorly

Antony thinks Lepidus "shall but bear them as the ass bears gold". Octavius has nothing further to recommend him. He meekly lets Antony "do your will".

8
TITINIUS

A brave and trusted soldier under Cassius

Titinius is an officer under Cassius. He is a brave and trusted soldier, and both Brutus and Cassius repose their faith in him. They know he does not have the qualities of a general, but they consider him intelligent enough to take his opinion regarding the strategies of battle. They trust him so much that he remains by the side of Brutus and Cassius when the two fight at Sardis.

He has immense love for Cassius

He has immense love for Cassius, almost as much as Antony has for Caesar. He loves Cassius so much that nothing is left in the world to attract him. "He lies not like the living, O my heart !" [V. iii. 59], he says when he sees Cassius dead lying infront of him. He thinks that the sun of Rome is set :

O setting sun,

As in thy red rays thou dost sink to night,

So in his red blood Cassius' day is set, —

The sun of Rome is set ! Our day is gone;

Clouds, dews, and dangers come; our deeds are done !

[V. iii. 60-64]

He ends his life with the same sword that killed Cassius

He ends his life with the same sword that killed Cassius, uttering:

Come Cassius' sword, and find Titinius' heart.   [V. iii. 90]

9
LUCILIUS

His loyalty for Brutus is unquestionable

Luclius is Brutus' friend and companion. Cassius too considers him a friend, though his affection for him declines as the play progresses. His loyalty

is so complete that he compromises his life so that Brutus can escape. He is
courageous enough to even challenge Mark Antony :

> I dare assure thee that no enemy
>
> Shall ever take alive the noble Brutus :   [V. iv. 21-22]

Antony orders that he be taken prisoner. He pays him glowing
compliments after he is arrested :

> This is not Brutus, friend; but, I assure you,
> A prize no less in worth; keep this man safe,
> Give him all kindness : I had rather have
> Such men my friends than enemies   [V. iv. 26-29]

Antony honours his sense of loyalty

Antony readily takes him into his service after he wins the battle. He
remained faithful to Antony till his death. Trust and loyalty are his trade
marks. He is a brave soldier and he is large-hearted enough to praise his
enemy. Such men are honoured by every kind of people, because they are in
short supply. It is not surprising that both Brutus and Antony give him so
much respect.

10
CICERO

He is a brave and blunt senator who favours republicanism

Shakespeare depicts Cicero as a dynamic, blunt and a highly respected
orator. He is a senator in Rome. He seems to have a very clear mind and
distinctly wants a republican form of government in Rome. Casca refers
contemptuously to his intellectual superiority; but Shakespeare restores parity
in the line "Those who understood him smiled at one another and shook their
heads" This line suggests that Cicero understands the problem that Rome is
facing due to Caesar's covetous desire to become king. It also suggests that
he could have contributed much to the conspiracy had the conspirators been
foresighted enough to include him in their enterprise. Brutus vetos Cicero's
inclusion because, in his opinion, Cicero is too independent minded to take
orders. This is to Brutus' loss, because his quiet wisdom would have been an
asset to a very complex assassination.

11
PORTIA

She is Brutus' wife

Portia is the wife of Brutus and the daughter of Cato, a well-known
Roman patriot and idealist, who fought with Pompey against Caesar. He was
defeated, and he finally killed himself rather than suffer ignoble captivity.

She is Brutus' softened reflection

Portia is a softened reflection of Brutus, and thus an exceptional companion for him. As he cannot forget that he is "Brutus" so she is filled with the consciousness of being:

A woman that Lord Brutus took to wife;
I grant I am a woman : but withal
A woman well-reputed, — Cato's daughter.   [II. i. 293-295]

She is acutely aware of her pedigree and responsibilities

The feeling that she is "so father'd and so husbanded" makes her acutely aware of her pedigree as well as her responsibilities. This also lends her a certain self-control, despite her inherent compassion. It is, however, less than what she presumes to have. She is truly a woman and her tenderness makes her an endearing wife. This surfaces in her anxiety for Burtus' safety. She loses much of her composure, under what can be considered extremely trying circumstances. She knows her husband has gone to the senate house. She has probably guessed that there is a conspiracy to kill Caesar. She does not try to stop Brutus. She is anxious primarily to learn if he has succeeded or failed. She never questions the morality of the assassination. She only chides herself for being weak :

Ay me, how weak a thing
The heart of woman is !   [II. iv 39-40]

She kills herself

She is unable to endure to strain of seeing the conspiracy reach its very end. The strain proves too great. She "falls distract "and kills herself by swallowing coals.

She creates a lasting impression despite her short appearance on stage

Portia appears only in two scenes in the play. Yet, she manages to figure prominently in our minds. We sincerely hope that the limitations of dramatic art have not deprived us the company of a magnificent woman. With mounting anxiety she observes Brutus' increasing preoccupation with an ominously dangerous and complex enterprise, and the terrible effect it has on him. She bears his altered disposition with praiseworthy understanding. She comes to her husband only after the conspirators have met secretly in their house. She insists to be included in the burden of grief which weighs him down. Brutus tries to evade the issue by saying that he is ill, but Portia refuses to be ignored. She appeals to his love and what she deserves to have as his wife :

No. my Brutus;
You have some sick offence within your mind,
Which by the right and virtue of my place

I ought to know of : and, upon my knees,
I charm you, by my once-commended beauty,
By all your vows of love, and that great vow
Which did incorporate and make us one.
That you unfold to me, yourself, your half,
Why you are heavy, and what men to-night
Have had resort to you, — for here have been
Some six or seven, who did hide their faces;
Even from darkness.   [II. i. 263-278]

She wants to reduce her husband's heavy burden

Portia does not merely want to know what is going on. She wants to
reduce the heavy burden that rests on her husband's heart. As Brutus' wife
and Cato's daughter she considers herself worthy of sharing her husband's
secrets. She reminds him of the time when she had stabbed herself to show
that she could endure pain. This means she has the courage to keep secrets.
Seeing her on her knees, the loving husband cries "O ye gods! / Render me
worthy of this noble wife!" A knocking on the door disturbs the two. Brutus
promises to share his secrets with her.

Her virtues are very endearing

She is not merely an embodiment of loyalty and compassion.
Shakespeare does not depict her only as a unidimensional character. She has
the virtues she inherited from her stoic father. Her anxiety for Brutus' safety
makes her very endearing. She almost gives her husband away and has to
make enormous efforts to control her tongue :

O constancy, be strong upon my side,
Set a huge mountain 'tween my heart and tongue!
I have a man's mind, but a woman's might,
How hard it is for women to keep counsel ! —   [II. iv. 6-9]

She almost gives herself away

Her words convey her anxiety as well as her frailty. She imagines to
hear noises from the senate house, as if it were "a bustling rumour, like a
fray". It is not surprising that Lucius hears nothing. She almost gives herself
away at the arrival of the soothsayer, and hurriedly goes indoors to hide her
fears and to control her anxiety.

She is not a stoic in practice

Shakespeare thus depicts Portia with many qualities, which are often
opposed to one another, but which put together makes her a very likable
woman. She kills herself, thus suggesting that she is not a stoic, despite her
husband and father ardently practicing it. Suicide may have been considered

a very brave thing, but in reality it is a cowardly escape from the pressures of existence.

One of her jobs is to display Brutus the private man

One crucial role of Portia is to show Brutus as a private man, who has a loving wife and a contented marriage. Brutus is delineated both as a public man of affairs and a private man, who is compassionate and loving. Brutus' existence besides Portia provides insight into him as a private man. He cannot put off her questions with simple falsehoods; she knows him too well. Brutus' withdrawal has already begun to disrupt his pleasant home life. After Caesar's assassination both the private and public Brutus will be completely destroyed.

She and Brutus could have had an ideal life

Portia and Brutus convey a perfect picture of what aught to be an ideal relationship between husband and wife. This absolute communion of souls is in sharp contrast to the shallow relationship that exists between Caesar and Calphurnia. Caesar treats Calphurnia as a child, to be humoured or to be left alone as per his wish. Portia demands attention and equal status. It is to her credit that Brutus is so ready to give it to her. We wish Brutus had not made that terrible error of joining the conspiracy. It shows how one error in our public life can ruin the happiness of our private life, and that of our near and dear ones.

12
CALPHURNIA

Shakespeare gives us a very sketchy picture of her

She is Julius Caesar's wife. Whereas Portia seems a reflection of the noblest part of her husband's nature, Calphurnia is contrastingly weaker in status and intelligence. Shakespeare gives us a very sketchy and uninspiring figure in the person of Caesar's wife. Nothing is known of her much. We know she has not borne any child to Caesar. Antony is asked by Caesar to touch her while running the course during the feast of Lupercal, so that she could become fertile. She herself does not utter a word during the entire scene.

She is terrified by the storm and by her dream

We next learn about her in the second scene of the second act, when she displays her terror at the portents of the storm and her dreams, wherein she had seen her husband's murder. It is, however, fair to accept that she is terrified for Caesar than for herself. She is convinced that the prodigies portend the death of some great man. She is further convinced that the man must be her husband :

When beggars die, there are comets seen;
The heavens themselves blaze forth the death of princes.

[II, ii. 30-31]

She is a reflection of Caesar

Calphurma is a reflection of her husband, but in a rather weak and unappetising manner. When Caesar talks about his own unmatched courage, her love for her husband gives her courage too. She tells Caesar that his wisdom is "consum'd in confidence." She has an instinctive urge to protect her husband. She repeatedly pleads to him not to go to the senate house, "Call it my fear that keeps you in house, and not your own", she tells him, and at last Caesar relents in order to indulge her in this "humour". It is a different matter that he changes his mind and goes to the senate house, partly out of greed and partly to avoid ridicule.

Text with
Modern English Rendering

DRAMATIS PERSONAE

JULIUS CAESAR.
OCTAVIUS CAESAR, ⎫
MARCUS ANTONIUS, ⎬ triumvirs after the death of Julius Caesar.
M. AEMILIUS LEPIDUS, ⎭
CICERO, ⎫
PUBLIUS, ⎬ senators.
POPILIUS LENA, ⎭
MARCUS BRUTUS, ⎫
CASSIUS, ⎪
CASCA, ⎪
TREBONIUS, ⎪
LIGARIUS, ⎬ conspirators against Julius Caesar.
DECIUS BRUTUS, ⎪
METELLUS CIMBER, ⎪
CINNA, ⎭
FLAVIUS and MARULLUS, tribunes.
ARTEMIDORUS of Cnidos, teacher of rhetoric.
A Soothsayer.
CINNA, a poet.
Another Poet.
LUCILIUS, ⎫
TITINIUS, ⎪
MESSALA, ⎬ friends to Brutus and Cassius.
Young CATO, ⎪
VOLUMNIUS, ⎭
VARRO, ⎫
CLITUS, ⎪
CLAUDIUS, ⎪
STRATO, ⎬ servants to Brutus.
LUCIUS, ⎪
DARDANIUS, ⎭
PINDARUS, servant to Cassius.
CALPURNIA, wife to Caesar.
PORTIA, wife to Brutus.
Senators, Citizens, Guards, Attendants, &c.

SCENE

*During a great part of the play of Rome; afterwards
near Sardis, and near Philippi.*

JULIUS CAESAR

ACT I

Scene I. *Rome. A street*

Enter Flavius, Marullus, *and certain Citizens*

Flav. Hence ! home, you idle creatures, get you home.
Is this a holiday? What ! know you not,
Being mechanical,[1] you ought not walk
Upon a labouring day without the sign[2]
Of your profession? Speak, what trade art thou? 5

First Citizen. Why, sir, a carpenter.

Marullus. Where is thy leather apron and thy rule?[3]
What dost thou with thy best apparel on?
You, sir, what trade are you?

Second Citizen. Truly, sir, in respect of a fine workman, I am
but, as you would say, a cobbler. 10

Marullus. But what trade art thou? answer me directly.

Second Citizen. A trade, sir, that I hope I may use with a safe
conscience; which is, indeed, sir, a mender of bad soles. 15

Marullus. What trade, thou knave? thou naughty knave,
what trade?

Second Citizen. Nay, I beseech you, sir, be not out[4] with me:
yet, if you be out,[5] sir, I can mend you.

Marullus. What meanest thou by that? mend me, thou
saucy fellow ! 20

Second Citizen. Why, sir, cobble you.

Flavius. Thou art a cobbler, art thou?

Second Citizen. Truly, sir, all that I live by is with the awl: I
meddle with no tradesman's matters, nor women's matters; but 25
withal[6] I am, indeed, sir, a surgeon to old shoes; when they are in
great danger, I re-cover[7] them. As proper men as ever trod upon
neat's[8] leather have gone upon my handiwork. 30

Flavius. But wherefore art not in the shop today?
Why dost thou lead these men about the streets?

Second Citizen. Truly, sir, to wear out their shoes, to get

---

1. *Mechanical*: mechanics or artisans. 2. *The sign*: The badges of your trade.
3. *Rule*: ruler. 4.*Out with me*: annoyed with me. 5. *If you be out*: if your shoes are
worn out. 6. *Withal* : pun on "with the awl" . 7. *Recover*: repair. 8. *Neat's*: cow's.

JULIUS CAESAR

ACT I

Scene I. *Rome. A street.*

Enter Flavius, Marullus, *and several Citizens*

Flavius. Go off ! Go home, you idle creatures, go home. Is there a public holiday? What, do you, who are artisans, not know that on a working day you are not allowed to walk about without wearing the badges of your trade? You there, what trade do you belong to ?

First Cit. Well, sir, I am a carpenter.

Marullus. Then where is your leather apron and your footrule? Why are you wearing your best clothes? You there, what is your trade?

Second Cit. Well sir, as far as I may be considered a fine workman, I am but, as you might say, a shoemaker (a repairer of shoes).

Marullus. What is your trade? Answer me directly.

Second Cit. A trade which a man may use with a clear conscience, for I am a mender of soles (soles of shoes: souls).

Marullus. What is your trade, you bad fellow? Your trade?

Second Cit. Now I beg of you, sir, do not lose your temper with me. Yet if you are out of temper (if your shoes are worn out) I can mend you.

Marullus. What do you mean by "mend me" you insolent fellow?

Second Cit. Why, sir, repair your shoes.

Marullus. So you are a cobbler of shoes?

Second Cit. Indeed, sir, all that I live by is my shoemaker's awl. I do not interfere with the affairs of other tradesmen, or those of women, but still (with my awl) I am indeed, sir, a repairer of old shoes. When they are in danger, I resole them. As good men as ever wore shoes have gone about in my work.

Flavius. But why are you not in your shop to-day? Why are you leading those men about in the streets?

Second Cit. Indeed, sir, it is to wear their shoes out so that I shall get

myself into more work. But indeed, sir, we make holiday,
to see Caesar and to rejoice in his triumph.   35

    Marullus.   Wherefore rejoice? What conquest brings he home?
What tributaries[1] follow him to Rome,
To grace in captive bonds his chariot-wheels?
You blocks, you stones, you worse than senseless things!   40
O you hard hearts, you cruel men of Rome,
Knew you not Pompey? Many a time and oft.
Have you climb'd up to walls and battlements,
To towers and windows, yea, to chimney-tops,
Your infants in your arms, and there have sat   45
The livelong day, with patient expectation,
To see great Pompey pass the streets of Rome :
And when you saw his chariot but appear,
Have you not made an universal shout,
That Tiber trembled underneath her banks,   50
To hear the replication[2] of your sounds
Made in her concave[3] shores?
And do you now put on your best attire?
And do you now cull out[4] a holiday?
And do you now strew flowers in his way
That comes in triumph over Pompey's blood?   55
Be gone !
Run to your houses, fall upon your knees,
Pray to the gods to intermit[5] the plague
That needs must light on this ingratitude.   60

    Flavius.   Go, go, good countrymen, and, for this fault,
Assemble all the poor men of your sort;[6]
Draw them to Tiber banks, and weep your tears
Into the channel, till the lowest stream
Do kiss the most exalted shores of all.   [*Exeunt Citizens*   65
See, whether their basest metal be not mov'd !
They vanish tongue-tied in their guiltiness.
Go you down that way towards the Capitol;
This way will I: disrobe[7] the images,
If you do find them deck'd with ceremonies.   70

    Marullus.   May we do so?
You know it is the feast of Lupercal,

    Flavius.   It is no matter; let no images

  ‑1. *Tributaries:* payers of tribute. 2. *Replication:* repetition; echo. 3. *Concave:* hollow. 4. *Cull out:* select 5. *Intermit:* stop; prevent. 6. *Sort:* class. 7. *Disrobe:* remove the decorations.

more work. We are holding a holiday in order to see Caesar and to rejoice at his triumph.

Marullus. Why should you rejoice? What gains has he brought home? What people compelled to pay tribute have followed him back to Rome, to decorate with their presence the wheels of his chariot in his triumphal return? You are stupid as blocks of wood or stones, and worse than senseless ! You are hard-hearted, you cruel men of Rome. Do you not remember Pompey? Many times and often have you climbed up walls and battlements, towers and windows, even to the tops of chimneys, with your babies in your arms, and have sat there all day patiently expecting to see great Pompey pass along the streets of Rome. When you saw his chariot appear, did you not raise such a general shout that even the river Tiber trembled within her banks to hear the repeated echoes of the sound in her hollow shores? Now you put on your best clothing and choose this day for a holiday, and you scatter flowers in the way of the man who comes in triumph after shedding Pompey's blood, Go, run to your houses and fall upon your knees; pray to the gods to halt the plague that is sure to fall upon men for such ingratitude.

Flavius. Go, my good fellow-citizens, and, because of this fault you have committed, assemble all poor men of your class and take them to the banks of the Tiber, letting your tears fall into the river till the lowest stream rises to the top of the bank. See how their base natures are moved ! They go off, silent in their sense of guilt. You go that way towards the Capitol. If you find the images with ceremonial robes, take them off.

Marullus. Is it proper for us to do so? You know it is the Festival of the Lupercal.

Flavius. It does not matter; do not allow any images to be dressed

Be hung[1] with Caesar's trophies. I'll about,
And drive away the vulgar from the streets: 75
So do you too, where you perceive them thick.
These growing feathers pluck'd from Caesar's wing
Will make him fly an ordinary pitch[2];
Who else would soar above the view of men,
And keep us all in servile fearfulness. [*Exeunt* 80

SCENE II. *A public place*

Enter, in procession, with music, Caesar; Antony, *for the course;* Calpurnia, Portia, Decius, Cicero, Brutus, Cassius *and* Casca; *a great crowd following, among them a* Soothsayer

Caesar, Calpurnia !

Casca.   Peace, ho ! Caesar speaks.

                        [*Music ceases*

Caesar.   Calpurnia !

Calpurnia. Here, my lord.

Caesar. Stand you directly in Antonius' way,
When he doth run his course[3]. — Antonius!

Antony. Caesar, my lord? 5

Caesar. Forget not, in your speed, Antonius,
To touch Calpurnia; for our elders[4] say
The barren[5] touched in this holy chase,
Shake off their sterile curse[6].

Antony.   I shall remember:
When Caesar says "Do this," it is perform'd. 10

Caesar. Set on; and leave no ceremony out. [*Music*

Soothsayer. Caesar!

Caesar. Ha! who calls?

Casca. Bid every noise be still: — peace yet again!

                        [*Music ceases*

Caesar. Who is it in the press[7] that calls on me? 15
I hear a tongue, shriller than all the music,
Cry "Caesar." Speak; Caesar is turn'd to hear.

Soothsayer. Beware the ides of March.

Caesar.   What man is that?

---

1. *Hung*: decorated. 2. *Pitch*: range; flight. 3. *Course*: act of running. 4. *Elders*: wise men. 5. *The barren*: women not bearing children. 6. *Sterile curse*: the curse of not bearing children. 7. *Press*: crowd; mob.

with triumphal decorations for Caesar. I'll go around and drive away the common people from the streets. You do the same, wherever you see them thickly assembled. If you pluck these, it will be like plucking the growing feathers from the wing of a young hawk, making him content to fly an ordinary flight, when otherwise he might fly right above men's heads and keep us all in a state of timorous servility.

SCENE II.   *A public place*

Enter in a procession with music, Caesar; Antony *for the course that is run by those celebrating the Lupercal;* Calpurnia, Portia, Decius, Cicero, Brutus, Cassius *and* Casca: *a great crowd following, among them a* Soothsayer.

Caesar. Calpurnia !

Casca.   Be silent, all ! Caesar is speaking.

(The Music stops.)

Caesar. Calpurnia !

Calpurnia.   I am here, my lord.

Caesar.   Stand right in the way of Antony when he is running his course.—Antony !

Antony. Yes, my lord Caesar.

Caesar. Do not forget, when you are running swiftly, Antony, to touch Calpurnia, for our elders say that barren women, if touched by one who runs this holy course, have their curse of barrenness removed.

(Music)

Antony. I shall remember. When Caesar gives an order, it is as good as done.

Caesar. Then, begin, and do not omit any ceremony.

Soothsayer. Caesar !

Caesar. Who is calling me?

Casca. Order all noise to stop: silence again. *(The music stops.)*

Caesar. Who is it in the crows that calls on me? I hear a voice, louder than all the music, cry "Caesar!" Speak, for Caesar is listening.

Soothsayer. Beware of the 15th of March.

Caesar.   Who is that man?

Brutus. A soothsayer bids you beware the ides of March,

Caesar. Set him before me; let me see his face. 20

Cass. Fellow, come from the throng; look upon Caesar.

Caesar. What say'st thou to me now? speak once again.

Soothsayer. Beware the ides of March.

Caesar. He is a dreamer; let us leave him:—pass.

[*Sennet. Exeunt all except Brutus and Cassius*

Cassius. Will you go see the order of the course? 25

Brutus. Not I.

Cassius. I pray you, do.

Brutus. I am not gamesome[1]. I do lack some part

Of that quick[2] spirit that is in Antony.

Let me not hinder, Cassius, your desires; 30

I'll leave you.

Cassius. Brutus, I do observe you now of late:

I have not from your eyes that gentleness

And show of love as I was wont[3] to have:

You bear too stubborn and too strange a hand[4] 35

Over your friend that loves you.

Brutus. Cassius,

Be not deceiv'd: if I have veil'd my look[5],

I turn the trouble of my countenance

Merely upon myself. Vexed I am

Of late with passions of some difference, 40

Conceptions only proper to myself,

Which give some soil, perhaps, to my behaviours;

But let not therefore my good friends be griev'd,—

Among which number, Cassius, be you one,—

Nor construe any further my neglect, 45

Than that poor Brutus, with himself at war,

Forgets the shows of love to other men.

Cassius. Then, Brutus, I have much mistook your passion;

By means whereof this breast of mine hath buried

Thouhts of great value, worthy cogitations[6]. 50

Tell me, good Brutus, can you see your face?

---

1. *Gamesome*: in a mood for play. 2. *Quick*: lively. 3. *Wont*: accustomed. 4. *A hand*: a bearing; manner. 5. *Veil'd my look*: shown nothing by my expression. 6. *Cogitations*: deep thought.

Brutus. It is a soothsayer who tells you to beware of the 15th of March.

Caesar. Bring him before me. Let me see his face.

Cassius. Man, come out of the crowd and appear before Caesar.

Caesar. Now what have you to say to me, Speak once more.

Soothsayer. Beware of the 15th of March.

Caesar. He is a dreamer. Let us not trouble with him. Pass on.

(*Sound of Trumpets. All go out except* Brutus *and* Cassius.)

Cassius. Will you go and see the arrangements for the devotees running the course?

Brutus. No I shall not.

Cassius. Do go, I beg of you.

Brutus. I am not in the mood for games. I require a share of the brisk spirit which Antony has. But do not let me stand in the way of your inclinations, Cassius. I'll leave you.

Cassius. Brutus, I have been observing you lately. I have not received from you the gentle looks of friendship and love that I have been accustomed to. You are too stiff and strange in your treatment of the friend who loves you.

Brutus. Cassius, do not make a mistake. If I have made my looks expressionless, it is merely because I have turned the trouble inward on myself. I have been troubled lately with conflicting emotions, moods which are purely personal to myself, and which may have given some grounds for my behaviors. But do not let my good friends be troubled — and, among them I look on you, Cassius, as one. Do not let them think otherwise of my neglect of them but that Brutus, having trouble within himself, forgets to pay his customary respects to others.

Cassius. Then, Brutus, I have greatly misunderstood your mood. Because of this, I have kept concealed in my breast very important thou-ghts and weighty deliberations. Tell me, Brutus, can you see your own face?

Brutus. No Cassius; for the eye sees not itself
But by reflection, by some other things.

    Cassius. 'Tis just :
And it is very much lamented, Brutus,   55
That you have no such mirrors as will turn
Your hidden worthiness into your eye,
That you might see your shadow. I have heard,
Where many of the best respect in Rome,—
Except immortal Caesar,—speaking of Brutus,   60
And groaning underneath this age's yoke[1],
Have wish'd that noble Brutus had his eyes.

    Brutus. Into what dangers would you lead me, Cassius,
That you would have me seek into myself
For that which is not in me?   65

    Cassius. Therefore, good Brutus, be prepar'd to hear :
And, since you know you cannot see myself
So well as by reflection. I, your glass,
Will modestly discover[2] to yourself
That of yourself which you yet know not of.   70
And be not jealous on me, gentle Brutus :
Were I a common laugher, or did use
To stale[3] with ordinary oaths my love
To every new protester[4], if you know
That I do fawn on men, and hug them hard,   75
And after scandal them; or if you know
That I profess myself in banqueting
To all the rout[5], then hold me dangerous.

                            [*Flourish and shout*

    Brutus. What means this shouting? I do fear, the people
Choose Caesar for their king.

    Cassius.   Ay, do you fear it?   80
Then must I think you would not have it so.

    Brutus. I would not, Cassius; yet I love him well—
But wherefore do you hold me here so long?
What is it that you would impart to me?
If it be aught toward the general good,   85
Set honour in one eye, and death i' the other,
And I will look on both indifferently;
For let the gods so speed me as I love
The name of honour more than I fear death.

--1. *The age's yoke*: the tyranny of our times. 2. *Discover*: reveal; make visible.
3. *Stale*: spoil; make dirty. 4. *Protester*: pretended friend. 5. *The rout*: the common
crowd.

Brutus. No, Cassius, just as the eye cannot see itself directly, but   ly reflected in some other object.

Cassius. That is correct. And it is greatly to be regretted that you have no mirrors to show your hidden merit to your own eye, that you may see the reflection of yourself. I have heard many of the most worthy people of Rome—except immortal Caesar—speaking of Brutus and complaining of the restrictions of the present time, say that they wished that the noble Brutus could but use his eyes.

Brutus. What dangerous thing do you want to suggest to me, Cassius, that you would have me think there are qualities in me which I do not really possess?

Cassius. Well, my good Brutus, be prepared to hear; and, since you know you cannot see yourself so well as you can by reflection (in a mirror), I shall be the mirror which will modestly reveal you to yourself and show you that of which you are not aware. Do not be suspicious of me, gentle Brutus. If I were a common trifler and were accustomed to spoil my love swearing vows with every new protester of friendship, if I were in the habit of fawning on great men, embracing them, and afterwards speaking ill of them, or if you knew me to be in the habit of professing my views to all the crowd at a banquet, then you might judge me to be dangerous.

                                                  (*Trumpets sound, shouting*)

Brutus. What is the meaning of this shouting? I am afraid the people are choosing Caesar for their king.

                                                  (*Trumpets: shouting*)

Cassius. You say you fear it? Then I must think that you are not in favour of such a thing?

Brutus. I am not, Cassius, although I love him well. But why do you detain me here so long, and what is it that you want to say to me? If it be anything in the public interest, then if it is a choice between death and honour, you will find that I will make the choice calmly. For I swear, as I wish the gods to help me, that my love for honour is greater than my fear of death.

Cassius.   I know that virtue to be in you, Brutus,   90
As well as I do know your outward favour[1].
Well, honour is the subject of my story.—
I cannot tell what you and other men
Think of this life; but, for my single self,
I had as lief[2] not be as live to be   95
In awe of such a thing as I myself.
I was born free as Caesar; so were you :
We both have fed as well; and we can both
Endure the winter's cold as well as he :
For once, upon a raw and gusty[3] day,   100
The troubled Tiber chafing[4] with her shores,
Caesar said to me, "Dar'st thou, Cassius, now
Leap in with me into this angry flood,
And swim to yonder point? Upon the word,
Accoutred[5] as I was, plunged in,   105
And bade him follow: so, indeed, he did.
The torrent roar'd, and we did buffet it
With lusty sinews, throwing it aside
And stemming it with hearts of controversy[6] :
But ere we could arrive the point propos'd,   110
Caesar cried, "Help me, Cassius, or I sink!"
I, as Aeneas, our great ancestor,
Did from the flames of Troy upon his shoulder
The old Anchises bear, so from the waves of Tiber
Did I the tired Caesar. And this man   115
Is now become a god; and Cassius is
A wretched creature, and must bend his body,
If Caesar carelessly but nod on him.
He had a fever when he was in Spain,
And, when the fit was on him, I did mark   120
How he did shake: 'tis true, this god did shake :
His coward lips did from their colour fly :
And that same eye, whose bend[7] doth awe the world,
Did lose his lustre : I did hear him groan :
Ay, and that tongue of his, that bade the Romans   125
Mark him, and write his speeches in their books,
Alas, it cried, "Give me some drink, Titinius."
As a sick girl. Ye gods, it doth amaze me
A man of such a feeble temper should
So get the start of the majestic world,   130

---

1. *Favour*: face. 2. *Had as lief*: would rather; would prefer. 3. *Gusty*: windy.
4. *Chafing*: dashing against. 5. *Accoutred*: fully dressed. 6. *Hearts of controversy*:
bold hearts. 7. *Bend*: glance.

Cassius. I know that you have that virtue, Brutus, as well as I know your face. Well, honour is the subject I wish to speak about. I cannot tell what you and other men think of this life, but, for my part, I would as soon not live at all as live to be in awe of one who is just a man like myself. I was born as free as Caesar, and so were you. We have fed as well, and we can both endure the winter's cold as well as he can. For once, on a cold and windy day, when the river Tiber was dashing against her banks, Caesar said to me, "Do you dare, Cassius, now to leap into this angry flood with me and swim to the point over there?" On these words, dressed just as I was, I jumped in and told him to follow me. Indeed he did so. The floor roared, and we beat it with out our strong muscles, throwing it aside and opposing it with resolute hearts. But before we could gain the point we had agreed upon, Caesar cried, "Help me, Cassius, or I shall sink!" Just as Aeneas, our great ancestor, carried his old father, Anchises, from the burning town of Troy upon his shoulders, so did I carry the tired Caesar from the waves of the Tiber. And this man is now as great as a God, and Cassius is a wretched creature who must humbly bow if Caesar only gives him a careless nod! He had a fever when he was in Spain, and when the ague-fit was on him, I noticed how this god did tremble. His cowardly lips lost their colour and that very eye, a look from which can frighten all the world, did lose its brightness and I heard him groan. That voice of his, which told the Romans to mark him and write down his speeches,—then it cried "Give me a drink, Titinius," just as if he had been a sick girl! Oh gods, it amazes me that a man of such a feeble nature should rise above all others in

And bear the palm[1] alone.   [*Flourish and shout*

    Brutus. Another general shout!
I do believe that these applauses are
For some new honours that are heap'd on Caesar.

    Cassius. Why, man, he doth bestride[2] the narrow world   135
Like a Colossus[3], and we petty men
Walk under his huge legs, and peep about
To find ourselves dishonourable graves.
Men at some time are masters of their fates :
The fault, dear Brutus, is not in our stars,   140
But in ourselves, that we are underlings[4].
'Brutus' and 'Caesar': what should be in that 'Caesar'?
Why should that name be sounded more than yours?
Write them together, yours is as fair a name ;
Sound them, it doth become the mouth as well ;   145
Weigh them, it is as heavy; conjure[5] with 'em,
'Brutus' will start a spirit as soon as 'Caesar.'
Now, in the names of all the gods at once,
Upon what meat doth this our Caesar feed,
That he is grown so great? Age, thou art sham'd!   150
Rome, thou hast lost the breed of noble bloods!
When went there by an age, since the great flood,
But it was fam'd with more than with one man?
When could they say, till now, that talk'd of Rome,
That her wide walls encompass'd[6] but one man?   155
Now is it Rome indeed, and room enough,
When there is in it but one only man.
O, you and I have heard our fathers say,
There was a Brutus once that would have brook'd[7]
The eternal devil to keep his state in Rome
As easily as a king.   160

    Brutus. That you do love me, I am nothing jealous[8];
What you would work me to, I have some aim[9] :
How I have thought of this, and of these times,
I shall recount hereafter; for this present,   165
I would not, so with love I might entreat you,
Be any further mov'd. What you have said,

---

    1. *Palm*: the prize of victory. 2. *Bestride*: stand with one foot on either side. 3. *Colossus*: a gigantic statue. 4. *Underlings*: subordinates. 5.*Conjure*: use as a charm or mantra. 6. *Encompass'd*: contained. 7. *Brook'd*: endured. 8. *Nothing jealous*: in no way doubtful. 9. *Aim*: idea.

this great world and bear off the victory's prize alone.

(Trumpets: more shouting)

Brutus.   Another general shout from the people ! I believe that this applause is for some new honour conferred upon Caesar.

Cassius.   Why, man, he stands over our narrow world as the Colossus statue (at Rhodes) bestrides the harbour. We miserable men walk far below him, and can look for nothing but a dishonorable death.   Men at some time in their lives have the direction of their own destinies. The fault, dear Brutus, is not in the stars but in ourselves, if we consent to be subordinates. Pronounce "Brutus" and "Caesar"; what special virtue is in "Caesar"? Why should that name be sounded more loudly than yours? Write them down together and yours is just as good a name. Pronounce them; yours sounds just as well in the mouth. Weight them; yours is just as heavy. Use them as charms, and Brutus has as much chance of calling up a spirit as Caesar. Now, by all the gods, what food has nourished this Caesar that he is grown so great? It is a shame to our age Rome has lost the race of noble souls she once produced. When was there ever an age, since the flood of Adam, that was not made famous by more than a single man? What would they say, who used to speak of Rome, if they could see her now made famous by a single man? Now, (to pun) we may say it is Rome where there is room for only one man! O, you and I have heard our fathers say that there was a Brutus once who would no more have endured seeing the immortal devil ruling in state in Rome than he would a king.

Brutus.   I have no doubt about your love for me, and I have some idea of what you are leading me up to. What I think of this, and of the present situation, I shall tell you afterwards. In the meantime, I do not wish, to be persuaded any further; and I ask you of your love to fall in with me in this;

I will consider; what you have to say,
I will with patience hear; and find a time
Both meet[1] to hear and answer such high things.   170
Till then, my noble friend, chew[2] upon this :
Brutus had rather be a villager
Than to repute himself[3] a son of Rome
Under these hard conditions as this time
Is like to lay upon us.   175

    Cassius.   I am glad
That my weak words have struck but thus much show
Of fire from Brutus.

    Brutus. The games are done, and Caesar is returning.

    Cassius.   As they pass by, pluck Casca by the sleeve;
and he will, after his sour fashion, tell you   180
What hath proceeded worthy note to-day.

      Re-enter CAESAR *and his Train*

    Brutus. I will do so. But look you, Cassius,
The angry spot doth glow on Caesar's brow,
And all the rest look a chidden train[4].
Calpurnia's cheek is pale; and Cicero   185
Looks with such ferret[5] and such fiery eyes
As we have seen him in the Capitol,
Being cross'd[6] in conference by some senators.

    Cassius. Casca will tell us what the matter is.

    Caesar. Antonius!   190

    Antony. Caesar?

    Caesar. Let me have men about me that are fat;
Sleek-headed men, and such as sleep o' nights :
Yond Cassius has a lean and hungry look;
He thinks too much: such men are dangerous.   195

    Antony. Fear him not, Caesar; he's not dangerous;
He is a noble Roman, and well given[7].

    Caesar. Would he were fatter!—but I fear him not :
Yet if my name were liable to fear,
I do not know the man I should avoid   200

---

1. *Meet*: suitable; convenient. 2. *Chew:* reflect; ponder over. 3. *Repute himself:* claim the honour of being. 4. *Chidden train*: group that has been scolded. 5. *Ferret*: an animal of the mongoose family. 6. *Cross'd in conference*: contra-dicted during a debate. 7. *Given*: disposed to us.

I shall consider what you have said, and I shall consider patiently what further you have to say, and I shall find a suitable time to hear and to reply to such important things. Till that time, my noble friend, ponder over this, that Brutus would rather be a villager than call himself a citizen of Rome under such conditions as we endure at present.

Cassius. I am glad that my feeble words have been sufficient to strike such a spark of the fire from Brutus.

Brutus. The games are over, and Caesar is returning.

Cassius. As they pass by, pull Casca by the sleeve and he will, in his sour manner, tell you of anything worthy of note that has happened to-day.

Re-enter Caesar and *his followers.*

Brutus. I shall do so. But see, Cassius! There is still a red flush of anger on Caesar's face. All the rest look like a following that has been scolded. Calpurnia's face is pale, and Cicero looks with the red eyes of a mongoose, as we have seen him in the Capitol when opposed in debate by some senators.

Cassius. Casca will tell us what it is all about.

Caesar. Antonius !

Antony. Caesar?

Caesar. I should like to be surrounded by men who are fat, men with smoothly-brushed hair, of the type that sleep soundly at nights. Cassius there looks a lean and hungry fellow. He thinks too much, and men of his kind are dangerous.

Antony. Do not fear him, Caesar. He is not dangerous. He is a noble Roman and well-disposed towards you.

Caesar. I wish he were fatter—but I do not fear him. Yet if it was in my nature to fear. I do not know any man I should want to avoid more than

So soon as that spare[1] Cassius. He reads much;
He is a great observer, and he looks
Quite through the deeds of men; he loves no plays,
As thou dost, Antony; he hears no music:
Seldom he smiles, and smiles in such a sort[2]   205
As if he mock'd himself[3], and scorn'd his spirit
That could be mov'd to smile at any thing.
Such men as he be never at heart's ease[4]
Whiles they behold a greater than themselves;   210
And therefore are they very dangerous.
I rather tell thee what is to be fear'd
Than what I fear; for always I am Caesar.
Come on my right hand, for this ear is deaf,
And tell me truly what thou think'st of him.
[*Sennet. Exeunt* Caesar *and all his Train, except* Casca

    Casca. You pull'd me by the cloak; would you speak
with me?   215
    Brutus. Ay, Casca; tell us what hath chanc'd to-day,
That Caesar looks so sad.
    Casca. Why, you were with him, were you not?
    Brutus. I should not, then, ask Casca what had chanc'd.
    Casca. Why, there was a crown offered him; and being   220
offered him, he put it by[5] with the back of his hand, thus; and then
the people fell a-shouting.
    Brutus. What was the second noise for?
    Casca. Why, for that too.   225
    Cassius. They shouted thrice: what was the last cry for?
    Casca. Why, for that too.
    Brutus. Was the crown offered him thrice?
    Casca. Ay, marry[6] was't, and he put it by thrice,   230
every time gentler than other; and at every putting-by mine
honest neighbours shouted.
    Cassius. Who offered him the crown?
    Casca. Why, Antony?
    Brutus. Tell us the manner of it, gentle Casca.
    Casca. I can as well be hanged as tell the manner of it :   235
it was mere foolery; I did not mark it. I saw Mark Antony offer
him a crown;—yet 'twas not a crown neither, 'twas one of these
coronets;—and, as I told you, he put it by once : but,

---

    1. *Spare*: lean; thin. 2. *Sort*: manner. 3. *Mock'd himself* : thought it unworthy
to smile. 4. *At heart's ease* : with a calm mind. 5. *Put it by*: pushed it from him.
6. *Marry*: by Mary; by the blessed Virgin.

that lean Cassius. He reads much, is a very observant fellow, and can read the characters of men that lie behind their acts. He does not love play-acting, as you do, Antony, and does not listen to music. He smiles seldom, and when he does, so in such a manner that you would think he mocked his own smile and scorned the spirit that could be induced to smile at anything. Such men as he are never quiet at heart when they see one greater than themselves, and so they are very dangerous. I am telling you the points about him that should be feared, but I do not say that I fear them, for I am always Caesar, the fearless. Come to my right side, for this left ear is deaf, and tell me truly what you think of him.

(Trumpet sounds: Caesar *and all followers depart, except* Casca.)

Casca.   You pulled my cloak: do you want to speak to me?

Brutus.   Yes, Casca. Tell us what has happened to-day that has made Caesar look so sad.

Casca.   You were there with him, were you not?

Brutus.   If I had been, Casca, I should not now be asking you what had happened.

Casca.   Well, there was a crown offered to him, and, when it was offered, he pushed it away with the back of his hand, like this, and all the people began to shout.

Brutus.   What was the reason for the second shout?

Casca.   It was for the same thing.

Cassius.   They shouted three times. What was the reason for the third cry?

Brutus.   Was the crown offered to him three times?

Casca.   Yes, indeed it was, and he pushed it away three times, every time more gently than before, and each time that he pushed it away the crowd shouted.

Cassius.   Who offered him the crown?

Casca.   It was Mark Antony.

Brutus.   Tell us how it happened, good Casca.

Casca.   It is as difficult to describe it as to be hanged. It was pure foolery and I hardly noticed it. I saw Mark Antony offer him a crown — yet it was hardly a crown, but rather one of those garlands, and, as I told you,

for all that, to my thinking[1], he would fain[2] have had it.   240
Then he offered it to him again; then he put it by again: but,
to my thinking, he was very loth[3] to lay his fingers off it. And
then he offered it the third time; he put it the third time by :
and still as he refused it, the rabblement[4] shouted, and   245
clapped their chapped[5] hands, and threw up their sweaty
nightcaps, and uttered such a deal of stinking breath because
Caesar refused the crown, that it had almost chocked Caesar;
for he swooned, and fell down at it : and for mine own part,   250
I durst not laugh, for fear of opening my lips and receiving
the bad air.

   Cassius.   But, soft, I pray you : what , did Caesar swoon?

   Casca.   He fell down in the market-place, and foamed at
mouth, and was speechless.   255

   Brutus.   'Tis very like; he hath the falling sickness.

   Cassius.   No, Caesar hath it not : but you, and I,
And honest Casca, we have the falling sickness.

   Casca. I know not what you mean by that; but, I am sure,   260
Caesar fell down. If the tag-rag[6] people did not clap him and hiss him,
according as he pleased and displeased them, as they use to do the
players in the theatre, I am no true man.

   Brutus. What said he when he came into himself?

   Casca. Marry, before he fell down, when he perceived the
common herd[7] was glad he refused the crown, he plucked me ope
his doublet, and offered them his throat to cut:—an I had been a
man of any occupation, if I would not have taken him at a word.
I would I might go to hell among the rogues:—and so he fell.
When he came to himself again, he said,   if he had done   270
or said any thing amiss, he desired their worships to think
it was his infirmity[8]. Three or four wenches[9], where I stood,
cried, 'Alas, good soul!" and forgave him with all their   275
hearts: but there's no heed to be taken of them; if Caesar
had stabbed their mothers, they would have done no less.

   Brutus. And after that, he came, thus sad, away?

   Casca. Ay.

   Cassius.   Did Cicero say any thing?   280

   Casca. Ay, he spoke Greek.

   Cassius.   To what effect?

---

   1. *To my thinking*: in my opinion. 2. *Would fain ...it*: would have liked to accept
it. 3. *Loth*: reluctant. 4. *Rabblement*: bazar crowd. 5. *Chapped*: roughened by cold
or toil. 6. *Tag-rag*: low class. 7. *Herd*: mob. 8. *Infirmity*: weakness. 9. *Wenches*:
young women.

he rejected, it once, but in spite of that, it is my opinion that he would have liked to have it. Then he offered it to him again, and he refused it again, but in my opinion he was very unwilling to take his hand away from it. Then he offered it the third time, and he pushed it away for the third time, and again, as he refused it, the mob shouted and clapped their toil-hardened hands and threw up their greasy caps and gave off so much bad-smelling breath, because Caesar had refused the crown, that it almost suffocated Caesar, for he fainted and fell down. As far as I was concerned, I dared not open my mouth to laugh for fear of breathing in the bad air.

Cassius. But wait, please. Did Caesar actually swoon?

Casca. He fell down in the market place, foamed at the mouth and was speechless.

Brutus. That is quite probable. He suffers from the falling sickness.

Cassius. No, Caesar has not got it. It is you and I, and honest Casca here, who have the falling sickness.

Casca. I do not know what you mean by that, but I am sure that Caesar fell down. If the ragged fellows did not applaud him and hiss him, according to whether he pleased or displeased them, as they do actors on the stage, then I am not speaking the truth.

Brutus. What did he say when he came to his senses again?

Casca. Indeed, before he fell down, when he saw that the common crowd was glad that he had refused the crown, he pulled his coat open and invited them to cut his throat. If I had been a working class man, then may I go to hell if I would not have taken him at his word. So he fell down. When he came to his senses again, he said that if he had done or spoken anything out of place, he hoped the gentlemen would understand it was because of his weakness. Three or four women where I stood cried, "O, the poor fellow!" and forgave him with all their hearts, but there need be no attention paid to them, for if Caesar had stabbed their mothers, they would have said the same thing.

Brutus. And after that he came away in this sad manner?

Casca. Yes.

Cassius. Did Cicero say anything?

Casca. Yes, he spoke Greek.

Cassius. What was it about?

Casca. Nay, an[1] I tell you that, I'll ne'er look you i' the
face again ; but those that understood him smiled at one another, 285
and shook their heads; but, for mine own part, it was Greek to me.
I could tell you more news too : Marullus and Flavius, for pulling
scarfs[2] off Caesar's images, are put to silence[3]. Fare you well. There
was more foolery yet, if I could remember it. 290

    Casca. No, I am promised forth[4].

    Cassius. Will you dine with me to-morrow?

    Casca. Ay, if I be alive, and your mind hold, and your 295
dinner worth the eating.

    Cassius. Good; I will expect you.

    Casca. Do so : farewell, both.   [*Exit.*

    Brutus. What a blunt fellow is this grown to be :
He was quick mettle[5] when he went to school. 300

    Cassius. So is he now, in execution
Of any bold or noble enterprise,
However he puts on this tardy form.
This rudeness is a sauce to his good wit,
Which gives men stomach[6] to digest his words 305
With better appetite.

    Brutus. And so it is. For this time[7] I will leave you:
To-morrow, if you please to speak with me,
I will come home to you; or, if you will,
Come home to me, and I will wait for you. 310

    Cassius. I will do so: till then, think of the world.
                [*Exit* Brutus.

Well, Brutus, thou art noble; yet, I see,
Thy honourable metal[8] may be wrought[9]
From that it is dispos'd : therefore 'tis meet
That noble minds keep ever with their likes; 315
For who so firm that cannot be seduc'd?
Caesar doth bear me hard[10], but he loves Brutus:
If I were Brutus now, and he were Cassius,
He should not humour me. I will this night,
In several hands, in at his windows throw, 320
As if they came from several citizens,
Writings all tending to the great opinion

---

    1. *An I tell you*: if I tell you. 2. *Scarfs*: decorations. 3. *Put to silence*: removed
from their posts. 4. *Forth*: to go out. 5. *Quick mettle*: lively spirits. 6. *Stomach*:
inclination. 7. *For this time*: for the present. 8. *Metal*: spirit; nature. 9. *Wrought*:
inclined or influenced. 10. *Bear me hard*: dislike me.

Casca. Now if I tell that, (I shall be telling a lie) I shall never be able to look you directly in the face again, but those who understood it smiled at each other and shook their heads, but as far as I was concerned, it was unintelligible. I can tell you more news : Marullus and Flavius, for pulling the decorations from Caesar's images, are deprived of their posts. Now, good-bye ! There was still more foolishness if I could only remember it.

Cassius. Will you dine with me to-night, Casca?

Casca. No, I have promised to go out.

Cassius. Will you dine with me to-morrow?

Casca. Yes, if I am still alive, and you still hold the same invitation, and if your dinner is worth eating.

Cassius. Good. I shall expect you.

Casca. You may, Good-bye, both of you! (*Casca goes*)

Brutus. What a dull fellow he has become! He was quite bright when he was at school.

Cassius. He still is in the execution of any bold or noble plan. However he puts on this appearance of laziness. His rudeness is like a sauce to his ready wit, and enables men to enjoy his words with more appreciation.

Brutus. That is so. Well, now, I shall leave you for the time being. If you care to have a talk with me tomorrow, I shall come home with you, or, if you choose, come to my home and I shall wait for you.

Cassius. I shall do so. Till then, think of your duty to the world.

                                        (Brutus *departs*)

Well, Brutus, you are noble. Yet I see that your honourable nature may be bent from its natural direction. Thus it is better that noble minds should always keep company with noble minds, for who is so determined that he cannot be led away? Caesar is unfriendly to me, but he loves Brutus. If I were Brutus, now, and he were Cassius, he should not influence me. I shall this very night throw in at his window letters written in various handwriting, as if they came from different citizens, and all mentioning the high opinion that

That Rome holds of his name; wherein obscurely
Caesar's ambition shall be glánced at :
And after this let Caesar seat him sure;　　　325
For we will shake him, or worse days endure.　　[Exit

SCENE III.　A street

Thunder and lightning. Enter, from opposite sides, Casca,
with his sword drawn, and Cicero

Cicero.　Good even, Casca : brought you Caesar home? Why
are you breathless? and why stare you so?

Casca.　Are not you mov'd, when all the sway[1] of earth
Shakes like a thing unfirm? O Cicero,
I have seen tempests, when the scolding winds　　5
Have riv'd the knotty oaks; and I have seen
The ambitious[2] ocean swell and rage and foam,
To be exalted with the threatening clouds :
But never till to-night, never till now.
Did I go through a tempest dropping fire.　　10
Either there is a civil strife in heaven;
Or else the world, too saucy[3] with the gods.
Incenses them[4] to send destruction.

Cicero.　Why, saw you any thing more wonderful?

Casca.　A common slave—you know him well by sight—　　15
Held up his left hand, which did flame and burn
Like twenty torches join'd; and yet his hand,
Not sensible of[5] fire, remain'd unscorch'd,
Besides—I ha' not since put up my sword—
Against[6] the Capitol I met a lion,　　20
Who glar'd upon me, and went surly by,
Without annoying me : and there were drawn
Upon a heap a hundred ghastly women,
Transformed with their fear; who swore they saw
Men all in fire walk up and down the streets.　　25
And yesterday the bird[7] of night did sit
Even at noonday upon the market-place,
Hooting and shrieking. When these prodigies
Do so conjointly[8] meet, let not men say,

---

1. *Sway*: system; creation. 2. *Ambitious*: swelling up with pride. 3. *Saucy*:
insolent; ill-behaved. 4. *Incenses them*: makes them so angry that. 5. *Sensible of*:
feeling. 6. *Against*: opposite. 7. *Bird of night*: the owl. 8. *Conjointly*: all at the same
time.

Rome holds of his name. In them, Caesar's ambition shall be hinted at. After that, let Caesar see that his position is sure, that we shall either shake his power or submit to the worse times that are likely to come.

SCENE III.   *A street*

Thunder and lightning. Enter, from opposite sides,

Casca *with his sword drawn, and* Cicero

Cicero. Good evening, Casca. Did you accompany Caesar home? Why are you out of breath and why are you looking so strangely?

Casca. Are you not affected, when all the natural law of the earth is shaking like an unsteady thing? O, Cicero, I have seen tempests when the angry winds have torn the tough oak-trees. I have seen the rising ocean swell and roar and froth as if trying to be raised aloft to the threatening clouds, but never till to-night have I experienced a tempest which dropped fire. Either civil war has started in heaven, or else the world, behaving too rudely to the gods, has provoked them to send down destruction.

Cicero. Why, have you seen something more wonderful?

Casca. A common slave — one that you know well by sight— held up his left hand, and it was seen to flame and burn, as fiercely as if twenty torches had been placed together. Yet his hand, not feeling the fire, remained unburnt. In addition—I am still carrying my sword drawn—beside the Capitol I met a lion, who looked fiercely at me and went angrily past without molesting me. There were huddled together in a crowd a hundred terrible-looking women, quite beyond themselves with fear, who declared that they saw men all afire walk up and down the streets. Yesterday an owl, that bird of night, sat even at mid-day in the market-place, hooting and shrieking. When these signs happen all together, it is of no use to say,

"These are their reasons; they are natural";   30
For, I believe, they are portentous[1] things
Unto the climate[2] that they point upon.
    Cicero. Indeed it is a strange-disposed time :
But men may construe[3] things after their fashion,
Clean from the purpose[4] of the things themselves.   35
Comes Caesar to the Capitol to-morrow?
    Casca. He doth; for he did bid Antonius
Send word to you he would be there to-morrow.
    Cicero. Good night, then, Casca: this disturbed sky
Is not to walk in.
    Casca.   Farewell, Cicero.   [*Exit* Cicero.   40
                Enter CASSIUS
    Cassius. Who's there?
    Casca.   A Roman.
    Cassius.   Casca, by your voice.
    Casca. Your ear is good. Cassius, what night is this!
    Cassius. A very pleasing night to honest men.
    Casca. Who ever knew the heavens menace so?
    Cassius. Those that have known the earth so full
                      of faults.   45
For my part, I have walk'd about the streets,
Submitting me unto the perilous night;
And thus unbraced[5], Casca, as you see,
Have bar'd[6] my bosom to the thunder-stone :
And when the cross blue lightning seem'd to open   50
The breast of heaven, I did present myself
Even in the aim and very flash of it.
    Casca. But wherefore did you so much tempt the heavens?
It is the part of men to fear and tremble,
When the most mighty gods by tokens send   55
Such dreadful heralds[7] to astonish us.
    Cassius. You are dull, Casca; and those sparks of life
That should be in a Roman you do want,
Or else you use not. You look pale, and gaze,
And put on fear, and cast yourself in wonder,   60
To see the strange impatience[8] of the heavens :
But if you would consider the true cause
Why all these fires, why all these gliding ghosts,

---

   1. *Portentous*: ominous; prophetic. 2. *Climate*: the country or State 3. *Consture*: explain; to account for. 4. *Clean...purpose*: with an entirely different explanation. 5. *Unbrac'd*: with dress unfastened. 6. *Bar'd*: exposed. 7. *Heralds*: messengers. 8. *Impatience*: disturbed state.

"There are perfectly natural reasons which can be given for them." I believe they are deeply significant signs to the country on which their influence is directed.

Cicero. Indeed it is a time when things are going strangely. But men may explain away things after their own ways, quite different from the real purpose of such happenings. Will Caesar come to the Capitol tomorrow?

Casca. He will, for he asked Antonius to send word to you that he would be there to-morrow.

Cicero. Good night, then, Casca. It is not good to walk about under this disturbed sky.

Casca. Good-bye, Cicero.

Enter Cassius

Cassius. Who's there?

Casca. A Roman.

Cassius. It is Casca, judging by your voice.

Casca. You have good hearing. Cassius, what night is this?

Cassius. A very pleasing night to honest men.

Casca. Who ever knew the heavens to be so threatening?

Cassius. Men who have had previous experience of a time when the earth was as full of faults as at present. For my part, I have walked about the streets, exposing myself to the perilous night with my dress unfastened, Casca, as you see, and have left my naked breast exposed to the thunder-bolts. When the blue, forked lightning seemed to open the heavens wide, I have exposed myself right in the path of its flash.

Casca. But why did you so expose yourself to the violence of the sky? It is the duty of men to fear and tremble when the most mighty gods by their signs send such dreadful messengers to astonish us.

Cassius. You are dull, Casca, and you either lack the bright courage that should be in a Roman, or else you fail to use it. You look pale and gaze and put on a look of fear and throw yourself into amazement to see the strange anger of the heavens. But if you would consider the true cause, why all these fires and these gliding ghosts appear, why

Why birds and beasts from quality[1] and kind,
Why old men fool and children calculate,   65
Why all these things change from their ordinance[2]
Their natures and pre-formed faculties[3]
To monstrous quality;—why, you shall find
That heaven hath infus'd them with these spirits,
To make them instruments of fear and warning   70
Unto some monstrous state[4].
Now could, I, Casca, name to thee a man
Most like this dreadful night,
That thunders, lightens, opens graves, and roars
As doth the lion in the Capitol.—   75
A man no mightier than thyself or me
In personal action; yet prodigious[5] grown,
And fearful, as these strange eruptions are.
    Casca. 'Tis Caesar that you mean, it is not, Cassius?
    Cassius. Let it be who it is : for Romans now   80
Have thews and limbs like to their ancestors;
But, woe the while! our fathers' minds are dead,
And we are govern'd with our mothers' spirits :
Our yoke and sufferance show us womanish.
    Casca. Indeed, they say the senators to-morrow   85
Mean to establish Caesar as a king;
And he shall wear his crown by sea and land,
In every place, save here in Italy.
    Cassius. I knodw where I will wear this dagger, then;
Cassius from bondage will deliver Cassius :   90
Therein, ye gods, you make the weak most strong;
Therein, ye gods, you tyrants do defeat :
Nor stony tower, nor walls of beaten brass,
Nor airless dungeon, nor strong links of iron,
Can be retentive[6] to the strength of spirit;
But life, being weary of these worldly bars,
Never lacks power to dismiss itself.
If I know this, know all the world besides,
That part of tyranny that I do bear
I can shake off at pleasure.   *[Thunder still*
    Casca.   So can I :   100
So every bondman[7] in his own hand bears
The power to cancel his captivity.

---

    1. *From quality:* behaving unnaturally. 2. *Ordinance:* usual fixed course. 3. *Pre-formed faculties:* existing qualities. 4. *Monstrous state:* of some unnatural condition or happening. 5. *Prodigious:* unnatural; excessive. 6. *Retentive:* able to hold or detain. 7. *Bondman:* serf; slave.

birds and beasts behave in a way opposed to their natural inclinations and instincts, why old men are foolish while children reason wisely, why all these things change from their fixed natures and settled actions to assume a monstrous disposition, — why, you shall find that heaven has filled them with such spirits to make them signs of fear and a warning against some unnatural state of things. Now, Casca, I could name to you a man who resembles this dreadful night, that thunders, lightens, open graves and roars like the (captive) lion in the Capitol. He is a man no stronger than you or I in bodily acts, but has grown enormous and fearful, like these outbreaks of Nature.

Casca. It is Caesar that you mean : it is not Cassius?

Cassius. No matter who it is. Romans now have muscles and limbs as their ancestors had. But alas! The courageous minds of our fathers have died out of us and we are rather inspired by our mothers' spirits. Our burden and the way we submit to it show that we are womanly.

Casca. Indeed they say that the senators to-morrow mean to set up Caesar as a king. He shall wear his crown by sea and land, everywhere except in Italy here.

Cassius. I know where I shall place my dagger then (in my own heart). Thus shall I deliver myself from bondage; in the power to do this, Oh gods, you have made weak men strong. By this, O gods, you have defeated tyrants. No tower of stone, no walls of hammered brass, no airless prison-cell nor strong iron chains can enclose the powerful spirit. For life, when it tires of those worldly limitations, never lacks power to set itself free. If I know this, then all the rest of the world may know that, whatever tyranny I may bear, I can free myself from it whenever I choose.

(*Sound of thunder*)

Casca. So can I. So every prisoner carries in his own hand the means of ending his captivity.

     Cassius. And why should Caesar be a tyrant, then?
Poor man! I know he would not be a wolf,
But that he sees the Romans are but sheep: 105
He were no lion, were not Romans hinds[1].
Those that with haste will make a mighty fire
Begin it with weak straws: what trash is Rome,
What rubbish, and what offal[2], when it serves
For the base matter[3] to illuminate   110
So vile a thing as Caesar! But, O grief,
Where hast thou led me? I perhaps speak this
Before a willing bondman : then I know
My answer[4] must be made; but I am arm'd,
And dangers are to me indifferent.   115
     Casca. You speak to Casca; and to such a man
That is no fleering[5] tell-tale. Hold, my hand :
Be factious[6] for redress of all these griefs;
And I will set this foot of mine as far
As who goes farthest.   120
     Cassius.   There's a bargain made.
Now know you, Casca, I have mov'd already
Some certain of the noblest-minded Romans
To undergo with me an enterprise
Of honourable-dangerous consequence;
And I do know, by this, they stay for me   125
In Pompey's porch: for now, this fearful night,
There is no stir or walking in the streets;
And the complexion of the element
In favour's[7] like the work we have in hand,
Most bloody, fiery, and most terrible.   130
     Casca. Stand close awhile, for here comes one in haste.
     Cassius. 'Tis Cinna,—I do know him by his gait;
He is friend.

              Enter CINNA
         Cinna, where haste you so?
     Cinna. To find out you. Who's that? Metellus Cimber?
     Cassius. No, it is Casca; one incorporate[8]   135
To our attempts. Am I not stay'd for, Cinna?
     Cinna. I am glad on't. What a fearful night is this!
There's two or three of us have seen strange sights.

---

    1. *Hinds:* female deer. 2. *Offal:* the inferior parts of meat, discarded by the
butcher. 3. *For the base matter:* as the dull background of Caesar's glory. 4. *My
answer:* my excuse or explanation. 5. *Fleering:* mischievous; scornful. 6. *Factious:*
in rebellious mood; mutinous. 7. *Favour:* appearance. 8. *Incorporate:* a member; a
sharer in.

Cassius. Why, then, should Caesar be a tyrant? Poor man, I know he has no wish to behave like a fierce wolf, only that he sees how the Romans behave like sheep. He would not be like a lion if the Romans were not like deer. Those who wish quickly to build up a great fire start it with slight straws. What poor stuff is Rome, what refuse, what dirt when it serves as the vile background to set off such a vile tyrant as Caesar! But O, into what words has my grief led me? I may be speaking thus before one who welcomes his bondage. Then I know that I shall be called upon to answer for my words. But I am armed, and therefore can be indifferent to danger.

Casca. You speak to Casca, and to a man who is no grinning tell-tale. Take my hand. Be active in seeking reform of all our grievances, and I shall follow you as far as the most bold of all who take part.

Cassius. That is agreed, then. Now you should know, Casca, that I have already taken steps to move certain of the most noble of the Romans to join with me in an enterprise of honour, though possibly dangerous in its consequences. I know that, by this time, they will be waiting for me in Pompey's porch, for now, on this terrible night, there is no movement and nobody walking in the streets. The appearance of the heavens is very similar to the work we have in hand,— bloody, fiery and terrible.

Casca. Keep back for a while. Here comes some one in a hurry.

Cassius. It i s Cinna. I know his way of walking. He is a friend.

Enter Cinna

Cinna, where are you going in such haste?

Cinna. To find you. Who's that? Is it Metellus Cimber?

Cassius. No, it is Casca, one who is a sharer in our plans. Are they awaiting me, Cinna?

Cinna. I am glad to hear what you say. What a fearful night it is! There are two or three of us who have seen strange sights.

Cassius.   Am I not stay'd for? tell me.

Cinna.   Yes, you are.—

O Cassius, if you could

But win the noble Brutus to our party—   140

Cassius.   Be you content: good Cinna, take this paper,

And look you lay it in the paretor's[1] chair,

Where Brutus may but find it; and throw this

In at his window; set this up with wax   145

Upon old Brutus' statue: all this done,

Repair[2] to Pompey's porch, where you shall find us.

Is Decius Brutus and Trebonius there?

Cinna.   All but Metellus Cimber; and he's gone

To seek you at your house. Well, I will hie[3],   150

And so bestow these papers as you bade me.

                                              [Exit Cinna

Come, Casca, you and I will yet, ere day,

See Brutus at his house: three parts of him

Is ours already; and the man entire   155

Upon the next encounter[4], yields him ours.

Casca.   O, he sits high in all the people's hearts :

And that which would appear offence in us,

His countenance, like richest alchemy[5],

Will change to virtue and to worthiness.   160

Cassius. Him, and his worth, and our great need of him,

You have right well conceited[6]. Let us go,

For it is after midnight, and ere day

We will awake him and be sure of him.

                                              [Exeunt

ACT II

SCENE I. *Rome.* BRUTUS' *Orchard*
Enter BRUTUS

Brutus.   What, Lucius, ho!—

I cannot, by the progress[7] of the stars,

Give guess how near to day, — Lucius, I say !—

I would it were my fault to sleep so soundly.—

When, Lucius, when? awake, I say! what, Lucius!   5

                          Enter Lucius

Lucius.   Call'd you, my lord?

Brutus.   Get me a taper in my study, Lucius :

When it is lighted, come and call me here.

Lucius.   I will, my lord.

                                              [Exit

---

1. *Proetor*: a Roman magistrate. 2. *Repair*: make your way. 3. *Hie*: go.
4. *Encounter*: meeting. 5. *Alchemy*: magical transforming power. 6. *conceited*:
judged; estimated. 7. *Progress*: changed positions.

Cassius. Are they waiting for me? Tell me.

Cinna. Yes, you are awaited. O Cassius, if you could only win over the noble Brutus to our side.

Cassius. Be content. Good Cinna take this paper and place it in the praetor's chair, where only Brutus will find it. Throw this one in through his window. Fix this one with wax to the statue of the older Brutus. When you have done all this, come to Pompey's porch and you will find us there, Are Decius Brutus and Trebonius there?

Cinna. All are there except Metellus Cimber, and he has gone to look for you at your house. Well, I shall go and deal with these papers as you have told me.

Cassius. Having done that, come to Pompey's theatre.

[Cinna *departs*

Come, Casca. You and I shall, before daybreak, see Brutus at his house. He has already gone three quarters of the way to joining us. Upon our next meeting, the whole of him will be ours.

Casca. O, he has a high place in the hearts of all the people, and a thing which would appear bad in us will by his countenance, as if a magic transformation, be changed to virtue and merit.

Cassius. You have correctly estimated him and his worth, and also our great need of him. Let us go, for it is past midnight. We shall awaken him before daybreak and make sure of him.

ACT II

SCENE I. *Rome,* BRUTUS'S *Orchad*

Enter Brutus

Brutus. Are you there, Lucius! I cannot from the appearance of the stars say how long it is before daybreak. Lucius! I wish I had this fault of sleeping too deeply. When are you coming? Waken up, I say, Lucius!

Enter Lucius

Lucius. Did you call, my lord?

Brutus. Place a candle for me in my study, Lucius, When it is lighted, come here and tell me.

Lucius. I will, my lord. (Lucius *goes out*)

Brutus. It must be by his death: and, for my part,　　　　10
I know no personal cause to spurn[1] at him,
But for the general. He would be crown'd :—
How that might change his nature, there's the question :
It is the bright sun that brings forth the adder[2],
And that craves[3] wary walking. Crown him?—that;—　　15
And then, I grant, we put a sting in him,
That at his will be may do danger with.
The abuse of greatness is, when it disjoins[4]
Remorse from power: and, to speak truth of Caesar,
I have not known when his affections sway'd　　　　20
More than his reason. But 'tis a common proof,
That lowliness[5] is young ambition's ladder.
Whereto the climber-upward turns his face;
But when he once attains the upmost round.
He then unto the ladder turns his back,　　　　25
Looks in the clouds, scorning the base degrees
By which he did ascend. So Caesar may;
Then, lest he may, prevent. And, since the quarrel
Will bear no colour for the thing he is,
Fashion it thus; that what he is, augmented[6],　　30
Would run to these and these extremities[7].
And therefore think him as a serpent's egg,
Which, hatch'd, would, as his kind[8], grow mischievous,
And kill him in the shell.

Re-enter Lucius

Lucius. The taper burneth in your closet, sir.　　　35
Searching the window for a flint, I found
This paper, thus seal'd up; and, I am sure,
It did not lie there when I went to bed.　　　　*[Gives him the letter*
Brutus. Get you to bed again; it is not day.
Is not to-morrow, boy, the ides of March?　　　40
Lucius. I know not, Sir.
Brutus. Look in the calendar, and bring me word.
Lucius. I will, sir.　　　　　　　　　*[Exit*
Brutus. The exhalations[9] whizzing in the air
Give so much light that I may read by them.　　　45
　　　　　　　　　[Opens the letter and reads
"Brutus, thou sleep'st : awake, and see thyself.
Shall Rome, &c. Speak, strike, redress!"—

---

1. *Spurn at*: attack. 2. *Adder*: a poisonous snake. 3. *Craves*: requires; calls for.
4. *Disjoins*: separates. 5. *Lowliness*: an assumed humility. 6. *Augmented*: when
grown mature. 7. *These ... extremities*: to certain disastrous results. 8. *As his kind*: as
his nature is. 9. *Exhalations*: vapours and gases.

Brutus. It must be done by his death. For my part I have no personal reason to reject him: it is for the public good. He would like to be crowned king. How far that might change his nature : that is the question! It is the heat of the sun that brings the serpent from its hiding place. This requires that one should move carefully. If he is crowned, then we have armed him with a sting that may be used to work mischief with, when he chooses. The bad side of greatness comes when it separates the kindly feelings and leaves the power (of a tyrant). To speak truly of Caesar, I have not known him to be guided by his feelings rather than by his intellect. But it is commonly seen that humility is used as a stepping-stone by an ambitious young man, and that he moves with his eyes upwards. But when he has attained the highest point, then he has no more use for the ladder by which he has risen, and still looks upwards, scorning the humble things which helped him to rise. So may Caesar do. Lest he do this, he should be prevented. But since a movement against him is not justified by the position he holds now, let us state the case thus, that what he is, plus an increase of power, would bring about the extreme evils we fear. So let us think of him as a serpent's egg, which, when hatched, would grow dangerous as is natural to serpents; therefore let us kill him in the shell.

Re-enter LUCIUS

Lucius. The taper is burning in your study, sir. While I was looking for a flint (to make a light) I found this paper, sealed up as it is. I am sure it was not lying there when I went to bed.

(*Gives letter to* Brutus)

Brutus. Go to bed again: it is not daylight yet. Is not tomorrow the 15th of March, my boy?

Lucius. I do not know, sir.

Brutus. Look at the calendar and come back and tell me.

Lucius: I will, Sir   (Lucius *goes out*)

Brutus. These luminous gases in the air to-night give so much light that I can read by them.   (*Opens the letter and reads*)

"Brutus, you are asleep. Awake and see yourself. Shall Rome, &c .....
Speak, strike, redress !"

"Brutus, thou sleep'st : awake!"
Such instigations[1] have been often dropp'd
Where I have took them up.   50
"Shall Rome, &c." Thus must I piece[2] it out;
Shall Rome stand under one man's awe[3]? What, Rome?
My ancestors did from the streets of Rome
The Tarquin drive, when he was call'd a king.   55
"Speak, strike, redress!"[4] Am I entreated
To speak and strike? O Rome, I make thee promise,
If the redress will follow, thou receivest
Thy full petition[5] at the hand of Brutus!

       Re-enter Lucius

  Lucius. Sir, March is wasted fifteen days.

             [*Knocking within*

  Brutus. 'Tis good. Go to the gate; somebody knocks.   60

             [*Exit* Lucius
Since Cassius first did whet[6] me against Caesar.
I have not slept.
Between the acting of a dreadful thing
And the first motion[7], all the interim[8] is
Like a phantasma[9] or a hideous dream :   65
The Genius[10] and the mortal instruments
Are then in council; and the state of man,
Like a little kingdom, suffers then
The nature of an insurrection.

       Re-enter LUCIUS

  Lucius. Sir, 'tis your brother Cassius at the door.   70
Who doth desire to see you.

  Brutus.   Is he alone?

  Lucius. No, sir, there are more with him.

  Brutus.   Do you know them?

  Lucius. No, sir; their hats are pluck'd about their ears,
And half their faces buried in their cloaks.
That by no means I may discover them   75
By any mark of favour[11].

  Brutus.   Let 'em enter. [*Exit Lucius*

---

  1. *Instigations*: promptings; urge to take action. 2. *Piece it out*: understand it
to be. 3. *Awe*: dominations. 4. *Redress*: Reform; undo the wrongs. 5. *Full petition*:
the utmost you plead for. 6. *Whet*: sharpen my enmity. 7. *Motion*: conception or
plan. 8. *Interim*: the intervening time. 9. *Phantasma*: a ghostly vision. 10. *Genius*:
guiding spirit. 11. *Of favour*: of their faces.

They say that I am sleeping! Such hints have often been dropped to me, and I have perceived them. "Shall Rome, &c."

This I must think out. Shall Rome remain in terror of one man? Rome? It was my ancestors who drove Tarquin from the streets of Rome when he was called a king. "Speak, strike, redress!" Are they asking me to speak and strike? O Rome, I promise you that if redress will follow this, you will have your request granted by the hand of Brutus.

Re-enter Lucius

Lucius. Sir, fifteen days of March have gone.

(*Knocking at the door*)

Brutus. That's all right. go to the door: some one is knocking.

(Lucius *goes out*)

Since Cassius first sharpened my feelings against Caesar, I have not slept. Between the performance of a dreadful act and the first conception of it, all the interval is like a nightmare or a horrible dream. The soul of the man and his mortal senses are then deliberating together. The man is then like a little kingdom in which there is a rebellion.

Re-enter Lucius

Lucius. Sir, your dear friend, Cassius, is at the door and wishes to see you.

Brutus. Is the alone?

Lucius. No, sir, there are more with him.

Brutus. Do you know them?

Lucius. No, sir, their hats are pulled down over their ears and half their faces are concealed in their cloaks, so that by no means could I recognise them by any sight of their faces.

Brutus. Let them come in.   (Lucius *goes out*)

They are the faction. O conspiracy,
Sham'st thou to show thy dangerous brow by night,
When evils are most free? O then, by day
Where wilt thou find a cavern dark enough   80
To mask thy monstrous visage? Seek none, conspiracy;
Hide it in smiles and affability :
For if thou path, thy native semblance on,
Not Erebus[1] itself were dim enough
To hide thee from prevention[2].   85

> *Enter* Cassius, Casca, Decius, Cinna, Metellus
> Cimber, *and* Trebonius

    Cassius. I think we are too bold[3] upon your rest :
Good morrow, Brutus; do we trouble you?
    Brutus. I have been up this hour, awake all night.
Know I these men that come along with you?
    Cassius. Yes, every man of them; and no man here   90
But honours you; and every one doth wish
You had but that opinion of yourself
Which every noble Roman bears of you.
This is Trebonius.
    Brutus.   He is welcome hither.
    Cassius. This, Decius, Brutus.   95
    Brutus.   He is welco e too.
    Cassius. This, Casca; this, Cinna : and this, Metallus Cimber.
    Brutus. They are all welcome,—
What watchful cares do interpose themselves
Between your eyes[4] and night?
    Cassius. Shall I entreat a word?   100

> [Brutus *and* Cassius *whisper*

    Decius. Here lies the east : doth not the day break here?
    Casca. No.
    Cinna. O, pardon sir, it doth; and you gray lines
That fret[5] the clouds are messengers of day.
    Casca. You shall confess that you are both deciv'd.   105
Here, as I point my sword, the sun arises;
Which is a great way growing on the south,
Weighing[6] the youthful season of the year.

---

1. *Erebus*: Hell. 2. *From prevention*: from being discovered and checked.
3.*Too bold*: i.e., "too bold in disturbing". 4. *Between your eyes, &c.*: between you and
your sleep. 5. *Fret*: to mark with streaks. 6. *Weighing.... season*: considering the early
stage of the year.

This is the party. O' conspiracy, you are afraid to show the dangers of your face by night, when evil things are usually free! Then by day where will you find a cave dark enough to hide your dangerous face? Do not try to find one, O conspiracy : hide your face in smiles and pleasantness for if you walk about with your natural appearance, not even Hell would be dark enough to prevent you from being opposed.

Enter Cassius, Casca, Decius, Cinna, Metellus

Cimber, *and* Trebonius

Cassius. I think we are too bold in breaking in on your leisure. Good morning, Brutus : are we a trouble to you?

Brutus. I have been up for an hour and awake all night. Do I know these men who have come with you?

Cassius. Yes, every man of them, and there is no man here who does not honour you. Every one wishes that you had the same high opinion of yourself that every noble Roman has of you. This is Trebonius.

Brutus. He is welcome here.

Cassius. This is Decius, Brutus.

Brutus. He is welcome too.

Cassius. This is Casca and here is Cinna and here Metellus Cimber.

Brutus. They are all welcome. What affairs requiring wakefulness have kept you from closing your eyes in the sleep of night?

Cassius. May I have a word? (Brutus *and* Cassius *whisper*)

Decius. This is the east. Is it here that the day breaks?

Casca. No.

Cinna. Forgive me, sir, but it does, and the gray lines which mark the sky yonder are the first signs of day break.

Casca. I shall make you admit that you are both mistaken. This way, where I point my sword, is where the sun rises, which is a good deal towards the south, considering that this is the early season of the year.

Some two months hence, up higher toward the north
He first presents[1] his fire : and the high east   110
Stand, as the Capitol, directly here.

  Brutus. Give me your hands all over, one by one.

  Cassius. And let us swear our resolution.

  Brutus. No, not an oath : if not the face of men,
The sufferance[2] of our souls, the time's abuse[3],—   115
If these be motives weak, break off betimes[4] ,
And every man hence to his idle bed;
So let high-sighted tyranny range on,
Till each man drop by lottery[5]. But if these,
As I am sure they do, bear fire enough   120
To kindle cowards, and to steel with valour
The melting spirits of women; then, countrymen,
What need we any spur but our own cause,
To prick us to redress? what other bond
Than secret Romans, that have spoke the word,   125
And will not palter[6]? And what other oath
Than honesty to honesty engag'd,
That this shall be, or we will fall for it?
Swear priests, and cowards, and men cautelous[7],
Old feeble carrions[8], and such suffering souls   130
That welcome wrongs; unto bad causes swear
Such creatures as men doubt : but do not stain
The even virtue[9] of our enterprise,
Nor the insuppressive mettle of our spirits,
To think that or our cause or our performance   135
Did need an oath; when every drop of blood
That every Roman bears, and nobly bears,
Is guilty of a several bastardy,
If he do break the smallest particle
Of any promise that hath pass'd from him.   140

  Cassius. But what of Cicero? shall we sound him?
I think he will stand very strong with us.

  Casca. Let us not leave him out.

  Cinna.   No, by no means.

  Metellus. O, let us have him; for his silver hairs
Will purchase us a good opinion.   145
And buy men's voice to commend[10] our deeds :

---

 1. *He first presents*: he will first show his light. 2. *Sufferance*: suffering.
3. *Time's abuse*: the hardship of the times. 4. *Be-times*: early; soon. 5. *By lottery*:
by mere chance. 6. *Palter*: behave frivolously. 7.*Cautelous*: mean and worthless.
8. *Carrions*: dead and decaying bodies. 9. *Even virtue*: the steadfast justice and
right. 10. *Commend*: approve of.

Two months after this, he will first display his beams higher up towards the
north. The direct east is towards the Capitol, in this direction.

Brutus. Give me your hands all of you, one by one.

Cassius. And let us swear to what we have resolved.

Brutus. No, let there be no oath. If the sad faces of men, the sufferings
of our souls, the evils of the time — if all these are not motives enough to bind
you, then break this discussion off in time and let each man get back to his
empty bed. Then let arrogant tyranny march on till every man drops before
it when his fate calls. But if these men — *causes* as I am sure they do — have spirit
enough to stimulate cowards and to strengthen with valour the gentle spirits
of women, then, my countrymen what need is there of any other urging on but
our own cause to make us try for justice? What other bond is required but the
fact that we are Romans who have met in secret and have passed our word and
will not trifle with it? What other oath is required than the word of honest man
to honest man that we shall bring this about or fall in the attempt? Let priests
and cowards swear oaths, and untrustworthy men, old worthless creatures and
suffering souls who are pleased with their wrongs. Swear by oath in bad
causes such people as you are doubtful of, but do not stain the pure virtue of
our enterprise nor the indomitable courage of our spirits by thinking that our
cause or our will to execute it requires an oath. Every drop of blood in the
veins of every Roman noble would be guilty of a separate treachery if he were
to break the smallest part of any promise made by him here.

Cassius. But what of Cicero? Shall we try him? I think he will be
strongly inclined to our side.

Casca. Do not let him be left out.

Cinna. By no means.

Metellus. O' let us have him. His white hairs will make men think well
of us and lift their voices to praise our deeds. It will be said that his mature

It shall be said, his judgment rul'd our hands;
Our youths and wildness shall no whit appear,
But all be buried in his gravity.

    Brutus. O, name him not; let us not break with[1] him;
For he will never follow any thing
That other men begin.

    Cassius.   Then leave him out.

    Casca. Indeed he is not fit.

    Decius. Shall no man else be touch'd but only Caesar?

    Cassius. Decius, well urg'd :— I think it is not meet[2]
Mark Antony, so well belov'd of Caesar,
Should outlive Caesar : we shall find of him
A shrewd contriver[3]; and, you know, his means,
If he improve them, may well stretch so far
As to annoy us all : which to prevent,   160
Let Antony and Caesar fall together.

    Brutus. Our course will seem too bloody, Caius Cassius,
To cut the head off and then hack the limbs,—
Like wrath in death and envy afterwards;
For Antony is but a limb of Caesar :   165
Let us be sacrificers, but not butchers, Caius.
We all stand up against the spirit of Caesar;
And in the spirit of men there is no blood :
O that we, then, could come[4] by Caesar's spirit,
And not dismember[5] Caesar! But, alas,   170
Caesar must bleed for it! And, gentle friends,
Let's kill him boldly, but not wrathfully;
Let's carve him as a dish fit for the gods,
Not hew him as a carcase fit for hounds :
And let our hearts, as subtle masters do,   175
Stir up their servants to an act of rage,
And after seem to chide[6] 'em. This shall make
Our purpose necessary and not envious :
Which so appearing to the common eyes,
We shall be call'd purgers[7], not murderers.   180
And for Mark Antony, think not of him;
For he can do no more than Caesar's arm
When Caesar's head is off.

---

  1. *Break with*: reveal our plans to. 2. *Meet*: desirable. 3. *Contriver*: plotter.
4. *Come by*: strike at. 5. *Dismember*: break the body of. 6. *Chide*: rebuke. 7. *Purgers:*
cleansers; physicians.

judgment guided our actions, and your youth and rash natures will be forgotten in the effect produced by his gravity.

Brutus. O, do not mention his name. Let us not open our plans to him, for he will never follow out any scheme that has been started by other men.

Cassius. Then leave him out.

Casca. Indeed he is not fit.

Decius. Is it agreed that no other man is to be harmed but Caesar?

Cassius. Decius, that is a good point. I think it is not advisable that Mark Antony, so well beloved by Caesar, should be allowed to outlive him. We shall find in him a shrewd schemer, and you know that the means at his disposal, if he make the best of them, may go so far as to trouble us all. To prevent this, let Antony and Caesar be slain together.

Brutus. Our acts will then seem too bloody, Caius Cassius. It is as if we cut off a man's head and then cut off his limbs; like anger in life followed by envy after death, for Antony is only a limb of Caesar. Let us slay like priests making a sacrifice, but not like butchers, Cassius. It is the spirit of Caesar to which we are opposed, and in the spirit of men there is no blood. I would that we could conquer Caesar's spirit without harming Caesar's body. But alas, Caesar must bleed because of his spirit. So, dear friends, let us kill him boldly but not savagely. Let us slay him as if an offering to the gods, and not like a carcase that is being cut up to feed the hounds. Let our hearts, as some crafty masters do, stir up their servants (our hands) to an act of anger and then appear to rebuke them for it. This shall make it appear that we were impelled by necessity and not by envy; and when it appears thus to the public, we shall be called cleansers of the State and not murderers. As for Mark Antony, do not think of him; for he can do no more than Caesar's arm after Caesar's head is cut off.

    Cassius.   Yet I fear him;
For in the ingrafted[1] love he bears to Caesar—

    Brutus. Alas, good Cassius, do not think of him :   185
If he love Caesar, all that he can do
Is to himself,—take thought and die for Caesar;
And that were much he should; for he is given
To sports, to wildness, and much company.

    Trebonius. There is no fear in him; let him not die;   190
For he will live, and laugh at this hereafter.

                                  [Clock strikes

    Brutus. Peace! count the clock.

    Cassius,   The clock hath stricken three.

    Trebonius. 'Tis time to part.

    Cassius.   But it is doubtful yet,
Whether Caesar will come forth to-day or no;
For he is supersitious grown of late;   195
Quite from[2] the main opinion he held once
Of fantasy, of dreams and ceremonies[3] :
It may be, these apparent prodigies,
The unaccustom'd terror of this night,
And the persuasion of his augurers[4],   200
May hold him from the Capitol to-day.

    Decius. Never fear that : if he be so resolv'd
I can o'ersway him; for he loves to hear
That unicorns may be betray'd with trees,
And bears with glasses, elephants with holes,   205
Lions with toils, and men with flatterers :
But when I tell him he hates flatterers,
He says he does,—being then most flattered.
Let me work;
For I can given his humour[5] the true bent[6],   210
And I will bring[7] him to the Capitol.

    Cassius. Nay, we will all of us be there to fetch him.

    Brutus. By the eighth hour: is that the uttermost[8]?

    Cinna. Be that the uttermost, and fail not then.

    Metellus. Caius Ligarius doth bear[9] Caesar hard,   215
Who rated him for speaking well of Pompey :
I wonder none of you have thought of him.

---

    1. *Ingrafted*: deeply rooted. 2. *Quite from*: quite different from. 3. *Ceremonies*: signs and omens. 4. *Augurers*: fortunetellers. 5. *Humour*: mood. 6. *Bent*: direction or inclination. 7. *Bring*: conduct; lead. 8. *Uttermost*: latest. 9. *Doth bear hard*: is hostile to.

Cassius.   Yet I fear him, because of the deeply-rooted love he bears for Caesar.

Brutus.   Alas, good Cassius, do not think of him. If he loves Caesar, then all that he can do is to himself, he can make up his mind to die for Caesar's sake. It would be a good thing for him to do that, for he is greatly addicted to sports, wild life and social company.

Trebonius.   There is no need to fear him. Do not kill him, for he will live on to laugh at this business afterwards.

(Clock strikes)

Brutus.   Hush! Count the strokes.

Cassius. The clock has struck three.

Trebonius. It is time for us to disperse.

Cassius. But it is still doubtful whether Caesar will come out to-day or not, for he has grown superstitious lately, quite different from the strong opinion which he once held about the supernatural, about dreams and ceremonies. It may be that these apparent supernatural happenings, the unusual terrors of this last night, and the advice of his priestly advisers will prevent him from going to the Capitol to-day.

Decius. Do not be afraid of that. If he decides that way, I can persuade him otherwise, for he loves to hear how unicorns may be captured by getting them to charge a tree, bears by placing mirrors to captivate them, elephants by holes dug in the ground, and men by flattery. Then, when I tell him that he hates flattery, he says that he does, although I am then flattering him more than all. Let me work on him, for I know how to direct his peculiarities into the proper channel : and I shall bring him to the Capitol.

Cassius. No, we had better all go to escort him.

Brutus. By eight o'clock : is that the time limit?

Cinna. Let that be the latest time and do not be later than that.

Metellus. Caius Ligarius feels strongly against Caesar, who rebuked him for speaking well of Pompey. I wonder that none of you thought of him.

Brutus. Now, good Metellus, go along by him:
He loves me well, and I have given him reasons;
Send him but hither, and I'll fashion him.   220

    Cassius. The morning comes upon's; we'll leave you,
      Brutus:—
And friends, disperse yourselves; but all remember
What you have said, and show yourselves true Romans.

    Brutus. Good gentlemen, look fresh and meerily;
Let not our looks put on¹ our purposes;   225
But bear it as our Roman actors do,
With untir'd spirits and formal constancy :
And so, good morrow to you every one.   [*Exeunt all except* Brutus
Boy! Lucius!—Fast asleep? It is no matter;
Enjoy the honey-heavy dew of slumber;   230
Thou hast no figures nor no fantasies²,
Which busy care draws in the brains of men;
Therefore thou sleep'st so sound.

Enter Portia

    Portia.   Brutus, my lord!

    Brutus. Portia, what mean you? wherefore rise you now?   235
It is not for your health thus to commit
Your weak condition to the raw cold morning.

    Portia.   Nor for yours neither. You've ungently³, Brutus,
Stole from my bed: and yesternight, at supper,
You suddenly arose, and walk'd about,
Musing and sighing, with your arms across⁴;   240
And when I ask'd you what the matter was,
You star'd upon me with ungentle looks :
I urg'd you further; then you scratch'd your head,
And too impatiently stamp'd with your foot :
Yet I insisted, yet you answer'd not;   245
But, with an angry wafture⁵ of your hand,
Gave sign for me to leave you : so I did;
Fearing to strengthen that impatience
Which seem'd too much enkindled; and withal
Hoping it was but an effect of humour⁶,   250
Which sometime hath his hour with every man.
It will not let you eat, nor talk, nor sleep;
And, could it work so much upon your shape⁷
As it hath much prevail'd on your condition⁸,
I should not know you, Brutus. Dear my lord,   255

---

1. *Put on*: reveal. 2. *Fantasies*: illusions. 3. *Ungently*: unkindly. 4. *Arms across*: with arms folded.   5. *Wafture*: wave. 6. *Humour*: mood or temper. 7. *Shape*: bodily form. 8. *Condition*: mental state.

Brutus. Now, my good Metellus, you go along to him. He likes me, and I have given him cause to do so. Send him here and I shall influence him.

Cassius. The morning comes upon us: we shall leave you, Brutus. Disperse, my friends: but all remember what you have said, and show yourselves to be true Romans.

Brutus. Good gentlemen, look bright and cheerful. Do not let our looks reveal our gloomy intentions, but behave as our Roman actors do, with tireless spirits and ordinary calmness of manner. So good-morning to each one of you! *(All go, except* Brutus) Boy ! Lucius ! Fast asleep? It does not matter. Enjoy the sweet rest of deep sleep. You have no apparitions and no strange appearances which anxiety causes in the minds of men, and so you sleep soundly.

Enter Portia.

Portia.   Brutus, my lord !

Brutus.   Portia, what is the meaning of your rising just now? It is not for the good of your health to expose yourself in your weak condition to the damp, cold morning.

Portia.   Nor is it good for you. You have most unkindly, Brutus, stolen away from me. Last night at supper you suddenly arose and walked about, thinking deeply and sighing, with your arms folded. When I asked you what the matter was, you looked on me with bad-tempered looks. I pressed you further, and you scratched your head and then very impatiently stamped your foot. I continued to press you, but you did not answer, but with an angry wave of your hand signed for me to leave you, and I did so. I feared to make you even more irritated, as you seemed overexcited. I hoped that it was but a temperamental upset, which sometimes affects every man for an hour or so, But it does not allow you to eat, to talk or to sleep. If it could act upon your looks as much as it has upon your mental condition, then I should not recognise you, Brutus. My dear lord,

Make me acquainted with your cause of grief.
   Brutus. I am not well in health, and that is all.
   Portia. Brutus is wise, and, were he not in health,
He would embrace¹ the means to come by it.
   Brutus. Why, so I do.—Good Portia, go to bed. 260
   Portia. Is Brutus sick? and is it physical
To walk unbraced², and suck up the humours³
Of the dank morning? What, is Brutus sick,
And will he steal out of his wholesome bed,
To dare the vile contagion of the night, 265
And tempt the rheumy⁴ and unpurged air
To add unto his sickness? No, my Brutus;
You have some sick offence within your mind,
Which by the right and virtue of my place
I ought to know of: and, upon my knees, 270
I charm you, by my once-commended beauty,
By all your vows of love, and that great vow
Which did incorporate and make us one.
That you unfold to me, yourself, your half,
Why you are heavy; and what men to-night 275
Have had resort to you,—for here have been
Some six or seven, who did hide their faces
Even from darkness.
   Brutus.   Kneel not, gentle Portia.
   Portia. I should not need, if you were gentle Brutus.
Within the bond of marriage, tell me, Brutus, 280
Is it excepted⁵ I should know no secrets
That appertain⁶ to you? Am I yourself
But, as it were, in sort or limitation,—
To keep with you at meals, comfort your bed,
And talk to you sometimes? Dwell I but in the suburbs⁷ 285
Of your good pleasure? If it be no more,
Portia is Brutus' harlot, not his wife.
   Brutus. You are my true and honourable wife;
As dear to me as are the ruddy drops
That visit my sad heart. 290
   Portia. If this were true, then should I know this secret.

---

1. *Embrace the means*: take the right steps. 2. *Unbraced*: to walk with clothing unfastened. 3. *Humours*: moisture. 4. *Rheumy*: causing rheumatism. 5. *Excepted*: stated as an exception. 6. *Appertain to*: concern. 7. *Suburbs:* the outer fringe.

confide in me the reasons for your anxiety.

Brutus.   My health is a little upset: that is all.

Portia.   I know that you are a wise man, and that if there were anything wrong with your health, you would take steps to have it put right.

Brutus.   That is what I am doing. Good Portia, go to bed.

Portia.   Are you unwell, Brutus, and is it good for health to walk with clothing unfastened to absorb the cold airs of this damp morning? Are you unwell, and yet you go stealthily from your warm bed to risk the unhealthy infection of the night, allowing the rheumatic-causing and unwarmed air to increase your sickness? No, Brutus, you have some cause of sickness which is in your mind, which it is my right to know, by virtue of my position as your wife. Upon my knees I implore you, by my beauty which you once praised so much, by all your vows of love, and that great marriage vow which joined us together and united us into one, that you reveal to me — who am yourself, half of you, why you are so moody, and what men they were who come to you this night, for there have been six or seven here who hid their faces even though it was dark.

Brutus.   Do not kneel to me, dear Portia.

Portia.   I should not need to, if you were gentle, O Brutus. Tell me, within the bond of secrecy that exists between man and wife: Is there any exception made that I am not to know any secrets that concern you? Am I what I am only with limitations, to sit with you at table and to sleep with you and talk to you at times? Do I live only on the outer edges of your pleasure? If I am no more than that, then I am your harlot, not your wife.

Brutus.   You are my true and honourable wife, as dear to me as the very life-blood of my heart.

Portia.   If that were true, then you would tell me this secret. I admit

I grant I am a woman; but withal.
A women that Lord Brutus took to wife;
I grant I am a woman : but withal
A woman well-reputed,—Cato's daughter.   295
Think you I am no stronger than my sex[1],
Being so father'd and so husbanded?
Tell me your counsels[2]; I will not disclose 'em :
I have made strong proof of my constancy[3],
Giving myself a voluntary wound   300
Here, in the thigh : can I bear that with patience,
And not my husband's secrets?
       Brutus.   O ye gods,
Render me worthy of this noble wife!   *[Knocking within*
Hark, hark! one knocks: Portia, go in awhile;
And by and by thy bosom shall partake[4]   305
The secrets of my heart :
All my engagements I will construe to thee,
All the charactery[5] of my sad brows:—
Leave me with haste. [*Exit* Portia.]—Lucius, who's that knocks?
         Re-enter Lucius *with* Ligarius

     Lucius.   Here is a sick man that would speak with you. 310
     Brutus.   Caius Ligarius, that Metellus spake of. —
Boy, stand aside,—Caius Ligarius! how?
     Ligarius. Vouchsafe good-morrow from a feeble tongue.
     Brutus. O what a time have you chose out, brave Caius,
To wear a kerchief[6] ! Would you were not sick!   315
     Ligarius.   I am not sick, if Brutus have in hand[7]
Any exploit worthy the name of honour.
     Brutus.   Such an exploit have I in hand, Ligarius.
Had you a healthful ear to hear of it.
     Ligarius.   By all the gods that Romans bow before,   320
I here discard my sickness! Soul of Rome!
Brave son, deriv'd from honourable loins[8]!
Thou, like an exorcist[9], hast conjur'd up
My mortified[10] spirit. Now bid me run,
And I will strive with things impossible;   325
Yea, get the better of them. What's to do?
     Brutus.   A piece of work that will make sick men whole.
     Ligarius.   But are not some whole that we must make sick?

---

    1. *Than my sex:* than women in general. 2. *Counsels:* problems. 3. *Constancy:* determination. 4. *Part-ake:* share. 5. *Charactery:* interpretation. 6. *Wear a kerchief:* the badge of sickness. 7. *In hand*: now to be done. 8. *Loins*: father. 9. *Exorcist*: man able to drive away evil spirits. 10. *Mortified*: dying.

I am only a woman, but still a woman that Brutus thought worthy to be his wife; I admit I am a woman, but at the same time a woman of some reputation, the daughter of Cato. Do you not think I am stronger than the rest of my sex, when I have such a husband and such a father? Tell me your plans: I shall not give them away : I have given proof of my reliability, once inflicting a wound on my own thigh. If I was able to bear that calmly, can I not keep my husband's secrets?

Brutus. O gods, I hope you will make me worthy of such a noble wife! (*A knocking is heard*) Listen ! Some one is knocking. Portia go indoors for a while, and afterwards you shall share in all the secrets of my heart. I shall explain all the engagements I have entered into, and the sadness which is written on my face. But leave me quickly. (*Portia goes*) Lucius, who is it that is knocking?

Re-enter Lucius *with* Ligarius

Lucius. Here is a sick man who wants to speak to you.

Brutus. Caius Ligarius, to whom Metellus spoke ! Boy, stand aside. Caius Ligarius ! How are you?

Ligarius. I wish you good morning, though my voice is weak.

Brutus. What an unsuitable time have you chosen, brave Caius, to wear the muffler of sickness! I wish you were not sick !

Ligarius. I am not sick if Brutus requires me for any deed which can be described as honourable.

Brutus. I have such a deed on hand, Ligarius. Is your ear strong enough to hear it ?

Ligarius. I swear by all the gods that the Romans worship that I here cast off my sickness. O, Brutus, soul of Rome! Brave son of an honourable father! You, like a magician, have summoned up my dying spirit. Tell me to run, and I shall strive against the most impossible odds, and even overcome them. What is to be done?

Brutus. A piece of work that will make sick men well again.

Ligarius. But are there not some men well at present, whom we must make sick?

Brutus.   That must we also. What it is, my Caius,
I shall unfold¹ to thee, as we are going   330
To whom it must be done.

    Ligarius.   Set on your foot²,
And with a heart new-fir'd³ I follow you,
To do I know not what: but it sufficeth
That Brutus leads me on.

    Brutus.   Follow me, then.   *[Exeunt*

SCENE II. *A room in* Caesar's *house*

Thunder and lightning. Enter Caesar, *in his nightgown*

    Caesar.   Nor⁴ heaven nor earth have been at peace tonight :
Thrice hath Calpurnia in her sleep cried out.
"Help, ho! they murder Caesar!"—Who's within?

Enter a Servant

    Servant.   My lord?

    Caesar.   Go bid the priests do present sacrifice⁵,   5
And bring me their opinions of success.

    Servant. I will, my lord.   *[Exit*

Enter Calpurnia

    Calpurnia.   What mean you, Caesar? think you to
        walk forth?
You shall not stir out of your house to-day.

    Caesar. Caesar shall forth: the things that threaten'd me   10
Ne'er look'd but on my back⁶, when they shall see
The face of Caesar, they are vanished.

    Calpurnia. Caesar, I never stood on ceremonies,
Yet now they fright me. There is one within⁷,
Besides the things that we have heard and seen,   15
Recounts most horrid sights seen by the watch.
A lioness hath whelped⁸ in the streets;
And graves have yawn'd and yielded up their dead;
Fierce fiery warriors fought upon the clouds,
In ranks and squadrons and right form⁹ of war,   20
Which drizzled¹⁰ blood upon the Capitol;
The noise of battle hurtled¹¹ in the air,
Horses did neigh, and dying men did groan;
And ghosts did shriek and squeal about the streets.
O Caesar, these things are beyond all use¹²,   25
And I do, fear them !

---

1. *Unfold*: explain; reveal. 2. *Set ... foot*: walk on. 3. *New fir'd*: freshly inspired.
4. *Nor*: neither. 5. *Present sacrifice*: a sacrifice immediately. 6. *On my back*: when
unseen behind me. 7. *One within*: a person inside here. 8. *Whelped*: given birth to
young ones. 9. *Form*: military formations. 10. *Drizzled*: showered down. 11. *Hurtled*:
flew, noisily. 12. *All use*: all former experience.

Brutus. That also we must do. What it is, my Caius, I shall reveal to you, as we are going towards the man to whom this is to be done.

Ligarius. March on, and with a heart newly inspired I shall follow you, though I know not what is to be done. It is sufficient for me that Brutus is my leader.

Brutus. Follow me then.   *(They go out.)*

Scene II. *A room in Caesar's house.*

Tlunder and lightning. Enter Caesar *in his night-robe.*

Caesar. Neither heaven nor earth has been peaceful tonight. Three times in her sleep has Calpurnia called out, "Help, help! They are murdering Caesar! Who's there!"

Enter a Servant.

Servant. My lord?

Caesar. Go, tell the priests to sacrifice an animal to the gods now, and then bring me their opinions as to the chances of success.

Servant. I will, my lord.

Enter Calpurnia

Calpurnia. What do you intend, Caesar? Do you mean to go out? You shall not leave your house to-day.

Caesar. I shall go out. The things that have threatened me could only do so behind my back. Whenever they see my face, they disappear.

Calpurnia. Caesar, I have never believed in omens, but now they frighten me. There is a person inside who, in addition to the things that we have heard and seen, describes most dreadful sights seen by the night-watchmen. A lioness has given birth to young in the streets; graves have opened and let the dead come out. Fierce warriors of fire were seen fighting in the clouds, in lines and troops and proper formations of battle, from which blood dropped down on the Capitol. The noise of battle rushed through the air, horses neighed and dying men groaned, while ghosts shrieked and screamed in the streets. O Caesar, these things are beyond all experience, and I fear them.

Caesar.   What can be avoided
Whose end is purpos'd[1] by the mighty gods?
Yet Caesar shall go forth; for these predictions
Are to the world in general[2] as to Caesar.

    Calpurnia. When beggars die, there are no comets seen;   30
The heavens themselves blaze[3] forth the death of princes.

    Caesar. Cowards die many times before their deaths;
The valiant never taste of death but once.
Of all the wonders that I yet have heard,
It seems to me most strange that men should fear;   35
Seeing that death, a necessary end,
Will come when it will come.

Re-enter Servant

                              What say the augurers[4]?

    Servant. They would not have you to stir forth to-day.
Plucking the entrails of an offering[5] forth,
They could not find a heart within the beast.   40

    Caesar. The gods do this in shame of cowardice :
Caesar should be a beast without a heart,
If he should stay at home to-day for fear.
No, Caesar shall not. Danger knows full well
That Caesar is more dangerous than he :   45
We are two lions litter'd[6] in one day,
And I the elder and more terrible :
And Caesar shall go forth.

    Calpurnia.   Alas, my lord.
Your wisdom is consum'd[7] in confidence.   50
Do not go forth to-day; call it my fear
That keeps you in the house, and not your own.
We'll send Mark Antony to the senate-house;
And he shall say you are not well to-day :
Let me, upon my knee, prevail in this.

    Caesar. Mark Antony shall say I am not well :   55
And, for thy humour[8]. I will stay at home.

Enter Decius

Here's Decius Brutus, he shall tell them so.

---

    1. *Purpos'd*: intended; ordained. 2. *In general*: to all men. 3. *Blaze forth*: show
by fiery signals. 4. *Auguers*: the priests who interpreted omens. 5. *Offering*: an
animal killed as a sacrifice. 6. *Litter'd*: born. 7. *Consum'd in*: destroyed by 8. *For
thy humour*: because of your mood.

Caesar. What thing can be avoided if it has been willed by the mighty gods? Yet I shall go forth, for those omens may apply to all the world as well as to me.

Calpurnia. When beggars die, no comets proclaim the fact: but the heavens show by mighty signs the death of princes.

Caesar. Cowards die in imagination many times before their death; brave men only once feel the pains. Of all the strange things I have met with, it seems to me most strange that men should fear death, since it is a necessary end to all which comes at the appointed time.

Re-enter Servant.

What do the augurers say?

Servant. They do not want you to go out to-day. When they pulled out the entrails of a sacrificed animal, they found that the beast had not a heart.

Caesar. The gods have done this to shame men for cowardice. Caesar would be a beast without a heart if he were to stay at home to-day because of fear. Caesar shall not do so. Dangerous men know that I am more dangerous to them (than they to me). Danger and I are like two lions born on the same day, and I am the more terrible of the two. So I shall go out.

Calpurnia. Alas, my lord! Your wisdom is destroyed by your over-confidence. Do not go out to-day; say it is my fears which keep you in the house, and not your own. We shall send Mark Antony to the Senate House, and he will say that you are not well. Let me beg of you on my knees to have my own way in this.

Caesar. Mark Antony shall say that I am not well, and, because of your mood, I shall stay at home.

Enter Decius

Here's Decius Brutus; he shall tell them so.

Decius. Caesar, all hail ! good morrow, worthy Caesar :
I come to fetch you to the senate-house.

    Caesar. And you are come in very happy[1] time,   60
To bear my greeting to the senators,
And tell them that I will not come to-day :
Cannot, is false : and that I dare not, falser :
I will not come to-day—tell them so, Decius.

    Calpurnia. Say he is sick.   65

    Caesar.   Shall Caesar send a lie?
Have I in conquest stretch'd mine arm so far,
To be afeard[2] to tell graybeards[3] the truth?
Decius, go tell them Caesar will not come.

    Decius. Most mighty Caesar, let me know some cause,
Lest I be laugh'd at when I tell them so.   70

    Caesar. The cause is in my will,—I will not come;
That is enough to satisfy the senate.
But, for your private[4] satisfaction,
Because I love you, I will let you know :
Calpurnia here, my wife, stays[5] me at home;   75
She dreamt to-night she saw my statue,
Which, like a fountain with an hundred spouts,
Did run pure blood; and many lusty[6] Romans
Came smiling, and did bathe their hands in it :
And these does she apply for warnings, and portents,
And evils imminent[7], and on her knee   80
Hath begg'd that I will stay at home to-day.

    Decius. This dream is all amiss[8] interpreted;
It was a vision fair and fortunate :
Your statue spouting blood in many pipes[9],   85
In which so many smiling Romans bath'd,
Signifies that from you great Rome shall suck
Reviving blood; and that great men shall press
For tinctures[10], stains, relics, and cognizance[11],
This by Calpurnia's dream is signified.   90

    Caesar. And this way have you well expounded[12] it.

---

1. *Happy*: appropriate. 2. *Afeard*: afraid. 3. *Graybeards*: old men. 4. *Private*:
personal. 5. *Stays*: keeps; detains. 6. *Lusty*: strong. 7. *Imminent*: soon to happen.
8. *Amiss*: wrongly. 9. *Pipes*: spouts. 10. *Tinctures*: stains, articles stained in Caesar's
blood. 11. *Cognizance*: mementos. 12. *Expounded*: explained; interpreted.

Decius. Greeting, Caesar, Good morning, worthy Caesar. I have come to take you to the Senate House.

Caesar. You have come just at the right time to convey my greetings to the senators and tell them that I shall not come to-day. It would be false to say "cannot come" and more false to say "dare not" I will not come to-day; tell them so, Decius.

Calpurnia. Say he is sick.

Caesar. Shall I send a lying message? Have I stretched my arm over the world in military conquest, to be afraid now to tell the truth to grey-bearded senators? Decius, tell them that Caesar will not come (no more).

Decius. Most mighty Caesar, give me some proper explanation or else they will laugh at me when I tell them.

Caesar. The reason is that I have willed it : I will not come. That is enough to satisfy the senate. But to explain to you privately, because I love you, I may inform you that it is my wife Calpurnia who keeps me at home. She dreamed last night that she saw my statue, from which blood was pouring as if from a fountain with a hundred spouts. Many strong Romans were coming smiling to bathe their hands in the blood. This dream she takes to be a warning and a prophetic sign of coming evils, and on her knees she has begged that I shall stay at home to-day.

Decius. She has interpreted the dream quite wrongly. It is a fair and favourable dream. Your statue, spouting blood from many pipes, in which so many smiling Romans were bathing, signifies that from you Rome shall draw new life-blood, and that great men shall press to get handkerchiefs coloured and stained in it as relics and mementos. This is what is meant by Calpurnia's dreams.

Caesar. And you have given a worthy interpretation.

Decius. I have, when you have heard what I can say:
And know[1] it now,—the senate have concluded
To give, this day, a crown to mighty Caesar.
If you shall send them word you will not come,   95
Their minds may change. Besides, it were a mock
Apt to be render'd[2], for some one to say,
"Break up the senate till another time,
When Caesar's wife shall meet with better dreams."
If Caesar hide himself, shall they not whisper,   100
"Lo, Caesar is afraid"?
Pardon me, Caesar; for my dear dear love
To your proceeding bids me tell you this;
And reason to my love is liable[3].

    Caesar. How foolish do your fears seem now,
                          Calpurnia!   105
I am ashamed I did yield to them.
Give me my robe, for I will go :—

       Enter Publius, Brutus, Ligarius. Metellus, Casca,
                Trebonius *and* Cinna
And look where Publius is come to fetch me.
    Publius, Good morrow, Caesar.
    Caesar.   Welcome, Publius.—
What, Brutus, are you stirr'd so early too?—   110
Good morrow. Casca. —Caius Ligarius,
Caesar was ne'er so much your enemy
As that some ague[4] which hath made you lean.
What is o'clock?
    Brutus.   Caesar, 'tis strucken eight.
    Caesar. I think you for pains and courtesy.   115
             Enter Antony
See! Antony, that revels long o'nights,
Is notwithstanding up[5]. Good morrow, Antony.
    Antony. So to most noble Caesar.
    Caesar.   Bid them prepare within;
I am to blame to be thus waited for[6].
Now, Cinna:— now, Metellus:—what, Trebonius!   120
I have an hour's talk in store[7] for you;
Remember that you call on me to-day:
Be near me that I may remember you.

---

1. *Know it*: hear this from me. 2. *Apt to be render'd*: likely to be passed or said.
3. *Is liable*: is influenced by. 4. *Ague*: feverish shivering fit. 5. *Notwithstanding up*:
is nevertheless arisen. 6. *Waited for*: making you wait for me. 7. *In store*: arranged
for; reserved.

Decius. I shall have done so, when you have heard all I have to say. So hear it now: the Senate have decided to give to-day a crown to mighty Caesar. If you send them word that you will not come, they may change their minds. Besides it makes it possible for some one to mock, saying, "Dismiss the Senate till another time, when Caesar's wife shall have had better dreams." If Caesar hides, will they not whisper, "See, Caesar is afraid!" Forgive me, Caesar, because of my great devotion to your interests which makes me tell you this, and my reason has to give way to my devotion.

Caesar. How foolish your fears seem now, Calpurnia. I am ashamed that I yielded to them. Give me my robe, for I shall go :—

Enter Publius, Brutus, Ligarius, Metellus, Casca,

Trebonius *and* Cinna.

See, here Publius has come to take me.

Publius. Good morning, Caesar.

Caesar. Welcome, Publius. What, Brutus, are you arisen so early too? Good morning, Casca, Caius Ligarius, Caesar was never so unfriendly to you as the fever which has made you thin. What time is it?

Brutus. Caesar, it has struck eight.

Caesar. I thank you for your trouble and your courtesy.

Enter Antony.

See, Antony who feasts so late at night is, nevertheless arisen, Good morning, Antony.

Antony. The same to you, most noble Caesar.

Caesar. Tell those in the house to make ready. I am to balme for thus making the Senate wait for me. Now, Cinna, Metellus: — what, Trebonius! I want to have an hour's friendly talk with you: please remember to call on me today. Be near me so that I may remember you.

Trebonius. Caesar, I will:— [*Aside*] and so near will I be,
That your best friends shall wish I had been further.   125

     Caesar. Good friends, go in, and taste some wine with me;
And we, like friends, will straightway go together.

     Brutus. [*Aside*] That every like is not the same, O Caesar,
The heart of Brutus yearns[1] to thin upon!   [*Exeunt*

SCENE III. A street near the Capitol

Enter Artemidorus, reading a paper

     Artemidorus. "Caesar, beware of Brutus; take heed of
Cassius; come not near Casca; have an eye to Cinna; trust not
Trebonius; mark well Metellus Cimber; Decius Brutus loves thee
not: thou hast wronged Caius Ligarius, There is but one mind in all
these men, and it is bent[2] against Caesar. If thou beest not immortal,   5
look about you : security gives way to conspiracy.
The mighty gods defend there ! Thy lover, Artemidorus.
Here will I stand till Caesar pass along,
and as a suitor[3] will I give him this.
My heart laments that virtue cannot live   10
Out of the teeth of emulation[4].
If thou read this, O Caesar, thou mayst live;
If **not**, the Fates with traitors do contrive[5].   [*Exit*

SCENE IV. Another part of the same street,

before the house of Brutus

Enter Portia and Lucius

     Portia. I prithee, boy, run to the senate-house;
Stay not **to** answer me, but get thee gone;
Why dost thou stay?

     Lucius.   To know my errand, madam.

     Portia. I would have had thee there, and here again,
Ere I can tell thee what thou shouldst do there.—   5
[*Aside*] O constancy[6], be strong upon my side,
Set a huge mountain 'tween my heart and tongue!
I have a man's mind, but a woman's might[7],
How hard it is for women to keep counsel!—
Art thou here yet?

---

     1. *Yearns*: is sore and regretful. 2. *Bent*: turned against. 3. *A suitor*: one with
a petition. 4. *Emulation*: out of the grasp of jealousy, &c. 5. *Do contrive*: are plotting.
6. *Constancy;* a steady spirit. 7. *Might*: physical strength.

Trebonius. Caesar, I will. (*Speaking aside*) I shall be so close to you that your best friends will wish I had been further away.

Caesar. Good friends, will you come in and drink some wine with me? Then we will all go off together like good friends.

Brutus. (*Aside*) Things which are "like" are not the same thing, O Caesar, a sad fact for my heart to think upon! (*They go*)

SCENE III

A street near the Capitol. Enter Artemidorus

reading a paper

Artemidorus. "Caesar, beware of Brutus; be careful of Cassius, do not come near Casca: keep a watch on Cinna; do not trust Trebonius; keep watch on Metellus Cimber; Decius Brutus does not like you, you have wronged Caius Ligarius. All these men are of one mind, and that is opposed to Caesar. If you are not proof against death keep watch about you: your security is threatened by conspiracy. May the mighty gods defend you! Your admirer, Artemidorus."

I shall stand here till Caesar passes along, and I shall give him this as if I were a petitioner. My heart is said to think that virtue cannot live beyond the power of jealousy. If you read this, Caesar, you may live: it not, then Destiny is allied with traitors. (*He goes out*)

SCENE IV

Another part of the same street, before the house of Brutus,

Enter Portia *and* Lucius

Portia. I pray you, boy, run to the Senate House. Do not stay to answer me, but go. Why are you staying?

Lucius. To know what my errand is, madam.

Portia. I would have liked you to be there and back again before I shall be able to tell you what you are to do there. (*Aside*) O, self-control, help me! Put a barrier between the feelings of my heart, and my tongue which would utter them. I have a man's brain but only a woman's emotions. It is hard for a woman to keep silence on what she knows. Are you here yet?

     Lucius. Madam, what should I do?   10
Run to the Capitol, and nothing else?
And so return to you, and nothing else?
     Portia. Yes, bring me word, by, if thy lord look well.
For he went sickly[1] forth: and take good note
What Caesar doth, what suitors press to him.   15
Hark, boy! what noise is that?
     Lucius. I hear none, madam.
     Portia.   Prithee, listen well :
I hear a bustling rumour[2], like a fray[3],
And the wind brings it from the Capitol.
     Lucius. Sooth, madam, I hear nothing.   20

                Enter Soothsayer

     Portia. Come hither, fellow: which way hast thou been?
     Soothsayer. At mine own house, good lady.
     Partia. What is't o'clock?
     Soothsayer.   About the ninth hour, lady.
     Portia. Is Caesar yet gone to the Capitol?
     Soothsayer. Madam, not yet: I go to take my stand,   25
To see him pass on to the Capitol.
     Portia. Thou hast some suit[4] to Caesar, hast thou not ?
     Soothsayer. That I have, lady: if it will please Caesar
To be so good to Caesar as to hear me,
I shall beseech him to be friend himself.   30
     Portia. Why, know'st thou any harm's intended
               towards him?
     Soothsayer, None that I know will be, much that I
               fear may chance[5].
Good morrow to you—Here the street is narrow :
The throng that follows Caesar at the heels,
Of senators, of praetors[6], common suitors[7],   35
Will crowd a feeble man almost to death:
I'll get me place more void[8], and there
Speak to great Caesar as he comes along   [*Exit*
     Portia. I must ago in.—[*Aside*] Ay me, how weak a thing
The heart of woman is ! O Brutus,   40
The heavens speed[9] thee in thine enterprise!—
Sure, the boy heard me,—Brutus hath a suit
That Caesar will not grant—O, I grow faint.—
Run, Lucius, and commend[10] me to my lord;

---

1. *Sickly forth*: went out like a sick man. 2. *Bustling rumour*: a roar of voices.
3. *Fray*: a fight or disturbance. 4. *Suit*: petition. 5. *Chance*: happen. 6. *Praetors*:
minor officials. 7. *Suitors*: petitioners. 8. *More void*: less crowded. 9. *Speed*:
prosper. 10. *Commend*: give my regards.

Lucius. Madam. what am I to do : Run to the Capitol, and no more? And then return to you, and no more than that ?

Portia. Yes, and bring me news, boy, whether your master looks well, for he went away rather unwell. Take good note of what Caesar is doing and what petitioners are pressing round him. Listen, boy! What noise is that?

Lucius. I hear none, madam.

Portia. I pray you, listen well. I hear a confused murmur like a conflict, and the wind brings it from the direction of the Capitol.

Lucius. Truly, madam, I hear nothing.

Enter Soothsayer

Portia. Come here, fellow. By which way have you come?

Soothsayer. From my own house, good lady.

Pornia. What time is it?

Soothsayer. About the ninth hour, lady.

Portia. Has Caesar gone to the Capitol yet?

Soothsayer. No, madam, not yet. I am going to take up a position where I can see him pass to the Capitol.

Portia. You have some application to make to Caesar, have you not?

Soothsayer. That I have, lady. If it will please Caesar to consult his own interests by hearing me. I shall beg to him to look after his own safety.

Portia. Why, do you know of any harm that is aimed against him.

Soothsayer. None that I know definitely will happen, but much that I fear is possible. Good morning to you. The street is narrow here, and the crowd that follows at the heels of Caesar—senators, praetors, common petitioners, will crowd a weak man almost to death. I shall get along to a more empty place, and there shall speak to great Caesar as he comes along. (*He goes*)

Portia. I must go in. (*Aside*) Oh, how weak a thing the heart of a women is ! O Brutus, may the heavens prosper you in your enterprise! Sure the boy Lucius heard me. Brutus has a request that Caesar will not grant. O, I am growing faint. Run, Lucius, and give my compliments to your master.

Say I am merry[1], come to me again.
And bring me word what he doth say to thee.   43

                              [Exeunt severally

ACT III

SCENE I. *Before the Capitol; the* Senate
sitting above

*A crowd of people in the street leading to the Capitol;
among them* Artemidorus *and the* Soothsayer[2]. *Flourish.*
Enter Caesar, Brutus, Cassius, Casca, Decius, Metellus,
Trebonius, Cinna, Antony, Lepidus, Popilius, Publius, *and
others.*

Caesar. The ides of March are come.

Soothsayer. Ay, Caesar; but not gone.

Artemidortus. Hail, Caesar ! read this schedule[3].

Decius. Trebonius doth desire you to o'er-read,
At your best leisure, this his humble suit.   5

Artemidorus. O Caesar, read mine first; for mine's a suit
That touches[4] Caesar nearer: read it, great Caesar.

Caesar. What touches us ourself shall be last serv'd.

Artemidorus. Delay not, Caesar; read it instantly.

Caesar. What, is the fellow mad?   10

Publius.   Sirrah, give place[5].

Cassius. What, urge[6] you your petitions in the street?
Come the the Capitol.

Caesar goes up to the Senate-House, the rest following

Popilius. I wish your enterprise to-day may thrive.

Cassius. What enterprise, Popillius?

Popilius.   Fare you well.

[Advances to Caesar

Brutus. What said Popilius Lena?   15

Cassius. He wish'd to-day our enterprise might thrive,
I fear our purpose is discovered.

Brutus. Look, how he makes to Caesar; mark him.

Cassius. Casca, be sudden, for we fear prevention[7].—
Brutus, what shall be done? If this be known,   20
Cassius or Caesar never shall turn back,
For I will slay myself.

---

1. *Merry*: cheerful; happy. 2. *Soothsayer*: fortune-teller. 3. *Schedule*: document.
4. *Touches*: concerns; affects. 5. *Give place*: made way. 6. *Urge you*: do you press.
7. *We fear Prevention*: fear we will be stopped.

Tell him I am in good spirits, and then return and tell me what he says to you.

(*They go out separately*)

ACT III

SCENE I. *Before the Capitol; the Senate*
sitting above

A crowd of people in the street leading to the
Capitol; among them Artemidorus *and the*
Soothsayer. *A sound of trumpets. Enter* Caesar,
Brutus, Cassius, Casca, Decius, Metellus.
Trebonius, Cinna, Antony. Lepidus,
Popilius, Publius, *and others.*

Caesar. The ides of March have come.

Soothsayer. Yes, Caesar, but not finished.

Artemidorus. Hail, Caesar! Read this paper.

Decius. Trebonius wishes you to read over this humble petition of his at your leisure.

Artemidorus. O Caesar, read mine first, for mine is an application that concerns Caesar more personally. Read it, great Caesar.

Caesar. What concerns me personally will be the last to receive attention.

Artemidorus. Do not delay, Caesar. Read it at once.

Caesar. What, is the fellow mad?

Publius. Get out of the way, fellow.

Cassius. Why are you pressing your petitions in the street? Come to the Capitol.

(Caesar *goes up to the Senate House, the rest following*)

Popilius. I wish that your enterprise to-day may be successful.

Cassius. What enterprise, Popilius?

Popilius. Good-bye. (*He goes towards Caesar*).

Brutus. What did Popilius Lena say?

Cassius. He hoped that our enterprise to-day might succeed. I fear our intentions have been discovered.

Brutus. See how he goes towards Caesar; watch him!

Cassius. Casca, be quick, for we fear they may prevent us. Brutus, what is to be done? If this should become known, then either Cassius or Caesar will not return from here, for I shall slay myself.

Brutus   Cassius, be constant.
Popiloius Lena speaks not of our purposes;
For, look, he smiles, and Caesar doth not change.

    Cassius.   Trebonius knows his time; for, look you, Brutus   25
He draws Mark Antony out of the way.

                [Exeunt Antony and Trebonius

    Decius.   Where is Metellus Cimber ? Let him go.
And presently prefer[1] his suit to Caesar.

    Brutus.   He is address'd[2]: press never and second[3] him.

    Cinna.   Casca, you are the first that rears[4] your hand.   30

    Caesar.   Are we all ready?   What is now amiss
That Caesar and his senate must redress?

    Metellus.   Most high, most mighty, and most puissant[5] Caesar,
Metellus Cimber throws before thy seat
An humble heart,—   *[Kneeling*

    Caesar.   I must prevent thee, Cimber.   35
These couching[6] and these lowly courtesies
Might fore the blood of ordinary men.
And turn pre-ordinance and first decree[7]
Into the law of children. Be not fond[8],
To think that Caesar bears such rebel blood   40
That will be thaw'd from the true quality
With that which melteth fools; I mean, sweet words.
Low-crooked[9] court'sies and base spaniel–fawning.
Thy brother by decree is banished:
If thou dost bend and pray and fawn for him,   45
I spurn thee like a cur[10] out of my way.
Know, Caesar doth not wrong, nor without cause.
Will he be satisfied.

    Metellus.   Is there no voice more worthy than my own,
To sound more sweetly in great Caesar's ear
For the repealing[11] of my banish'd brother?

    Brutus.   I kiss thy hand but not in flattery, Caesar;
Desiring thee that Publius Cimber may
Have an immediate freedom of repeal[12].

    Caesar.   What, Brutus!   55

    Cassius.   Pardon. Caesar: Caesar, pardon :
As low as to thy foot doth Cassius fall,

---

1. *Prefer*: present; submit.   2. *Address'd*: is addressing him.   3. *Second*: support.   4. *Rears your hand*: strikes.   5. *Puissant*: mighty.   6. *Couchings*: low bows. 7. *Preordinance and first decree*: laws and regulations.   8. *Fond* : foolish.   9. *Low-crooked*: with knees bent low.   10. *Cur*: pariah dog.   11. *Repealing*: recalling from exile.   12. *Freedom of repeal*: freecdom to return.

Brutus. Cassius, be calm. Popilius Lena is not speaking of our intention to Caesar, for, see, he is smiling and Caesar has not changed his expression.

Cassius. Trebonius knows that the time for his action has come, for, see, he is drawing Mark Antony away.

(Antony *and* Trebonius *go out*)

Decius. Where is Metellus Cimber? Let him go soon and put up his application to Caesar.

Brutus. He is addressing. Push closer and support him.

Cinna. Casca, you are the first to raise your hand.

Caesar. Are we all ready? What now is there that is wrong, for Caesar and his Senate to put right?

Metellus. Most high, most mighty, and most powerful Caesar, Metellus Cimber approaches your throne with a humble heart.—

Caesar. I must stop you, Cimber. Those bows and bendings down low might excite the natures of ordinary men, and turn predestined things and basic rules into the laws of children. Do not be so foolish as to think that Caesar has such an unstable nature that it can be swayed from the proper course by that which influences fools.—I mean by sweet words, low-bending bows and base and spaniel-like servility. Your brother has been banished by an edict. If you are going to bow down and beg and flatter on his behalf, I push you out of my way like a mongrel dog. Understand that Caesar does no wrong act, and he will not be satisfied without sound reasons.

Metellus. Is there no one with a voice more influential than mine, which will get a better reception from Caesar, to ask for the recall of my banished brother?

Brutus. I kiss your hand, though in no spirit of flattery, Caesar, asking of you that Publius Cimber may immediately have freedom by being allowed to come back from banishment.

Caesar. What, you Brutus!

Cassius. Pardon me, great Caesar. Even at your feet does Cassius fall

To beg enfranchisement[1] for Publius Cimber.

    Caesar. I could be well move'd, if I were as you;
If I could pray to move, prayers would move me :
But I am constant as the northern star,   60
Of whose true-fix'd and resting quality[2]
There is no fellow[3] in the firmament.
The skies are painted with unnumber'd sparks[4],
They are all fire, and every one doth shine;
But there's but one in all doth holl his place :   65
So in the world,—'tis furnish'd well with men,
And men are flesh and blood, and apprehensive :
Yet in the number I do know but one
That unassailable holds on his rank[5].
Unshake'd of motion[6]: and that I am he,   70
Let me a little show it, even in this,—
That I was constant Cimber should be banish'd.
And constant do remain to keep him so.

    Cinna.   O Caesar.—

    Caesar.   Hence ! wilt thou lift up Olympus[7]?

    Decius. Great Caesar,—

    Caesar.   Doth not Brutus bootless[8] kneel?   75

    Casca. Speak; hands, for me!

    Casca *stabs* Caesar *in the neck. He is then stabbed by*
    several other Conspirators, and last by Marcus Brutus.

    Caesar.   Et tu, Brute!—Then fall, Caesar!

        [*Dies. The Senators and People retire in confusion.*]

    Cinna. Liberty ! Freedom ! Tyranny is dead!—
Run hence, proclaim, cry it about the streets.

    Cassius.   Some to the common pulpits[9], and cry out,   80
"Liberty, freedom, and enfranchisement!"

    Brutus. People and senators, be not affrighted :
Fly not; stand still:—ambition's debt is paid[10].

    Casca. Go to the pulpit, Brutus.

    Decius.   And Cassius too.

---

    1. *Enfranchisment*: restoring to freedom   2. *True-fix'd &c*: exact and regular
nature. 3. *Fellow*: equal. 4. *Unnumbered sparks*: numerous points of light. 5. *Holds
on his rank*: keeps on in his course. 6. *Of motion*: in his career. 7. *Lift up Olympus*:
remove a mountain. 8. *Botless*: in vain. 9. *Pulpits*: lecture platforms. 10. *Ambition's debt.
&c.*: the punishment for ambition is complete.

to beg for restoration of freedom for Publius Cimber.

Caesar. It would be possible to move me easily, if I were like you. If I could lower myself to pray to other people, then prayers move me. But I am as fixed in my course as the Pole star, of the same fixed and immovable nature as makes it without equal in the heavens. The skies are dotted with numerous small stars; they are all stars and all shed their light. But there is only one among them all which holds its place unchangingly. So it is in the world. It is well filled with men, and all men are made of flesh and blood and are intelligent. Yet of them all I only know one who holds on his career, no matter how he is assailed, unshaken in his course, and I am that man. Let me show it even in this case; I was constant in my resolve that Cimber should be banished, and I remain constant in my resolve to keep him banished.

Cinna. O Caesar.

Caesar. Begone! You might as well try to move Mount Olympus.

Decius. Great Caesar, —

Caesar. Has not Brutus knelt in vain?

Casca. Now let my hands speak for me!

(Casca *stabs* Caesar *in the neck. He is then stabbed by the other*

conspirators, last of all by Brutus)

Caesar. And you too, Brutus! Then let Caesar fall!

[*Caesar dies. The senators and people retire in confusion*].

Cinna. Liberty! Freedom! Tyranny is dead! Run from here, announce it, shout it out in the streets.

Cassius. Let some go to the public speaking-platforms, and cry out. "Liberty, freedom, and deliverance !"

Brutus. Citizens and senators, do not be afraid. Do not run away, but stand still. Caesar has paid the price of his ambition.

Casca. Go on the platform, Brutus.

Decius. And Cassius also.

Brutus. Where's Publius?   85

Cinna. Here, quite confounded with the mutiny.

Metellus. Stand fast together, lest some friend of
        Caesar's should chance—

Brutus. Talk not of standing.—Publius, good cheer :
There is no harm intended to your person,   90
Nor to no Roman else[1]: so tell them, Publius.

Cassius. And leave us, Publius; lest that the people,
Rushing on us, should do your age some mischief.

Brutus. Do so:— and let no man abide[2] this deed,
But we the doers

                    Re-enter Trebonius

Cassius. Where's Antony?

Trebonius.   Fled to house amaz'd :
Men, wives, and children stare, cry out, and run
As it were domsday.

Brutus.   Fates, we will know your pleasures :
That we shall die, we know; 'tis but the time,
And drawing days out, that men stand upon.   100

Cassius. Why, he that cuts off twenty years of life
Cuts off so many years of fearing death.

Brutus. Grant that, and then is death a benefit :
So are we Caesar's friends, that have abridg'd[3]
His time of fearing death.—Stoop, Romans, stoop,   105
And let us bathe our hands in Caesar's blood
Up to the elbows, and besmear our swords :
Then walk we forth, even to the market-place,
And, waving our red weapons o'er our heads,
Let's all cry, "Peace, freedom, and liberty!"   110

Cassius. Stoop, then, and wash.—How many ages hence
Shall this our lofty scene be acted over
In states unborn and accents[4] yet unknown !

Brutus. How many times shall Caesar bleed in sport,
That now on Pompey's basis[5] lies along   115
Now worthier than the dust !

Cassius.   So oft as that shall be.
So often shall the knot[6] of us be call'd
The men that gave their country liberty.

Decius. What, shall we forth?

---

1. *No Roman else*: no other Roman. 2. *Abide*: be responsible for. 3. *Abridg'd*:
cut short. 4. *Accents*: languages. 5. *Pompey's basis:* the base of Pompey's pillar
6. *Knot*: group.

Brutus. Where's Publius !

Cinna. Here, quite amazed by this uprising.

Metellus. Let us remain firmly together, lest some friend of Caesar's should —

Brutus. Do not talk of standing still. Publius, be cheerful. There is no personal harm intended towards you, or to any other Roman. Tell them so, Publius.

Cassius. You should leave us, Publius, lest the people should attack us and do harm to one so young.

Brutus. Yes, do so. Let no man be responsible for this deed except those who have done it.

Re-enter Trebonius

Cassius. Where's Antony?

Trebonius. Fled to his house in great confusion. Men women, and children are staring, crying out, and running as if it were the day of judgment.

Brutus. Now Destiny, we shall know what you propose for us. That we shall die, we know well. It is only a case of the time, and prolonging their days that men are concerned with.

Cassius. And he who loses twenty years of his life only loses so many years of miserable fear of death.

Brutus. If that be assumed, then death is a benefit. So we, who are Caesar's friends, have shortened his period of fearing death. Bend down, ye Romans, and bathe your hands in Caesar's blood up to the elbows, and smear it on your swords. Then let us walk forth, even to the market place, waving our red swords over our heads and shouting, "Peace, Freedom, and Liberty!"

Cassius. Bend down, then, and bathe. How often in future ages will this lofty scene be acted over again, in countries which are as yet unformed and in languages which are not yet spoken !

Brutus. How many times shall Caesar's death be shown in sport (on the stage), he who now lies at the base of Pompey's statue, of no more value than dust.

Cassius. And, as often as that happens, so often shall this group of us be called the men who gave their country liberty.

Decius. Well, shall we go out?

Cassius.   Ay, every man away :
Brutus, shall lead; and we will grace his heels   120
With the most boldest and best hearts of Rome.

Brutus.   Soft! who comes here?

Enter a Servant
A friend of Antony's.

Servant.   Thus, Brutus, did my master bid me kneel;
Thus did Mark Antony bid me fall down;
And, being prostrate, thus he bade me say:—   125
Brutus is noble, wise, valiant, and honest :
Caesar was mighty, bold, royal, and loving;
Say I love Brutus and I honour him;
Say I fear'd Caesar, honour'd him, and lov'd him.
If Brutus will vouchsafe that Antony   130
May safely come to him. and be resolv'd
How Caesar has deserv'd to lie in death.
Mark Antony shall not love Caesar dead
So well as Brutus living; but will follow
The fortunes and affairs of noble Brutus   135
Thorough the hazards of this untrod[1] sate
With all true faith. So say my master Antony.

Brutus.   Thy master is a wise and valiant Roman;
I never thought him worse.
Tell him, so please him come unto this place,   140
He shall be satisfied; and, by my honour,
Depart untouch'd.

Servent.   I'll fetch him presently.   [*Exit*

Brutus.   I know that we shall have him well to friend.

Cassius.   I wish we may: but yet have I a mind
That fears him much; and my misgiving[2] still   145
Falls sherewdly to the purpose[3].

Brutus.   But here comes Antony.

Re-enter Antony.

Welcome, Mark Antony.

Antony.   O mighty Caesar! dost thou lie so low?
Are all the conquests, glories, triumphs, spoils,
Shrunk to this little measure ? Fare thee well.—   150
I know not, gentlement, what you intend,
Who else must be let blood, who else is rank[4]:

---

1. *Untrod*: untried. 2. *Misgiving*: doubts. 3. *Falls.... purpose*: hits the nail on the head. 4. *Rank*: in need of blood-letting.

Cassius. Yes, every man away! Brutus shall lead, and we shall form a dignified following of the boldest and best men of Rome.

Brutus. Stop, who comes here?

Enter a Servant.

A friend of Antony's.

Servant. In this way, Brutus, did my master Antony order me to kneel: thus did he tell me to tall down before you, and in this position he told me to say "Brutus is noble, wise, valiant and honest. Caesar was mighty, bold, royal, and loving. Antony loves Brutus and honours him: he feared Caesar, honoured him and loved him. If Brutus will grant that Antony may come to him in safety and have it explained how Caesar has deserved to lie dead, then Mark Antony shall not love the dead Caesar so well as he will love the living Brutus. He will rather follow the fortunes and actions of noble Brutus through the dangers of the untrodden path he is upon, with the fullest confidence." That is what my master, Antony, says.

Brutus. Your master is a wise and valiant Roman, and I never thought of him as less than that. Tell him, if he will please come to my house, I shall satisfy his doubts, and, on my word of honour, he shall be allowed to depart unharmed.

Servant. I shall bring him soon. (*Goes out*).

Brutus. I wish that we might have him as a friend.

Cassius. I wish that also. But there is something in my mind which fears him greatly, and my fears usually seem to hit the truth.

Brutus. But here comes Antony.

Re-enter Antony.

Welcome, Mark Antony !

Antony. O mighty Caesar, do you lie so low there? Are all your gains, your glories, your triumphs and plunder reduced to this little space? Good-bye! I do not know, gentlemen, what you intend, who else is required to shed his blood, who else is too strong. If it is myself, there is no hour

If I myself, there is no hour so fit
As Caesar's death's hour; nor no instrument
Of half that worth as those your swords, made rich   155
With the most noble blood of all this world.
I do beseech ye if you bear me hard[1],
Now, whilst your purpled hands do reek[2] and smoke,
Fulfil your pleasure. Live a thousand years,
I shall not find myself so apt[3] to die :   160
No place will please me so, no mean of death,
As here by Caesar, and by you cut off,
The choice and master spirits of this age.

    Brutus. O Antony, big not your death of us.
Though now we must appear bloody and cruel,   165
As, by our hands and this our present act,
You see we do; yet see you but our hands,
And this the bleeding business they have done :
Our hearts you see not,—they are pitiful;
And pity to the general wrong of Rome——   170
As fire drives out fire, so pity pity—
Hath done this deed on Caesar. For your part,
To you our swords have leaden[4] points, Mark Antony :
Our arms, in strength of malice, and our hearts
Of brothers' temper, do receive you in   175
With all kind love, good thoughts, and reverence.

    Cassius. Your voice shall be as strong as any man's
In the disposing of new dignities[5].

    Brutus. Only be patient till we have appeas'd
The multitude, beside themeslves with fear,
And then we will deliver[6] you the cause,
Why I, that did love Caesar when I struck him,
Have thus proceeded.

    Antony.   I doubt not of your wisdom.
Let each man render me his bloody hand :
First Marcus Brutus, will I shake with you;—   185
Next Caius Cassius, do I take your hand;
Now, Decius Brutus, yours;—now yours, Metellus;
Yours, Cinna;—and, my valiant Casca, yours;—
Thou last, not least in love, yours, good Trebonius.
Gentlemen all,—alas, what shall I say ?   190
My credit[7] now stands on such slippery[8] ground,

---

1. *Bear me hard*: are hostile to me. 2. *Reek* : give off steam. 3. *Apt*: ready.
4. *Leaden*: dull and harmless. 5. *Dignities*: appointments. 6. *Deliver*: explain.
7. *Credit;* reputation. 8. *Slippery*: insecure.

so fit for me to die as Caesar's death hour. No instruments (to cause my death) could be half so valuable as your swords, enriched as they are by the most noble blood in the world. I beseech you, if you bear hard feelings against me, now while your red hands still steam with the blood of Caesar, carry out your wishes. If I live a thousand years, I shall never find myself more ready for death. No other place will please me so well: no other way of death will be so good as to be here beside Caesar, and slain by you, the foremost and greatest spirits of our time.

Brutus. O Antony, do not ask for death from us. Though now we must appear bloody and cruel, as by our (blood-stained) hands and the deed we have done, you see that we do, yet you only see our hands and the bloody deed which they have done. You cannot see the motives of our hearts, and they are full of pity. It is pity for the public wrongs of Rome which has done this deed to Caesar, for as fire puts out fire, so has that pity put out the pity we had for him. But as concerns you, our swords are as harmless as if made of lead, Mark Antony. Our arms, strong in their ill-feeling to Caesar and our hearts, full of brotherly love for our friends, alike welcome you with kind love, good thoughts and with respect.

Cassius. Your opinion shall be as influential as any man's in making new appointments.

Brutus. Only be patient till we have calmed the multitude now in a state of great fear, and then we shall explain to you the causes which made me, who loved Caesar, act as I did.

Antony. I do not doubt your wise judgment. Let each man give me his blood-stained hand. First, Marcus Brutus, I shake hands with you. Next do I take your hand Caius Cassius, and now Decius Brutus, and Metellus, and your's Cinna, and then your hand, valiant Casca. Then last, though not the least in my love for him, good Trebonius. Gentlemen, what am I to say? My credit with you is now a difficult dilemma, for you must form one or other of

That one of two bad ways you must conceit me,
Either a coward or a flatterer.
That I did love thee, Caesar, O, 'tis true :
If, then, thy spirit look upon us now,   195
Shall it not grieve thee dearer[1] than thy death,
To see thy Antony making his peace,
Shaking the bloody fingers of thy foes,
Most noble! in the presence of thy corse?
Had I as many eyes as thou hast wounds,   200
Weeping as fast as they stream forth thy blood,
It would become me better than to close[2]
In terms of friendship with thine enemies.
Pardon me, Julius,—Here wast thou bay'd[3] brave hart,
Here didst thou fall; and here thy hunters stand,   205
Sign'd in thy spoil, and crimson'd in the lathe[4].
O world. thou wast the forest to this hart;
And this, indeed, O world, the heart of thee.—
How like a deer, strucken by many princes,
Dost thou here lie!   210

    Cassius.   Mark Antony,—

    Antony.   Pardon me, Caius Cassius :

The enemies of Caesar shall say this;
Then, in a friend, it is cold modesty.

    Cassius.   I blame you not for praising Caesar so;
But what compact mean you to have with us?
Will you be prick'd in number of our friends;
or shall we on, and not depend on you?

    Antony.   Therefore I took your hand, but was, indeed,
Sway'd from the point, by looking down on Caesar.
Friends am I with you all, and love you all;   220
Upon this hope, that you shall give me reasons
Why and wherein Caesar was dangerous.

    Brutus.   Or else were this a savage spectacle;
Our reasons are so full of good regard[5].
That were you, Antony, the son of Caesar,   225
You should be satisfied.

    Antony.   That's all I seek :
And am moreover suitor that I may
Produce his body to the market-place;

---

1. *Dearer*: more. 2. *Close*: come terms with. 3. *Bay'd*: bought to the last stand.
4. *Lethe*: life-blood. 5. *Regard*: intentions.

two bad opinions of me — either as a coward or a flatterer. It is true that I loved you, O Caesar, if your spirit is looking at us now, it will be grieved more deeply than by your death to see Antony making peaceful terms and shaking the blood-stained hands of your foes, O noble one, in the presence of your dead body. Had I as many eyes as you have wounds, and if they were shedding tears as fast as your wounds shed blood, that would be more proper for me than to be entering into friendship with your enemies. Pardon me, Julius. Here you turned at bay like a noble deer, and here were you slain: and here stand your hunters, bearing the marks of your death and reddened with your life-blood. O, the whole world was the forest of this deer, and you were the heart (hart) of the world. How like a deer which has been slain by many princes you look as you lie here!

Cassius. Mark Antony!

Antony. Pardon me, Caius Cassius; even the enemies of Caesar shall say what I am saying, so in a friend the words are cold and moderate.

Cassius. I do not blame you for thus praising Caesar, but what bargain do you mean to make with us? Will you be enrolled among the number of those friendly to us, or shall we proceed alone, not depending on your assistance?

Antony. It was with that purpose that I took your hands, but I was led away from my point by looking down on Caesar. I am friends with you all and love all of you. But I have the hope that you will give me your reasons for having considered Caesar to be so dangerous.

Brutus. (If we had not) then this would be a savage sight. Our reasons are so full of strong argument that, even if you were Caesar's son, O Antony, they would satisfy you.

Antony. That is all I ask. I also wish to ask permission to show his body

and in the pulpit, as becomes a friend,
Speak in the order of his funeral.   230

    Brutus, You shall, Mark Antony.

    Cassius. Brutus, a word with you.
[*Aside to Brutus*] You know not what you do: Do not consent
That Antony speak in his funeral :
Know you how much the people may be mov'd
By that which he will utter?

    Brutus.   By your pardon;—
I will myself into the pulpit first,
And show the reason of our Caesar's death :
What Antony shall speak, I will protest[1]
He speaks by leave and by permission;
And that we are contented Caesar shall   240
Have all true rites and lawful ceremonies.
It shall advantage[2] more than do us wrong.

    Cassius. I know not what may fall; I like it not.

    Brutus, Mark Antony, here, take you Caesar's body.
You shall not in your funeral speech blame us,   245
But speak all good you can devise[3] of Caesar;
And say you do't by our permission;
Else shall you not have any hand at all
About his funeral : and you shall speak
In the same pulpit whereto I am going,   250
After my speech is ended.

    Antony.   Be it so;
I do desire no more

    Brutus. Prepare the body, then, and follow us.
                     [*Exeunt all except* Antony

    Antony. O, pardon me, thou bleeding piece of earth.
that I am mek and gentle with these butchers !   255
Thou art the ruins of the noblest man
That ever lived in the tide of times.[4]
Woe to the hands that shed this costly blood !
Over thy wounds now do I prophesy,—
Which, like dumb mouths, do ope their ruby lips,   260
To beg the voice and utterance[5] of my tongue,—
A curse shall light upon the limbs of men :
Domestic fury[6] and fierce civil strife

---

    1. *Protest* : state. 2. *Advantage* : benefit; profit. 3. *Devise* : make up. 4. *Tide of times*: all the ages. 5. *Utterance:* expression. 6. *Domestic fury*: disturbance in the home.

in the market-place, and, on the platform, as is fitting for a friend, speak a few words at his funeral.

Brutus. You shall, Mark Antony.

Cassius. Brutus, let me speak with you. (*Aside to* Brutus) You do not know what you are doing. Do not permit Antony to speak at Caesar's funeral. Do you know how much the people may be affected by what he says?

Brutus. If you will excuse me, I shall myself go into the pulpit first and explain the reasons for the death of Caesar. I shall say that whatever Antony speaks is by our-permission, and that we are satisfied that Caesar should have the proper rites and the correct ceremonies. This will favour us, rather than do us harm.

Cassius. I do not know what may happen, but I do not like it.

Brutus. Mark Antony! Here, you may take Caesar's body. You must not in your funeral speech put blame on us, but you may speak as much good as you like about Caesar, and say that you do it by our permission. Otherwise you will not have any part at all in his funeral. You shall speak on the same platform to which I am going, after my speech is over.

Antony. All right, I ask for no more.

Brutus. Prepare the body, then, and follow us.

(*All leave except* Antony)

Antony. O, pardon me, you bleeding piece of earth, for having been meek and gentle with your murderers. You are the ruined remains of the noblest man that ever lived in the highest point of progress. Cursed be the hands that shed your precious blood! Over your wounds now do I prophesy—as they, open themselves, red edged, like dumb mouths to beg my tongue to speak on their side—I prophesy that a curse shall fall upon the limbs of men. There shall be anger at home and civil war shall impede

Shall cumber[1] all the parts of Italy;
Blood and destruction shall be so in use,   265
And dreadful objects so familiar,
That mothers shall but smile when they behold
Their infants quarter'd[2] with the hands of war;
All pity chok'd with custom[3] of fell deeds:
And Caesar's spirit, ranging for revenge,   270
With Ate by his hole come hot from hall.
Shall in these confines with a monarch's voice
Cry "Havoc," and let slip the dogs of war;
That this foul deed shall smell above the earth
With carrion[4] men, groaning for burial.   275

Enter a Servant

You serve Octavius Caesar, do you not?

   Servant. I do, Mark Antony.

   Antony. Caesar did write for him to come to Rome.

   Servant. He did receive his letters, and is coming;
and bid me say to you by word of mouth—   280
O Caesar!—   *[Seeing the body*

   Antony, Thy heart is big, get thee apart and weep.
Passion, I see, is catching[5]; for mine eyes.
Seeing those beads of sorrow stand in thine,
Began to water. Is thy master coming?   285

   Servant. He lies to-night within seven leagues of Rome.

   Antony. Post back with speed, and tell him what hath chanc'd[6];
Here is a mourning Rome, a dangerous Rome,
No Rome of safety for Octavius yet;
Hie[7] hence, and tell him so, Yet, stay awhile;   290
Thou shalt not back till I have borne this corse
Into the market-place: there shall I try[8],
In my oration, how the people take
The cruel issue[9] of these bloody men;
According to the which, thou shalt discourse   295
To young Octavius of the state of things.
Lend me your hand.   *[Exeunt with* Caesar's body.

SCENE II. *The Forum*

Enter Brutus *and* Cassius. *and a throng of* Citizens,
Citizens. We will be satisfied: let us be satisfied.

---

   1. *Cumber*: lie heavily on. 2. *Quarter'd* : cut into four. 3. *With custom*: by
familiarity with. 4. *Carrion*: decayed in death. 5.*Catching*: infectious. 6. *Chanc'd*:
happend. 7. *Hie*: go. 8. *Try*: test; find out. 9. *Issue*: result; consequences.

progress everywhere in Italy. Blood and destruction shall be so frequent, and dreadful objects shall be so familiar that mothers will merely smile when they see their children cut up by the cruel hands of soldiers. All pity shall die as foul deeds become the general custom. The spirit of Caesar, hunting for revenge, with the rash Goddess Ate by his side, just come from Hell, shall in our boundaries with a mighty voice cry "Destruction!" and let loose the horrors of war. This foul deed shall shed an evil smell over the earth, along with the rotting bodies of men urgently needing burial.

Enter a Servant

You serve Octvius Caesar, do you not?

Servant. I do, Mark Antony.

Antony. Caesar had written to him to come to Rome.

Servant. Octavius did receive his letter, and he is coming; and he ordered me to say to you verbally —   (*He sees the body*).

O, Caesar!

Antony. Your heart is full of emotion. Draw aside and weep. Passion, I see, is infectious, for my eyes, seeing these drops of water in yours, begin to water. Is your master coming?

Servant. He halts to-night within twenty-one miles of Rome.

Antony. Travel back to him speedily and tell him what has happened. Rome is a place of mourning, a place of danger. There is no safety here for Octavius yet. Go off and tell him so. Yet wait a little. You shall not go back till I have carried this corpse into the market place. There I shall try in my speech how the people view the cruel action of these bloody men, and according to what happens you shall inform young Octavius of the state of affairs. Give me your hand to help.

(*They go, carrying* Caesar's *body*.)

SCENE II. *The Forum*

Enter Brutus *and* Cassius, *and a crowd of* citizens.

Citizens. We wish satisfactory reasons: let us have them.

Brutus.   Then follow me, and give me audience[1], friends.—
Cassius, go you into the other street.
And part the numbers—
Those that will hear me speak, let 'em stay here;   5
Those that will follow Cassius, go with him;
And public reasons shall be rendered
Of Caesar's death.
        First Citizen : I will hear Brutus speak.
        Second Citizen.   I will hear Cassius; and compare their
reasons.   10
When severally[2] we heaar them rendered.
                    [*Exit* Cassius *with some of the Citizens.*
                    Brutus goes into the pulpit

        Third Citizen.   The noble Brutus is ascended : silence!
        Brutus.   Be patient till the last.
Romans, countrymen, and lovers! hear me for my cause[3], and be   15
silent, that you may hear: believe me for mine honour, and have
respect to mine honour, that you may believe: censure[4] me in your
wisdom, and awake your senses, that you may the better judge.
If there by any in this assembly, any dear friend of Caesar's, to
him I say, that Brutus' love to Caesar was no less than his. If, then, 20
that friend demand why Brutus rose against Caesar, this is my
answer,—Not that I loved Caesar less, but that I loved Rome more.
Had you rather Caesar were living and die all slaves, than that
Caesar were dead, to live all free men? As Caesar loved me, I   25
weep for him; as he was fortunate, I rejoice at it; as he was valiant,
I honour him; but, as he was ambitious, I slew him. There is tears
for his love; joy for his fortune; honour for his valour; and death
for his ambition. Who is here so base that would be a bondman[5]?   30
If any, speak; for him have I offended. Who is here so rude that
would not be a Roman? If any, speak; for him have I offended.
Who is here so vile that will not love his country? If any, speak :
for him have I offended. I pause for a reply.   35
        Citizens. None, Brutus. none.
        Brutus. Then none have I offended. I have done no more to
Caesar than you shall do to Brutus. The question of his death is   40
enrolled[6] in the Capitol: his glory not extenuated[7], wherein he was
worthy; nor his offences enforced[8], for which he suffered death.

        Enter Antony *and others, with* Caesar's *body.*

---

    1. *Audience*: a hearing. 2. *Severally*: separately. 3. *Cause*: my explanation.
4. *Censure*: judge. 5. *Bondman*: slave. 6. *Enrolled*: recorded. 7. *Extenuated*: made
less. 8. *Enforced*: stressed; exaggerated.

Brutus. Then follow me and give me a hearing, friends.

Cassius, you go into the other street, after dividing the numbers. Those who wish to hear me speak, let them stay here. Those who want to go with Cassius, let them follow him, and a public explanation will be given of Caesar's death.

First Citizen. I shall hear Brutus speak.

Second Citizen. I shall hear Cassius, and we shall compare their reasons when we hear them given separately.

(Cassius goes out with some of the citizens:
Brutus *ascends the platform.)*

Third Citizen. The noble Brutus has ascended the platform. Silence!

Brutus. Be patient till I have finished. Romans, fellow-countrymen, and friends ! Hear me speak for my cause, and, so that you may hear, be silent. Believe me as I am a man of honour, and respect my honour that you may believe me. Judge me with your wisdom and sharpen your wits that you may be the better able to judge. If there be any one in this gathering who was a dear friend of Caesar's, to him I say that Brutus' love for Caesar was no less than his. If, then, that friend ask why Brutus rose against Caesar : this is my answer, not that I loved Caesar the less, but that my love for Rome was greater. Would you rather have Caesar alive and all of you be slaves, or have Caesar dead and all be free men? As Caesar was a loved friend, I weep for him : when he was fortunate, I rejoiced at it : when he was brave, I honoured him : but, because he was ambitious, I slew him. There are tears for his love, joy for his good fortune, respect for his bravery, but death because of his ambition. Who is here so base a man that he would wish to be a slave? If there is anyone, speak for such a man I have offended. Who is here so rough that he does not glory in being a Roman? If there is anyone, speak, for I have offended such a one. Who is so wicked that he does not love his country? If there is such a man, let him speak, for I have offended him. I pause for a reply.

Citizens. There are no such men, Brutus.

Brutus. Then I have offended no one. I have done no more to Caesar than you are at liberty to do to Brutus. The matter of his death will be recorded in the Capitol, his glory not lessened in anything in which he was worthy, nor his offences exaggerated, for which he suffered death.

Enter Antony *and others, with* Caesar's *body.*

Here comes his body, mourned by Mark Antony: who,   45
though he had no hand in his death, shall receive the benefit of his
dying, a place in the commonwealth; as which of you shall not?
With this I depart,—that, as I slew my best lover for the good of
Rome, I have the same dagger for myself, when it shall please my
country to need my death.

    Citizens.   Live, Brutus! live, live!   50
    First Citizen. Bring him with triumph[1] home unto his house.
    Second Citizen. Give him a statue with his ancestors.
    Third Citizen. Let him be Caesar.[2]
    Fourth Citizen.   Caesar's better parts   55
Shall be crown'd[3] in Brutus.
    First Citizen.   We'll bring him to his house with shouts and
clamours.
    Brutus.   My countrymen,—
    Second Citizen.   Peace, silence! Brutus speaks.
    First Citizen. Peace, ho!
    Brutus,   Good countrymen, let me depart alone,   60
And, for my sake, stay here with Antony :
Do grace to Caesar's corpse, and grace his speech
Tending[4] to Caesar's glories; which Mark Antony
By our permission, is allow'd to make.
I do entreat you, not a man depart,   65
Save I alone, till Antony have spoke.   [*Exit*
    First Citizen. Stay, ho ! and let us hear Mark Antony.
    Third Citizen. Let him go up into the public chair;
We'll hear him.— Noble Antony, go up.
    Antony. For Brutus' sake, I am beholding[5] to you.   70
                         [*Goes up into the pulpit*
    Fourth Citizen. What does he say of Brutus?
    First Citizen.   He says. for Brutus' sake.
He finds himself beholding for us all.
    Fourth Citizen. 'Twere best he speak no harm of Brutus heare.
    First Citizen.   This Caesar was a tyrant.
    Third Citizen.   Nay, that's certain
We bless'd that Rome is rid of him.   75
    Second Citizen. Peace! let us hear what Antony can say.
    Antony. You gentle Romans,—
    Citizens.   Peace, ho ! let us hear him.
    Antony. Friends, Romans, countrymen, lend me your ears;

---

    1. *With triumph*: in a procession. 2.*Caesar*: emperor. 3. *Crown'd*: completed
4. *Tending to*: dealing with. 5. *Beholding:* grateful.

I have come to assist in Caesar's burial, not to deliver praise of him. The evil deeds that man do remain after their deaths: their good actions are forgotten. Let it be so with Caesar. The noble Brutus has told you that Caesar was ambitious. If that was true, it was a severe fault and Caesar has paid a heavy penalty for it. Here, by permission of Brutus and the others — for Brutus is an honourable man, as the others are also honourable men, — have I come to speak at Caesar's funeral. He was my friend, faithful and true to me. But Brutus says he was ambitious, and we must remember that Brutus is an honourable man. Caesar has brought many prisoners of war back to Rome, and the money paid for their liberation went into the public treasury. Did this seem ambitious on Caesar's part? When poor people have suffered, Caesar has wept for them. Ambition should show a harder nature than that. Yet Brutus says he was ambitious, and Brutus is an honourable man. You all saw how, on the Festival of the Wolf, I three times offered him a royal crown, which he did three times refuse. Was this ambition? Yet Brutus says he was ambitious, and certainly he is an honourable man. I am not trying to contradict what Brutus has said, but I am only telling you what I know for myself. You all loved him once, and not without good reason. What reason is t here now that should prevent you from mourning him? O, common intelligence has become the property of animals, for men have lost their reason. Be patient with me: my heart is full of grief for Caesar there in his coffin, and I must wait till I am calm again.

First Citizen. It seems to me there is much in what he says.

Second Citizen. If you consider the matter fully, Caesar has been greatly wronged.

Third Citizen. He has, my friends, and I fear that a worse man may come in his place.

> *Fourth Citizen.* Mark'd ye his words? He would not take the
> crown;
> Therefore 'tis certain he was not ambitious.
>> *First Citizen.* If it be found so, some will dear abide[1] it.
>> *Second Citizen.* Poor soul ! his eyes are red as fire
>> with weeping.   120
>> *Third Citizen.* There's not a nobler man in Rome than
>> Antony
>> *Fourth Citizen.* Now mark him, he begins again to speak.
>> *Antony.* But yesterday the word of Caesar might
> Have stood against the world; now lies he there.
> And none so poor to do him reverence[2].   125
> O masters, if I were dispos'd to stir
> Your hearts and minds to mutiny and rage,
> I should do Brutus wrong, and Cassius wrong,
> Who, you all know, are honourable men :
> I will not do them wrong: I rather choose   130
> To wrong the dead, to wrong myself, and you.
> Than I will wrong such honourable men.
> But here's a parchment[3] with the seal of Caesar;
> I found it in his closet[4],—'tis his will :
> Let but the commons[5] hear this testament,[6]—   135
> Which, pardon me, I do not mean to read,—
> And they would go and kiss dead Caesar's wounds,
> And dip their napkins in his sacred blood;
> Yea, beg a hair of him for memory,
> And, dying, mention it within their wills,   140
> Bequeathing it as a rich legacy[7]
> Unto their issue[8].
>> *Fourth Citizen.* We'll hear the will : read it, Mark Antony.
>> *Citizens.* The will, the will! we will hear Caesar's will.
>> *Antony.* Have patience, gentle friends, I must not read it; 145
> It is not meet[9] you know how Caesar lov'd you.
> You are not wood, you are not stones, but men:
> And, being men, hearing the will of Caesar,
> It will inflame you, it will make you mad :

---

1. *Abide it:* be held responsible. 2. *Reverence*: treat him with respect. 3. *Parch-ment*: document. 4. *Closet*: private room. 5. *Commons*: the common people. 6. *Testament*: written declaration. 7. *Legacy*: anything left to another by the will of a deceased person. 8. *Issue*: children. 9. *Meet*: suitable; desirable.

Fourth Citizen. Did you notice what he said? Caesar would not accept the crown, so it is certain that he was not ambitious.

First Citizen. If it is true, then some will pay dearly for this.

Second Citizen. Poor fellow, his eyes are red as fire with weeping.

Third Citizen. There's not a nobler man in Rome than Antony.

Fourth Citizen. Now attend to him. He is going to speak again.

Antony. Only yesterday, the word of Caesar might have controlled the whole world. Now he lies here, and there is not even the poorest man to pay respect to him. O my friends, if I were inclined to stir you up to rebellion and fury, I should do a wrong to Brutus and to Cassius, who, as you know, are honourable men. I shall not do them wrong. I prefer to wrong the dead, to wrong myself and you, rather than to wrong such honourable men. But here is a document with Caesar's seal on it. I found it in his private room: it is his will. If the common people only hear this will, which, pardon me, I am not going to read, then they would go and kiss dead Caesar's wounds. They would dip their handkerchiefs in his sacred blood and beg to have but one hair from his head in memory of him, and, when they died, would mention this hair in their wills, leaving it as a priceless inheritance to their sons.

Fourth Citizen. We must hear the will. Read it, Mark Antony.

Citizens. The will, the will ! You must read us Caesar's will.

Antony. Be patient, my good friends, I must not read it. It is not fitting that you should know how much Caesar loved you. You are not senseless things like wood and stone, but you are men, and, since you are men, when you hear the will of Caesar it will inflame your passion; it will make you mad.

'Tis good you know not that you are his heirs;   150
For, if you shoul, O, what would come of it!

    Forth Citizen. Read the will; we'll hear it, Antony;
You shall read us the will,—Caesar's will.

    Antony. Will you be patient? will you stay awhile?
I have o'ershot[1] myself to tell you of it ;   155
I fear I wrong the honourable men
Whose daggers have stabb'd Caesar; I do fear it.

    Fourth Citizen. They were traitors: honourable men!

    Citizens. The will ! the testament !

    Second Citizen. They were villains, murderers : the will !   160
       read the will.

    Antony. You will compel me, then, to read the will ?
Then make a ring about the corpose of Caesar,
And let me show you him that made the will.
Shall I descend? and will you give me leave?

    Citizens. Come down.   165

    Second Citizen. Descend.

    Third Citizen. You shall have leave.

                           [Antony comes down

    Fourth Citizen. A ring; stand round.

    First Citizens. Stand from the hearse[2], stand from the body.

    Second Citizen. rom for Antony,—most noble Antony. 170

    Antony. Nay, press not so upon me; stand far off.

    Citizens. Stand back; room; bear back.

    Antony. If you have tears, prepare to shed them now.
You all do know this mantle: I remember
The first time ever Caesar put it on;   175
'Twas on a summer's evening, in his tent,
That day overcome the Nervii[3].
Look, in this place ran Cassius' dagger through;
See what a rent the envious Casca made :
Through this the well - beloved Brutus stabb'd;   180
And, as he pluck'd his cursed steel away,
Mark how the blood of Caesar follow'd it,
As rushing out of doors, to be resolv'd[4]
If Brutus so unkindly knock'd, or no;
For Brutus, as you know, was Caesar's angel[5]:   185

---

1. *O'ershot myself*: gone too far; said more than I intended. 2. *Hearse*: the bier;
platform for a dead body. 3. *Nervii*: an enemy tribe. 4. *To be resolv'd*: to find out.
5. *Angel*: guiding spirit.

It is better for you not to know that you are his heirs, for if you should learn this, what might happen?

Fourth Citizen. Read the will. We shall hear it, Antony.

Antony. Will you be patient and wait a little longer ? I have gone further than I intended in telling you of it. I fear I have wronged the honourable men whose daggers have stabbed Caesar. I fear I have done this!

Fourth Citizen. They were traitors ! Honourable men, indeed!

Citizens. Read us Caesar's will and testament.

Second Citizen. They were villains and murderers. Read the will.

Antony. Will you compel me then to read the will? Then form a ring round the corpse of Caesar and let me show you the man that made the will. Shall I come down from here? Do you allow me?

Citizens. Come down.

Second Citizen. Descend.

Third Citizen. You have our permission.

[*Antony comes down.*

Fourth Citizen. Form a ring. Stand around.

First Citizen. Stand away from the coffin. Stand away from the body.

Second Citizen. Make room for Antony, the most noble Antony.

Antony. Now do not press so closely upon me. Keep further off.

Citizens. Stand back and make room. Keep back.

Antony. If you are able to shed tears, prepare to do so now. You all know this cloak, I remember the first time Caesar ever wore it. It was on a summer evening in his tent, on the day he defeated the tribe called the Nervii. Look, here is the place where the dagger of Cassius pierced it. See, what a tear in it the envious Casca made ! Through this hole the well-beloved friend, Brutus, stabbed Caesar; and, as he pulled the cursed dagger out again, note how Caesar's blood followed it, as if rushing outside to be assured whether it was Brutus who had stabbed him or not, for Brutus, as you know, was Caesar's

Judge, O you gods, how dearly Caesar lov'd him !
This was the most unkindest cut[1] of all ;
For when the noble Caesar saw him stab,
Ingratitude, more strong than traitors' arms[2],
Quite vanquished him: then burst his mighty heart   190
And, in his mantle muffling up his face,
Even at the base of Pomey's statue,
Which all the while ran blood, great Caesar fell.
O what a fall was there, my countrymen !
Then I, and you, and all of us fell down,   195
Whilst bloody treason flourish'd over us.
O, now you weep; and, I perceive, you feel
The dint[3] of pity: these are gracious drops.
Kind souls, what, weep you when you but behold
Our Caesar's vesture[4] wounded ? Look you here,   200
Here is himself, marr'd[5], as you , with traitors.

    First Citizen. O piteous spectacle !

    Second Citizen. O noble Caesar !

    Third Citizen. O woful day !

    Fourth Citizen. O traitors, villains !   205
    First Citizen. O most bloody sight !
    Second Citizen. We will be revenged.
    Citizens. Revenge ! About ! Seek ! Burn ! Fire ! Kill ! Slay !
Let not a traitor live !

    Antony. Stay, countrymen.   210
    First Citizen. Peace there ! hear the noble Antony.

    Second Citizen. We'll hear him, will follow him,
      we'll die with him.

    Antony. Good friends, sweet friends, let me not stir
      you up
To such a sudden flood of mutiny.   215
They that have done this deed are honourable :
What private griefs[6] they have, alas, I know not,
That made them do't; they are wise and honourable,
And will, no doubt, with reasons answer you.
I come not, friends, to steal away your hearts :   220
I am no orator, as Brutus is;
But, as you know me all, a plain blunt man,
That love my friend; and that they know full well
That gave me public leave to speak of him :

---

1. *Cut*: wound. 2. *Arms*: weapons. 3. *Dint*: stroke; impact. 4. *Vesture*:
garments. 5. *Marr'd*: spoiled; mutilated. 6. *Griefs*: grievances.

dearest friend. O, gods, consider how dearly Caesar loved him! This was the most unkind of all the wounds, for when the noble Caesar saw Brutus stab him, the ingratitude of Brutus, more strong than the daggers of the traitors, quite broke his mighty heart. Wrapping his mantle around his face, just by the base of Pompey's statue, which meanwhile was flowing with his blood, great Caesar fell. O, what a terrible fall that was, my countrymen! It was a fall for you and for me, while bloody treachery triumphed over us. O, now you weep, and I see that you feel the impression of pity. These are kind tears. Good people, do you weep when you but look on Caesar's mantle wounded? Look here! Here is Caesar himself, spoiled as you see by traitors.

(*Uncovers Caesar's Body*).

First Citizen. O piteous sight !

Second Citizen. O noble Caesar !

Third Citizen. O day of woe !

Fourth Citizen. O traitors, villains !

First Citizen. O, most bloody sight !

Second Citizen. We will be avenged.

Citizens. Revenge ! Turn about ! Seek for them: burn them with fire! Slay them : leave not a traitor alive !

Antony. Stay, my countrymen !

First Citizen. Stop, hear the noble Antony.

Second Citizen. We shall hear him; we shall follow him and die with him.

Antony. Good friends, dear friends, let me not arouse you to a sudden outburst of mutiny. Those who have done this are honourable men. What private grievances they may have had, I do not know, which impelled them to do it. They are wise and honourable and will doubtless answer you with satisfactory reasons, I do not come, my friends, to win you over. I am not a fluent speaker like Brutus, but, as you all know, a plain, downright fellow, loving my friend. That they knew very well when they gave me permission to speak of him

For I have neither wit[1], nor words, nor worth,   225
Action nor utterance, nor the power of speech,
To stir men's blood: I only speak right on;
I tell you that which you yourselves do know;
Show you sweet Caesar's wounds, poor poor dumb mouths,
And bid them speak for me: but were I Brutus,   230
And Brutus Antony, there were an Antony
Would ruffle[2] up your spirits, and put a tongue
In every wound of Caesar, that should move
The stones of Rome to rise and mutiny.

    Citizens. We'll mutiny :   235

    First Citizen. We'll burn the house of Brutus.

    Third Citizen. Away, then ! come, seek the conspirators.

    Antony. Yet hear me, contrymen: yet here me speak.

    Citizens. Peace, ho! hear Antony, —most noble Antony.

    Antony. Why, friends, you go to do you know not what :
Wherein hath Caesar thus deserv'd your loves?
Alas, you know not,——I must tell you, then :
You have forgot the will I told you of.

    Citizens. Most true; the will; let's stay and hear the will.

    Antony. Here is the will, and under Caesar's seal :   245
To every Roman citizen he gives,
To every several[3] man, seventy-five drachmas.

    Second Citizen. Most noble Caesar !—we'll revenge his
        death.

    Third Citizen, O royal Caesar !

    Antony. Hear me with patience.

    Citizens. Peace, ho !   250

    Antony. Moreover, he hath left you all his walks,
His private arbours[4] and new-planted orchards,
On this side Tiber; he hath left them you,
And to your heirs for ever,—common pleasures[5]   255
To walk abroad, and recreate[6] yourselves.
Here was a Caesar ! when comes such another ?

    First Citizen. Never, never,—Come, away, a way !
We'll burn his body in th holy place,   260
And with the brands[7] fire the traitors' houses.
Take up the body.

    Second Citizen. Go fetch fire.

---

1. *Wit:* cleverness. 2. *Ruffle:* stir up; disturb. 3. *Several:* single; individual.
4. *Arbours:* gardens or groves. 5. *Common pleasures:* public pleasure grounds.
6. *Recreate:* refresh. 7. *Brands:* pieces of burning wood.

in public, for I have neither quick wit, eloquent words, nor any merit of my own, I have no acts or expression, I have no power of fluent speech to stir up the passions of men. I only speak in a straightforward way as words come to me. I am but telling you things that you know already; I show you dear Caesar's wounds, poor dumb mouths, and ask them to speak for me. But if I were Brutus and he were Antony, then he would be able to stir up your spirits and make a fluent tongue for every wound of Caesar's that would make the very stones of the road in Rome rise up in rebellion.

Citizens. We shall rebel.

First Citizen. We shall burn the house of Brutus.

Third Citizen. Let us go away and look for the conspirators.

Antony. Hear me further, countrymen. Let me speak.

Citizens. Silence! Hear Antony, the most noble Antony !

Antony. Why, friends, you do not know what you are about to do. In what respect has Caesar so much deserved your love? Alas, you do not know! I must tell you, then. You have forgotten the will of which I told you.

Citizens. Very true. Let us stay and hear the will.

Antony. Here is the will, with Caesar's seal upon it. To every Roman citizen he gives — to each individual — seventy-five drachmas.

Second Citizen. Most noble Caesar ! We shall have revenge for him.

Third Citizen. O royal Caesar !

Antony. Hear me with patience.

Citizens. Silence !

Antony. Moreover he has left you all his private roads, his groves of trees and newly-planted orchards on this side of the river Tiber. He has left them to you and your heirs for ever,— common pleasure- grounds in which you may walk about and refresh yourselves. What a Caesar he was! when shall we have another such !

First Citizen. Never, never. Come, away and let us burn his body in the holy temple, and with the burning logs we shall set fire to the houses of the traitors. Take up the body.

Second Citizen. Go, bring fire.

Third Citizen. Pluck down benches.

Fourth Citizen. Pluck down forms, windows, anything.

[Exeunt Citizens with the body

Antony. Now let it work. Mischief, thou art afoot,   265
Take thou what course thou wilt !

Enter a Servant

How now, fellow!

Servant. Sir, Octavius is already come to Rome.

Antony. Where is he ?

Servant. He and Lepidus are at Caesar's house.

Antony. And thither will I straight to visit him :   270
He comes upon a wish¹. Fortune is merry²,
And in this mood will give us any thing.

Servant. I heard him say, Brutus and Cassius
Are rid³ like madmen through the gates of Rome.

Antony. Belike⁴ they had some notice of the people,   275
How I had mov'd them. Bring me to Octavius.   *[Exeunt*

SCENE III. *A Street*

Enter Cinna *the poet*

Cinna. I dreamt to-night that I did feast with Caesar,
And things unluckily charge my fantasy⁵:
I have no will⁶ to wander forth of doors,
Yet something leads me forth.

Enter Citizens

First Citizen. What is your name?   5

Second Citizen. Whither are you going ?

Third Citizen. Where do you dwell ?

Fourth Citizen. Are you a married man or a bachelor ?

Second Citizen. Answer every man directly.

First Citizen. Ay, and briefly.   10

Fourth Citizen. Ay, and wisely.

Third Citizen. Ay, and truly, you were best.

Cinna. What is my name? Whither am I going ?
Where do I dwell ? Am I a married man or a bachelor ?
Then, to answer every man directly and briefly, wisely and
truly;—wisely I say, I am a bachelor.

Second Citizen. That's as much as to say, they are fools
that marry:—you'll bear me a bang⁷ for that, I fear.   20
Proceed: directly.

---

1. *Upon a wish*: just as I wished for him. 2. *Merry*: kind; generous. 3. *Are rid*:
have ridden. 4. *Belike*: probably. 5. *Fantasy*: dream. 6. *Will*: wish or desire. 7. *Bear
me a bang*: suffer a blow from me.

Third Citizen. Tear down the benches for wood.

Fourth Citizen. Tear down seats, benches, windows, —anything.

(The citizens go out with the body).

Antony. Now let the movement proceed. Spirit of Trouble I have started you: now take your own course.

Enter a Servant.

What is it, fellow?

Servant.   Sir, Octavius has already arrived in Rome.

Antony.   Where is he?

Servant.   He and Lepidus are at Caesar's house.

Antony.   I shall go at once and visit him there. He comes just as I was wishing for him. Fortune is indeed gay, and in her mood will give us any success.

Servant.   I heard him say that Brutus and Cassius have ridden madly away through the gates of Rome.

Antony.   Probably they had seen some signs from the people of the way in which I had moved them. Take me to Octavius.   *(They go)*

SCENE III. *A street.*

Enter Cinna *the poet*

Cinna. I dreamed last night that I was feasting with Caesar, and my mind is filled with unfortunate influences. I have no desire to go outside, but something impels me to go.

Enter Citizens

First Citizen. What is your name?

Second Citizen. Where are you going?

Third Citizen. Where is your house?

Fourth Citizen. Are you a married man or a bachelor?

Second Citizen. Answer every man directly.

First Citizen. Yes, and briefly.

Fourth Citizen. Yes, and sensibly.

Third Citizen. Yes, it will be better for you to obey.

Cinna. What is my name? Where am I going? Where do I live? Am I a married man or a bachelor? Then to answer every man directly and briefly, sensibly and truly; well, wisely, I reply that I am a bachelor.

Second Citizen. That is the same as saying that they are fools who marry. You will get a blow from me for that, I doubt. Go on!

Cinna. Directly, I am going to Caesar's funeral.

First Citizen. As a friend or an enemy ?

Cinna. As a friend.

Second citizen. That matter is answered directly.   25

Fourth Citizen. For your dwelling,—briefly.

Cinna. Briefly, I dwell by the Capitol.

Third Citizen. Your name, sir, truly.

Cinna. Truly, my name is Cinna.

First Citizen. Tear him to pieces; he's a conspirator.   30

Cinna. I am Cinna the poet. I am Cinna the poet.

Fourth Citizen. Tear him for his bad verses, tear him for
    his bad verses.

Cinna. I am not Cinna the conspirator.

Fourth Citizen. It is no matter, his name's Cinna; pluck
but his name out of his heart, and turn him going[1].

Third Citizen. Tear him, tear him ! Come, brands, oh !
fire-brands : to Brutus', to Cassius'; burn all; some to Decius'
house, and some to Casca's; some to Ligarius'; away, go !   40

[Exeunt

ACT IV

SCENE I. *A house in Rome*

Antony, Octavius, and Lepidus, *seated at a table*

Antony. These many, then, shall die; their names are prick'd[2].

Octavius. Your brother too must die; consent you, Lepidus?

Lepidus. I do consent,—

Octavius.   Prick him down, Antony

Lepidus. Upon condition[3] Publius shall not live, Who is
your sister's son, Mark Antony.   5

Antony. He shall not live; look, with a spot I damn him.
But, Lepidus, go you to Caesar's house;
Fetch the will hither, and we shall determine
How to cut off some charge in legacies.

Lepidus. What, shall I find you here ?   10

Octavius.   Or here, or at
The Capitol.   *[Exit Lepidus*

Antony. This is a slight unmeritable[4] man,
Meet to be sent on errands; is it fit,
The threefold world divided, he should stand
One of the three to share it ?   15

---

1. *Turn him going*: let him go. 2. *Prick'd*: marked with a 'tick' on the list.
3. *Upon condition*: on the condition that.... 4. *Unmeritable*: Undeserving.

Cinna. I am going to Caesar's funeral.

Second Citizen. As a friend or an enemy?

Cinna. As a friend.

Second Citizen. That point has been answered directly.

Fourth Citizen. Now, briefly, where is your dwelling?

Cinna. I dwell beside the Capitol.

Third Citizen. And your name? Speak truly.

Cinna. Truly my name is Cinna.

First Citizen. Tear him to pieces ! He is a conspirator.

Cinna. I am Cinna, the poet.

Fourth Citizen. Then tear him because of his bad poetry.

Cinna. I am not Cinna the conspirator.

Fourth Citizen. It does not matter; his name is Cinna. So just tear off his name and send him away.

Third Citizen. Tear him ! Tear him ! Come, burning torches ! Come on the fire carriers ! To the house of Brutus, of Cassius, burn everything ! Some to Decius' house, some to Casca's some to Ligarius. Off you go !

ACT IV

SCENE I. *A house in Rome.*

Antony, Octavius, *and* Lepidus *seated at a table.*

Antony. So many, then, shall die. Their names have been ticked off.

Octavius. Your brother, too, must die. Do you agree, Lipidus?

Lepidus. Yes, I agree.

Octavius. Tick him off, Antony.

Lepidus. But upon the condition that Publius, also, is not allowed to live, who is your nephew, Antony.

Antony. He shall not live. Look with a stroke of the pen I condemn him. But, Lepidus, you go to Caesar's house. Bring the will here, and we shall settle how to reduce some of the expenditure in legacies.

Lepidus. Shall I find you still here?

Octavius. Either here or at the Capitol. (Lepidus *goes out*).

Antony. Lepidus is a feeble man of no merit. He is fit only to be used for errands. Is it fitting, now the world is to be divided between three rulers, that he should be one of the three?

Octavius.   So you thought him,
And took his voice who should be prick'd to die,
In our black sentence and proscription[1].

    Antony. Octavius, I have seen more days than you :
And though we lay these honours on this man,
To ease ourselves of divers slanderous loads[2],   20
He shall but bear them as the ass bears gold,
To groan and sweat under the business,
Either led or driven, as we point the way;
And having brought our treasure where we will,
Then take we down his load, and aturn him off,   25
Like to the empty ass[3], to shake his ears,
And graze in commons[4].

    Octavius.   You may do your will :
But he's tried and valiant soldier.

    Antony. So is my horse, Octavius; and for that
I do appoint[5] him store of provender[6] :   30
It is a creature that I teach to fight,
To wind, to stop, to run directly on,
His corporal[7] motion govern'd by my spirit.
And, in some taste, is Lepidus but so;
He must be taught, and train'd, and bid go forth;   35
A barren-spirited fellow; one that feeds
On abjects, orts[8] and imitations,
Which, out of use and stal'd[9] by other men,
Begin his fashion: do not talk of him
But as a property[10]. And now, Octavius,   40
Listen great things:— Brutus and Cassius
Are levying powers[11] : we must straight make head :
Therefore let our alliance be combin'd,
Ourt best friends made, our means stretch'd;
And let us presently go sit in council,   45
How covert matters[12] may be best disclos'd,
And open perils surest answered.

    Octavius. Let us do so: for we are at the stake,
And bay'd[13] about with many enemies;
And some that smile have in their hearts, I fear,   50
Millions of mischiefs.   *[Exeunt*

---

    1. *Proscription*: list of the guilty. 2. *Divers....loads*: various masses of slander.
3. *Empty ass*: an ass when unloaded. 4. *Commons*: ordinary land. 5. *Appoint*:
arrange. 6. *Provender*: food. 7. *Corporal*: bodily. 8. *Abjects, orts*: common things
and scraps of food left over. 9. *Stal'd*: soiled by being used. 10. *Property*: part of
our possessions. 11. *Levying powers*: raising troops. 12. *Covert matters*: things
secret. 13. *Bay'd*: surrounded and made to fight.

Octavius. You thought this about him, and yet you took his vote as to who be marked off to die, in our black list of those who are sentenced!

Antony. Octavius, I am an older man than you. Though we lay those responsibilities on this man, and get rid of certain tasks which will create slander, he will be like the donkey who carries the gold, groaning and sweating under the labour, being led or driven in whatever direction we wish. When he has carried the load to the place we select, then we take it from him and send him off, like the ass deprived of everything, to shake his ears and eat grass on the common land.

Octavius. You may do as you choose; but he is a proved brave soldier.

Antony. So is my horse, Octavius, and for being so, I set aside for him a supply of food. He is a creature that I teach to fight, to turn, to stop, or to run directly on, the motions of his body being controlled by my spirit. And to some extent, such is Lepidus. He must be taught and trained and ordered to go out, a fellow devoid of true spirit. He is one who lives on rejected scraps, things left by other people, and imitations of others. Things no longer used and put aside by other men are then used by him (as if fashionable): do not talk of him except as a piece of furniture. Now, Octavius, hear great news: Brutus and Cassius are raising armies. We must immediately muster our resources, so let us form a firm alliance; let us make the best allies we can and stretch our resources as far as possible. Meanwhile we must immediately sit in deliberation as to how hidden things may be best exposed and open dangers most easily encountered.

Octavius. Let us do so, for we are like the bear which is tied to the stake, and fighting against a ring of dogs. Some who smile on us have, I fear, in their secret hearts, great capacity for mischief.

SCENE II. *Camp near Sardis. Before* Brutus' *tent*
Drum. Enter Brutus, Lucilius, Titinius, *and* Soldiers;
Pindarus *meeting them;* Lucius *at some distance*

Brutus. Stand, ho!

Lucilius. Give the word, ho! and stand.

Brutus. What now, Lucilius ! is Cassius near ?

Lucilius. He is at hand; and Pindarus is come
To do you salutation[1] from his master.   5

                    [*Pindarus gives a letter to Brutus*

Brutus. He greets me well.—Your master, Pindarus, ➤ *Cassius's slave/servant*
In his own charge[2], or by ill[3] officers,
Hath given me some worthy cause to wish
Things done undone: but, if he be at hand,
I shall be satisfied.

Pindarus.   I do not doubt   10
But that my noble master will appear
Such as he is, full of regard and honour.

Brutus. He is not doubted.—A word, Lucilius;
How he receiv'd you, let me be resolv'd[4].

Lucilius. With courtesy and with respect enough;   15
But not with such familiar instances,[5]
Nor with such free and friendly conference,
As he hath us'd of old.

Brutus.   Thou hast describ'd
A hot friend cooling: ever note, Lucilius,
When love begins to sicken and decay,   20
It useth an enforced ceremony.[6]
There are no tricks in plain and simple faith :
But hollow[7] men, like horse hot at hand,[8]
Make gallant show and promise of their mettle;
But when they should endure the bloody spur, ·   25
They fall their crests,[9] and, like deceitful jades[10],
Sink in the trial. Comes his army on?

Lucilius. They mean this night in Sardis to be quarter'd;
The greater part, the horses in general,
Are come with Cassius.   [*March within*   30

Brutus.   Hark ! he is arriv'd :—
March gently on to meet him.

---

1. *Do... salutation*: greet you. 2. *In his own charge*: by his own actions. 3. *Ill*: bad. 4. *Resolv'd*: informed. 5. *Familiar instances*: friendly actions. 6. *Enforced ceremony*: formal politeness. 7. *Hollow*: false. 8. *Hot at hand*: lively when being led by hand. 9. *Crests*: heads. 10. *Deceitful jades*: unreliable horses.

SCENE II. *The Camp near Sardis. Brutus' tent.*

Sound of drum. Enter Brutus, Lucilius, Titinius, *and*

Soldiers. Pindarus *meets them.* Lucius *near by.*

Brutus. Stand, whoever comes!

Lucilius. Give the pass-word, and stand still.

Brutus. What, is it you, Lucilius? is Cassius near?

Lucilius. He is near by, and Pindarus has come to bring you salutations from his master.

(Pindarus *gives a letter to* Brutus)

Brutus. He greets me in a friendly manner. Your master, Pindarus, either by his own actions or by bad officers of his, has given me strong cause to regret some things he has done. But if he is here now, I shall be given explanations.

Pindarus. I have no doubt that my worthy master will appear, being so courteous and honourable.

Brutus. I do not doubt it. A word with you, Lucilius; let me know fully how he received you.

Lucilius. With sufficient courtesy and respect, but not with such examples of familiarity nor with such free and friendly confidence as he had used before.

Brutus. You have described a warm friend who is becoming cold. Always observe, Lucilius, when friendship begins to grow weak and to die, it uses a kind of forced politeness. There are no tricks in plain and simple honesty. But insincere men, like horses, full of spirit when they are hand-led, make a great show and promise of their high quality. But when they are made to feel the spur of action, their high heads fall and, like deceptive and worn-out horses, they fail when put to the test, Is his army coming?

Lucilius. They mean this night to occupy quarters in Sardis. The greater part, all of the cavalry, have come with Cassius.

(*The sound of marching*)

Brutus. Listen! He has arrived. March gently on to meet him.

Enter Cassius *and* Soldiers

Cassius, Stand, ho !

Brutus. Stand, ho! Speak the word along.

Within. Stand !

Within. Stand !   35

Within. Stand !

Cassius. Most noble brother, you have done me wrong.

Brutus. Judge me, you gods ! wrong I mine enemies ?
And if not so, how should I wrong a brother ?

Cassius. Brutus, this sober form¹ of yours hides wrong;   40
And when you do them—

    Brutus.   Cassius, be content;
Speak your griefs softly,—I do know you well.
Before the eyes of both our armies here,
Which should perceive nothing but love from us,
Let us not wrangle: bid them move away;
Then in my tent, Cassius, enlarge² your grief,   45
And I will give you audience.

    Cassius.   Pindarus,
Bid our commanders lead their charges³ off,
A little from this ground,

    Brutus. Lucius, do you the like; and let no man   50
Come to our tent till we have done our conference.
Lucilius and Titinius guard our door.   *[Exeunt*

SCENE III. *Within the tent of* Brutus
Enter Brutus *and* Cassius

Cassius. That you have wrong'd me doth appear in this :
You have condemn'd and noted⁴ Lucius Pella
For taking bribes here of the Sardians;
Wherein my letters, praying on his side,
Because I knew the man, were slighted off.⁵   5

Brutus. you wrong'd yourself to write in such a case.

Cassius. In such a time as this it is not meet.
That every nice⁶ offence should bear his comment.

Brutus. Let me tell you, Cassius, you yourself

Are much condemn'd to have an itching palm⁷;   10
To sell and mart⁸ your offices for gold
To undeservers.

---

1. *Sober form*: grave appearance. 2. *Enlarge*: state fully your grievances.
3. *Charges*: the groups under their command. 4. *Noted*: made an unfavourable note of.
5. *Slighted off*: treated as if of no importance. 6. *Nice offence*: an offence only in the
eyes of a nice of fastidious person. 7. *Itching palm*: hand greedy for bribes. 8. *Mart*:
sell in the market.

Enter Cassius *and* Soldiers

Cassius. Halt, there!

Brutus. Halt. Pass the word along.

Soldiers. Halt ! Halt ! Halt !

Cassius. Most noble brother, you have wronged me.

Brutus. May the gods judge whether I have done so! I do not wrong my enemies, so why should I wrong a brother.

Cassius. Brutus, this grave appearance of yours hides wrong dealing, and, when you act thus —

Brutus. Cassius, be patient. Speak quietly of your complaints: I know you well enough for that. Do not let us quarrel before the eyes of both our armies here, which should see nothing but friendship between us. Tell them to move away. Then in my tent, Cassius, you may open out all your grievances, and I shall give you my attention.

Cassius. Pindarus, tell our officers to lead off their men a little from this place.

Brutus. Lucius, you do the same, and let no man come to our tent till our discussion is finished. Lucius and Titinius keep watch on our door.

SCENE III. *Inside the tent of* Brutus

Enter Brutus *and* Cassius

Cassius. That you have wronged me is obvious in this matter: you have condemned and made public Lucius Pella for taking bribes from the Sardians here, and in this my letters, appealing in his favour because I knew the man, were treated with contempt.

Brutus. You did wrong to yourself, to write in such an undeserving case.

Cassius. In such a time as this it is not fitting that every trifling offence should be strictly gone into.

Brutus. Let me tell you, Cassius, you yourself are much criticised as having a hand greedy for rewards, and for selling and giving for gold your appointments to undeserving people.

   Cassius.   I an itching palm !
You know that you are Brutus that speaks this,
Or, by the gods, this speech were else your last.
   Brutus. the name of Cassius honours this corruption[1], 15
And chastisement[2] doth therefore hide his head.
   Cassius. Chastisement !
   Brutus. Remember March, the Ides of March remember :
Did not great Julius bleed for justice's sake ?
What villain touch'd his body, that did stab,   20
And not for justice ? What, shall one of us,
That struck the foremost man of all this world
But for supporting robbers, shall we now
Contaminate[3] our fingers with base bribes,
And sell the mighty space[4] of our large honours   25
For so much trash as may be grasped thus ?
I had rather be a dog, and bay[5] the moon,
Than such a Roman.
   Cassius.   Brutus, bay not me;
I'll not endure it : you forget yourself
To hedge[6] me in; I am a soldier, I,   30
Older in practice, abler than yourself
To make conditions.
   Brutus.   Go to; you are not, Cassius.
   Cassius. I am.
   Brutus. I say you are not.
   Cassius. Urge me no more, I shall forget myself; 35
Have mind upon your health, tempt me no further.
   Brutus. Away, slight[7] man !
   Cassius. Is't possible ?
   Brutus.   Hear me, for I will speak.
Must I give way and room to your rash choler[8] ?   40
Shall I be frighted when a madman stares ?
   Cassius. O ye gods, ye gods ! must I endure all this ?
   Brutus. All this ! ay, more : fret till your proud heart break;
Go show your slaves how choleric you are,
And make your bondmen tremble. Must I budge[9] ? 45
Must I observe you ? must I stand and crouch[10]
Under your testy humour ?[11] By the gods,
You shall digest the venom of your spleen[12].

---

1. *Honours this corruption*: makes this corruption seem honest. 2. *Chastisement*: punishment. 3. *Contaminate:* to make soiled or dirty. 4. *Space*: amount. 5. *Bay*: bark at. 6. *Hedge me in*: restrict my authority. 7. *Slight*: puny; weak. 8. *Choler*: bad temper. 9. *Budge*: give way. 10. *Crouch*: cower; kneel. 11. *Testy humour*: quick-tempered mood. 12. *Spleen*: bad temper arising from one's own organs.

Cassius. I greedy for gold! You know that you are privileged when you say this, Brutus, or I swear by the gods that such speech would be your last.

Brutus. The name of Cassius covers up this dishonest practice, and on that account punishment is averted.

Cassius. Punishment !

Brutus. Remember March, remember the Ides of March. Was it not to satisfy justice that great Caesar died? Of all the villains who touched his body, there was not one who did not stab in the name of justice. Now shall one of us, who struck down the greatest man in the world only for supporting robbers, shall we now soil our hands with vile bribes, and sell the great honours we have gained for so much worthless gold as may be grasped in a hand like this? I would rather be a dog and bark at the moon than be a Roman like that.

Cassius. Brutus, do not make me turn at bay (do not bark at me); I shall not endure it. You forget yourself, to restrict my powers like this. I am a soldier, more experienced and more efficient than yourself in making conditions (of appointments).

Brutus. Indeed you are not, Cassius.

Cassius. I am.

Brutus. I say you are not.

Cassius. Do not press me any further or I shall lose my temper. Be careful of your safety and do not provoke me any more.

Brutus. Away, feeble man !

Cassius. Is it possible (that Brutus speaks like this)?

Brutus. Hear me, for I shall speak. Must I yield and give way before your rash temper? Have I to be frightened by the angry looks of a madman?

Cassius. O gods, must I submit to all this?

Brutus. Yes, and to more. Anger yourself till your proud heart breaks. Go and show your slaves how ill-tempered you are, and make your servants tremble. Must I give way? Must I study how to please you? Must I stand and bend down before your irritable mood? By the gods, you will have to swallow the poison of your own bad temper, though it should burst your body apart.

Though it do split you; for, from this day forth,
I'll use you for my mirth, yea, for my laughter,
When you are waspish.   50

    Cassius.   It is come to this ?

    Brutus. You say you are a better soldier :
Let it appear so : make your vaunting[1] true,
And it shall please me well : for mine own part,
I shall be glad to learn of noble men.

    Cassius. You wrong me every way; you wrong me,   55
        Brutus;
I said, an elder solder, not a better :
Did I say "better" ?

    Brutus.   If you did, I care not.

    Cassius. When Caesar liv'd he durst not thus have mov'd me.

    Brutus. Peace, peace! you durst not so have temped[2] him.   60

    Cassius. I durst not!

    Brutus. No.

    Cassius. What, durst not tempt him !

    Brutus.   For your life you durst not.

    Cassius. Do not presume too much upon my love; I may
do that I shall be sorry for.

    Brutus. You have done that you should be sorry for.   65
There is no terror, Cassius, in your threats;
For I am arm'd so strong in honesty,
That they pass by me as the idle wind,
Which I respect[3] not. I did send to you
For certain sums of gold, which you denied[4] me;—   70
For I can raise no money by vile means :
By heaven, I had rather coin my heart,[5]
And drop my blood for drachmas, than to wring
From athe hard hands of peasants their vile trash
By any indirection[6], —I did send   75
To you for gold to pay my legions,
Which you denied me; was that done like Cassius ?
Should I have answer'd Caius Cassius so ?
When Marcus Brutus grows so covetous,
To lock such rascal counters[7] from his friends,   80
Be ready, gods, with all your thunderbolts;
Desh him to pieces!

---

1. *Vaunting*: boast. 2. *Tempted*: provoke; challenged. 3. *Respect not*: do not care for. 4. *Denied*: refused. 5. *Coin my heart*: turn my heart into coins. 6. *Indirection*: dishonest means. 7. *Rascal counters*: dirty pieces of metal.

From this day, I shall regard you as an object of mirth and laughter when you become ill-tempered.

Cassius. Has, it come to this?

Brutus. You say you are a better soldier? Let it be shown that this is true, and justify your boast. I shall be well pleased if you do. For my part, I am only too pleased to learn something from great men.

Cassius. You wrong me in every way; indeed you wrong me, Brutus. I said "an older soldier" and not "a better soldier."

Brutus. It makes no difference to me.

Cassius. When Caesar was alive, he dared not have angered me thus.

Brutus. Be quiet. you dared not so have provoked him.

Cassius. You say that I dared not!

Brutus. No.

Cassius. What, I dared not anger him?

Brutus. Even for your life's sake, you dared not.

Cassius. Do not take undue advantage of our friendship. You may make me do something I shall be sorry for.

Brutus. You have already done things you should be sorry for. There is nothing in your threats to frighten anyone, Cassius. I am so well protected by my sense of honesty that they pass by me as harmlessly as the wind, for which I care nothing. I sent to you for certain sums of money in gold, and you refused me, —for I am not able to raise money by dishonourable means. By heaven, I would rather turn my own heart into coins and have my blood made into drachmas than by any unjust measures extort vile money from the toil-hardened hands of peasants. I sent to you for gold to pay my regiments, and you refused me. Was that an act worthy of Cassius? Should I have sent Cassius such an answer? When Marcus Brutus becomes so greedy as to lock away his dirty coins from his friends, be ready, O gods, to dash him to pieces with your thunderbolts.

Cassius.   I denied you not.

Brutus. You did.

Cassius. I did not: he was but a fool that brought

My answer back, — Brutus hath riv'n[1] my heart;   85

A friend should bear his friend's infirmities[2], → *weaknesses*

But Brutus makes mine greater than they are.

Brutus. I do not, till you practise them on me.

Cassius. You love me not.

Brutus.   I do not like your faults.

Cassius. A friendly eye could never such faults.   90

Brutus. A flaterer's would not, though they do appear

As huge as high Olympus.

Cassius. Come, Antony, and young Octavius, come,

Revenge yourselves alone on Cassius,

For Cassius is aweary of the world;   95

Hated by one he loves; brav'd by his brother;

Check'd like a bondman[3]; all his faults observ'd,

Set in a note-book, learn'd, and conn'd by rote[4],

To cast into my teeth[5], O, I could weep

My spirit from mine eyes!—There is my dagger,   100

And here my naked breast; within, a heart

Dearer than Plutus'[6] mine, richer than gold;

If that thou be'st a Roman,take it forth;

I, that denied thee gold, will give my heart :

Strike, as thou didst at Caesar; for, I know,   105

When thou didst hate him worst, thou lov'dst him better

Than ever thou lov'dst Cassius.

Brutus.   Sheath your dagger;

Be angry when you will, it shall have scope[7];

Do what you will, dishonour shall be humour[8].

O Cassius, you are yoked with a lamb   110

That carries anger as the flint bears fire;

Who, much enforced[9], shows a hasty[10] spark,

And straight is cold again.

---

1. *Riv'n*: torn; wounded. 2. *Infirmities*: errors; faults. 3. *Check'd......bondman*; reprimanded like a slave. 4 . *Conn'd by rote;* learnt by heart. 5. *Into my teeth*: to throw in my face. 6. *Pluto*: god of the underworld. 7. *Scope*: freedom without check. 8. *Humour:* only a personal fad. 9. *Enforced*: struck with the steel. 10. *Hasty spark*: momentary flash.

Cassius. I did not refuse you.

Brutus. You did.

Cassius. I did not. He was a foolish fellow who brought my answer to you. Brutus, you have broken my heart. A friend should be patient with the weaknesses of a friend, but you are making mine greater than they are.

Brutus. I do not, until you employ them against me.

Cassius. You do not love me.

Brutus. I do not like your faults.

Cassius. A friendly eye could never see such faults.

Brutus. The eye of a flatterer would not see them, they were obviously as high as mount Olympus.

Cassius. All right, Antony and young Octavius may now come and avenge themselves alone on me. For I am tired of this world, in which I am hated by one whom I love, defied by my brother, rebuked like a servant, and all my faults examined, written down as if in a note-book, studied and learned by heart to throw in may face afterwards. O, I could weep till my soul flowed with tears from my eyes ! Here is my dagger and here is my naked breast. Inside is my heart dearer to me than the wealth of the god Pluto, more precious than gold. If you are indeed a Roman, cut it out. I, who refused you gold, will give you my heart. Strike at me, as you did at Caesar, for I know that when you hated him most, you loved him more than you love Cassius.

Brutus. Sheathe your dagger. Be angry when you like; your anger shall have liberty. Do what you like; dishonourable words from you shall be deemed humorous. O Cassius, you are the partner of a man as gentle as a lamb. I have anger within me only as the flint holds latent fire. With great force, I show a hasty spark of temper, and immediately am cold again.

Cassius.   Hath Cassius liv'd
To be but mirth and laughter to his Brutus,
When grief, and blood ill-temper'd, vexeth him ?   115

Brutus.   When I spoke that, I was ill-temper'd too.

Cassius.   Do you confess so much ? Give me your hand.

Brutus.   And my heart too.

Cassius.   O Brutus,—

Brutus.   What's the matter ?

Cassius.   Have not you love enough to bear with me,
When that rash humour[1] which my mother gave me   120
Makes me forgetful?

Brutus.   Yes, Cassius; and, from henceforth,
When you are over-earnest with your Brutus,
He'll think your mother chides, and leave you so.

Poet. [*Within*] Let me go in to see the generals;
There is some grudge[2] between 'em, 'tis not meet   125
They be alone.

Lucilius. [*Within*] You shall not come to them.

Poet. [*Within*] Nothing but death shall stay me.

     Enter Poet, *followed by* Lucilius, Titinius, *and* Lucius.

Cassius.   How now! what's the matter?

Poet.   For shame, you generals! what do you mean?   130
Love, and be friends, as two such men should be;
For I have seen more years, I'm sure, than ye.

Cassius.   Ha, ha ! how vilely doth this cynic[3] rhyme !

Brutus.   Get you hence, sirrah; saucy fellow, hence !

Cassius.   Bear with him, Brutus 'tis his fashion.   135

Brutus.   I'll know his humour, when he knows his time[4];
What should the wars do with these jigging[5] fools?—
Companion, hence!

Cassius.   Away, away, away, be gone !   [*Exit Poet*

Brutus.   Lucilius and Titinius, bid the commanders
Prepare to lodge their companies to-night.   140

Cassius.   And come yourselves, and bring Messala with you.
Immediately to us.   [*Exeunt Lucilius and Titinius*

Brutus.   Lucius, a bowl of wine !

Cassius.   I did not think you could have been so angry.

Brutus.   O Cassius, I am sick of many griefs.

---

1. *Rash humour*: headstrong nature. 2. *Grudge*: unfriendliness. 3. *Cynic*: one
who follows the severe rationlistic philiosophy of the Cynics. 4. *Knows his time*:
expresses his wit at a suitable time. 5. *Jigging*: rhyming.

Cassius. Has Cassius lived to become nothing but a subject for mirth and laughter to Brutus, when grief and indisposition of the body troubles him?

Brutus. When I said that, I too was in bad temper.

Cassius. Do you admit so much? give me your hand.

Brutus. And my heart also.

Cassius. O Brutus!

Brutus. What is the matter?

Cassius. Have you not love enough to be patient with me when that rashness of nature troubles me, which I inherited from my mother?

Brutus. Yes, Cassius, and from this time, when you are too serious with me, I shall think it is your mother scolding, and leave you alone.

Poet (*Outside the tent*). Let me go in to see the generals. There is some ill-feeling between them. it is not right that they should be alone.

Lucilius (*Outside*). You cannot go in to them.

Poet. Nothing but death shall stop me.

    Enter Poet, *followed by* Lucilius, Titinius and Lucius.

Cassius. Hulloa! What is the matter?

Poet. Be ashamed of yourselves, generals? What is the meaning of this? You should love and be friends, as two such men should be. I who say this am older by years than you.

Cassius. Ha, ha! how badly does this cynic philosopher rhyme!

Brutus. Go away, you! Insolent fellow, get out!

Cassius. Be patient with him, Brutus. It is only his manner.

Brutus. I shall understand his humour when he understands the proper time for it. What use is there in war time for such rhyming fools? Now, friend, get out!

Cassius. Yes, away with you. Go!   (*Poet goes*)

Brutus. Lucilius and Titinius, order your commanders to quarter their men for the night.

Cassius. And come back yourselves, and bring Messala immediately to us. (*Lucilius and* Titinius *go out*)

Brutus. Lucius, will you have a cup of wine?

Cassius. I did not think it was possible for you to be so angry.

Brutus. O Cassius, many sources of trouble have made me sick.

Cassius. Of your philosophy you make no use, 145
If you give place to accidental evils.[1]

Brutus. No man bears sorrow better: — Portia is dead.

Cassius. Ha ! Portia !

Brutus. She is dead.

Cassius. How 'scap'd[2] I killing when I cross'd[3] you so? 150
O insupportable and touching loss!—
Upon what sickness?

Brutus.　　　　　　　Impatient of my absence,
And grief that young Octavius with Mark Antony
Have made themselve so strong;— for with her death
That tidings come;—with this she fell distract[4], 155
And, her attendants absent, swallow'd fire[5].

Cassius. And died so?

Brutus.　　　　　　　Even so.

Cassius.　　　　　　　　　　　O ye immortal gods !

　　　　　Re-enter Lucius, *with wine and taper*

Brutus. Speak no more of her.—Give me a bowl of wine.
In this I bury all unkindness, Cassius.　　　　　[*Drinks.*

Cassius. My heart is thirsty for thet noble pledge.— 160
Fill, Lucius, till the wine o'erswell[6] the cup;
I cannot drink too much of Brutus' love.　　　[*Drinks.*

Brutus. Come in. Titinius !　　　　　　　[*Exit Lucius*

　　　　　Re-enter Titinius *with* Messala
　　　　　　　　　　　　　Welcome, good Messala.
Now sit we close about this taper here,
And call in question[7] our necessities. 165

Cassius. Portia, art thou gone?

Brutus.　　　　　　　No more, I pray you.—
Messala, I have here received letters,
That young Octavius and Mark Antony
Come down upon us with a mighty power[8],
Bending[9] their expedition toward Philippi. 170

Messala. Myself have letters of the selfsame tenour[10].

Brutus. With what addition ?

---

　　1. *Accidental evils*: misfortunes which happen and are inevitable. 2. *'Scap'd I*: did I escape. 3. *Cross'd*: opposed. 4. *Distract*: insane. 5. *Fire*: a corrosive poison. 6. *O'erswell*: brims over. 7. *Call in question*: take up the matter of. 8. *Power*: army. 9. *Bending*: directing. 10. *Selfsame tenour*: with the very same news.

Cassius. You are not practising your own philosophy, if you give way to chance misfortunes.

Brutus. No man endures sorrow better than I. Portia is dead.

Cassius. What, Portia !

Brutus. She is dead.

Cassius. How did I escape being killed, when I thwarted you in such circumstances ? O, unbearable and heavy loss ! What was her sickness ?

Brutus. Not able to endure my absence, and grieving that young Octavius and Mark Antony have made themselves so strong, for news of that has come along with news of her death, she became deeply upset, and while her attendants were out, swallowed poison.

Cassius. And died of this ?

Brutus. Yes, even thus.

Cassius. O you immortal gods !

Re-enter Lucius *with wine and taper.*

Brutus. Speak no more of her. Give me a howl of wine. In this cup, I drink away all unfriendliness, Cassius. (*Drinks*)

Cassius. My heart is longing for those noble words of your pledge. Fill it up, Lucius, till the wine runs over the edge of the cup. I cannot drink too deeply of Brutus' love. (*Drinks*)

Brutus. Come in, Titinius !   (Lucius *goes out*)

Re-enter Titinius *and* Messala.

Welcome, good Messala. Now let us sit closely together round the candle here, and discuss the things that are necessary.

Cassius. Portia, are you indeed gone ?

Brutus. No more of her, I pray you. Messala, I have received letters here telling me that young Octavius and Mark Antony are coming down upon us with a great force, directing their expedition towards Philippi.

Messala. I have myself received letter to the same effect.

Brutus. And any further news ?

  Messala. That by proscription[1] and bills of outlawry[2],
Octavius, Antony, and Lepidus,
Have put to death an hundred senators.   175
  Brutus. Therein our letters do not agree;
Mine speak of seventy senators that died
By their proscriptions, Cicero being one.
  Cassius. Cicero one !
  Messala.   Cicero is dead,
And by that order of proscription.—   180
Had you your letters from your wife, my lord ?
  Brutus. No, Messala.
  Messala. Nor nothing in your letters writ of her ?
  Brutus. Nothing, Messala.
  Messala.   That, methinks, is strange.
  Brutus. Why ask you ? hear you aught[3] of her in yours ? 185
  Messala. No, my lord.
  Brutus. Now, as you are a Roman, tell me true.
  Messala. Then like a Roman bear the truth I tell :
For certain she is dead, and by strange manner.
  Brutus. Why, farewell, Portia.—We must die, Messala; 90
With meditating that she must die once,
I have the patience to endure it now.
  Messala. Even so great men great losses should endure.
  Cassius. I have as much of this in art[4] as you,
But yet my nature could not bear it so.   195
  Brutus. Well, to our work alive. What do you think
Of marching to Philippi presently[5] ?
  Cassius. I do not think it good.
  Brutus.   Your reason ?
  Cassius.   This it is :
'Tis better that the enemy seek us :
So shall he waste his means, weary his soldiers,   200
Doing himself offence[6]; whilst we, lying still,
Are full of rest, defence, and nimbleness.
  Brutus. Good reasons must, of force, give place to better.
The people 'twixt Philippi and this ground
Do stand but in a forc'd affection[7];   205
For they have grudg'd us contribution[8] :
The enemy, marching along by them,

---

  1. *Proscription:* an edict confiscating a person's property to Government.
2. *Bill of outlawry:* edicts declaring certain persons at outlaws, in effect condemnig
them to death. 3. *Aught:* anything. 4. *In art:* in theory, though I may be weak in
practice. 5. *Presently;* soon. 6. *Offence;* injuring himself. 7. *Forc'd affection;*
unwilling support. 8. *Contribution:* supplies, money, etc.

Messala. That by an order of doom and an edict outlawing men, Octavius, Antony and Lepidus have put to death a hundred senators.

Brutus. In that your letters do not agree with mine. Mine speak of seventy senators who died under their order of doom, Cicero being one.

Messala. Cicero is dead, and by that order of proscription. Did you have letters from your wife, my lord ?

Brutus. No, Messala.

Messala. And nothing written about her in any of your letters ?

Brutus. Nothing, Messala.

Messala. That, it seems to me is strange.

Brutus. Why do you ask? Have you heard anything about her in any of your letters?

Messala. No, my lord.

Brutus. Now I bid you, on your ward as a Roman, tell me truly.

Messala. Then you must bear the truth I tell in a Roman manner. For it is certain that she is dead, and in a strage manner.

Brutus. Then, farewell, Portia. We must all die, Messala. Having meditated on the fact that she must surely die one day, I am now able to bear it.

Massala. That is the way in which great men should bear great losses.

Cassius. I have as much of this philosophy in theory as you, but yet my nature could not bear it in such a way.

Brutus. Well, let us get to our work with the living. What do you think of the scheme of marching to Philippi soon ?

Cassius. I do not think it good.

Brutus. What is your reason?

Cassius. It is this : It is better to let the enemy look for us. So will he spend his resources and tire his soldiers, doing himself harm. We, remaining still, shall be full of strength from resisting, strong in defensive power and mobility.

Brutus. Good reasons, but they must yield to better onces. The people between Philippi and here are only attached to us by compulsion. They have only contributed to us with reluctance. If the enemy marches through them,

By them shall make a fuller number up[1],
Come on refresh'd, new-added, and encourag'd;
From which advantage shall we cut him off,   210
If at Philippi we do face him there,
These people at our back.

      Cassius.   Hear me, good brother.

     Brutus. Under your pardon.—You must note beside,
That we have tried the utmost of our friends,
Our legions are brim-full, our cause is ripe[2]:   215
The enemy increaseth every day;
We, at the height, are ready to decline[3],
There is a tide in the affairs of men,
Which, taken the flood, leads on to fortune;
Omitted[4], all the voyage of their life   220
Is bound in shallows[5] and in miseries.
On such a full sea are we now afloat;
And we must take the current when it serves,
Or lose our ventures[6].

      Cassius.   Then, with your will, go on;
We'll along ourselves, and meet them at Philippi.   225

     Brutus. The deep of night is crept upon our talk,
And nature must obey necessity;
Which we will niggard[7] with a little rest.
There is no more to say ?

      Cassius.   No more. Good night :
Early to-morrow will we rise, and hence.   230

     Brutus, Lucius! [*Enter Lucius.*] My gown. [*Exit Lucius.*]
                Farewell, good Messala:—
Good night, Titinius;—noble, noble Cassius,
Good night, and good repose.

      Cassius.   O my dear brother !
This was an ill[8] begining of the night :
Never come such division[9] 'tween our souls !   235
Let it not, Brutus.

     Brutus. Every thing is well.

     Cassius. Good night, my lord.

     Brutus.   Good night, good brother.

     Titin. Mess. Good night, Lord Brutus.

     Brutus.   Farewell, every one.
            [*Exeunt Cassius, Titinius and Messala*

---

1. *A fuller number up:* shall increase his numbers by recruiting. 2. *Ripe:* at its strongest point. 3. *Decline:* lose strength. 4. *Omitted:* if missed. 5. *Shallows:* dengers. 6. *Ventures:* risks we have taken. 7. *Niggard:* stisfy sparingly. 8. *Ill:* bad. 9. *Division:* stife; a quarrel.

they shall receive a fuller number of recruits, and then come on refreshed, reinforced and encouraged. We shall cut him off from these advantages if we go on and face him at Philippi, leaving those people behind us.

Cassius. Hear me, good brother.

Brutus. Pardon me,—you must note also that we have tried our utmost with our friends, our regiments are full up, our case is at full strength. The enemy is increasing every day, but we, at the height of our strength, are more likely to fall off. There is a certain current of affairs in men's lives which, if taken when at its highest point, leads to success. If that moment is missed, then all their future course will be in disaster and suffering. We are now moving on such full current, and we must take the opportunity when it is offered or else lose all we have risked.

Cassius. Then, if that is your decision, go on. We shall also go and meet them at Philippi.

Brutus. The darkness of night has come on while we were talking. Nature must obey the necessary call (to sleep); so we shall obey the call with a niggardly (small) amount of rest. There is no more to discuss?

Cassius. No more. Good night. Early to-morrow we shall arise and leave here.

Brutus. Lucius! (*Enter* Lucius) Bring my robe. (Lucius *goes out*) Farewell, good Messala. Good night, Titinius : noble Cassius, good night and pleasant rest to you.

Cassius. O my dear brother ! This night began badly. Never let such a quarrel come between our souls again ! Do not allow it, Brutus.

Brutus. Everything is all right.

Cassius. Good night, my lord.

Brutus. Good night, good brother.

Titin., Messala. Good night, Lord Brutus.

Brutus. Farewell, everyone.

(*Cassius, Titinius and* Messala *go*)

Re-enter Lucius *with the gown*

Give me the gown. Where is thy instrument[1] ?

Lucius. Here in the tent.

Brutus.   What, thou speak'st drowsily[2] ?   240

Poor knave, I blame thee not; thou art o'er-watch'd[3].

Call Claudius and some other of my men;

I'll have them sleep on cushions in my tent.

Lucius. Varro and Claudius !

Enter Varro *and* Claudius

Varro. Calls my lord ?   245

Brutus. I pray you, sirs, lie in my tent and sleep;

It may be I shall raise[4] you by and by

On business to my brother Cassius.

Varro. So please you, we will stand and watch your
          pleasure.

Brutus. I will not have it so: lie down, good sirs;   250

It may be I sall otherwise bethink me[5].—

Look, Lucius, here's the book I sought for so;

I put it in the pocket of my gown.

                          [*Varro and Claudius lie down*

Lucius. I was sure your lordship did not give it me.

Brutus. Bear with me, good boy, I am much forgetful.   255

Canst thou hold up[6] thy heavy eyes awhile,

And touch thy instrument a strain or two?

Lucius. Ay, my lord, an't please you.

Brutus.   It does, my boy;

I trouble thee too much, but thou art willing.

Lucius. It is my duty, sir,   260

Brutus. I should not urge thy duty past thy might[7];

I know young bloods look for a time of rest.

Lucius. I have slept, my lord, already.

Brutus. It was well done : and thou shalt sleep again;   265

I will not hold thee long : if I do live,

I will be good to thee.

          [*Music, and song, towards the end of which Lucius falls asleep*

This is a sleepy tune :— O murderous[8] slumber,

Lay'st thou thy leaden mace[1] upon my boy,

---

1. *Ins-trument*: a lute or lyre. 2. *Drowsily*: as if sleepy. 3. *O'er-watch'd*: kept awake to late. 4. *Raise*: rouse; call. 5. *Otherwise bethink me*: decide otherwise. 6. *Hold up*: keep open. 7. *Past thy might*: beyond your strength. 8. *Murderous*: because it induces unconsciousness.

Re-enter Lucius *bringing the robe.*

Give me the gown. Where is your musical instrument ?

Lucius. Here in the tent.

Brutus. O, you speak as if drowsy ? Poor boy, I do not blame you; you are tired with remaining awake. Call Claudius and some others of my men. I shall have them sleep on cushions in my tent.

Enter Varro *and* Claudius

Varro. Did you call, my lord ?

Brutus. I pray you, gentlemen, lie in my tent and sleep. It is possible that I shall call you bye and bye, to take some message to my brother Cassius.

Varro. Sir, if you allow, we shall remain standing and wait for your wishes.

Brutus. No. I should not like that. Lie down, good gentlemen. It may be I shall change my mind. See, Lucius : here is the book I looked for so hard. I had put it in the pocket of my robe.

*(*Varro *and* Claudius *lie down)*

Lucius. I am sure, sir, that you did not give it to me.

Brutus. Be patient with me, good lad. I am very forgetful. Can you keep your sleepy eyes open for a little longer, and touch a few notes of music on your instrument ?

Lucius. Yes, my lord, if such is your wish.

Brutus. It is, my boy. I trouble you too much, but you are always willing.

Lucius. It is my duty, sir.

Brutus. I should not make your duty more than your strength can bear. I know young fellows need a time of rest.

Lucius. I have slept already, my lord.

Brutus. You were right to do so, and you shall sleep again. I shall not detain you long. If I live after all this, I shall be very good to you.

Music and a song, towards the end of which Lucius falls asleep.

This is a tune which makes one sleepy. O sleep, that kills the senses, have

That plays thee music?—Gentle knave², good night;
I will not do thee so much wrong to wake thee :   270
If thou dost nod³, thou break'st thy instrument;
I'll take it from thee; and, good boy, good night.—
Let me see, let me see; is not the leaf turn'd down
Where I left reading ? Here it is, I think.

Enter the Ghost of Caesar

How ill this taper burns! —Ha! who comes here?   275
I think it is the weakness of mine eyes
That shapes this monstrous apparition.⁴
It comes upon me—Art thou anything?
Art thou some god, some angel, or some devil,
That mak'st my blood cold, and my hair to stare⁵   280
Speak to me what thou art.

 Ghost. Thy evil spirit, Brutus.

 Brutus. Why comest thou?

 Ghost. To tell thee thou shalt see me at Philippi.

 Brutus. Well; then I shall see thee again?   285

 Ghost. Ay, at Philippi.

 Brutus. Why, I will see thee at Phllippi, then.

[Ghost vanishes

Now I have taken heart⁶ thou vanishest :
Ill spirit, I would hold more talk with thee.—
Boy, Lucius!—Varro! Claudius—Sirs, awake;—   290
Claudius!

 Lucius. The strings⁷, my lord, are false⁸.

 Brutus. He thinks he still is at his instrument—
Lucius, awake!

 Lucius. My Lord?   295

 Brutus. Didst thou dream, Lucius, that thou so criedst out?

 Lucius. My lord, I do not know that I did cry.

 Brutus. Yes, that thou dist : didst thou see anything?

 Lucius. Nothing, my lord.

 Brutus. Sleep again, Lucius—Sirrah⁹ Claudius!—   300
[*To Varro.*] fellow thou, awake!

 Varro. My lord?

 Claudius. My lord?

---

1. *Leaden mace;* dull stupefying influence. 2. *Gentle knave*: good boy. 3. *Nod*:
drop your head. 4. *Apparition*: appearance; spectre. 5. *To stare*: to bristle; stand up.
6. *Have taken heart*: have summonded my courage. 7. *Strings*: wires of the harp.
8. *False*: not sounding properly. 9. *Sirrah*: fellow.

you laid your heavy power over the boy who plays you music? good boy,
good night. I shall not disturb you by waking you. But, if you fall over, you
may break your instrument. I shall take if away from you. Good night, good
boy. Let me see, did I not mark, by turning the leaf down, the place in my book
where I was reading? Here it is, I think.

Enter the Spirit of Caesar

How badly the candle burns ! Hulloa, who is it that comes ! I think it is the
weakness of my own eyes which creates this terrible appearance. It comes
towards me. Have you real existence ? Are you god, angel or devil ? You make
my blood turn cold and my hair stand upright. Tell me who you are.

Spirit. I am your evil spirit, Brutus.

Brutus. Why have you come ?

Spirit. To tell you that you will see me at Philippi.

Brutus. Well, I am to see you again ?

Spirit. Yes, at Philippi.

Brutus. So be it. I shall see you at Philippi.

The Spirit disappears.

Now, I have become more bold when you have vanished. Evil spirit,
I should like to speak further with you ! Boy ! Lucius ! Varro ! Claudius!
Awake, gentlemen ! Claudius !

Lucius. The strings of my instrument are not tuned.

Brutus. He imagines that he is still playing his instrument. Lucius,
awake !

Lucius, My lord ?

Brutus. Were you dreaming, Lucius, when you cried out so ?

Lucius. My lord, I was not aware that I had cried.

Brutus. Yes, indeed you did. Did you see anything ?

Lucius. Nothing, my lord.

Brutus. Sleep again, Lucius. You, Claudius ! You, Varro ! Awake !

Varro. My lord ?

Claudius. My lord ?

Brutus. Why did you so cry out, sirs, in your sleep?

Var., Clau. Did we, my lord?

Brutus.   Ay : saw you any thing?   305

Varro. No, my lord, I saw nothing.

Claudius.   Nor I, may lord.

Brutus. Go and commend me¹ to my brother Cassius;
Bid him set on his powers² betimes³ before,
And we will follow.

      Varro, Claudius. It shall be done, my lord.   *[Exeunt*

ACT V

SCENE I. *The plains of Philippi*

Enter Octavious, Antony *and their* Army

Octavious. Now, Antony, our hopes are answered :
You said the enemy would not come down,
But keep the hills and upper regions;
It proves not so; their battles⁴ are at hand;
They means to warn us at Philippi here,   5
Answering before we do demand of them.

    Antony. Tut, I am in their bosoms⁵, and I know
Wherefore they do it: they could be content
To visit other places; and come down
With fearful bravery⁶, thinking by this face⁷   10
To fasten in our thoughts that they have courage;
But 'tis not so.

Enter a Messenger

    Messenger. Prepare you, generals;
The enemy comes on in gallant show;
Their bloody sign of battle⁸ is hung out,
And something to be done immediately.   15

    Antony. Octavius, lead your battle softly on,
Upon the left hand of the even field.

    Octavius. Upon the right hand I; keep thou the left.

    Antony. Why do you cross me in this exigent⁹?

    Octavius. I do not cross you; but I will do so.   20

                                 [March

Drum. Enter Brutus, Cassius, *and their* Army;
Lucilius, Titinius, Messala, *and others*

---

1. *Commend me*: give my regards. 2. *Powers*: army; forces. 3. *Betimes*: early; in good time 4. *Battles*: armies. 5. *In their bosoms*: familiar with their thoughts. 6. *Fearful bravery*: bravery that is inspired by fear. 7. *This face*: this show or parade. 8. *Sign of battle*: the signal given by a flag or otherwise. 9. *Exigent*: critical time.

Brutus. Why did you cry out, gentlemen, in your sleep?

Varro. Claud. Did we, my lord?

Brutus. Yes. Did you see anything?

Varro. No, my lord. I saw nothing.

Claudius. Nor did I, my lord.

Brutus. Go and give my compliments to my brother Cassius. Tell him to start off with his forces some time beforehand. I shall follow after.

Varro, Claudius. It shall be done, my lord.   (*They go out*)

ACT V

SCENE I. *The plains of Philippi*

Enter Octavius, Antony, *and their* Army

Octavius. Now, Antony, our hopes have been realised. You said that the enemy would not come down to the plain, but would stay in the hills and on the higher ground. It is not so. They mean to summon us to battle at Philippi here, answering our challenge before we have made it.

Antony. Oh, I am in the secrets of their hearts and I know why they have done this. They would be pleased to go to other places, and to come down with a kind of fear and bravery, thinking in this way to make us think that they have courage. But they have none.

Enter a Messenger

Messenger. Prepare yourselves, generals. The enemy is advancing in bold array. Their red flag of battle is displayed and action must be taken at once.

Antony. Octavius, lead your army slowly on, on the left side of the level plain.

Octavius. No, I shall advance on the right. You keep to the left.

Antony. Why do you contradict me at this critical time?

Octavius. I do not contradict you, but I shall do as I said.

(*They march*)

Sound of drums. Enter Brutus, Cassius, *and* Army :
Lucilius, Titinius, Messala *and others*

Brutus. They stand, and would have parley[1].

Cassius. Stand fast, Titinius. We must out and talk.

Octavius. Mark Antony, shall we give sign of battle?

Antony. No, Caesar, we will answer on their charge.
Make forth; the generals would have some words.   25

Octavius. Stir not until the signal.

Brutus. Words before blows : is it so, countrymen?

Octavius. Not that we love words better as you do.

Brutus. Good words are better than bad strokes[2], Octavius.

Antony. In your bad strokes, Brutus, you give good words;   30
Witness the hole you made in Caesar's heart,
Crying, "Long live ! hail, Caesar !"

Cassius.   Antony.
The posture[3] of your blows are yet unknown;
But for your words, they rob the Hybla bees,
And leave them honeyless.   35

Antony.   Not stigless too.

Brutus. O, yes, and soundless too;
For you have stol'n their buzzing[4], Antony,
And very wisely threat before you sting.

Antony. Villains, you did not so, when your vile daggers

Hack'd[5] one another in the sides of Caesar;   40
You show'd your teeth like apes, and fawn'd[6] like hounds,
And bow'd like bondmen, kissing Caesar's feet;
Whilst damend Casca, like a cur, behind
Struck Caesar on the neck. O you flatterers !

Cassius. Flatterers !— Now, Brutus, thank yourself :   45
This tongue had not offerded so to-day,
If Cassius might have rul'd.[7]

Octavius. Come, come, the cause : if arguing make us sweat,
The proof of it[8] will turn to redder drops.
Look,
I draw a sword against conspirators;   50
When think you that the sword goes up[9] again ?
Never, till Caesar's three-and-thirty wounds
Be well aveg'd; or till another Caesar[10]
Have added slaughter to the sword of traitors.   55

---

1. *Parley*: a discussion or talk 2. *Strokes*: blow. 3. *Posture:* nature; quality.
4. *Stol'n their buzzing*: imitated the buzzing of bees. 5. *Hock'd*: notched. 6. *Fawn'd*:
cowered. 7. *Might have rul'd*: had been allowed to advise you. 8. *Proof of it*: settling
it by fighting. 9. *Goes up*: is returned to its sheath. 10. *Another Caesar*: Octavius
himself.

Brutus. They halt, and want to have a discussion.

Cassius. Stand firmly by, Titinius. We must go foward and talk.

Octivius. Mark Antony, shall we give the signal to start the battle ?

Antony. No, Caesar. We shall respond to their invitation. Let us go forth. The generals wish to hold some discussion.

Octivius. Do not move until the signal is given.

Brutus. A discussion before fighting. Do you agree, countrymen ?

Octavius. Yes, but not because we like words better than fighting, as you do.

Brutus. Good words are better than bad blows, Octavius.

Antony. Along with your bad blows, you give good words, Brutus. For example, when you struck Caesar through the heart, you did it while crying "Long live ? Hail, Caesar!"

Cassius. Antony, the nature of the blows you give is yet to be seen. But your words are as sweet as if they had taken away all the honey from the bees of Hybla.

Antony. But they have not also taken their stings.

Brutus. Yes, and their buzzing noise too. You have stolen the buzzing of the bees, and wisely threaten before you sting.

Antony. Villains, you did not do so when your vile daggers hit against each other in the body of Caesar. You showed your teeth like monkeys and humbled yourselves before him like dogs, and bowed down like slaves, kissing Caesar's feet, while damned Casca, attacking, like a cur from behind, struck Caesar in the neck. O, what flatterers you are !

Cassius. Flatterers! Now Brutus, it is due to you that the tongue of Antony is so able to insult us to-day, which would not have been possible if you had listened to me.

Octavius. Come, come, to work ! If to argue makes us sweat, then the proof of action will produce red drops of blood. See ! I draw my sword against conspirators. When do you think that my sword will be put in its sheath again ? Never until Caesar's three and thirty wounds are all avenged, or till another Caesar has also been slaughtered by the swords of traitors.

Brutus. Caesar, thou canst not die by traitors' hands
Unless thou bring'st them with thee.

    Octavius.   So I hope;
I was not born to die on Brutus's sword.

    Brutus. O, if thou wert the noblest of thy strain[1],
Young man, thou couldst not die more honourable.   60

    Cassius. A peevish schoolboy, worthless of such honour,
Join'd with a masker[2] and a reveller!

    Antony. Old Cassius still!

    Octavius.   Come, Antony; away!—
Defiance, traitors, hurl we in your teeth :
If you dare fight to-day, come to the field;
If not, when you have stomachs[3].   65

    [Exeunt Octavius, Antony, and their Army

    Cassius. Why, now, blow wind, swell billow[4], and swim bark[5]!
The storm is up; and all is on the hazard.

    Brutus. Ho, Lucilius! hark; a word with you.

    Lucilius.   My lord?

    [Brutus and Lucius converse apart

    Cassius. Messala !

    Messala.   What says my general?   70

    Cassuis.   Messala,
This is my birth-day : as this very day
Was Cassius born. Give me thy hand, Messala :
Be thou my witness that, against my will,
As Pompey was, am I compell'd to set[6],   75
Upon one battle all our liberties.
You know that I held Epicurus strong,
And his opinion : now I change my mind,
And partly credit things that do presage[7].
Coming from Sardis, on our former ensign   80
Two mighty eagles fell; and there they perch'd,
Gorging and feeding from our soldiers hands;
Who to Philippi here consorted us[8].
This morning are they fled away and gone;
And in their steads[9] do ravens, crows, and kites,   85
Fly o'er our heads, and downward look on us,
As we were sickly prey[10] their shadows seem

---

1. *Strain:* family: community. 2. *Masker:* one taking part in masked entertainments.
3. *Stomachs:* inclination. 4. *Swell billow:* may the waves rise. 5. *Bark:* a ship. 6. *Set:*
to stake or venture. 7. *Presage:* show forthcoming events. 8. *Consorted us:*
accompanied us. 9. *Their steads:* their place. 10. *Sickly prey:* a sick animal likely to
become their prey.

Brutus. Caesar, you cannot die at the hands of traitors, unless you have brought some with you.

Octivius. I hope so. Fate did not destine me to die by the sword of Brutus.

Brutus. If you were the noblest of all your family, young man, you could not die a more honourable death.

Cassius. He is an ill-tempered school-boy, quite unworthy of such an honour, allied as he is with one who frequents masques and revels.

Antony. Still the same old Cassius !

Octavius. Come, Antony, let us go! Traitors, we throw our defiance in your faces. If you have courage enough to fight today, come to the battle-field. If not, come when you are more fit.

Octavius, Antony *and their forces depart.*

Cassius. Well, now may the winds blow, the waves rise and the ship sail along ! The storm has started and all depends on the decision of destiny.

Brutus. Lucilius, listen! Let me have a word with you.

Lucilius. My lord?

Brutus *and* Lucilius *talk apart.*

Cassius. Messala !

Messala. Yes, generaí?

Cassius. Messala, this is my birth-day: the very on which Cassius was born. Give me your hand, Messala. You will be my witness to the fact that, like Pompey, I have been unwillingly compelled to risk the liberties of all of us on the result of one battle. You know that I believed strongly in Epicurus and his philosophy. Now I have changed my mind and partly believe in omens which foretell the future. Coming from Sardis, two great eagles alighted on our foremost standard, and there they perched, devouring and swallowing food from the hands of the soldiers. They accompanied us to Philippi here, but this morning they have flown away and gone. In their places, ravens, crows and kites fly over our heads and look down on us as if we were sick animals marked as their prey. Their shadows overhead seem

A canopy[1] most fatal, under which
Our army lies, ready to give up the ghost.
    Messala. Believe not so.   90
    Cassius.   I but believe it partly;
For I am fresh of spirit and resolv'd
To meet all perils very constantly.
    Brutus. Even so, Lucilius.
    Cassius.   Now, most noble Brutus,
The gods to-day stand friendly, that we may,
Lovers[2] in peace, lead on our days to age!   95
But since the affairs of men rest still uncertain[3]
Let's reason with the worst that they may befall,
If we do lose this battle, then is this
The very last time we shall speak together;
What are you, then, determined to do?   100
    Brutus. Even by the rule of that philosophy
By which I did blame Cato for the death
Which he did give himself : — I know not how,
But I do find it cowardly and vile,
For fear of what might fall[4], so to prevent[5]   105
The time of life:— arming myself with patience
To stay the providence[6] of some high powers
That govern us below.
    Cassius.   Then, if we lose this battle
You are contented to be led in triumph
Through the streets of Rome?   110
    Brutus. No, Cassius, no, think not, thou noble Roman,
That ever Brutus will go bound to Rome;
He bears too great a mind. But this same day
Must end that work the ides of March begun;
And whether we shall meet again I know not.   115
Therefore our everlasting farewell take :
For ever, and for ever, farewell, Cassius !
If we do meet again, why, we shall smile;
If not, why, then, athis parting was we made.
    Cassius, For ever, and for ever, farewell, Brutus !   120
If we do meet again we'll smile indeed;
If not, 'tis true this parting was well made.
    Brutus. Why, then, lead on.—O, that a man might know
The end of this day's business ere it come !
But it sufficeth that the day will end.   125

---

1. *Canopy*: overhead cover. 2. *Lovers*: friends. 3. *Rest still uncertain*: are always uncertain. 4. *Fall*: happen. 5. *To prevent*: to cut short; to interfere with. 6. *Providence*: arrangements; the will.

a fatal canopy under which our army lies, ready to give up its life.

Messala. Do not believe it.

Cassius. I only partly believe it. I am still strong in courage and resolved to meet all dangers very steadily.

Brutus. Exactly so, Lucilius.

Cassius. Now, most noble Brutus, may the gods today befriend us, so the we, close friends in peaces, may go on happily to old age. But since the fortunes of men are always uncertain, let us sketch the worst that can happen to us. If we should lose this battle, then this will have been the last time that we had to speak with each other. What have you resolved to do?

Brutus. Even to remain faithful to the same philosophy by which I blamed Cato for the death which he inflicted on himself. I cannot explain it, but I hold it to be a cowardly and vile action, for fear of the consequences, to shorten our own lives. I shall arm myself with patience to endure whatever is provided by the high deities who govern the lives of men on the world below.

Cassius, Then, if we lose this battle, you are content to be led in a triumphal procession through the streets of Rome ?

Brutus. No, Cassius, no. Do not think, O noble Roman, that ever Brutus will go as a prisoner to Rome. He has too lofty a mind. But this very day must complete the work that was commenced on the Ides of March. Whether we shall meet again or not, I do not know. So let us take the final farewell of each other : farewell, for ever and ever, Cassius ! If we do chance to meet again, then we shall smile (at this talk); if not, then it is well that we have made this farewell parting.

Cassius. Farewell for ever and ever, Brutus ! If we meet again, we shall smile at this. If not, it will be as well that we have made this parting.

Brutus. Then lead on. O, I wish that one could know that the result of this day's work beforehand ! But it is sufficient to know that the day will end

And then the end is known.— Come, ho! away!   *[Exeunt*

SCENE II. *The same. The field of battle*
Alarums. Enter Brutus *and* Messala

Brutus. Ride, ride, Messala, ride, and give these bills[1]
Unto the legions on the other side :
Let them set on at once; for I perceive
But cold demeanour[2] in Octavius' wing[3],
And sudden push gives them the overthrow.   5
Ride, ride, Messala: let them all come down.   *[Exeunt*

SCENE III. *Another part of the field.*
Alarums. Enter Cassius *and* Titinius

Cassius. O, look, Titinius, look, the villains fly!
Myself have to mine own turn'd enemy :
This ensign[4] here of mine was turning back;
I slew the coward, and did take it from him.

Titinius. O Cassius, Brutus gave the word too early;   5
Who, having some advantage on Octavius,
Took it too eagerly: his soldiers fell to spoil[5],
Whilst we by Antony are all enclose'd[6].

Enter Pindarus

Pindarus. Fly further off, my lord, fly further off;
Mark Antony is in your tents, my lord;   10
Fly, therefore, noble Cassius, fly far off.

Cassius. This hill is far enough.—Look, look, Titinius :
Are those my tents where I percive the fire ?

Titinius. They are, my lord.

Cassius.   Titinius, if thou lov'st me.
Mount thou my horse, and hide[7] thy spurs in him,   15
Till he have brought thee up to yonder troops,
And here again; the I may rest assur'd
Whether yond troops are friend or enemy.

Titinius. I will be here again, even with a thought.   *[Exit*

Cassius. Go, Pindarus, get higher on that hill: 20
My sight was ever thick[8], regard Titinius,
And tell me what thou not'st about the field.

[Pindarus ascends the hill

---

1. *Bills:* messages; written orders. 2. *Cold demeanour*: lack of will to fight.
3. *Wing*: the flank or side commanded by Octavius. 4. *Ensign*: the flag or standard
bearer. 5. *Spoil*: looting. 6. *Enclos'd*: surrounded. 7. *Hide*: *apply*; dig in deeply.
8. *Thick*: dim or misty.

and then the result will be known. come, let us go ! (*They go out*)

SCENE II The battlefield. Noises of battle

Enter Brutus and Messala

Brutus. Ride, ride, Messala, and give these written orders to the regiments on the other side. Let them make the attack at once, for I see only a half-hearted spirit on Octavius's side of the field, and a sudden attack will give them a defeat, Ride, ride, Messala; and let them all come to the attack.

(They go)

Scene III, Another part of the field

Sounds of battle. Enter Cassius and Titinius

Cassius. O, look, Titinius, the villains are running away ! I have become an enemy of my own troops. This standard-bearer of mine was turning back, so I slew the coward and took the ensign from him.

Titinius. O Cassius, Brutus gave the order for attack too early. He had gained some advantage over Octavius' army, but he took it too rashly. His soldiers commenced to loot, and now we are surrounded by Antony's men.

Enter Pindarus

Pindarus. Retreal further off, my lord, retreat further. Mark Antony has already entered your camp, my lord. so retreat for off, noble Cassius.

Cassius. This hill is far enough for me. Look, Titinius ! Are those my tents where I see a fire burning?

Titinius. They are, my lord.

Cassius. Titinius, if you love me, mount my horse and drive your spurs into him till he carries you up to those troops, and then back here again. I must know with certainty whether those troops are our friends or the enemy.

Titinius. I shall be back here with the speed of th ght.

(He goes off)

Cassius. Go, Pindarus, and mount higher up that hill. My eyesight has always been weak. Look, Titinius, and tell me what you see of the battle.

(Pindarus ascends the hill)

This day I breath'd first[1]: time is come round,
And where I did begin, there shall I end;
My life is run its compass[2].—Sirrah, what news?   25
    Pindarus. [*Above*] O my lord!
    Cassius. What news?
    Pindarus. [*Above*] Titinius is enclosed round about
With horsemen, that make to him on the spur;—
Yet he spurs on.—Now they are almost on him.   30
Now, Titinius!....Now some light[3]. O, he lights too
He's ta'en[4]; [*Shout*] and, hark ! they shout for joy.
    Cassius. Come down, behold no more.
O, coward that I am to live so long,
To see my best friend ta'en before my face !   35

Pindarus descends

Come hither, sirrah :
In Parthia did I take there prisoner;
And then I swore thee, saving of thy life,
That whatsoever I did bid thee do,
Thou shouldst attempt it. Come now, keep thine oath;   40
Now be a freeman[5]; and with this good sword,
That ran through Caesar's bowels, search[6] this bosom.
Stand not to answer: here, take thou the hilts[7];
And when my face is cover'd, as 'tis now,
Guide thou the sword. [*Pindarus stabs him.*] Caesar, thou
    art reveng'd,   45
Even with the sword that kill'd thee.   *[Dies*
    Pindarus. So, I am free; yet would not so have been,
Durst I have done my will[8]! O Cassius!
Far from this country Pindarus shall run,
Where never Roman shall take note of him. *[Exit*   50

Re-enter Titinius with Messala

    Messala. It is but change[9], Titinius; for Octavius
Is overthrown by noble Brutus' power[10],
As Cassius' legions are by Antony.
    Titinius. These tidings will well comfort Cassius.
    Messala. Where did you leave him?

---

    1. *Breath'd first*: was born. 2. *Run its compass*: completed its course. 3. *Light*: are alighting— dismounting. 4. *Ta'en*: taken; captured. 5. *Freeman*: I release you from your bondage to me   6. *Search*: pierce. 7. *Hilts*: handle. 8. *Done my will*: followed my own wishes. 9. *Change*: exchange, victory on one side, defeat on the other. 10. *Power*: army.

This is the day on which I commenced to live. The cycle of time is completed, and on this date of my beginning, I shall die. My life has complete its course. Well, Sir, what news ?

Pindarus. (Above) O, my lord !

Cassius. What news ?

Pindarus. (Above) Titinius is surrounded by horsemen who are spurring towards him. Yet he spurs his horse on. Now they are almost upon him. Now, Titinius ! Now some of them are alighting from their horses. O, he is alighting too ! He is captured. (*Shouting is heard*) Listen, they are shouting for joy.

Cassius. Come down; and watch no more. What a coward I am, to live so long as this, and see my best friend taken prisoner before my face !

Pindarus comes down.

Come here, sir. It was in Parthia that I took you prisoner, and I made you swear a vow, after I saved your life, that no matter what I ordered you to do, you should attempt it. Come, now, keep your promise. Now become a freeman. With this good sword of mine, that ran through Caesar's body, stab into my breast. Do not try to answer me. Take the hilt of the sword, and, when my face is covered as it is now, plunge in the sword. (Pindarus *stabs him*). Now Caesar, you are avenged, and by the very same sword which killed you. (Cassius *dies.*)

Pindarus. So now I am free. Yet I would not have been so had I dared to follow my own wishes. O Cassius ! I shall flee far from this country, where no Roman shall ever see me.   *(He goes)*

Re-enter Titinius and Messala

Messala. It is but a change, Titinius, for Octavius has been defeated by the army of our noble Brutus, just as the legions of Cassius have been defeated by Antony.

Titinius. The news will be a great comfort to Cassius.

Messala. Where did you leave him?

    Titinius.   All disconsolate.   55
With Pindarus his bondman, on this hill.
      Messala. Is not that he that lies upon the ground?
      Titinius. He lies not like the living. O my heart!
      Messala. Is not that he?
      Titinius.   No, this was he, Messala.
But Cassius is no more.—O setting sun,   60
As in thy red rays thou dost sink to night,
So in his red blood Cassius' day is set,—
The sun of Rome is set ! Our day is gone;
Clouds, dews, and dangers come; our deeds are done!
Mistrust[1] of my success hath done this deed.   65
      Mesala. Mistrust of good success hath done this deed.
O hateful Error, Melancholy's child,
Why dost thou show to the apt[2] thoughts of men
The things that are not ? O Error, soon conceiv'd,[3]
Thoy never com'st unto a happy birth,   70
But kill'st the mother that engender'd thee!
      Titinius. What, Pindarus! where art thou, Pindarus?
      Messala. Seek him, Titinius, whilst I go to meet
The noble Brutus, thrusting this report
Into his ears: I may say, thrusting it;   75
For piercing steel and darts envenom'd[4]
Shall be as welcome to athe ears of Brutus
As tidings of this sight.
      Titinius.   Hie[5] you. Messala,
And I will seek for Pindarus the while.   *[Exit Messala*
Why didst thou send me forth, brave Cassius?   80
Did I not meet thy friends ? and did not they
Put on my brows this wreath of victory,
And bid me give it thee ? Dist thou not hear their shouts?
Alas, thou hast misconstru'd[6] every thing!
But, hold thee, take this garland on thy brow;   85
Thy Brutus bid me give it thee, and I
Will do his bidding.—Brutus, come apace[7],
And see how I regarded Caius Cassius.—
By your leave, gods :—this is a Roman's part[8];
Come, Cassius' sword, and find Titinius' heart.   90
                            [Kills himelf

---

   1. *Mistrust*: etc., doubt as to whether I should succeed, 2. *Apt*: *ready;* quick
to receive. 3. *Conceiv'd*: born. 4. *Envenom'd*: poisoned. 5. *Hie*: go. 6. *Misconstru'd*:
misunderstood. 7. *Apace*: quickly. 8. *Part*: duty; custom.

Titinius. Quite down-hearted with his slave, Pindaruas on this hill.

Messala. Is not that he lying on the ground ?

Titinius. He does not lie as a living man would. O, my heart !

Messala. Is not that he ?

Titinius. No, it *was* he, Messala. But Cassius is no more. O setting sun!
just as you sink in a flood of red fire at sunset, so has Cassius ended his life's
course in his own red blood. The Sun of Rome has set. Now clouds, dews and
dangers may come; our deeds are ended. His want of confidence that I would
succeed has led to this act.

Messala. Want of trust in our good success had led to it. O, Spirit of
Error, child of Melancholy, who do you allow the ready thoughts of men to
see things which do not exist? O Error, easily formed, but yet you never have
a happy birth but always kill the mother in whom you are formed!

Titinius. Pindarus ! Where are you, Pindarus?

Messala. Look for him, Titinius, while I go to meet the noble Brutus,
to thrust this news into his ears. I say, "thrusting" because pointed steel and
poisoned darts would be a disagreeable to the ears of Brutus as the news of
this sad sight.

Titinius. you go, Messala, and I shall look for Pindarus in the meantime.
(Messala goes) Why did you send me out, brave Cassius? Did I not meet your
friends, and did not they put on my forehead this garland of victory, telling
me to give it to you ? Your friend Brutus told me to give it to you, and I shall
carry out his request. Brutus, come soon, and see how much regard I had for
Caius Cassius. Forgive me, O gods, this is a Roman act. now let the sword of
Cassius pierce my heart also.   *(Kills himself)*

Alarums. Re-enter Messala *with* Brutus, *young* Cato,
Strato, Volumnius, *and* Lucilius

Brutus. Where, where, Messala, doth his body lie?
Messala. Lo yonder; and Titinius mourning it.
Brutus. Titinius' face is upward.
Cato.   He is slain.
Brutus. O Julius Caesar, thou are mighty yet!
Thy spirit walks abroad, and turns our swords   95
In our own proper entrails[1].   [*Low alarums*
Cato.   Brave Titinius !
Look, whether he have not crown'd dead Cassius !
   Brutus. Are yet two Romans living such as these?—
The last of all the Romans, fare thee well !
It is impossible that ever Rome   100
Should breed thy fellow[2].—Friends, I owe more tears
To this dead man than you shall see me pay.—
I shall find time, Cassius, I shall find time.—
Come, therefore, and to Thasos send his body :
His funerals[3] shall not be in our camp,   105
Lest it discomfort[4] us. —Lucilius, come;—
And come, young Cato; let us to the field.—
Labeo and Flavius, set our battles[5] on:—
'Tis three o'clock; and, Romans, yet ere night
Whe shall try fortune in a second fight.   [*Exeunt*   110

SCENE IV. *Another part of the field*
Alarums. Enter fighting Soldiers *of both armies; then*
Brutus, *young* Cato, Lucilius, *and others*

Brutus. Yet, countrymen, O, yet hold up your heads !
Cato. What bastard doth not ? Who will go with me?
I will proclaim my name about the field:—
I am the son of Marcus Cato, ho!
A foe to tyrants, and my country's friend;   5
I am the son of Marcus Cato, ho!
              [*Charges the enemy*
   Brutus. And I am Brutus, Marcus Brutus, I;
Brutus, my country's friend; know me for Brutus !
         [*Exit, charging the enemy. Cato
            is overpowered, and falls*
   Lucilius. O young and noble Cato, art thou down?
Why, now thou diest as bravely as Titinius;   10
And mayst be honour'd, being Cato's son.

---

1. *Proper entrails*: our own bodies. 2. *Fellow*: equal. 3. *Funerals*: burial
ceremonies. 4. *Discomfort us*: upset the troops. 5. *Battles*: forces; legions.

Sounds of battle. Re-enter Messala, *with* Brutus,
young Cato, Strato, Volumnius, *and* Lucilius.

Brutus. Where, O where does his body lie, Messala?

Messala. Over there, and Titinius beside, mourning for him.

Brutus. The face of Titinius is turned upwards.

Cato. He is dead.

Brutus. O julius Caesar. (*though dead*) you are still mighty! Your spirit
walks about and turns our swords into our own bodies.

Cato. Brave Titinius ! See, has he not garlanded dead Cassius !

Brutus. Are there two Romans left alive as great as these ? Farewell to
you, the last of the Romans ! It is impossible that Rome shall ever produce
their equals. Friends, I owe more tears to this dead friend than you shall see
me shed. But I shall yet find time, Cassius; I shall find time. Come, then, and
let us send his body to Thasos. His funeral ceremonies shall not be in our
camp, lest they should upset our troops. Come, Lucilius and you, young Cato.
Let us make our way to the battlefield. Labeo and Flavius, set our forces in
movement. It is three o'clock. Romans, and before night we shall risk our
fortune in a second battle.   (*They go out*)

SCENE IV. *Another part of the field*

Sounds of fighting, Enter fighting soldiers *of both armies* :

then Brutus, *young* Cato, Lucilius *and others.*

Brutus. My countrymen, hold up your heads yet awhile!

Cato. Who is so unworthy as not to do so? Who will follow me? I shall
announce my name over the battlefield. I am the son of Marcus Cato, an
enemy to tyrants and a friend to my country. I am the son of Marcus Cato!
(*Charges the enemy*)

Brutus. And I am Brutus, Marcus Brutus. I am Brutus, the friend of my
country. Let everyone know me for Brutus. (*He goes out and charges the
enemy.* Cato *is overpowered and falls down*).

Lucilius. O young and noble Cato, have you fallen? Well, now you have
died as bravely as Titinius, and have earned honour as the son of Cato.

First Soldier. Yield, or thou diest.

Lucilius.   Only I yield to die :

There is so much that thou wilt kill me straight[1];

                                        [*Offering money*

Kill Brutus, and be honour'd in his death.

First Soldier. We must not.— A noble prisoner !   15

Second Soldier. Room, ho ! Tell Antony, Brutus is ta'en.[2]

First Soldier. I'll tell the news:—here comes the general.

                         Enter Antony

Brutus is ta'en, Brutus is ta'en, my lord.

Antony. Where is he ?

Lucilius. Safe, Antony; Brutus is safe enough :   20

I dare assure thee that no enemy

Shall ever take alive the noble Brutus :

The gods defend him from so great a shame !

When you do find him, or alive or dead[3]

He will be found like Brutus, like himself.   25

    Antony. This is not Brutus, friend; but, I assure you,

A prize no less in worth: keep this man safe,

Give him all kindness : I had rather have

Such men my friends than enemies. Go on,

And see whether Brutus be alive or dead;   30

And bring us word unto Octaivius' tent

How every thing is chanc'd[4].   [*Exeunt*

              SCENE V. *Another part of the field*

                 Enter Brutus, Dardanius, Clitus, Strato,

                         and Volumnius

Brutus. Come, poor remains of friends, rest on this rock.

Clitus. Statilius show'd the torch-light; but, my lord,

He came not back : he is or ta'en or slain.[5]

Brutus. Sit thee down, Clitus : slaying is the word;

It is a deed in fashion. Hark thee, Clitus.   5

                                        [*Whispers him*

Clitus. What, I, my lord ? No, not for all the world.

Brutus. Peace, then ! no words.

Clitus.   I'll rather kill myself.

Brutus. Hark thee, Dardanius.   [*Whispers him*

Dardanius.   Shall I do such a deed?

---

1. *Kill me straight*: if you will but kill me at once. 2. *Ta'en*: captured. 3. *Or alive or dead*: whether alive or dead. 4. *Is chanc'd*: has happened. 5. *Or ta'en or slain*: either captured or killed.

First Soldier. Yield, or you shall die.

Lucilius. I yield myself, only to die. Here is so much money, if you will kill me at once. (*Offers the soldier money*). Kill Brutus, and it will be an honour for you to have caused his death.

First Soldier. We must not. This is a noble prisoner.

Second Soldier. Make room there! Tell Antony that Brutus is captured.

First Soldier. I shall tell him the news. Here comes the general.

Enter Antony.

Brutus is captured, my lord.

Antony, Where is he?

Lucilius. He is safe, Antony. Brutus is safe enough, I can assure you that no enemy will ever capture the noble Brutus alive. May the gods protect him from so great a disgrace! When you do find him, whether alive or dead, he shall be found in such a fitting stage as is worthy of Brutus himself.

Antony. This is not Brutus, my friend, but I can assure you he is a prisoner of no less importance. Keep this man safe and treat him with kindness : I would rather have such men my friends than my enemies. Go on and see whether Brutus be alive or dead. Then bring me news, to the tent of Octavius, how everything has turned out.   (*They go*)

SCENE V. *Another part of the field*

Enter Brutus, Dardanius, Clitus, Strato *and* Volumnius.

Brutus. Come, you who are the poor remaining friends. Rest on the rock.

Clitus. Statilius showed the signal of the torch-light, but he did not come back, my lord. He is either captured or killed.

Brutus. Sit down, Clitus, "Slaying" is the proper word to use; it is very common at present. Listen, Clitus. (*Whispers to him.*)

Clitus, what, I, my lord? No, not for all the world.

Brutus. Keep silent, then! Say no words.

Clitus. I would rather kill myself.

Brutus. Listen, Dardanius. (*Whispers to him*).

Dardanius. Shall I do such a deed?

Clitus. O Dardanius!

Dardanius. O Clitus!   10

Clitus. What ill request did Brutus make to thee?

Dardanius. To kill him, Clitus. Look, he meditates.

Clitus. Now is that noble vessel full of grief,

That it runs over even at his eyes.

  Brutus. Come hither, good Volumnius; list a word.   15

  Volumnius. What says my lord?

  Brutus.   Why, this, Volumnius :

The ghost of Caesar hath appear'd to me

Two several[1] times by night; at Sardis once,

And, this last night, here in Philippi fields :

I know my hour[2] is come.

  Volumnius.   Not so, my lord.   20

  Brutus. Nay, I am sure it is, Volumnius.

Thou seest the world. Voluminius, how it goes;

Our enemies have beat us to the pit[3]:   *[Low alarums*

It is more worthy to leap in ourselves,

Than tarry[4] till they push us. Good Volumnius,   25

Thou know'st that we two went to school together :

Even for that our love of old, I prithee,

Hold thou my sword-hilts[5], whilst I run on it.

  Volumnius. That's not an office for a friend, my lord.

          [Alarums still

  Clitus. Fly, fly, my lord; there is no tarrying here.   30

  Brutus. Farewell to you;—and you;—and you Volumnius.—

Strato, thou hast been all this while asleep;

Farewell to thee too, Strato.—Countrymen,

My heart doth joy[6] that yet in all my life

I found no man but he was true to me.   35

I shall have glory by this losing day,

More than Octavius and Mark Antony

By this vile conquest shall attain unto.

So, fare you well at once; for Brutus' tongue

Hath almost ended his life's history :   40

Night hangs upon mine eyes; my bones would rest,

That have but labour'd to attain this hour.

     [Alarums. Cry within, "Fly, fly, fly !"

  Clitus. Fly, my lord, fly.

Brutus.   Hence ! I will follow.

     [Exeunt Clitus, Dardanius, and Volumnius

---

  1. *Several:* separate; different. 2. *My hour:* the hour of my death. 3. *The pit:* the trap laid for us. 4. *Tarry:* wait. 5. *Sword hilts:* handle of my sword. 6. *Joy:* rejoice.

Clitus. O Dardanius ?

Dardanius. O Clitus !

Clitus. What terrible thing did Brutus ask of you ?

Dardanius. That I should kill him, Clitus. See he is mediating.

Clitus. Now the noble man is full of grief, which overflows in the form of tears from his eyes.

Brutus. Come here my good Volumnius. Hear my words,

Volumnius. What say you, my lord ?

Brutus. Only this, Volumnius : the spirit of Caesar has appeared to me, two different times by night. Once was at Sardis, and then last night, here in the field of Philippi. I know that my hour of death has come.

Volumnius. Not so, my lord.

Brutus. No, I am sure it is so, Volumnius. You see the ways of the world, Volumnius, and how things happen. Our enemies have driven us like animals which the hunters have pursued to a pit dug in the ground. It is more worthy now to leap in of our own accord than to wait for them to push us in. Good Volumnius, you know that the two of us went to school together. For the sake of that old time love of ours, I pray you to hold fast the handle of my sword, till I run on the blade.

Volumnius. That is not a service for a friend to do, my lord.

(Still sounds of battle)

Clitus. Flee, lord. It will not do to remain here.

Brutus. Farewell to you : and you, and you, Volumnius. Strato, you have been asleep all this time. Farewell to you too, Strato. My countrymen, my heart rejoices that even till now, in all my life I have found no man who was not true to me. I shall gain fame by this day of defeat more than Octavius and Mark Antony shall get from their vile victory. So farewell at once, for my tongue has almost ended its life's work. A darkness falls upon my eyes and my tired bones long for rest. They have only laboured to lead up to this hour.

(Sounds of war. Cries Fly! Fly!)

Clitus. Fly, my lord, fly.

Brutus. You go. I shall follow.

(Clitus, Dardanius and Volumnius *depart)*

I prithee[1], Strato, stay thou by thy lord :
Thou art a fellow of a good respect[2];   45
Thy life hath had some santch[3] of honour in it :
Hold, then, my sword, and turn away thy face,
While I do run upon it. Wilt thou, Strato ?

    Strato. Give me your hand first; fare you well, my lord.

    Brutus. Farewell, good Strato, — Caesar, now be still :   50
I kill'd not thee with half so good a will.
                [He runs on his sword, and dies
      Alarums. Retreat. Enter Octavius, Antony, Messala,
                Lucilius, *and* Army

    Octavius. What man is that?

    Messala. My master's man.—Strato, where is thy master?

    Strato. Free from the bondage you are in, Messala :
The conquerors can but make a fire of him;   55
For Brutus only overcame himself,
And no man else hath honour by his death[4].

    Lucilius. So Brutus should be found : I thank thee, Brutus.
That thou hast proved Lucilius' saying true.

    Octavius. All that serv'd Brutus, I will enteratain them[5].   60
Fellow, wilt thou bestow thy time[6] with me?

    Strato. Ay, if Messala will prefer[7] me to you.

    Octavius. Do, so, good Messala.

    Messala. How died my master, Strato?

    Strato. I held the sword, and he did run on it.   65

    Messala. Octavius, then take him to follow thee,
That did the latest service[8] to my master.

    Antony. This was the noblest Roman of them all :
All the conspirators, save only he,
Did that they did in envy of great Caesar;   70
He only, in a general honest thought.[9]
And common good to all, made one of them
His life was gentle, and the elements[10]
So mix'd in him, that Nature might stand up
And say to all the world, "This was a man !"   75

---

    1. *Prithee:* beg of you. 2. *Respect;* character. 3. *Snatch:* amount; measure. 4. *By his death*: of having killed him. 5. *Entertain them:* thake them into my employment. 6. *Bestow thy time*: enter my service. 7. *Prefer:* recommend. 8. *Latest service*: the last service, of helping him to die. 9. *General honest thought*: honestly thinking of the public good. 10. *Elements;* qualities.

I pray you, Strato, stay beside your lord. You are a man of good and noble conduct, and your life has had a trace of honour in it. You hold my sword, and look away while I run upon it. Will you do so, Strato?

Strato. Give me your hand first. Farewell, my lord.

Brutus. Farewell, good Strato. Caesar, now you may rest in peace. I did not kill you with half so much willingness as I kill myself.

(He runs on the sword and dies)

Sounds of fighting. Trumpets blowing retreat.
Enter Octavius, Antony, Messala, Lucilius *and* Army

Octavius. Who is that man ?

Messala. My master's servant. Strato, where is your master ?

Strato. He is free from the captivity in which you are, Messala. His conquerors can only burn his body, for Brutus was overcome by nobody except himself. No other man gains any honour from his death.

Lucilius. This is the way in which Brutus should be found. I thank you, Brutus, for you have proved that what Lucilius said was true.

Octavius. I shall employ all who served under Brutus. Fellow, will you give your service to me ?

Strato. Yes, if Messala will recommend me to you.

Octavius. Do so, good Messala.

Messala. How did my master die, Strato ?

Strato. I held his sword for him to run upon it.

Messala. Octavius, take the man to be your follower who did the last service to his master.

Antony. This Brutus was the noblest of all the Romans. All the conspirators, with the exception of him, did what they did because they envied Caesar. He only, thinking honestly of the good of the people, became one of them. His life was gentle, and the various qualities were so combined in him that Nature might stand up and say to all the world, "This was indeed a Man."

  Octavius. According to his virtue let us use him.
With all respect and rites of burial.
Within my tent his bones to-night shall lie,
Most like a soldier, order'd honourably.—
So, call the field¹ to rest: and let's away,   80
To part² the glories of this happy day.   *[Exeunt*

---

1. *Field*: all the soldiers. 2. *Part*: share.

Octavius. Let us treat him according to his virtue, and give him all due honours and ceremonies of burial. His body shall lie inside my tent to-night, arranged with honour as is most fitting for a soldier. So call the soldiers to rest. Let us go now, to divide up the honours of this day of victory.

(They depart)

NOTES

ACT I. Scene I

2. *Is this a holiday?* Flavius means that they should not be rejoicing in the streets when the day is not a "calendar' holiday.

3. *mechanical,* labourers; artisans. The word has not this meaning in our times.

4-5. *without a sign.... profession,* the law said that on ordinary working days, a labourer should carry the signs of his trade upon him.

7. *thy rule,* the ruler, which a carpenter would normally carry with him.

8. *best apparel,* his best clothes, which should not normally be worn on a working day.

10-11. *in respect of,* if regarded as. *a cobbler,* we see here one of the great forms of Elizabethan wit, the pun or double meaning, so little used now. A cobbler is in the usual sense "a repairer of shoes." But the literal meaning is a bungler, or "one who spoils his work." Such plays on double meanings were looked upon as the latest wit by the uneducated audience of the time.

15. *mender of bad soles,* again the play on words, "sole" and "soul." In *Merchant of Venice,* when the Jew is sharpening his knife, one of the character says to him :

> "Not on thy sole but on thy soul, harsh Jew,
>
> Thou makest thy knife keen."

16. *naughty,* this is a word which has now a mild meaning, and is applied to the misconduct of little children. But in Shakespeare's days, it was a stronger word, meaning "bad" or "wicked."

18. *out with me,* out of temper with me : angry with me.

19. *mend you,* repair you, i.e., your shoes.

24. *with the awl,........withal I am,* again a pun or a play on the similar sounds of words, *with awl* and *withal.* The awl is the pointed instrument which the shoe-maker use to make holes in leather.

27. *re-cover,* again the play upon words, the usual meaning of "recover" being set against the literal sense of "to put a new covering of leather on the shoes."

29. *proper,* fine; handsome. An old meaning of the word. *neat's*

leather, leather made from the skin of oxen. *Neat* is an Old English word for an ox or cow.

35. *in his triumph,* when a Roman general returned victorious or a statesman distinguished himself, he was accorded a public procession and ceremonies, called a "triumph."

37. *tributaries,* conquered chiefs, who in the future would be compelled to pay tribute or taxes to the conquerors.

39. *To grace..... wheels,* it was the custom for a victorious general to bring back prisoners of war, and they had to walk on foot in the procession through the city beside the chariot of the victorious conqueror.

43. *battlements,* the coping or raised edge of a roof, behind which cover might be taken in old-time warfare.

47. *pass the streets,* the preposition "through" is understood.

51. *replication,* repetition, i.e. echo.

52. *concave shores,* the hollow rocks which formed the bank of the Tiber.

55. *cull out,* to "cull" is to pick out or select an object from a number of them. They had carefully selected that day for a holiday.

55. *over Pompey's blood,* over the two sons of Pompey, Cnaeus and Sextus, whom Caesar had just defeated in battle, the former of them having been killed.

59. *intermit,* to stop, or literally, to come between the people and the plague which is about to fall on them as a punishment.

62. *of your sport,* in your class or community.

64. *the lowest stream,* the water at its deepest part.

66. *See whether.... mov'd,* 'You can see that even their base natures are deeply moved."

69. *disrobe the images,* strip off the coloured scarfs, mentioned in 1, 2, 289, which had been placed on the stone statues to make decorations for the holiday. *decked with ceremonies,* adorned with ceremonial decorations.

72. *feast of Lupercal,* the Lupercalia was an important festival held in Rome. Legend had it that the founders of Rome, Romulus and Remus, were fed by a she-wolf; (Latin, *lupus,* a wolf). The men who celebrated the festival were called the Luperci, and they ran a course round the city wall, carrying thongs and whips with which they struck at the people as they passed. Those thongs were made from the skins of the sacrificed animals, and called *februa.* This has given us the name of the month, February. The Lupercal was a ceremony of purification.

74. *trophies,* decorations.

75. *vulgar*, common people.

77. *Those growing feathers etc.*, the metaphor is from the sport of falconry, the hunting of game by means of trained hawks. A *pitch* was a technical term of falconry for the height to which a hawk flew. Shakespeare draws often on this sports for his illustrations, which would be well understood by an Elizabethan audience.

Scene II

Antony for the course, Antony was one of the celebrants called the Luperci, and so was preparing to run the allotted course round the city wall.

6-9. *Forget not, etc.*, it was an old superstition that a barren woman would be cured and would have children if touched by the thongs of the Luperci. Educated Romans like Brutus would think little of such old beliefs, but it is a proof that Caesar is "superstitious grown," that he should believe such things. *sterile curse*, the curse of not having any children.

15. *press*, crowd; mob.

18. *Ides of March*, the Ides fell on the 15th Day in the month of March. May, July, October. In other months, on the 13th. Cf. the Muslim festival of Id.

19. *soothsayer*, literally "truth-teller." They were semi-religious mystics with powers of prophecy and divination.

28. *gamesome*, inclined for sport or games.

30. *hinder your desire*, stand in the way of your wishes.

32-36. *Brutus, I do observe etc.*, Plutarch mentions that there had been some coldness between Cassius and Brutus, because they had been rivals for the post of Praetor. Brutus having been preferred to Cassius. *Bear too stubborn... hand*, the metaphor is that of controlling a horse with a tight and heavy rein, keeping it under firm guidance. *strange*, unfriendly.

39. *merely*, only; entirely.

40. *passions of some difference*, passions which are in conflict with each other. He probably means his love for Caesar and his love for Rome, and the difficulty of bringing them into agreement with each other.

41. *proper*, personal. (Latin, *proprius*, one's own).

42. *soil*, stain, blemish. *behaviours*, conduct. The abstract noun "behaviour" has no plural in modern usage; here we may read it as "acts."

45. *Nor construe etc.* "and do not interpret my neglect as meaning any more than that, etc."

49. *By means whereof*, because of which.

54. *'Tis just*, that is so.

58. *your shodow*, a true picture or reflection of yourself. The object which Cassius has in mind is to arouse jealousy in Brutus, and make him feel that he is just as worthy to rule as Caesar.

59. *Where may, etc.*, "where" is not, as usual, an adverb of place, but rather a conjunction meaning "that".

61. *this age's yoke*, the burden worn by the people of this age.

64. *seek into myself*, look into my own nature.

68-69. *I, your glass*, Cassius will be the looking-glass, which will truly reveal to Brutus an unexaggerated picture of himself.

73. *a common laugher*, an ordinary frivolous or flippant man.

73. *to stale*, to soil : to make cheap or common.

74. *every new protestor*, each newcomer who makes protestations of friendship.

75. *fawn*, the word usually describes the humble licking and crouching of a dog trying to be friendly.

76. *after*, afterwards.

77. *profess myself*, exposing the thoughts of my mind.

78. *the rout*, the common crowd.

86. *in one eye*, on one hand.

87. *indifferently*, **unmoved**; impartially. Brutus means that he will be quite unaffected by personal considerations of honour or safety.

88. *speed*, prosper : help. The old expression "God speed you !" was a wish for God to send prosperity, "and had no" idea of haste or swiftness as is now associated with the verb "to speed".

91. *favour*, then had its ordinary meaning of "face".

95. *had as lief*, "would as soon." This old English word in not much used now.

101. *The troubled Tiber etc*. When the troubled or stormy Tiber (was) fighting against her boundaries.

105. *accoutred*, dressed or equipped. They made no change or adjustment of dress before swimming.

107. *buffet*, the word means "to strike a blow." Here it signifies that they met the fast river with strong swimming strokes.

109. *stemming*, facing; opposing and holding one's own against any force. *hearts of controversy*, bold or resolute hearts.

110. *arrive*, understand, "arrive at".

112. *as Aeneas etc.* The old story of the Trojan war recounted that, after the Greeks had succeeded in entering Troy by the stratagem of the wooden horse, they set fire to the city. Aeneas, the great Trojan leader, was compelled to make a hurried flight from the city, so he carried his aged father on his back. After many hardships and wanderings, he founded the Roman people. This history of the beginnings of the Roman people forms the theme of Virgil's *Aenied*.

120. *mark*, observe.

122. *did from their colour fly*, "lost their colour." The regimental flag is called "the colours" and so Caesar is described as being like a coward who deserts his flag.

123. *bend*, look; glance. *awe*, frighten. (vb.)

125-6 *and write his speeches*, the Roman writer, Suetonius, says that Caesar remarked that men should pay attention to his words whenever he spoke, "and should regard what he said as laws."

129. *temper*, nature.

130. *get the start*, get far in front of others, like a man leading in a foot race. *bear the palm*, carry off the prize.

133. *applauses*, according to the rules of abstract nouns, we could not now use this word in the plural form.

136. *Colossus*, the word, originally from the Greek and meaning any gigantic statue, came to be applied to the great statue of Apollo in the harbour of the town of Rhodes. It was said to be ninety feet high, and to stand with one leg on each side of the entrance to the harbour, so that ships coming in could sail between the two great legs. Ships, of course, were not so very big in those early times.

139-40 *Men ot some time...., underlings*, in Shakespeare's days, there was a general belief in astrology. The stars were thought to have a strong effect on the fortunes of men, and it was customary to have horoscopes drawn up at birth, as is still done by many people in India. All throughout the plays we see references to the powerful influences of the stars, though the present passage is often quoted to prove that Shakespeare himself was no great believer. He held that a man's destiny is influenced by his own character, and not by any stars which happen to be in the heavens at the time of his birth.

146. *conjure with them*, in those days of belief in the supernatural, it

was thought that certain combinations of words had magical power and could be used to conjure or summon up spirits.

149　*meat*, food.

150.　*Age*, the men of the time: this generation.

152.　*the great flood*, the original story of the flood sent by God on the world was known to all the old world, sometimes the two survivors being Deucalion and Pyrrha sometimes Noah and his wife in the Bible story.

156.　*Rome..... room*, again the attempt to make a pun, so common in Shakespeare's days, by using the similarity of sounds in the two words. It is in moments of emotion that Shakespeare's characters pun like this.

159.　*brook'd*, tolerated; endured. *a Brutus*, the reference is to Junius Brutus, who headed the popular movement which expelled the last of the Roman kings, Tarquin, in the year B.C. 510. It was to reinstate Tarquin that the army came which was defied by Horatius on the bridge.

160　*the eternal devil*, the devil who is always to be feared, who works without ending. *to keep his state*, to set up his court.

162.　*nothing jealous*, not at all doubtful.

163.　*work*, persuade. *aim*, idea; understanding

166.　*so with love etc.*, If in a friendly manner I might, etc.

171.　*chew*, reflect; ponder. We have taken the word *ruminate* and used it in the sense of to ponder or think over some subject, whereas it originally meant the activity of a ruminant animal in chewing grass which was swallowed previously.

173.　*repute himself*, carry the name and the reputation of being.

176.　*have struck .....fire from Brutus*, the metaphor is that of striking sparks from flint by means of a piece of steel, which was the method of starting a fire before the modern invention of matches.

180.　*sour*, serious; grave.

181.　*proceeded*, happened.

184.　*a chidden train*, a group of followers, quiet because of having been rebuked or scolded.

186.　*ferret*, an animal very similar to the mongoose, and used in Britain by sportsmen to make rabbits bolt from their holes. The ferret is yellow in colour, with reddish or pink eyes.

188.　*Being cross'd in conference*, when he has been obstructed in the debate.

194.　*Yond*, that.

199. *my name* = I myself.

204. *As thou dost, Antony etc.*, Plutarch wrote of Antony: "In his house they did nothing but feast, dance and mask; and himself passed away the time in hearing of foolish plays."

208. *Such men... be,* in Old English, the third person, plural of the verb "to be" was *beon,* and it was commonly used side by side with "are" for long as it still is in poetic diction.

209. *whiles,* when.

217. *sad,* grave; serious.

221. *put it by,* rejected it.

229. *marry,* a simple oath, used commonly in Shakespeare's times, being a contraction for "By Mary."

236. *one of these coronets,* we learn from Plutarch that it was a garland of laurel leaves, encircled by a band of white cloth, this being a symbol of royalty.

238. *did not mark,* it did not pay attention to it.

240. *fain,* gladly.

242. *loth,* reluctant, unwilling.

245. *rabblement,* mob.

246. *chopped,* chapped i.e., with the skin broken and roughened by labour.

247. *sweaty nightcaps,* Englishmen in Shakespeare's time wore night caps to protect the head from the cold when asleep. But the man who wore the same cap by day was looked upon as an ill-behaved fellow of no culture. It is hard to say what mental picture Shakespeare had of the head-dress of old-time Romans. Perhaps he did not think much about it, as he never thought local colour an important point in his plays. *stinking breath,* here we see what Shakespeare thought of the common people. They were dirty in clothing and deficient in personal hygiene. It is no wonder that he has been charged with being an aristocratic writer, and, indeed, all Shakespeare's great characters are of high rank and noble family.

256. *the falling sickness,* the name that was then applied to the disease of epilepsy. North says : "Caesar was often subject to headache, and sometime to the falling sickness, which took him the first time in Cordova, a city in Spain."

257-8. *No Caesar hath it not etc.* Cassius means that it is the people of Rome who have another kind of falling sickness, for they have all fallen completely before the power and the eloquence of Caesar.

260. *tag-rag people*, the mob; the rabble, people who are only "odds and ends".

263. *true man*, honest man.

265. *Marry*, See Note, line 229.

267. *plucked me ope his doublet*, "pulled open his coat." The doublet was the upper garment like a jacket, worn by the people of that age, with long stockings or "hose". *me* is superfluous, being an obsolete grammatical construction.

269. *of any occupation*, belonging to any of the labouring trades.

274. *Amiss*, wrong; out of place.

275. *to think it was his infirmity*, to attribute it to his illness.

275. *wenches*, women.

284. *an I tell you that*, *an* was an old fashioned form with the sense of "if."

287. *it was Greek to me*, it is still a colloquialism in English, when we hear anything that we do not understand at all, to say "This is Greek to me."

290. *put to silence*, reduced to impotence; dismissed to private life. Plutarch tells us that, for this offence, the tribunes in question were deprived of their offices.

293. *promised forth*, already engaged to go out.

295. *your mind hold*, if your intention to invite me still holds.

299. *blunt*, this adjective in our own times means "out-spoken" or very direct in speech, but Shakespeare used it rather in the sense of "dull" or "stupid."

300. *quick mettle*, of sharp intelligence.

303. *puts on his tardy form*, assumes this appearance of slowness.

311. *think of the world*, to the Romans, the world was Rome. This appeal to his sense of public duty is the strongest that could have been made to Brutus.

314. *from that it is disposed*, from its own natural inclination. *meet*, fitting; appropriate.

317. *bear me hard*, bears ill will against me.

318-19.   *If I were Brutus etc.* Cassius says, "If I were Brutus and he were Cassius, he would not influence me as I am now influencing him." It seems that he looks on Brutus as being rather easily led away from his loyalty to Caesar. But the explanation lies in Brutus' high sense to public duty, and not in any weakness of character.

320. *In several hands*. In different hand writings.

323. *obscurely*, indirectly; in veiled language. *Glanced at*, hinted at.

325-6. *And, after this, etc.*, notice that, after the long period of blank verse, the scene is now terminated with a rhymed couplet. This is a common device in Shakespeare : it helped to show the audience that the scene was ended, and so to some extent took the part of the fall of the curtain, which terminates the action on the modern stage.

SCENE III

1. *brought*, accompanied.

3. *sway*, rule : government;

5. *scolding*, boisterous : rough;

6. *rived*, torn: split;

12. *saucy*, insolent; disrespectful.

13. *incenses*, angers.

14. *more wonderful*, the sense is "very wonderful," and there is no comparison with anything, unless it be with the normal state of things.

18. *Not sensible of*, not feeling.

19. *put up my sword*, returned my sword to its sheath.

20. *Against*, opposite; beside. *a lion*, lions were never found in a state of freedom in Italy, but in the days of the Romans captive lions were frequently brought from North Africa. The Romans then being fond of seeing fights between wild animals in the arena.

22. *annoying*, harming; interfering with;

23. *Upon a heap*, in a crowd; in a huddled group;

26. *the bird of night*, the owl was a bird looked upon as of ill-omen and it was a particularly unnatural thing that an owl should appear by daylight.

29. *do so conjointly meet*, do all happen thus at the same time.

31. *portentous things*, things which portend the future, and are ominous.

32. *climate*, country.

34. *construe*, explain; interpret. *after their fashion*, according to every man's own taste.

35. *clean from the purpose*, quite different from the real meaning.

47. *Submitting*, exposing myself.

48. *unbraced*, with dress unfastened.

49. *the thunder-stone*, the scientific knowledge of those days was not highly advanced, and men were not sure what happened when a flash of

lightning was followed by a report of thunder. But the popular opinion was that a missile or stone was discharged against the earth, called sometimes a "thunder-bolt."

50. *cross blue lightning*, lightning with a zig-zag or "forked" course.

54. *part*, duty; natural place.

56. *heralds*, messengers.

61. *impatience*, anger; disturbed state. *Cast yourself in wonder*, throw yourself into a state of wonderment.

64. *from quality and kind*, this is Shakespearean condensation. We must supply a verb after "beasts" and read, 'behave differently from their natures and normal standards."

65. *old men...... calculate*, that is, "age behaves childishly and childhood shows the wisdom of age." In Macbeth, too, we as shown that a disturbed condition in the political affairs of men is reflected in Nature, and birds and beasts, etc. all behave in a manner quite different from that which is natural to them. Similarly in *Midsummer Night's Dream*, the quarrel between Oberon and Titania upsets all natural things, so that snow comes in summer and roses bloom in winter.

66. *their ordinance*, their guiding principles or rules.

67. *pre-formed faculties*, their well-ordered natures and powers.

71. *Unto some, monstrous state*, "pointing to some unnatural state of things."

75. *in the Capitol*, there has been some difference of opinion among editors as to whether this phrase should go with "roars" or with "lion." We prefer the second, though either will give good sense.

81. *thews*, muscles. *woe the while* ! alas for our times !

84. *Our yoke and sufferance*, our servitude and our toleration of it. *womanish*, effeminate and weak.

85-8. *Indeed they say....in Italy*, at this time. Caesar was about to set out on a warlike expedition against the Parthian tribe, who had defeated the Romans in 55 B.C. Plutarch says that there was an old prophecy that only forces led by king could conquer the Parthians and that was the reason for the Senate wishing to make Caesar a king, but only outside the boundaries of Italy.

91. *Therein*, In this point, namely that man has the power of ending his own life. The Romans, like the modern Japenese, looked on self-killing as a brave and a noble act.

94. *Nor stony tower, etc.*, in Shakespeare's time, the usage *Nor.... nor* was used to give the meaning of *Neither ....nor*.

95. *Can be retentive*, can succeed in retaining or holding.

102. *to cancel his captivity*, a slave could be made a free man of his master drew up a formal document cancelling the rights which he had over him. Similarly the slave could cancel his own captivity by ending his life with his dagger.

106. *He were*, he would be.

109-110. *when it serves for the base matter, etc.*, i.e., Rome is not looked upon as having an end and worthy existence in itself, but Rome and Romans are being made entirely subservient to the glory and the ambition of Caesar.

114. *my answer must be made*, I shall be called upon for an explanation.

117. *fleering*, grinning; smiling maliciously.

118. *factious*, the sense here is "active" or "energetic," though normally there is a bad sense of "rebellious" attached to the word. *griefs*, injustices; grievances.

120. *who*, the man who.

123. *undergo*, undertake.

124. *Of honourable....dangerous consequences*, Shakespearean brevity. By making this compound adjective, he shows that the undertaking will be an honourable nature but that it is also be accompanied by danger.

125. *by this*, by this time; now.

126. *Pompey's porch*, the portico or outer porch leading into Pompey's theatre. A porch is a vestibule or entrance-hall.

128. *complexion of the element*, general apperance of the weather.

129. *in favour*, literally " in its face or outer appearance." This is, then, a repetition of "complexion."

132. *Cinna*, it is doubtful if Cinna took an active part in the conspiracy, though he was in sympathy with it. His sister Cornelia was Caesar's first wife, and Caesar had appointed him Praetor.

134. *Metellus Cimber*, actually Lucius Tillius Cimber, who had been made Governor of Bithynia by Caesar.

135. *incorporate*, at one with us; allied.

141. *the noble Brutus*, it is obvious that all the conspirators think it important to gain the support of Brutus, because of the high reputation he holds among the people or Rome.

144. *Where Brutus may find it,* the limiting adverb *but* should apply to *Brutus* and not to *find*, i.e. where only Brutus may find it.

146. *old Brutus*, the ancestor of the present Brutus, who had been prominent in the fight against the kings of Rome before they were driven out. *Cp. 1, 2, 159.*

148. *Decius Brutus*, the correct name of the conspirator was Decimus, but Shakespeare copied an error which had arisen because of a misprint in North's translation of Plutarch. This man had been appointed Governor of Cisalpine Gaul by Caesar. He was one of the leaders of the people in whom Caesar placed utmost confidence. *Trebonius*, another of Caesar's officers in the Gallic campaign, who received great benefits from the leader against whom he was now conspiring.

150. *hie*, go. (Old English, *higian*, to go).

152. *repair*, make your way; go. *Pompey's Theatre*, a great building built of stone, first opened to the people in 55 B.C. There was a great open portico or court in front of it, with lawns and trees in the centre.

156. *encounter*, meeting. *yields him ours*, will give himself to our cause.

159. *coumenance*, support. *like richest alchemy*, the chemists of the olden days tried to practise alchemy, by which they understood the art of changing common metals into gold. It is was always believed that repeated experiments would find a means of turning lead into gold. Similarly the magic of Brutus' presence will t urn the base appearance of their plot into something golden in the eyes of the people.

162. *conceited*, estimated.

ACT II

Scene I

3. *give guess*, make a guess.

5. *When...when ?*, i.e. when are you going to come ?

10. *It must be etc.*, Brutus is thinking loud. He has been pondering on the best way to prevent Caesar from accepting the kingship, which is the "It" in his mind.

11. *I know no personal cause*, again emphasises the fact that the part played in the conspiracy by Brutus was not in the least due to personal grudges, as in the case of some of the plotters, but dictated solely by patriotism. *the general*, the public good. *the adder*, the poisonous snake called the viper. In cold countries, it never comes into the open except on warm, sunny days.

15. *craves wary walking*, requires that we proceed warily. *Crown him*, Brutus shows a deep and doctrinaire horror at the very idea of a king being set up the Rome again. the old kings had been unpopular tyrants, and

he seems to take it for granted that to revive the kingship will bring back the old evils. In fact, Caesar was already so powerful as dictator that it would have made little difference, and the idea of a limited and benevolent monarchy never seems to have occurred to Brutus.

16. *sting*, a continuation of the metaphor of the adder.

19. *when it disjoins Remorse from power*, "remorse" is not quite the same in meaning as we now understand, but rather "compassion" or "feelings of humanity." Brutus thinks that to have the power of a king makes a man forget those gentler qualities. It is hard to see how a change of title could have been expected to change Caesar's nature to such an extent, especially as he was at the time of his death a man of fifty six years of age.

21. *a common proof*, a thing often proved in practice, *that lowliness............ ladder*, that humility is used as a stepping stone by young men who are ambitious.

24. *round*, rung or step of the ladder.

26. *degrees*, steps; stages.

28. *prevent*, i.e. let us prevent or stop him.

29. *Will bear no colour .....he is*, our motives will not be justified because of what he is at present.

30. *Fashion it thus*, let us word it as follows.

33. *his kind*, the class to which he belongs, i.e. serpents.

36. *a flint, in those days*, there were no matches to make a light easily, and the favourite method was a flint and steel, the steel striking a spark from the flint into tinder or some similar inflammable material.

44. *exhalation*, the word suggests "gases" which are giving off light. At the same time Shakespeare uses the word in *Henry IV, Part I, II, 4, 352*, as follows: ".......do you see these meteors? do you behold these exhalations?" so that he indicates solid bodies rather than gases.

49. *instigations*, messages to instigate or inspire him to act.

51. *piece it out*, complete the sense.

59. *wasted*, spent; gone. *fifteen days*, some change this to *fourteen*, on the ground that the historical event of the murder of Caesar took place on the 15th, so that fourteen and not fifteen days of March had gone. But the Romans usually included the current date in such calculations.

59. *whet*, urge me on. Literally "what" is to sharpen a knife and so make it ready for use.

64. *the first motion*, the first time it was formed or planned in the mind.

65. *phantasma*, an unreal vision.

66. *the Genius*, some take this to mean "the mind" or "the intellectual powers." Verity thinks that Shakespeare follows the Roman belief according to which every man has his own guardian spirit, called by the Romans his Genius, and that "the mortal instruments" allude to his own inward powers. But this ignores the fact that there were two spirits attending on a man, according to the ancients, one working for good and one for evil, so that they would presumably be on opposite sides. The ghost which later appears to Brutus announces himself as Brutus' evil spirit.

67. *The state of man*, the kingdom or governed unit which every man is in miniature.

69. *The nature of*, something in the nature of.

70. *Your brother*, he was actually the brother-in-low, since he had married Junia, the half-sister of Brutus.

72. *moe*, old-fashinoed form of "more."

73. *plucked*, pulled tight.

75. *discover*, find them out.

76. *by any mark of favour*, by any features of the faces. "favour" had quite a different sense in those days, which it has now lost.

77. *faction*, party of the conspiracy.

83. *path*, is here used as a verb, with the sense "to walk about." Shakespeare often makes one part of speech work as another part.

84. *Erebus*, in the classical writers, Erebus was a dark and terrible place between earth and Hades. "Hell" is near enough.

86. *upon your rest*, understand some verb, such as "To intrude upon your time of rest."

91. *But honours* you = who not; i.e. who does not honour you.

101. *here lies the east etc.* we have seen that, on the Elizabethan stage, there were no scenic or lighting effects. It is intended here to show the conspirators meeting in the dark hours of the morning before day-break. Since this cannot be shown to the eye, Shakespeare does it in the conversation of his characters, and the discussion of the exact point where the sun will first arise is to create in the mind the illusion of a dark cold morning.

104. *fret*, to mark with lines or bars.

107. *Which is..... the south*, a glance at the map of Italy and its relation to the equator will show that, in the middle of March, the sun will not first be seen so far to the east as it will three months later, but will be south-east.

108. *weighing the youthful season*, considering the early stage.

110. *high east*, due east.

114. *if not the face of men*, he means, "If these are not enough, the sad face of men, the suffering, etc."

116. *betimes*, early; while there is still time.

117. *every man hence*, here is Shakespeare's customary omission of the verb of motion. We must understand "get" or "go" hence.

119. *by lottery*, by mere chance; when the lot falls to him.

123. *What need we*, what need is there. *spur*, stimulus.

124. *To prick us*, the metaphor of horse being urged on by sharp spurs is continued.

125. *Than secret Romans*, we have here a good illustration of Shakespeare's brevity and concentration of meaning into a few words. We have to read from these three words the idea "Than that of Romans who have met secretly...... or who are pledged to secrecy."

126. *Palter*, trifle; behave unworthily.

129. *Swear priests*, the verb is a subjective plural, i.e. "Let priests swear, etc."

129. *cautelous*, deceitful. An old word of Latin origin, not now in modern usage.

130. *carrions*, usually refers to a body not only dead and worthless but actually in a state of decay. We do not use the plural now.

133. *even virtue*, complete or perfect virtue. *unsuppressive mettle*, indomitable courage.

135. *or our cause*, again the old fashioned usage of *or....or*, meaning *either......or*.

138. *several*, separate. *bastardy*, that is, if any man betrayed his trust, then he would have proved himself a bastard and not of true Roman parentage.

141. *Sound him*, test his feelings or views.

145. *a good opinion*, will earn a good opinion from the public.

146. *no whit*, in no way.

150. *Let us not break with him*, an unusual sense of "break," viz. "Let us not open out or reveal our intentions to him."

155. *well urg'd*, you have raised a good point.

156. *Mark Antony*, Cassius has made a shrewd estimate of the character of Antony. He knows Antony to be a real man of action and genius, and knows that it will be dangerous to leave him at large. But he is overruled by Brutus, and from this error of Brutus spring all the disasters which later fall on the conspirators.

158. *contriver*, schemer.

160. *annoy*, harm.

169. *could come by Caesar's spirit*, could manage to strike at Caesar's spirit.

170. *dismember*, literally, cut up into the various parts or members of the body.

173. *as a dish fit for the gods*, again the contrast between the killing of a victim as a sacrifice as opposed to a more brutal killing.

175-77. *Let our hearts, as subtle masters etc.*, In *Richard II*, Bolingbroke encourages Exton to kill king Richard, and afterwards rebukes him for the deed.

176. the servants of the heart are the physical powers of the body, which execute its resolves and turn them into action. *necessary but not envious*, an act of necessity and not impelled by personal grudges. *purgers*, men who have purged the hand of evil.

187. *take thought and die*, after thinking, realise that all he can do is to die for Caesar.

188. *and that were much ..... etc.* "and it would be a great thing for him to do." The following line explains that, as Antony is a man given to fast living, it is hardly to be expected that he will go so far as to die for Caesar's sake.

190. *no fear in him*, no reason to fear him.

Stage direction. Clock strikes, this is an anachronism, for the Romans had no clocks which struck the hour. They had certain dials, such as sundials and water-clocks, but none with a striking device.

193. *The clock hath stricken three*, Shakespeare deliberately marks the passage of time all through this scene, right up to the hour of Caesar's death. By so doing, he heightens the suspense and keeps the interest of the audience on the stretch.

196. *Quite from the main opinion*, quite different from the general views.

197. *ceremonies*, signs and portents. The old-time Romans used to consult the soothsayers and augurers when in need of guidance for the future. Many of the portents and omens were found by studying the entrails of sacrificed animals, which were slain ceremonially in the temple.

198. *apparent*, outstanding; very clear.

200. *augurers*, the priests who read the omens from the slaughtered animals.

203. *o'ersway him*, persuade him the other way.

204-5.   *That unicorns. etc.,* the unicorn was a fabulous animal, depicted as having one long sharp horn in the middle of its forehead. Old tales gave the best way to capture a unicorn: when it was made to pursue a man, he would dodge behind a tree, and the impetuous unicorn, running full at him, would find its horn stuck fast in the tree and then could easily be captured. *bears with glasses*, it is said that bears can be captured by putting up a looking glass. The animal will stare at its reflection in the glass, giving the hunter a chance to come near and shoot. *elephants with holes*, elephants are caught by digging deep holes in the ground, into which they fall. *toils*, traps.

210. *give his humour the true bent*, I can play upon his own natural tendency, i.e. a weakness for flattery.

213. *the eighth hour*, that would be about one hour after mid-day or noon.

214. *the uttermost*, the very latest time.

215. *Ligarius*, this Roman had taken the side of Pompey against Caesar and had been banished afterwards, then forgiven and allowed to return to Rome. *doth bear Caesar hard*, has hard or hostile feelings against Caesar.

218. *by him*, to him: to his residence. *reasons*, i.e. for loving me.

220. *fashion him*, influence him.

225. *put on*, i.e. wear our intentions openly, and so reveal them.

226. *bear it*, behave. The *it* is impersonal, an old fashioned construction. *formal constancy*, a formal and steady manner.

230. *honey-heavy dew*, sleep is often compared to dew, which falls on the earth to refresh it. *honey-heavy* = heavy with sweetness like honey.

231. *figures.... fantasies*, imagined things and visions.

235. *commit*, expose; entrust. *canaition*, physical health.

238. *yesternight*, literally "yesterday night." (German, *gestern*, yesterday). This has not survived along with the common word "yesterday."

240. *across*, folded on your breast.

245. *yet*, still.

246. *wafture*, wave.

248. *to strengthen that impatience*, to increase your irritation.

249. *enkindled*, inflamed to activity; actively burning.

250. *an effect of humour*, something arising out of a mood or whim.

253. *shape*, physical appearance.

255. *Dear my lord*, this inverted form of address for "My dear lord" is very common in Shakespeare.

261. *physical*, good for physical health.

262. *unbraced*, with your robe unfastened. *humours*, moistness; damp air.

265. *contagion of the night*, the Elizabethans had the old-fashioned prejudice against night air, holding that it was unhealthy and not to be breathed without risk to the health.

266. *rheumy*, causing the flow of rheum in the body; moist. *unpurged*, the night air is only purged of its harmful impurities when the sun arises.

268. *sick offence*, condition of sickness; harmful condition.

269. *virtue*, privilege. Repetition of "right".

273. *incorporate*, literally "formed us into one body."

274. *your half*, it is a common idea that man and wife being one in the unity of marriage, each is one half of the whole. It is a common jest to call a man's wife his "better half".

280. *Within the bond*, in the confidential secrecy of the marriage union.

283. *in sort or limitation*, only after a style and within limits.

285. *in the suburbs*, on the fringe or the outskirts, just as a man living just outside the town in not actually in it. We see no justification for Verity's idea that Shakespeare is thinking of the rather poor repute of the suburbs of London at that time.

293. *to wife*, a common idiom for "as his wife."

295. *Cato's daughter*, Cato, the father of Portia, was one of the most honourable and distinguished of public figures in Rome.

305. *shall partake*, shall share in.

307. *construe*, explain.

308. *all the characters*, we speak of the letters of the alphabet as characters in such a phrase as "Hindi characters." Brutus means: "all the things that have written lines of sadness on my face."

313. *Vouchsafe*, accept; receive.

315. *to wear a kerchief*, this was a custom which was purely Elizabethan, for a sick man to wear on his head a scarf or handkerchief, and shows how Shakespeare used the customs of his own country in Roman play rather than striving to give it a Roman "colour."

322. *deriv'd from honourable loins*, offspring of a noble father.

323. *an exorcist*, a worker in magic, who claimed to have the power to control or summon up the spirits by means of charms or conjuration, *my mortified spirit*, my spirit that is dead within me.

328. *that we must make sick?* he suspects that the plan aims at some injury to Caesar. *whole* = healthy or well.

332. *New fir'd,* alight. with fresh hope.

Scene II

1. *Nor....nor,* neither...nor.

5. *priests,* the augurers, who were supposed to sacrifice an animal, and then study the organs and intestines to see whether the omens were favorable, *present,* immediate.

11. *Ne'er looked....back,* like cowardly enemies who only dared attack him in the back.

13. *I never stood on ceremonies,* I never paid attention to omens.

16. *Recounts,* (who) relates. *the watch,* the London streets were then patrolled by night-watchemen, and the idea is applied to Rome.

17. *whelped,* given birth to young.

21. *drizzled,* dripped down.

22. *hurtled,* clashed, like a material thing.

24. *And ghosts did shriek etc.,* the portents must have affected the imagination of Shakespeare. In *Hamlet, I, I, 113-18,* when speaking of supernatural happenings, he said :

> "In the most high and palmy state of Rome,
> And little ere the mightiest Julius fell,
> The graves stood tenantless and the sheeted dead
> Did squeak and gibber in the Roman streets."

In classical literature, the spirits of the dead were described as making a thin, squeaking sound like bats.

25. *beyond all use,* quite outside all our experience.

29. *Are to the world,* may apply to the whole world.

30-1. *When beggars die, etc.,* Plutarch mentions a great comet which "was seen very bright after Caesar's death." A comet was traditionally held to be an omen signifying change and disaster. Milton spoke of the appearance of a comet which "with fear of change, perplexes nations."

32-5. *Cowards die many times etc.,* Plutarch records that, not long before his death Caesar said that, "it was better to die once than always to be afraid of death."

41. *in shame of cowardice,* because the heart was supposed to be the physical seat of courage, so to be without a heart was a sign of cowardice. According to Plutarch, it was Caesar himself who made the sacrifice and found that there was no heart in the animal.

46. *litter'd*, born (of an animal).

54. *prevail*, have my own way.

55. *for thy humour*, to please your whim.

60. *in very happy time*, at a very convenient time.

67. *afeard*, an old form of "afraid".

69. *cause*, reason.

75. *stays,* keeps; detains. *tonight*, instead of the modern sense of "the night which is to come," the Elizabethans used this phrase as we do "last night."

80. *does she apply for*, she interprets as.

81. *imminent*, about to happen.

83. *amiss*, wrongly.

89. *Tinctures...... congnizance*, he suggests that men will colour or dye (tincture) their handkerchiefs, to leave a stain upon them, and keep them as souvenirs or relics, to honour him (by cognizance). At the execution of prominent men, notably Charles I and the Duke of Montrose, those present strove to get a bloodstain on a scarf of handkerchief to keep as a relic. A congnisance is a badge, something by which one is identified or recognised.

96. *a mock apt to be rendered*, a mocking remark which some one is likely to make.

104. *And reason....liable*, and my reason, though it warns me not to speak so plainly to Caesar, must be overruled by my love.

106. *Calpurnia*, she does not speak, having realised that she has lost the struggle. Her beautiful figure is seen no more in the play, in which she has so brief a part.

116. *that revels long etc.*, Cp. II. O, 188-89.

119. *To be thus waited for*, to keep the Senate waiting for me like this.

124. *so near will I be, etc.*, dramatic irony, in which a deep meaning is apparent to the audience which is not known to the other characters on the stage.

128. *That every like*, Brutus sadly reflects that to be like a thing is not to be that thing. They will go of like friends, but how far from friends they really are! *yearns*, mourns: grieves.

SCENE III

5. *beest*, old English form of the verb.

6. *security gives way to conspiracy*, your feeling of careless security leaves the way open to conspirators.

7. *lover*, friend.

11. *out of the teeth of*, out of the power of jealousy. *contrive*, plot.

SCENE IV

2. *get thee gone*, "thee" would be the customary address to an inferior, while to his lady he replies "you" (*tum* and *ap* in Hindustani).

6. *Constancy*, personified as the virtue of steadiness and cool courage, which a woman is traditionally not supposed to possess to the same extent as a man.

7. *Set a huge mountain etc.*, a woman is emotional, and the feelings of her heart are freely expressed by her tongue. In the present need to be secret and silent, Portia wishes for something to come between her heart and tongue to make her remain silent.

9. *to keep counsel*, "to keep anything secret." Women have never ceased to challenge this view of Shakespeare's.

14. *went sickly forth*, went away rather unwell.

15. *What suitors press to him*, in the beginning of the next Act, we see the various petitoners pressing around Caesar.

18. *rumour*, here means a vague and confused noise, suggesting the bustling or movement of numbers of people. *fray*, fight; quarrel.

20. *Sooth*, In truth.

29. *to be so good to Caesar*, to consult his own intersts to such an extent.

30. *to befriend himself*, to look after himself.

34. *at the heels*, after his heels, i.e. just behind him.

35. *praetors*, were officials connected with civil administration.

37. *void*, roomy; spacious.

42. *Brutus hath a suit*, Portia fears that she has let something escape of her secret to the boy Lucius, so she invests this suit of Brutus' as an explanation for her anxiety. Professor Dowden says : "Portia does not appear again; Shakespeare purposely lets us see her but seldom; otherwise an interest alien to the main action of the play might have grown too prominent.

ACT.III

SCENE I

The Senate usually met in the Forum.

3. *schedule*, written paper.

4. *over-read*, to read over.

7. *that touches Caesar never*, that affects you more intimately.

8. *touches us*, affects me.

11. *sirrah*, the usual peremptory address to an inferior.

14. *enterprise*, it seems as if Popilius had some suspicions that a plan was on foot. Yet he speaks so carelessly that he may be referring to some minor matter, and not to the main point. It may be only by accident that he gives the conspirators a few anxious minutes, but the point is not cleared up by Shakespeare.

18. *makes to*, goes towards.

19. *sudden*, quick; speedy.

21. *Cassius or Caesar......back*, either one or the other shall not leave this place.

24. *doth not change*, there is no change in his face to show that he is listening to such a serious thing as the revelation of a plot to kill him.

28. *presently*, at once. *prefer*, submit; offer.

29. *address'd*, ready. *second*, support.

30. *rears*, raises to strike.

32. *Caesar and his Senate*, rules of European courtesy should have impelled him to say, "Caesar's Senate, and himself." That he mentions himself first shows that he does not treat the Senate with much respect.

33. *puissant*, all-powerful.

35. *prevent*, interrupt.

36. *couchings*, literally "laying down." *courtesies*, this word literally meant "the act of bending," which sense it still has in the form "curtsey" so the sense is the same as in *couching*.

37. *fire the blood*, inflame the pride.

38. *And turn pre-ordinace, &c.*, turn what is laid down and decreed from the beginning into laws which can be set aside as easily as the laws of little children.

39. *Be not fond*, do not be so foolish. *rebel blood*, blood which can be affected so as to interfere with the rule of his reason. *thaw'd from the true quality*, turned aside from true lines of conduct by the flattery which affects fools.

43. *spaniel fawning*, the spaniel is a dog which is very affectionate and servile in behaviour, always licking and bending or couching before its master.

47-48. *Caesar doth not wrong &c.*, Ben Jonson wanted to make the line: "Caesar did never wrong but with just cause."
but there is no need to interfere with the original text of the early editions, especially as it gives good meaning.

51. *repealing,* strictly one repeals an order or law; one *recalls* a man who has been banished, and the latter is the meaning.

54. *freedom of repeal,* the words are still in a strange usage. "freedom of appeal" would have given better sense, but the general sense of 'freedom to return' may be accepted.

57. *enfranchisement,* the franchise is the right of the citizen to the vote and all else that belongs to citizenship. By his banishment, Cimber is without these things, and "enfranchisement' signifies the restoration of civic rights.

59. *If I could pray,* If I were capable of making prayers to move others, then I might also be capable of being moved by appeals.

60. *constant,* as regular and fixed.

61-2. *Of whose true-fix'd,* of whose truly regular and unchanging course there is no equal in the heavens.

65. *but one in all,* only one among them all i.e. the north star.

67. *apprehensive,* having apprehension or understanding.

69. *holds on his rank,* keeps on his course.

70. *unshak'd of motion,* quite unaffected in his movements.

72. *constant,* firm in my opinion.

74. *Olympus,* Mount Olympus was the great Mountain of Greece on which all the gods were supposed to have their abode. Caesar, not very modestly, says that he is as immovable and impossible to shake as Mount Olympus.

75. *bootless,* in vain, Caesar means, "If Brutus pleads in vain, what chance have your words ?

77. *Et tu, Brute*! the literal meaning of the Latin words is "You too, Brutus!" The words are not found in Plutarch, who does not say that Caesar made any remark on being stabbed by Brutus, and we cannot say what impelled Shakespeare to this original and striking phrase.

80. *pulpits,* platforms, from which announcements were made to the public. We have adapted the word to mean the box from which a priest delivers his sermon in church. The Latin word was *tribunalia* and there were several such platforms round about the Forum, from which orators were accustomed to address the people of Rome. The chief of these was called the Rostra, because it was adorned with 'rostra", the beaks or sharp bows of conquered enemy ships. It was on the Rostra that Caesar actually refused the crown.

86. *confounded,* confused and bewildered, *mutiny,* uprising.

91. *No......nor*, this is a double negative. In Shakespeare, the two negatives do not cancel out, but rather give emphasis.

91. *Publius*, it is not clear who this young man, Publius, was.

94. *abide*, answer for; be held responsible for.

96. *amazed*, in a state of confusion.

98. *doomsday*, the last day, on which, according to the Bible, the world will end.

100. *stand upon*, are concerned with.

104. *abridg'd*, shortened; lessened,

107. *swords*, the picture of the killing is that Caesar was killed with daggers, such as would be easily concealed beneath robes, but Shakespeare makes no distinction.

114. *in sport*, i.e. on the stage, to entertain audiences in the theatre.

115. *on Pompey's basis lies along*, lies along the base of Pompey's statue.

117. *knot*, group,

119. *shall we forth*? another example of how Shakespeare leaves the verb of motion "go" to be understood.

120. *grace his heels*, form a dignified following behind him.

121. *most boldest*, this double superlative is a liberty which Shakespeare frequently takes for the sake of emphasis. It was possible at a time when rules of grammar were not so firmly defined as they are now.

130. *vouchsafe*, grant; permit.

131. *May safely come to him*, may come to him without being harmed.

131. *resolv'd*, informed.

136. *thorough*, the same as "through." *this untrod state*, "this unknown path along which they are travelling." The sense is that Brutus and his friends have broken away from the straight road and have taken to an untrodden path which may be full of hazards.

140. *so please him come*, if he will please to come.

141. *shall be satisfied*, shall be given reasons which will satisfy him.

143. *to friend*, as a friend.

145-6.   *my misgiving..... the purpose*, and my suspicions are often most accurately realised. *still*, always.

152. *must be let blood*, "must have his blood shed." In the old days when medicine was in its infancy, the only remedy that doctors could think of for a variety of ailments was "blood letting", by which they meant to draw away a quantity of blood from a patient. *rank*, a patient said to be

"rank" when the old-fashioned doctors decided that he was too full of blood, and required to have some taken away.

157. *if you bear me hard,* if you have unfriendly feelings towards me.

158. *purpled,* reddened. *reek,* the same as "smoke."

159. *Live a thousand years,* again Shakespeare's use of abbreviation. Read, "If I should live, etc."

160. *apt,* ready.

161. *mean,* this is a singular form, but nowadays "means" in this sense has no singular. Shakespeare often uses this singular.

162. *by Caesar,* beside Caesar.

168. *business,* work; deed.

170. *the general wrong,* the wrong to the general public.

171. *so pity pity,* so pity for the people of Rome has driven out all pity for Caesar.

173. *leaden points,* harmless points, because lead is a soft metal and cannot be given a sharp point.

174. *Our arms, in strength of malice, etc.,* a passage which is very difficult to follow, and no satisfactory improvement has been given. The nearest is "Our arms intense in hatred of Caesar's tyranny, and our hearts, full of brotherly love to all Romans, do receive you."

178. *dignities,* appointments to posts in the new administration.

180. *beside themselves which fear,* almost out of their minds with fear.

183. *proceeded,* acted.

191. *on such slippery ground,* in such an uncertain condition.

192. *conceit me,* think of me.

196. *dearer,* more deeply.

202. *to close,* to come to agreement.

204. *bay'd,* a term from deer hunting, which had a language of its own and was well known to Elizabethans. A deer which ceased to flee, but turned to face its pursuers, was said to be brought to bay or to stand at bay. *hart,* a deer.

206. *Signed in thy spoil,* bearing signs of the way in which they have destroyed you. *lethe,* here "life blood." Literally the meaning is "death". The word is said to have been a technical term for the blood of the deer shed at the final killing, and it has no connection with the similar word *Lethe* which was the name of one of the rivers in the classical underworld.

208. *the heart of thee,* observe that, even in this moment of emotion,

Shakespeare introduces a pun on the similar sounds of the words "hart" and "heart". The world was the forest in which Caesar was the hart: similarly Caesar was so great and important that he might be called the heart of the world.

213. *it is cold modesty*, it is a calm and moderate statement from a friend, not at all a glowing tribute.

215. *compact*, bargain.

216. *prick'd*, marked down. The picture is that of someone with a list of names, pricking or 'ticking off' the names of those who were friendly.

217. *shall we on*, again the Shakespearean omission of "go".

218. *Therefore,* with that object in view (which you have stated).

221. *Upon this hope*, though I hope.

223. *Or else were this, &c.,* we must complete Brutus' thought : "we do have such reasons to give you, or else this would be, etc."

224. *regard*, reason; significance.

227. *And an moreover suitor that, &c.,* and moreover I make an application that etc."

229. *Produce his body.... market place*, in Rome, when a great man died, a speech in his praise was usually spoken at the funeral. The funeral came in procession to the Forum and stopped at the public platform or pulpit, on which a relative of the dead man would ascend to deliver the speech. If the dead man was a great public figure, the speech used to be delivered by a magistrate or other official, and so Antony had quite a claim to speak at Caesar's funeral. His request would be a natural one.

230. *in the order of*, in the arrangements of the funeral.

231. *You shall, &c.,* Brutus, with his generous and unsuspicious nature, agrees without reflecting. The more shrewd Cassius is far-sighted and sees what may happen. This is Brutus, second great mistake, leading to the disasters of the play.

238. *protest*, state; explain.

242. *advantage*, help, Shakespeare often makes a noun work as a verb. There is no verb "to advantage", but he cares little for that.

243. *fall*, befall; happen.

248. *hand*, share; part.

251. *after my speech is ended*, that is the very thing Antony would wish for, for he knows that the man who speaks last will have the best chance of influencing the people. Again Brutus shows the want of worldly wisdom, and that his philosophical learning cannot help him in practical affairs.

257. *in the tide of times*, "the times which come and go, just as the tide of the sea rises and falls." But the expression and its exact meaning are not clear.

261. *utterance*, speech; expression.

262. *limbs*, physical bodies, and not only arms and legs as the word usually signifies.

263. *Domestic fury... Italy*, this prophecy was realised, for after the death of Caesar, civil war and unrest prevailed all over Italy and the Empire.

269. *chok'd with custom of fell deeds*, feelings of pity shall cease to exist because foul deeds shall be such familiar things.

271. *Ate*, for the ancient world, Ate was the goddess of all kinds of mischief, and of revenge. She was a dweller in the underworld.

272. *in these confines*, within the boundaries of our land.

273. *cry Havoc*, proclaim destruction. They cry "Havoc" meant that no lives were to be spared in battle. *The dogs of war*, the metaphor is that War is a destructive hunter with fierce dogs helping him in the work.

275. *carrion men*, men who are dead and decaying.

281. *big*, full of emotion.

282. *catching*, infectious.

287. *Post back with speed*, the arrangements for post travel were that relays of fresh horses were ready at intervals along the route, and it was known in England in Shekespeare's times.

292. *Thou shalt not back*, again the typical Shakespearean omission of the verb of motion, leaving the reader to understand "go".

291. *corse*, a poetical form of "corpse."

295. *according to the which*, according to the result of my effort. *discourse*, speak.

297. *Young Octavius*, this was the nephew of Caesar, who afterwards become Emperor.

SCENE II

Scene. The Forum. The Forum of the Romans was four-sided area of about four acres in extent, in the centre of Rome, with great Public buildings on every side. Political gatherings usually assembled in the Forum and the business of the law courts was transacted there. It was the very heart of Rome and all official and public life centred round the Forum.

4. *part the numbers*, divide the crowd up into two.

7. *public reasons shall be rendered*, a public explanation shall be given.

9. *and compare their reasons*, if the second citizen hears only Cassius and not Brutus, then he cannot compare the reasons of the two speakers. The sense is that the two citizens are to meet afterwards and compare the reasons: but Shakespeare does not take pains to make his lines show this, by saying "and *we* shall compare their reason when *we* hear them given separately."

14. *Romans, countrymen, and lovers,* it is highly necessary for the reader who approaches *Julius Caesar* as educational study to look carefully into the contrast between this speech of Brutus and the oration of Antony which follows it. Shakespeare intended a very strong contrast between the two styles of speaking. In all the plays, Shakespeare uses poetry for beautiful and telling speeches, and prose for the commonplace conversation of the characters, when poetic beauty and effect are not wanted. The speech of Brutus is quite logical prose, almost like a lecturer in his classroom: while Antony knows every device of the skilful orator, every appeal to the emotions and the sensitive imagination of the common people. The result is a foregone conclusion. *for my cause,* Brutus' cause is abstract, that of patriotism: not so appealing as the concrete and personal appeal of Antony.

17. *censure*, this word meant originally to "judge" or "criticise" and that is the sense here. In our days, the meaning has changed till the word has come to mean "to reprimand." Notice that Brutus appeals purely to the thinking powers and not to the emotions. He places the same argument before the mob that he might have placed before the senators.

29. *There is tears, &c.,* Shakespeare takes all that follows as if it were one singular complement. He did not know the rule that a number of things linked together by "and" are considered plural.

31. *that would be,* that would like to be. *rude,* uncivilised.

41. *question*, fact; matter. *enrolled,* recorded.

41. *extenuated*, lessened.

43. *enforced*, stressed; magnified.

49. *With this*, with these words.

54. *Bring him with triumph*, the mob at once applauds. They agree with all that is said, but change quickly when the next speaker puts a contrary view before them. Brutus did not understand mob mentality, but Antony did.

55. *a statue........ancestors*, we have already seen that there was a statue of "old Brutus" somewhere about the house of Brutus, see *1, 3, 146.*

56. *Let him be Caesar*, it should be kept in mind that the name "Caesar" originally a proper name, gradually passed into a common name meaning "emperor." From it are derived the modern titles of kaiser and czar. But the words of the crowd show that they have completely failed to underst and the principle for which Brutus stands. He has destroyed Caesar for wanting to be a king, and at once they propose that Brutus should be made king. In their eyes, he is just an ambitious politician who has killed his rival in a personal bid for power, — which is exactly what Brutus was not. But the mob cannot understand principles or theories; they are only capable of understanding personalities. That is why they turn so quickly to Antony, who did understand how to sway them.

60. *let me depart alone*, this is the third great error of judgment. It has been a mistake to allow the clever Antony to address the fickle mob at all; but, having done so, it would still be all right if Brutus would but take the practical step of waiting to hear what Antony had to say. Then the clever eloquence would be kept in check. But Brutus is too much of a gentleman; incapable of double-dealing himself, he never suspects it in others.

63. *tending to*, dealing with.

68. *the public chair*, the platform for public speeches.

70. *beholding*, obliged. We use the past participle and say that we are "beholden" to a person for some favour. *For Brutus' sake*, i.e. in the name of Brutus, who has allowed him to speak.

78. *Friends, Roman &c.*, this is one of the most notable speeches in Shakespeare. He gets no help at all from Plutarch, who gives at different times varying accounts of what happened. The following in the outline : "Antony, making his funeral oration in praise of the dead, according to the ancient custom of Rome, and perceiving that his words moved the common people to compassion. He framed his eloquence to make their hearts yearn the more, and taking Caesar's gown all bloody in his hands, he laid it open to the sight of them all, showing what a number of cuts and holes it had upon it. Therewithal the people fell presently into such a rage and mutiny, that there was no more order kept among the common people. For some of them cried out, 'Kill the murderers! : others plucked up forms, tables and stalls about the market place, as they had done before at the funeral of Clodius, and having laid them all on a heap together, they set them on fire, and put thereon the body of Caesar and burned it in the midst of the most holy places. And furthermore, when the fire was thoroughly kindled, some here, some there, took burning firebrands and ran with them to the murderers' houses that had killed him, to set them on fire. Howbeit, the conspirators, foreseeing the danger before, had wisely provided for themselves and fled."

This was the bare outline from which Shakespeare made one of his most wonderful scenes. The gradual way in which Antony advances, feeling his way and growing more bold as he senses his success, is a marvel of naturalness. He starts with a hostile audience, is humble and apologetic, and then does exactly as he likes with them. Disclaiming any intention of praising Caesar, he nevertheless praises him indirectly and imperceptibly, without anyone realising what his aim is, till he has the fire well ablaze. There is no passage in literature or drama showing so well the effect of studied eloquence on a receptive audience. He begins quietly and with broken accents, the plain blunt man who is not used to such speech-making, and there is perfect irony, for every modest statement which he makes about his own intentions is untrue, and we know it to be so.

79. *not to praise him*, but the whole object of the funeral oration was to praise the dead! Antony sees that the praise, at the beginning, will be a mistake.

85. *answer'd it*, paid the penalty for it.

87-8. *For Brutus......honourable men*, in the beginning, this repeated compliment is made seriously and taken as serious, because the crowd has not commenced to be moved. Afterwards, there is a sneer and a shaft of sarcasm in every repetition of the phrase 'honourable men."

94. *ransoms..... general coffers*, wealthy prisoners of war were set free on payment of a high ransom, the money paid in this manner going into the public treasurey.

97. *sterner stuff*, i.e. men who are ambitious will be of harder natures than to weep.

113. *Methinks there is much reason, &c.* The opinion of the crowd is already changing round, and Antony's estimate of their fickleness is justified.

120. *abide it*, answer for it.

125. *And none so poor...... reverence*, "and now no man is so lowly that he will pay honour to Caesar." Yesterday he was highest of all; today, lowest.

133. *parchment*, the useful substance, paper, was not then known, but documents were written on paper substitutes, parchments often being of prepared lamb-skins.

134. *closet*, private room.

135. the document in which an Englishman records how his property is to be disposed of is still called his "last will and testament." *commons*, the common people, the *plebs vulgus* of Rome.

136. *I do not mean to read*, he knows enough of psychology to know

that by pretending to withhold knowledge of the will from the crowd, he will increase their interest and sharpen their curiosity in the matter.

138. *napkins*, handkerchiefs.

140-41. *mention it.....their issue*, see note on *II, II, 88, 89*. Those lucky enough to possess a hair of Caesar would leave it as a priceless thing to their heirs.

146. *meet*, appropriate.

149. *inflame*, set you on fire with anger.

150. *'Tis good.....his heirs*, pretending to conceal the nature of the will, he lets enough escape him to sharpen their curiosity and make them anxious for more.

155. *o'ershot myself*, gone further than I intended.

158. *the traitors*, the crowd speak the word traitors; after this, Antony is free to throw off pretence and go ahead more boldly with his accusations against the conspirators.

169. *hearse*, the hearse now-a-days is the carriage, horse-drawn or motor, in which the coffin is conveyed to the grave. But here it means the stretcher on which the body has been place.

171. *press not so upon me*, on the early stage, Antony used to show, though not openly, that his nose was offended by too close approach of the unwashed mob.

173-201. *If you have tears &c.*, it will be noted that Antony does not try to disprove the main charge against Caesar, that he was ambitious. He simply reminds the people of Caesar's services, and appeals to the natural feeling of sympathy which one feels on seeing a dead body. In fact, he make no effort to answer Brutus' charges of ambition. He knows that common men are not politicians; and do not care for general principles.

177. *the Nervii*, the battle of the Sambre was fought in the year 57 B.C. one of the greatest victories won by Caesar. Plutarch tells us that "the love of the people unto him made his victory much more famous." The Nervii were the most formidable tribal in Gaul, the north-west of modern France.

179. *Look, in this place &c.* As Antony was not present at the actual killing, it is by pure guess-work that he shows the separate cuts made by the different conspirators.

183. *As rushing*, as if it were rushing. *resolv'd*, answered; told.

185. *angel*, dearest friend.

187. *most unkindest*, again we have an example of the way in which Shakespeare doubles the superlative to secure emphasis.

189. *Ingratitude, more strong... arms*, the ungrateful conduct of Brutus

was more strong in making him fall than the weapons of the other conspirators.

191. *In his mantle......face*, Plutarch tells us: "when Caesar saw Brutus with his sword drawn in his hand, then he pulled his gown over his head and made no more resistance."

193. *which all the while ran blood*, in his recent edition, Professor Dover Wilson takes this to mean that there was a supernatural happening here, Pompey's statue itself shedding blood, because of sympathy for his old enemy. It is unlikely, and we think the sense is only that Caesar's own blood was flowing freely from so many wounds.

196. *bloody treason flourished, &c.*, Antony knows he has won, and he has now thrown aside all pretext of still calling the conspirators "honourable men."

198. *the dint*, the effect; influence. *gracious drops*, kindly tears.

200. *look you here*, here he draws the sheet from the corpse.

201. *marr'd*, spoiled.

217. *griefs*, grievances.

219. *with reasons*, he ingnores the fact that Brutus has already spoken and given his "reasons."

221. *I am no orator*, this is almost a sneer at the simple folks whom he has influenced so deeply, and it would appear that he deeply enjoys the part he is acting, in pretending to be what he is not.

226. *nor the power of speech.... blood*, but that is just what he has shown that he does possess! Under the circumstances, he seems to overact the part, or rather to delight in carrying it on so far as to make his hearers appear even more foolish and credulous than need be.

232. *ruffle*, stir. Understand "who would ruffle."

240. *wherein*, In what....?

247. *drachmas*, the drachma was a Greek silver coin, and the sum of seventy-five drachmas would be equal to about three pounds in sterling. It is a commentary on Antony's character that, as soon as his immediate purpose is achieved, he thinks of refusing to pay that legacy in question. (*Vide IV, 1, 8-9*).

several, separate; individual.

254. *On this side Tiber*, that would be in Latin *Cistiber*. But in Plutarch the expression was Trans Tiber, on the other side of the Tiber. But Amytot mistranslated it in the first place, so North and consequently Shakespeare, followed him in the error.

253. *arbours*, the Latin word, *arbor*, means "a tree." Here the sense is probably groves or plantations of trees.

255. *pleasures,* pleasure grounds or gardens. *abroad,* the meaning of this word is simply "out of doors."

256. *recreate,* refresh; amuse.

259. *the holy place,* would suggest the temple of Jupiter, but Plutarch says that the burning was done on the spot.

260. *brands,* burning pieces of wood.

270. *will I straight,* again the verb is left to be understood.

271. *upon a wish,* following upon my wish for his arrival.

274. *are rid,* have ridden. The past participles of verbs were not so clearly fixed then.

275. *Belike,* Probably. *some notice,* information.

Scene III

2. *things unluckily charge my fantasy,* an obscure line. Probably, "Events in an ill-omened manner confirm my dream" or "things of ill-fortune confirm my imaginings."

3. *will,* desire.

13. *you were best,* it will be better for you to do so.

20. *bear me a bang,* "get a blow from me." *me* is an old usage called the ethical dative.

33. *Tear him for his bad verses,* Shakespeare has added this touch of humour, instead of the murder described by Plutarch.

39. *pluck but his name..... going,* it is a stroke of imagination to think that a man's name can be torn out of his heart a jest which defies explanation.

turn him going, send him about his business.

ACT IV

Scene I

1. *prick'd,* marked off with a pencil.

2. *Your brother,* this refers to Paulus Lepidus, the brother in question, who had supported the party of Brutus. History tells us that he managed to escape.

4-5. *Publius,* We do not know who Publius may have been. The name comes into this play several times as if Shakespeare used it when in need of a name for any unimportant character. Perhaps Shakespeare had forgotten the name of Lucius Caesar, a relative of Antony, more probably an uncle than a "sister's son" said by Plutarch to have been condemned along with Cicero and Paulus.

6. *spot*, a stroke of the pen. *damn*, condemn.

9. *how to cut.... legacies*, the legacies had been useful to quote in his speech; now they are to be "cut." This well reveals the very unscrupulous character of Antony.

12. *slight*, weak unmarketable, worthless.

14. *threefold*, the Romans thought of the world as Europe, Africa and Asia, so that it was naturally suitable for division into three.

17-18. *And took his voice &c.* Octavius is startled to hear Antony's opinion of Lepidus, after having allowed him to vote on such an important matter as the names of those who were to be executed in the list of the outlawed. The Proscription was an official list of the people who, for their support of Brutus, were to lose their lives or property.

19. *these honours*, i.e. of being one of the responsible three.

20. *divers slanderous loads,* various loads of slander abuse, which will fall to the lot of anyone who has such a difficult responsibility to carry as that of the proscription and executions.

21. *the ass,* Shakespeare remembers an old proverb, "An ass is but an ass, though laden with gss,."

26. *like to the empty ass,* like any other unloaded ass.

27. *commons,* public ground where the grazing was free to all.

30. *appoint him....provender,* arrange for him a supply of food.

32. *to wind,* to turn. It was a point of horse-management to make a charger turn swiftly when in full gallop.

33. *corporal,* bodily.

34. *in some taste,* to some degree.

36. *barren-spirited,* a man of poor intelligence.

37. *On abjects, orts...fashion,* abjects are rejected morsels things flung away by other people: *orts* has the same sense of fragments left over by other people. The sense is that Lepidus is out of date. He takes up things too late, when other people have discarded them; is content to accept the leavings of others and to imitate them.

38. *stal'd,* used till they are stale and have lost their freshness.

39. *begin his fashion,* are taken up by him as if fashionable.

40. *property,* "a mere article of furniture on the stage of life." The word property is used technically to describe the movable scenery on the stage. The sense "a mere tool" is also suitable.

42. *make head,* this was technical term from military parlance for "to raise a force."

43. *alliance*, the league made up of all their supporters.

44. *Our means stretch'd*, the scansion of the line suggests that some phrase has been lost, e.g. "stretched to the full."

45. *presently*, immediately, *go sit in council*, we must understand, after *council*, some such verb as "and discuss."

47. *answered*, encountered; dealt with.

49-50. *at the stake ...bay'd about*, bear-baiting was a cruel sport in Shakespeare's times. A bear was fastened to a stake, and then attacked by dogs. Often several dogs were killed in the course of one bear-baiting. The bear had no chance of retreating, but had to fight. That is the point which appeals to Octavius. In a similar position, *Macbeth* said:

> "They have tied me to the stake: I cannot fly,
> But, bear-like, I must fight the course."

Macbeth, V, 7, 1-2

SCENE II

7. *In his own change...officers*, either through some change which has happened to him, or by bad conduct on the part of his officers.

10. *shall be satisfied*, shall receive a satisfactory explanation.

12. *Full of regard*, worthy of respect.

16. *familiar instances*, marks of friendly intercourse; signs of easy friendship.

17. *conference*, conversation; talk.

19. *a hot friend cooling*, a good friend who is becoming less friendly.

21. *enforced ceremony*, a forced and formal politeness.

22. *There are no tricks...faith*, there are no such things in plain and honest friendship.

23. *hollow*, insincere; unreliable. *horses hot at hand,* horses which prance about and make a great show of high spirits when they are only being led along by hand.

24. *promise of their mettle*, promise of being full of courage.

26. *They fall their crests*, "they drop their heads." The crest of a horse is the head and neck. In a high spirited horse, the crest is carried proudly aloft. When a horse is beaten in a race and loses courage, the crest is at once dropped. Here *fall* = let fall.

26. *jades*, the word "jade" applies to a worthless horse, sometimes to a worthless woman. *sink in the trial*, fall when put to the test.

38. *wrong I mine enemies*? do I do wrong, even to my enemies?

40. *sober form*, grave appearance.

42. *griefs,* grievances. *I do know you well,* the underlying meaning; "I am an old friend so there is no need to shout loudly at me."

46. *enlarge your griefs,* "bring out your grievances." Literally to "enlarge" is to set free something which has been kept shut in.

48. *their charges,* the troops under them.

50. *Lucius,* it seems strange that a boy servant should be given such a charge, as it would be the duty of an officer. It is thought that this is a misprint for "Lucilius," though it is perhaps possible to argue that there may have been another officer with the name Lucius.

Scene III

2. *noted,* make an unfavorable note against; put the case on record.

4. *Wherein,* in which case.

5. *were slighted off,* were set aside as of no importance.

7-8. *it is not meet....comment,* "it is not desirable that every slight offence should be gone into." A "nice" offence is one in which only a fastidious and over-critical judgment will decide that there has been an offence at all.

10. *condemn'd,* blamed, *to have,* for having. *an itching palm,* this is an idiomatic expression, for "a hand ready to accept money." *mart,* put up for sale.

15. *honours this corruption,* puts a covering of honour over this dishonesty.

16. *And chastisement....head,* "and before punishment is kept far off", *chastisement* is a strong word, suggesting physical beating, and so a strong word to use to the proud Cassius.

20-1. *What villain.....justice?* This is not quite in accordance with the motives that led the killing of Caesar. At no time did the conspirators say that it was for injustice that he was killed, and there was then no suggestion that Caesar was "supporting robbers." But Shakespeare was not concerned with preserving strict historical accuracy so much as with the matter of getting on with the play. It is from Plutarch that Shakespeare found: "Brutus answered that Cassius should remember the Ides of March, when they slew Caesar who neither robbed nor plundered the country, but only was a favorer of those that did rob by his countenance and authority."

25. *space,* amount. *so much trash....grasped thus,* here he makes the motion of closing his hand as if on a few gold coins.

25. *bay,* bark at.

30. *to hedge me in,* to lay restrictions on my authority.

31. *practice,* experience.

32. *to make conditions*, to settle the terms of appointments, etc.

35. *Urge* me, press me.

36. *Have mind upon your health*, take thought of your own safety, (which will be endangered if you anger me.)

37. *slight man*, feeble fellow!

39. *choler*, "bad temper." The choler was one of the liquids in the economy of the body, and an excess of choler was supposed to affect the temper. It is better known as the "bile." Plutarch describes Cassius as "choleric." We often use "liverish" to describe a hasty-tempered man.

44. *budge*, move from my place.

45. *Must I observe you*, i.e. must I watch carefully your fits of temper, so as to humour them? *testy*, easily offended.

47. *the venom of your spleen*, the people then were not sure of the functions of that organ of the body called the spleen but they thought that, like the choler from the liver, the spleen produced something which made man quick and hasty in temper.

50. *waspish*, spiteful; ill-tempered. The wasp, because of its ability to sting, has been taken as a symbol of hasty temper.

52. *vaunting*, boasting.

54. *to learn of noble men*, some think that it should be "able" or "abler" men, to correspond with the claim made by Cassius in line 31. The reading of the text would be more understandable if Cassius had claimed to be more noble than Brutus.

58. *mov'd*, angered; provoke.

59. *tempted*, provoked; angered.

69. *Which I respect not*, to which I pay no attention.

70. *denied*, in Shakespeare's time, the distinction between "deny" and "refuse" was not so clearly marked and words were used as if there were no difference between them.

71. *vile*, dishonest. *coin my heart;* make money from my heart. *wring*, export. *indirection*, injustice.

80. *rascal counters*, "vile coins." A counter is a round disc of metal shaped like a coin, used often for the purpose of counting. Gamblers often use a supply of counters representing money, the actual settlement being made afterwards.

84. *a fool that brought My answer*, that Lucilius (*IV, 2, 13-14*)

85. *riv'd*, broken; torn.

86. *bear*, put up with. *infirmities*, weaknesses; faults.

92. *Olympus*, Mount Olympus, on which the old classical gods were thought to live.

96. *brav'd*, defied; threatened.

97. *check'd* scolded; rebuked. *observ'd*, closely noted.

98. *conn'd by rote*, "learned by heart." This describes the committing of anything to memory by repeating it a number of times.

99. *into my teeth*, in my face.

102. *Plutus' mine*, some editions have "Pluto's mine." The sense is the same, as Plutus, the god of riches, and Pluto, king of the underworld, were the same deity under different aspects, according to the classics. Pluto in the underworld would naturally have easy access to mineral wealth. *Dearer*, richer.

103. *If that thou be's*t, if you are.

108. *it shall have scope*, your anger will have freedom; will not be opposed.

109. *dishonour shall be humour*, insult from you will be taken as a jest.

110. *yoked*, working together, as two bullocks are tied to the yoke of one wagon.

111. *That carries anger....cold again*, the flint is a cold stone, and yet a blow from steel sends a spark of fire from it. Then the stone is as cold as before. Brutus says that he is like this: a momentary spark of temper may be struck from him, and then he is a calm as before. *much enforced*, greatly provoked.

114. *To be but mirth &c.*, to be an object of mirth, etc.

115. *blood ill-temper'd vexeth him,* "when a ill-adjusted condition of his blood makes him irritable". The condition of the blood was thought to be the cause of bad temper and irritation. But we can also take blood, as meaning "passion" in a figurative sense. him, refers to Cassius.

119. *bear with me*, put up with me; be patient with me.

120. *rash humour,* quick temper. *my mother*, we have no historical record to show whether or not Cassius's mother was specially hasty of temper.

Enter Poet, Plutarch relates that, when all the officers were outside the tent, terrified at the sounds of quarrelling coming from the tow leaders, a certain eccentric poet called Phaonius forced his way into the tent, and quoted from Homer;

> "My lords, I pray you hearken both to me
> For I have seen more years than such three."

Shakespeare changes North's doggerel, probably finding the meaning of the second line obscure.

133. *cynic*, there was a school of philosophy called by this name, but the basic sense of "a rough and mannerless fellow" is all that is meant here.

134. *saucy*, impertinent.

135. *his fashion*, his usual way of behaving.

136. *I'll know his humour &c.*, I shall appreciate his wit better when he understands to introduce it only at a suitable time.

137. *What should the wars.....fools?* "what use is there in war-time for these rhyming follows?" *jigging* suggests a dancing step or a monotonous rhyme in verse.

138. *companion*, My friend.

140. *lodge their companies*, find quarters for their men.

146. *give place to accidental evils*, "give way to chance misfortunes." Cassius knew that Brutus believed in the Stoic philosophy, and that taught a calm acceptance of all the ups and downs of life. So, not knowing of Portia's death, he is puzzled to see the usually philosophic Brutus so disturbed in mind. Even death was not thought to justify emotion on the part of a true Stoic philosopher.

150. *How scap'd I......you so*, How did I escape being killed, when I opposed you at such a time?

152. *Impatient of*, unable to endure.

155. *fell distract*, became out of control; went mad.

154-5. *with her death that tidings come*, the news of Octavius and Antony raising such forces came at the same time as the report of Portia's death.

159. *In this I bury all unkindness*, in drinking this, I forget all our quarrelling.

161. *o'erswell the cup*, runs over the edge of the cup.

165. *call in question.....necessities*, discuss the matter of our needs.

169. *a mighty power*, a great army.

170. *Bending their expedition...Phillippi*, "and that their movements are directed towards Phillippi." Shakespeare use "expedition" to mean the progress or route of an army.

171. *the selfsame tenour*, to the same effect.

172. *with what addition?* with any further information?

173. *bills of outlawry*, bills or edicts which outlawed certain of their opponets. If a man was outlawed, he was outside the protection of the laws of the State, and anyone could kill him or seize his property without breaking the law, *proscription*, see Note, *IV, I, 15-17*. The proscription

was a general order or black list condemning all prominent supporters of the Brutus party.

183.   *write of her*, written about her.

185.   *ought*, anything.

187.   *As you are a Roman*, this appeal to a man's sense of nationality was a solemn and sacred one with Brutus.

189.   *By strange manner*, "in a strange manner." To swallow coals of fire was a strange and painful method of self-killing.

191.   *once*, "some time or other." As already mentioned, the Stoics were trained to accept death as an inevitable and ordinary thing. Macbeth, when told by his men that Lady Macbeth had died, simply said, "She would have died hereafter!" Death is certain, so it matters little whether it comes soon or late.

194-5.   *I have as much &c.*, I have as much of this philosophy in theory as you have, but because of my nature I could not bear it as calmly as you do.

196.   *to our work alive*, either "let us, the living, get on with our work," or "let us turn from the dead to our work with the living."

200.   *means*, resources; strength.

201.   *offence*, harm.

202.   *nimbleness*, mobility.

203.   *of force*, necessarily.

204.   *and this ground*, and the place where we are now.

205.   *forc'd affection*, that is, their attachment to Brutus was not voluntary, but because of compulsion.

206.   *For they....contribution*, they have going grudgingly the supplies etc. which we need.

207.   *along by them*, through their territory.

208.   *make a fuller number up*, increase his numbers by recruitment from them.

209.   *new-added*, with new additions to his strength.

213.   *Under your pardon*, "Forgive me: let me continue." Once again, because of his love for Brutus, Cassius is giving way although subsequent events are to show that again he is right and Brutus wrong.

214.   *tried the utmost of our friends*, tried all we can for the maximum that is to be got from our friends.

215.   *our cause is ripe*, our case is fresh and ready for action.

217.   *We at the height......decline*, we have reached the maximum of our power, and next thing is we shall begin to lose support.

218.   *There is a tide....fortune,* the tide rises and falls twice in every twenty-four hours. Sailors and people living by the sea speak of the "high water" and "low water". The former being when the tide has reached its highest level, the latter being the lowest. The highest point is also called the "flood." That is the sense here : after flood-tide, there will be a steady fall in the level of the water, and any work requiring the flood-tide must be tackled promptly.

220.   *Omitted,* if the chance is lost. *is bound is shallows,* the metaphor is that of a ship, which is in danger and trouble through having to sail through shallow and therefore difficult waters.

222.   *full sea,* full tide; high water. *current,* tide. *when it serves,* when it is suitable.

225.   *We'll along ourselves,* again the omission of "go".

226.   *is crept,* has fallen gently.

228.   *Which we will niggard.....rest,* there is a noun, "niggard," meaning a miserly or mean person, and the word can also be an adjective with the sense of miserly or very economical. But in his license, Shakespeare makes it work as a verb, meaning to deal or supply anything in a limited or sparing degree, i.e. "Nature feels that necessity of sleep, but we shall deal out a very scanty allowance of sleep to her."

235.   *Never comes such division,* may such a difference never come.

239.   *instrument,* Lucius played some musical instrument, probably the small stringed instrument called the lute.

240.   *drowsily,* as if sleepy.

241.   *knave,* has now come to mean "rascal." But in Shakespeare's time, the word meant "boy" and no more. It has kept the original sense in German (*der knabe,* the boy)

over-watch'd, tired through too much keeping watch or keeping awake.

247.   *raise,* arouse.

251.   *I shall otherwise bethink me,* I shall think of doing differently.

255.   *much forgetful,* we do not use *much* to modify an adjective in this way now, but the different uses between "much" and "very" were not so marked in Shakespeare's age.

256.   *hold up,* keep open.

257.   *Strain,* note.

258.   *an't please you,* if it is your pleasure.

262.   *bloods,* lads; people.

267.   *slumber,* is said to murder people, because in deep sleep man appear as if dead.

268. *thy leaden mace,* the procedure of the law, in Shakespeare's days, was that when the sergeant or bailiff went to arrest a man, he touched him on the shoulder with his short official staff or rod in token of arrest. The mace of slumber is called leaden because of the heaviness and deepness of sleep. Elsewhere Shakespeare speaks of "leaden slumbers." (*Rope of Lucrece*)

271. *nod,* drop the head or body, as one does when relaxed in sleep.

273. *is not the leaf turn'd down,* Plutarch says :

"Brutus, being in Pompey's camp, did nothing but study all day long.....Furthermore when others slept, or thought what would happen the morrow after, he fell to his book." The end of this scene brings out two points in the character of Brutus: (1) his scholarly tendencies, (2) his kindness and consideration for others, as seen in his regard for Lucius. But there is a slight anachronism, for in those days reading was done from rolls of parchment, and not from books with leaves which could be turned down.

Entet the Ghost of Caesar, the supernatural spirit is taken from Plutarch, who describes how "a wonderful strange and monstrous shape of a body came towards him and said never a word. So Brutus boldly asked what he was, a god or a man, and what cause brought him thither. The spirit answered him, 'I am thy evil spirit. Brutus, and thou shalt see me by the city of Philippes.' There is no suggestion that it was Caesar's spirit, but rather the evil genius which some classical writers allotted to every man. But it was much more in the European tradition to make it the ghost of the murdered Caesar, and this was more likely to be understood by Shakespeare's audience. So he made this change, but with characteristic carelessness or in his haste, allowed the dialogue to remain, unchanged. It is only the dialogue of *V, V, 16-20* that we learn that the apparition was the Ghost of Caesar, otherwise it might have remained the evil genius of classical tradition. A revengeful ghost, on the lines of Hamlet's father, was more suitable for Shakespeare's stage.

280. *stare,* stand erect, it is a physical fact that terror or strong emotion causes the hair to stand up.

288. *taken heart,* regained my courage.

289. *ill,* evil.

293. *The strings..... are false,* when the strings of an instrument give a wrong note, they are said to be "false" or out of tune. The boy is speaking in his slumber.

298. *didst thou see any thing?* Brutus is still confused and he doubts the reliability of his own sense. So naturally he tries to find whether Lucius has seen anything of the strange visitor who has just gone.

305. *saw you anything?* here he tries to get any confirmation of his vision that may be possible from the guards.

307. *commend me,* give my compliments; convey my respects.

308. *Bid him....before,* tell him to start his forces off at an earlier hour.

ACT V
SCENE I

1. *answered.* fulfilled.

3. *upper regions,* higher ground.

4. *battles,* the old meaning was "forces" or "armies." This is what Octavius means. *warn us,* this is also an unusual use of the word. It means "challenge us" or "call us to battle."

6. *Answering before....of them,* responding to our challenge before we have made it.

7. *in their bosoms,* fully acquainted with their plans.

9. *they could be content....places,* they would well like to go elsewhere and avoid us.

10. *with fearful bravery,* with a mixture of bravery and fear, the kind of bravery that is forced upon men who are compelled by circumstance to fight, though they have really no great enthusiasm for it. But bravery may also be taken to mean "display" or "ostentation." Plutarch says : "In truth Brutus' army was inferior to Octavius Caesar's in number of men; but for bravery and rich furniture, Brutus' arms far excelled Caesar's. For the most part of their armours were silver and gilt, which Brutus had bountifully given them." If this is the idea which Shakespeare had in mind, then we wou'd have to understand from *fearful bravery* "terrible splendour." *face,* show.

11. *To fasten in our thoughts,* to impress on us.

13. *in gallant show,* this might strengthen the argument for the second interpretation of *fearful bravery.*

14. *bloody sign of battle,* a signal given by a flag or some other symbol. Plutarch says: "The next morning by break of day, the signal of battle was set out in Brutus' and Cassius's camp, which was a scarlet coat."

16. *battle,* army; force.

17. *even field,* level ground.

19. *cross,* oppose; contradict. *exigent,* critical moment.

20. *but I will do so,* this may read either, "I shall do as you say," or, "I shall do what I have said." According to Plutarch there was a disagreement between Brutus and Cassius as to who should lead the right wing of the army. One editor says: "Shakespeare made use of this incident, but transferred it to the opposite camp, in order to bring out the character of Octavius."

21. *a parley*, a discussion; talk.

23. *sign*, the signal.

24. *we will answer on their charge*, may be "No, we will answer their invitation to talk." Or, if the invitation to a parley has not originated with Brutus's side, this may be "Do not start the battle now. We shall meet their charge or attack when they make it." Brutus speaks as if the invitation to parley had come from his opponents: in his words, "the generals would have some words," Antony speaks as if the invitation had come from Brutus and Cassius.

30. *In your bad strokes.....hail, Caesar!"* Antony cleverly takes up Brutus' remark and taunts him with having dealt treacherous blows to Caesar, while speaking words of flattery to him. But that is hardly a fair description of Brutus' share in the killing of Caesar.

31. *witness,* as for example.

33. *The posture of your blows are yet unknown*, "the nature of the blows you will deal in battle has yet to be found out." That is, Antony has not yet given proof of any skill in battle. *posture* meant the position of holding a weapon in drill exercises or in battle.

34-5. *they rob the Hybla bees*, Hybla, in Sicily, was famed for a breed of bees which produced very sweet honey. But, says Cassius, Antony can speak words so sweet that one would think he had taken away all the sweet honey from bees. The funeral oration gives some substance to this accusation.

not stingless.....before you sting, Antony retorts that he has not borrowed stings from the bees; and Brutus retorts bitterly that he has, and also the buzzing sound which the bees make, for he makes a speech before he attacks. The retort is weak, but Brutus has no gift of repartee.

40. *hacked one another*, there were so many daggers in Caesar's body that they were clashing or striking against each other.

42-39. *fawned like hounds, And bowed, &c.*, the "base spaniel fawning" has already been commented upon, while, in the murder scene, Metellus bowed down, Cassius did so at least in words, and Brutus kissed Caesar's hand. So Antony has fact on his side.

46-7. *This tongue....have ruled*, it is not often that Cassius indulges in the "I told you so!" that is so exasperating. But here he cannot resist from reminding Brutus that Mark Antony would not have been able to make such offensive speeches, if Cassius' advice had been taken.

48. *the cause*, the subject of our talk; the business on hand.

49. *The proof....redder drops*, to put these arguments to the proof by blows will produce bloodshed.

52. goes up again, a man was said to "put his sword up" when he returned it to its sheath, after having drawn it.

54. another Caesar, Octavius himself. His will be an additional death at the hands of the traitors who killed Julius.

57. Unless thou bring'st them, i.e. because there are no traitors present. So *I hope* he refers to the words "Thou canst not die."

60. honourable, honourably. Brutus has lost his temper in the war of words, and thinks that slights have been cast on the honour of his noble family.

61. peevish, "ill-mannered." *such honour,* such an honour as to die by the sword of Brutus.

62. masker....reveller, See *I, II, 204.*

63. Old Cassius still ! the same old sharp-tempered Cassius !

66. when you have stomachs, "when you have sufficient courage or inclination." It is still a current idiom to say of some unpleasant duty, "I have no stomach for the work."

67. swell billow, may the waves rise. *on the hazard,* at stake; trembling in the balance.

71. Plutarch writes, "Cassius said to Messala.....I am compelled against my will (as Pompey the Great was) to risk the liberty of our country to the hazard of a battle.....Cassius, having spoken these last words unto him, he bade him farewell, and willed him to come to supper with him the next night following, because it was his birthday." *as this very day,* "on this very date." At one time, *as* was used like this in phrases dealing with time.

75. As Pompey was, the war of 48 B.C. ended with the battle of Pharsalia in Thessaly. Pompey there wished to avoid matching his raw soldiers against the trained veterans of Caesar, but his hand was forced. The result was the complete defeat of Pompey.

77. hold Epicurus strong, "believe strongly in the philosophy of Epicurus." This was the philosophy at the opposite scale of thought from the Stoics, giving all importance to the satisfaction of the bodily senses and ignoring the claims of reason. The Epicureans did not believe in the significance of omens and portents. They did not believe that there was any supernatural or divine rule in the Universe.

80. Coming from Sardis. &c., it was in Plutarch again that Shakespeare found it recorded that : "two eagles....lighted upon two of the foremost ensigns and always followed the soldiers, who gave them meat and drink, until they come near the city of Philippes; and there, one day only before the battle, they both flew away....and yet further there was seen a marvellous number of birds of prey that feed upon dead carcases ....the which omens began somewhat to alter Cassius' mind from Epicurus' opinions, and hand put the soldiers also in a marvellous fear." *former ensign,* "our foremost standard." The Roman ensigns were already called "eagles" because they had carved reproductions of that bird.

81. *fell,* swooped down; alighted.

83. *consorted,* accompanied.

85. *stead,* place.

87. *As we were sickly prey,* the birds mentioned are eaters of dead animals, and if they ever see a sick beast, will keep by it in anticipation of it dying soon and becoming their prey. Thus it would be looked on as an omen of coming slaughter for the birds mentioned to follow the army.

88. *canopy,* an overhead shelter to keep off the rays of the sun.

89. *give up the ghost,* die.

92. *constantly,* with firmness.

94. *The gods stand friendly,* a wish is expressed, i.e. "may the gods today show themselves friendly to us !"

96. *rest,* remain.

97. *Let's reason....befall,* let us plan for the worst that can possibly happen to us.

98. *then is this*—then this is.

102. *By which I did blame Cato,* Plutarch reports Brutus to have said to Cassius : "I trust (I know not how) a certain rule of philosophy by which I did greatly blame Cato for killing himself as being no lawful nor godly act..... but being now in the midst of danger, I am of a contrary mind. For if it be not the will of god that this battle fall fortunate for us, I will look no more for hope.....but will rid me of this miserable world.

105-6. *For fear of what.....time of life,* for man, because he is afraid of the consequences, to shorten his period of life.

arming myself with patience, &c., Brutus thought that it was far more noble to wait patiently for whatever is arranged by the high powers who govern men's lives.

109. *led in triumph,* if Antony and Octavius were victorious, then they would be given a triumphal reception on their return to Rome. If Brutus then were alive, a prisoner of war, he would have to walk on foot in the procession beside the carriage of the triumphant Antony.

111. *think not..... that over Brutus &c.,* though his philosophy is all against the idea of suicide, yet the idea of being led through Rome as Antony's prisoner is so hateful to Brutus that there is no doubt he has resolved to take his own life if defeated in the coming battle. In *Antony and Cleopatra,* the news that Octavius may have her led as a captive along with

his triumphal chariot in Rome makes Cleopatra kill herself. But it had never been done to any Roman citizen !

113. *bear*, has.

125. *it sufficeth*, it is sufficient.

Scene II

1. *bills*, written papers, containing military orders in this case.

2. *the other side*, on the opposite side of the field.

4. *cold demeanour*, a half-hearted effort. Brutus saw the enemy faltering on the other side, and decided that a sudden sharp attack would probably drive them into cofusion.

Scene III

1. *the villains*, his own soldiers.

2. *Myself*, I.

3. *ensign*, standard-bearer.

4. *I slew the coward*, this is Shakespeare's addition. Plutarch only says that Cassius took the ensign and fastened it in the ground at his feet.

6. *Who*, he.

7. *fell to spoil*, stopped fighting to begin looting.

8. *enclosed,* surrounded.

10. *in your tents*, in Cassius's camp, a place which he thought to be safe from the enemy.

11. *for off*, further off.

15. *hide thy spurs-in him*, spur him sharply.

17. *here again*, and then back to me.

18. *yond troops*, the troops over there.

19. *even with a thought*, with the speed of thought.

21. *my sight was ever thick*, Plutarch furnishes the fact that Cassius had rather weak eye-sight.

22. *thou not'st*, what you see.

24. *where did I begin*, i.e. on the same date on which I was born.

25. *My life is run his compass*, life is regarded as a cycle, or the revolution of a wheel. Now the circuit has been completed and life is ended. In *King Lear*, Edmund says when dying "The wheel has come full cycle."

28. *enclosed*, surrounded. *on the spur*, spurring their horses to speed.

31. *some light,* some of them are dismounting.

32. *He's ta'en*, "he is taken captive." This was an error, since

Pindarus did not see that the horsemen where the victorious troops of Brutus. The error was to cost Cassius his life.

38. *I swore thee, saving of thy life,* I made you swear at that time when I saved your life.

41. *be a freeman,* Pindarus is a bondman, a higher standing than that of a slave, but still the property of Cassius and not a free man. Now Cassius offers him status as a free man in return for the service of rendering the last duty by killing his master.

42. *search this bosom,* pierce my breast.

43. *hilts,* the handle of the sword. It is used in the plural form although only one hilt is meant, but the hilt of a sword does consist of two guards.

46. *even with the sword that killed thee.* Shakespeare got this detail from Plutarch. and was quick to seize on any point of such dramatic effect.

Durst I have done my will, if I had dared exercise my own will be refusing to do this.

50. *Where never Roman...of him,* in the head note to the scene, we see that Plutarch says that Pindarus was never seen again.

51. *It is but change,* i.e. an exchange of defeats, the victory of one flank on each side being made up for by the defeat on the other wing.

61. *to night,* into darkness.

62. *set,* ended.

64. *Clods, dews...come,* Shakespeare always regards clouds, mists, dews and the like as unhealthy things, "poisonouns exhalations" which are hostile to men.

65. *Mistrust of my success,* "his lack of confidence in my gaining success has led to this deed." But the literal meaning of *success* is "result," in which case we have, " Doubt of the result on my side has caused this."

67-71. *O hateful error...engender'd thee.* Messala speaks in a strain of poetical personification. "Error" is hateful, and is said to be the child of melancholy in the sense that melancholy men are prone to commit errors. Messala asks, "Why do you imprint upon the ready minds of men things which do not actually exist?" Then he thinks of the man who commits an error as if he were a mother giving birth to a child, and says "O error, you are quickly born, but you never have a happy birth for you always kill the mother (erring person) who created you." This is an example of Elizabethan conceit. i.e., metaphor carried too far, so as to become fanciful, and even in Shakespeare's hands it is not successful.

74. *thrusting this report into his ears,* forcing this unwelcome news upon him.

76. *envenomed,* poisoned.

78. *Hie you*, go; make your way.

79. *the while*, in the meantime.

84. *misconstrued*, misunderstood, taken up wrongly.

85. *hold thee*, stop.

86. *bid,* told me. The past tense should be "bade," but these definite forms had not then been settled.

87. *apace*, quickly.

89. *By your leave, gods*, he asks permission of the gods to end his life before the time appointed by them.

a Roman's part, it was regarded as a duty to commit suicide if defeated, or a failure in any great undertaking. Till recent years we had similar ideas in the Japanese practice of *hari-kari*.

89-90. Note once again the rhyming couplet, showing that a certain action is ended and that another set of characters is about to come in. It is not always at the end of a scene, for remember that the arrangement into scenes is not Shakespeare's work, but has been done by later editors.

95. *abroad and turns our swords, &c.*, the prophecy of Antony, in III, I, 259-75, now seems to be fulfilled.

97. *Look, whether...Cassius!* "look ! why, he has actually garlanded dead Cassius!"

99. *The last of all the Romans*, this may be taken as referring to Cassius, as Titinius is hardly great enough to be included in such an eulogy.

101. *breed thy fellow,* produce your equal. *moe*, more. An antiquated form.

102. *than you shall see me pay,* they will not see the tears of Brutus; he will weep for Cassius in private.

104. *Thasos*, an inland in the Aegean sea, near the coast of Greece.

105. *funerals*, funeral ceremonies and rites.

106. *Lest it discomfort us*, the funeral of such well-known and honoured leader would have a disturbing effect on the morale of the troops. It is Plutarch who tells us that this was the main motive for sending the body to be buried at Thasos.

108. *battles*, forces; troops.

109. *'Tis three o'clock*, this hardly agrees with line 60, where it appeared that Titinius was looking at the setting sun. But Shakespeare has combined into one what were two different battles in Plutarch, and has probably forgotten to adjust this time item.

SCENE IV

2. *What bastard doth not?* "Who is the scoundrel who will not do so?" Cato insinuates that no true Roman would need such a reminder as Brutus has given, so if any man is not holding up his head bravely, he must be a bastard.

5. *A foe to tyrants.* This is because he is the son of Marcus Cato, who was one of the most bitter opponents of Julius Caesar.

8. *know me for Brutus,* Let everyone know that I am Brutus.

11. *being Cato's son,* as a worthy son of Cato.

14. *Kill Brutus...his death,* Lucilius in the hope of aiding Brutus to escape or of giving the leader time for further plans, tries to delay the soldiers by making them think that thy have captured Brutus.

16. *ta'en,* captured.

24. *or alive or dead,* whether alive or dead.

25. *like Brutus, like himself,* in a way that is worthy of Brutus and a honour to himself.

27. *a prize no less in worth,* it is surprising to hear Lucilius described as being a prize of equal value to the great Brutus. Perhaps Antony, of the wily tongue, is already trying to please and conciliate Lucilius. At any rate, Plutarch tells us : "Lucilius ever after served Antony faithfully even to his death."

32. *is chanc'd,* has gone or fallen out.

SCENE V

1. *poor remains of friends,* i.e. the poor remaining number of my friends, compared with the good number before the battle.

3. *or ta'en or slain,* either captured or killed.

4. *slaying is the word,* is the watch-word, the word which affects us all now. *a deed in fashion,* a deed which is now common.

7. *no words,* 'do not let the others hear what I have said to you.'

8. *Hark thee,* listen to me.

11. *ill,* evil.

13. *vessel,* is a common metaphor in the Bible. The word can mean any kind of jar or cup. Brutus is a vessel so full of grief that it is overflowing, in the form of tears from his eyes.

15. *list,* listen to me.

17. *the ghost of Caesar,* this is the first time that we are told that the apparition which appeared to Brutus was the ghost of Caesar. In the first description, the name of Caesar was not mentioned, and the spirit described himself as "Thy evil spirit, Brutus."

19. *here in Philippi fields*, this is the first time we have been told of the second appearance of the spirit, which Shakespeare has not shown on the stage. So we may surmise that it was on the second appearance that the spirit revealed itself to be the ghost of Caesar. But Plutarch says: "The night before the battle, it is reported that the monstrous spirit which had appeared before unto Brutus in the city of Sardis, did appear again unto him in the self-same shape and form, and so vanished away and said never a word."

23. *Our enemies....the pit,* this is thought to be a metaphor from the device of hunters, who dig a hole in the ground (pit) and cover it lightly over, afterwards driving the hunted animal towards this pit so that it falls in and is caught. Being on the edge of the pit, Brutus says that they may as well leap in to their destruction, as wait for the hunters to give them the push. In spite of the wide acceptance of this explanation, it seems difficult to understand how Shakespeare can have known of such a method of hunting, which was not practise in England of his time.

25. *tarry*, wait.

29. *sword-hilts*, the handle of my sword. See Note, *V, III, 43.*

29. *office*, service; duty.

34. *joy*, rejoice. *yet*, till the present time.

35. *but he was true to me*, who was not true or faithful to me.

36. *this losing day*, this day of defeat.

37-8. *More than Octavius. &c.,* Brutus thinks that history will say of Antony and Octavius that they had "slain good men, to usurp tyrannical power not pertaining to them." (North's *Plutarch*) They have won a "vile conquest" by defeating those who were fighting for the freedom of their country.

41-2. *Night hangs...... attain this hour,* this is the farewell speech of Brutus, spoken with all his usual dignity and serenity of spirit. His greatness and unselfish motives are seen most strongly when he prepares to leave the world and its trials behind him. It is with composure that he says: "The darkness of death rises before my eyes, and my bones long for the rest of the grave. They have laboured, only to attain this hour of failure." This is practically a confession from Brutus that his life's purpose has failed. Plutarch has no such words.

44. *stay thou by thy lord*, remain to assist your lord.

45. *of a good respect*, of good reputation; well respected by all.

46. *smatch*, usually spelt "smack," and dentoing "taste" or "savour." *i.e.* "Your life has always borne an atmosphere of honour."

49. *Give me your hand first*, Shake hands first in farewell.

Caesar......good a will, "Now, Caesar, thy spirit may rest. I did not slay thee with half the pleasure that I now slay myself." Brutus realises that he is vanquished by the spirit of dead Caesar, who has seemed to dominate the action of the play, even when dead.

52. *man,* has the sense of "servant" or "follower."

53. *The conquerors....fire of him,* "The most that the victors can do to him is to burn his body." It is related by Plutarch that they did indeed burn the body of Brutus in a fine funeral ceremony, and afterwards sent his ashes in honour to his mother.

56-7. *For Brutus......death,* For only Brutus conquered Brutus, and no man is able to boast of victory through his death.

58-9. *So Brutus......saying true,* (*See V, iv, 20-25*). "Yes, that is the way in which one would expect to find Brutus."

60-1. *All that....with me?* All who served Brutus I shall take into my service. You, Strato, will you now devote your time to my service?

62. *prefer me to you,* recommend me to you. Shakespeare sometimes uses "prefer" in the sense of "recommend," Cp. *Merchant of Venice :*

> "Shylock thy master spoke with me this day
> And hath preferr'd thee."

67. *latest service,* the last service on earth.

68-72. *This was....one of them,* Shakespeare makes Antony bear witness to the fact that Brutus only joined the conspiracy because of pure love of country, and not from selfish or ambitious motives like those of the other conspirators. The authority for this is found in Plutarch, and it shows the generous character which Antony possesses in such moments of deep feeling. He is very much moved by the feeling of the moment, and passes quickly from hate to sentiment.

69. *save only he,* with the exception of himself.

71. *in a general honest thought,* actuated by thoughts of honest concern for the general welfare of the state.

72. *and common good to all,* and the general good of the people.

made one of them, joined the conspirators.

73-5. *his life....a man,* His life was gentle, and the various qualities of nobility were so combined in him that Nature seemed to proclaim to all the world that here was the ideal man.

76-7. *According to.....burial,* In accordance with his valour, let us now treat him with honourable respect in the ceremonies of burial.

79. *order'd honourably,* "arranged in an honourable manner." *i.e.* his body would be laid out in a solemn manner, surrounded by his arms as was customary when a brave warrior died.

80-1. *So call the field...happy day,* "So now let us summon the soldiers to rest, and let us depart to divide up the glorious fruits of victory won on this happy day." Sometime Shakespeare uses "field" to denote a battle, but this is the only case where it denotes the troops. Possibly it is an imitation of the hunting metaphor, where all the huntsmen and dogs combined, who have been chasing the deer or fox, are called "the field."

In the drama of our modern age, the curtain usually falls on the catastrophe, and the action terminates at a point of high tension and emotion. But Shakespeare allowed a curtain falling-off to come after the climax, and his dramas, like those of the Greeks, end on a quiet and subdued note, which is agreed by most to be a procedure much more true to life.

GLOSSARY

All the words given here have already been commented upon in the Notes. Additional explanation is given in the case of words used in a sense different from present day usage, or obsolete. The following abbreviations are used : S.S. = Shakespearean Sense; M.E. = Modern English.

abide,   (III, I, 94; III, II, 119) to pay the penalty for, to atone. In M.E. the commone; meaning is to reside, to wait. But the former usage is still admitted.

abuse,   (II, I, 115) a dishonest or evil practice. (II, I, 18) an ill use, misuse. Both are now current.

addressed, (III, I, 29) the S.S. here is "ready" or "prepared." This is not current now, but the common sense in M.E. is "spoken to" or "having the address written on."

afeard,   (II, II, 67) an old form of "afraid."

affections, (II, I, 20) in S.S. here signifies inclinations or tendencies. But the sense in M.E. is always "love."

aim.   (I, II, 163) as a noun = guess or conjecture. (I, III, 52) the line of fire in shooting.

alarum,   (V, III, 90) and numerous Stage Direction. Summons to battle by trumpets, etc. Sometimes "The noise of fighting."

answer,   (III, II, 81) to pay the penalty for, (IV, I, 47; V, I, 24) to cope with, to deal with. (V, I, 6) to pay off, to settle a debt.

annoy,   (I, III, 22; II, I, 160) to molest or harm. In M.E. the sense is only to cause some slight feeling of anger or irritation.

apparent, (II, I, 198) manifest or clear. In M.E. also has the sense of "seeming" or "appearing to."

appoint,   (IV, I, 30) to supply with, to assign to. In M.E. the sense of putting a person into a post has become the commonest.

bay,   (IV, I, 49; IV, III, 27) to bark, (intr.), to bark at. (III, I, 204) to drive or bring to bay. Spoken of an animal when it turns in desperation to face its pursuers.

basis,   (III, I, 116) = base. The pedestal of a statue.

battle,   (V, I, 4, 16; V, III, 108) a force of men, an army. This old usage common in early English, is now obsolete.

beholding, (III, II, 70-72) obliged, indebted to. This S.S. is obsol. But in M.E. we use the participle "beholden" in that sense.

bent,   (I, II, 123) direction of the look, a glance. Obsol.

bizz,   (IV, III, 171) a decree. (V, II, I) a written paper.

blunt,   (I, II, 296). In S.S. "slow-witten" or "dull." But in M.E. always "abrupt or harsh in manner."

break with, (II, I, 150). S.S. make a disclosure; share a secret with. M.E. to sever relations with.

bootless, (III, I, 75) in vain, useless.

carrion, (III, I, 275) properly used of decaying flesh, but used as a term of insult to living persons in II, I, 130.

cautelous, (II, I, 129) deceitful or untrustworthy. The word is obsolete.

censure, (III, 2, 16) holds in Shak, the original Latin sense of "to judge" without implying whether favourably or not, but has since come to mean "to blame," or "to reprimand."

cast, (I, III, 60) to throw into a state or condition.

ceremony, sometimes in S.S. denotes an external rite or practice, and sometimes an omen or portent (II, II, 13).

change, S.S. exchange, (V, III, 51).

charactery, S.S. expression of thought by symbols or written characters. Here the wrinkles on his forehead. (II, I, 308).

charm, (II, I, 271) to lay a spell upon or to affect by magical means.

clean, completely, quite. (I, III, 35) Now colloquial in M.E. but quite literary usage for Shak.

climate, land or country. (I, III, 32)

charge, S.S. expense, (IV, I, 9) military command or body of troops under leader (IV, II, 48) load, fill, (III, III, 2).

close, S.S. come terms (III, I, 203).

closet, private room (II, I, 35).

cognizance, (II, II, 89) a term in heraldry for the device or distinguishing badge worn by the followers of a noble house.

colour, (II, I, 29) S.S. pretext or excuse.

con, (IV, III, 98) to learn by heart; to memories by repeated readings. Becoming obsolete.

conceit, (I, III, 162; III, I, 192) to judge, estimate. In M.E., "an overfavourable judgment of one's self."

couching, (III, I, 36) bending down, bowing. Obsolete.

confines, (3, I, 273) region or district, boundaries.

confound, (3, I, 87) strike with confusion or dismay.

conjure, (I, II, 146; II, I, 323), to call up spirit by magic power. In M.E. to perform tricks of juggling, etc.

consort, (vb.) (V, I, 82), to accompany. In M.E. with the same sense, but intr.

constancy, (2, I, 227; 2, I, 229; 2, IV, 6) self-control; firmness of mind.

contrive, (II, III, 15), to plot or conspire.

corse,   (III, I, 200), corpse. Poetic diction.

countenance, (I, III, 159), approval, sanction, M.E. face.

counters,   (IV, III, 80), round discs of common metal, used for counting.

crave,   (II, I, 15) need, ask for.

crest,   (IV, II, 26) horse's head.

cross,   (I, III, 50) forked, (adj) used to describe lightning.

cull.   (I, I, 53) to select, pick out.

curtsy,   (III, I, 43) a variant of "courtesy" = a bow.

cynic,   (IV, III, 133) originally "dog-like" because the Cynic philosophers disregarded all the polite customs of civilised life.

damn,   (IV, I, 6) to condemn.

danger,   (II, I, 17) harm or injury. S.S.

dear,   (III, I, 197; III, II, 115) deeply, to the heart, S.S.

degree,   (II, I, 26) a step or gradation.

deny,   (IV, III, 70, 77, 82) the same as "refuse" in S.S.

difference, (I, II, 40) strife, quarrel.

dint,   (III, II, 198) impression. S.S. Lit. "the mark left by a blow." M.E. dent.

discomfort, (V, III, 106) to discourage in S.S. In M.E. to make uncomfortable.

discover,   (I, II, 69) In S.S. "to reveal." In M.E. to find out.

distract,   (IV, III, 153) S.S. mad. M.E. in great mental confusion.

draw,   (I, III, 22) to gather or assemble.

doomsday, (III, I, 98) day or judgment for the world.

elem t,   (I, III, 128) the middle ages had a belief that four main parts go to make up all things: fire, water, air and earth, known as the four elements. In the body they appear as four moistures or "humours",—choler, phlegm, melancholy and blood. A man's nature depended on how the four elements were mixed in him. But "element" is often applied specially to the sky.

emulation, (II, III, 13) in S.S. = jealousy or rivalry. In M.E. can mean healthy competition, without the sense of jealousy.

enforce,   (III, II, 41) S. S. to exaggerate. (IV, III, III) to strike or provoke. In M.E. simply to compel or force.

enfranchisement, (III, I, 57) S. S. here is to recall from exile. In M.E. to confer the vote and other privileges of citizenship.

engage,   (II, I, 127) to pledge, promise.

enlarge,   (IV, II, 46) S.S. to give free play or scope.

ensign,   (V, I, 79) a standard. (V, III, III) a standard-bearer.

entertain,   (V, V, 60) to take into one's service. In M.E. to give hospitality, to receive as a guest.

even,   (II, I, 133) S.S. = honest. (V, I, 17) level.

exhalation,   (II, I, 44) meteor. In M.E. a gas or vapour given off.

exigent,   (V, I, 19) = critical moment. This is a case of adjective used as noun, equal to "exigency."

expedition,   (IV, III, 168) S.S. march forward, progress. In M.E. a force or party arranged for travel.

extenuate,   (III, II, 39) to diminish, understate.

extremity,   (II, I, 31) act of violence or savagery. In M.E. the end of anything, or, extreme need or distress.

faction,   (II, I, 77) supporters, not necessarily in a bad sense. But in M.E. a seditious or rebellious movement.

fantasy,   (II, I, 231) a short form of the same word is "fancy," *i.e.* that which is a product of the mind, and has no independent existence. So, a vision or phantom which is imagined.

favour,   (I, II, 91; II, I, 76) S.S. face or features. But in M.E. grace or kindness.

fell,   (III, I, 269) adj. fierce or cruel. Cognate with "felon!"

fleer,   (I, III, 117) to grin at or make faces. Not in use now.

fond,   (III, I, 39) S.S. is the old and original meaning, "foolish". In M.E. affectionate or loving.

field,   S.S. an army engaged in fighting. In hunting, all the hunters, hounds, etc. are collectively termed "the field." (V, V, 80)

fret,   (II, I, 104) to mark with mixed colours, or with bands of different colour. A *fret* was a small band; fretwork was a gilded pattern for hall roofs, made of gilt bands intersecting each other.

flood,   (I, II, 152) the great deluge of Noah, or Deucalion in classical story.

flourish,   a volume of trumpet sound (noun). Usually to announce the approach of royalty. (Stage Directions).

former,   (V, I, 79) foremost, most forward, S.S.

funerals,   (V, III, 105) the burial rites at a funeral. M.E. would mean a number of different burials.

gamesome,   (I, II, 28) fond of games or sport. Inclined for games.

general,   (V, V, 71) commonwealth, the public (n.) S.S.

genius,   (II, I, 66) guardian or presiding spirit, (old classical sense). M.E. great cleverness or intelligence.

given,   (I, II, 197) disposed, inclined to.

give place, (IV, III, 144) to give way or yield. S.S.

havoc,   (III, I, 273) when this cry was raised in battle; it meant that all the opposition were to be killed without mercy.

head,   (IV, I, 42) an armed force, or a force making successful resistance. S.S.

hearse,   (III, II, 169) either "coffin" or the bier on which the coffin rested. The only case where it is used in Shak. with this sense. In M.E. the coach which carries the coffin.

hedge in,   (IV, III, 30) to limit or restrict one's authority.

high,   (II, I, 110) exact. high east = due east. S.S.

high-sighted, (II, I, 118) arrogant, looking down on like a scornful conqueror. S.S.

hilts,   (V, III, 43; V, V, 28) the handle of a sword, in plural because handle is regarded as consisting of two, or three parts. In M.E. only considered as of one part, therefore used in singular for handle of one sword.

hind,   (I, III, 106) a female deer. The other sense of "peasants" is not intended here.

humour,   S.S. mood or disposition, (II, I, 210) whim or caprice, (II, I, 250) damp air, moisture (II, I, 262).

hurtle,   (II, II, 22) to clash, to fly through the air with a clatter.

impatient of, (IV, III, 150) unable to bear. Here S.S. is the direct Latin meaning of *impatiens*. In M.E. the meaning has changed to denote a mental attitude which is not disposed to wait.

improve.   (II, I, 159) S.S. to make good use of. M.E. to make anything better. S.S. was current usage in his time, given in *Old English Dictionary.*

incorporate, (I, III, 135) = incorporated, bound up with. This is an old form of the past participle, in imitation of the Latin.

indifferently, (I, II, 87) S.S. without concern or fear. In M.E. the meaning is "fairly" or "moderately," as in such a phrase as "indifferently well done."

indirection, (IV, III, 75) S.S. injustice; dishonesty. In M.E. if found at all, would mean "the wrong direction."

ingrafted, (II, I, 184) deeply rooted, grown into anything so as to become a part of it. Obsol.

instance,   (IV, II, 16) sign or proof. M.E. example.

instrument, (I, III, 70; II, I, 66) agent.

insupressive, (II, I, 134) that which cannot be suppressed. S.S. In M.E. the final *ible* or *able* is used rather than *-ive.*

intermit,   (I, I, 58) S.S. delay, postpone.

itching palm,   (IV, III, 10) Old English Dictionary gives "hankering after gain." Lit "a hand burning for money."

jade,   a worthless horse. This is universal in Old English, but in M.E. more commonly means "a worthless woman."

jigging,   (IV, III, 137) rhyming, (used in contempt).

keep,   (I, II, 315) keep company with.

kerchief,   (I, II, 315) a linen head cloth, used regularly by women, but by men only to wrap round the head in time of sickness.

kind,   (I, III, 64) S.S. nature. (II, I, 33) species.

knave,   (IV, III, 241, 269) in its original sense of "boy," as it is still used in German. No bad sense, M.E., "villain."

lay off,   (I, III, 243) take off, take away, S.S.

lie,   (III, I, 287) to remain in quarters for a halt, usually for a night.

limitation,   (II, I, 283) given in the Dictionary of Old English as a legal term, meaning, "the term that is laid down for the continuation of an office or appointment."

lover,   (II, III, 9; III, II, 18 and elsewhere). In the sense of "friend". This was common usage in Shakespeare's time.

mace,   (IV, III, 266) a law-officer's staff. Still used in the law courts. *make head,* (IV, I, 42) to organise resistance, or to raise armed opposition. Common in S.S. and in other writers of the time.

marry,   (I, II, 229) a corrupted form of the oath by which men used to swear in Catholic England, "By Mary." referring to the Blessed Virgin. So an Anachronism in *Julius Caesar.*

mart,   (IV, III, II) S.S. for this word, used as verb, is "to traffic in." In M.E. no verb, but the same word as noun = market.

masker,   (V, I, 62) one who take part in entertainments where masques are worn.

mechanical,   (I, I, 3) in S.S. "of the working classes." Now here is no such meaning, but M.E. sense is "as if done by a machine."

merely,   (I, II, 39) entirely, completely.

mettle,   (I, I, 65; I, II, 297; IV, II, 24) the same word as "metal". In S.S. and Old English generally, the material or substance of which a creature or person is made. Thus is often used in the sense of "courage" or "spirit".

moe,   (II, I, 72) old form of "more".

morrow,   (II, I, 228) in S.S. morning.

napkin, (III, II, 138) in S.S. is always "handkerchief," but in M.E. denotes the white linen cloth given to a guest or diner for use at table, to protect his clothing, etc.

native, (II, I, 83) natural.

naughty, (I, I, 17) in S.S. and Old English generally, a strong word meaning "good for nothing" i.e. = naught. In M.E. it has a mild sense of "behaving badly" when applied to the trifling offences of little children.

neat's leather, (I, I, 29) leather made from the skins of oxen. Old English, *neot,* cattle. Not used now.

new-added, (IV, III, 207) reinforced or strengthened by numbers.

nice, (IV, III, 8) S.S. fastidious, making too fine distinctions. At fist the word meant "foolish,"—then "foolish in taking too long to make a choice." Now in M.E. it is a much abused word, being loosely applied to anything or any person that is pleasant.

niggard, (IV, III, 226) here S.S. is of a verb, "to supply in small or sparing amount." There is no other example of it being used as a vb. In M.E. is always an adj. meaning, "mean or miserly," or a noun "a mean or miserly person."

night-gown, (II, II, Stage Direction) night-gown then meant a robe worn as we now wear a dressing-robe. Now it means a dress in which one sleeps.

note, (IV, III, II) to make notorious, to brand as an offender. S.S. In M.E. the only sense of the vb. note is to "take notice of."

observe, (IV, III, 45) to pay respect, to give close attention to a person's mood. S.S. But in M.E. "to see," or "to remark."

o'ershoot, S.S. a term of archery, meaning to go further than one had intended.

o'ersway, (II, I, 203) S.S.: to persuade a person, to influence the decision of another.

o'erwatched, (IV, III, 240) tired out by being kept awake too long. Only found once elsewhere, i.e. in *King Lear, IV, III, 240.*

offal, (I, III, 109) refuse or unwanted parts. S.S. Literally "the piece which falls off" like chips from the woodman's axe. In M.E. means the parts of an animal rejected as unfit to eat.

offend, (III, II, 30, 31, 33) to injure. S.S. But in M.E. means no more than "to give displeasure to."

opinion, (II, I, 145) S.S. reputation. (V, I, 77) outlook on life.

orchard, (III, II, 253) In S.S. simply "garden." In M.E. has come to denote specially a garden of fruit trees.

order, (V, V, 79) as a verb. In S.S. is usually "to treat with due respect."

orts, (IV, I, 37) the broken pieces of anything, left after a person has used it. An old Anglo-Saxon word, only used in poetic diction.

palm, (I, II, 131) the old emblem of victory.

palter, (II, I, 126) to deal in a shiftless and feeble fashion with anyone.

parley, (V, I, 21) a conference or talk, especially between enemies who wish to arrive at an agreement. French, *parler,* to talk.

passion, (I, II, 40, 48) S.S. as in Old English, any strong emotion such as love, hate, fear.

peevish, (V, I, 61) in S.S. is often "silly" or "childish," but in M.E. has more the idea of "bad-tempered."

phantasma, (II, I, 65) a horrible vision, a nightmare.

.piece-out, (II, I, 51) to eke out, to supplement.

pitch, (I, I, 77) a term from falconry, meaning the height to which a trained hawk flies. In M.E. can mean "degree" or "extent."

pleasure, (III, II, 252) a king of metonymy for "pleasure ground."

point upon, (I, III, 32) a term from astrology, meaning "to shed their influence upon."

post, (III, I, 288) to ride quickly, to hasten. The expression often signified the use of relays of fresh horses at stages.

posture, (V, I, 33) the movement of the position of a weapon, in drill or in fighting. (*Old English Dictionary*). In M.E. means the attitude or position of a person, the manner in which he is standing.

power, (IV, I, 42; IV, III, 167, 305) a body of armed men, a force. This was the general sense in Middle English.

praetor, (I, III, 143; II, IV, 34) a magistrate working under a consul elected annually for the administration of the law in Rome and in the provinces.

prefer, (V, V, 62) to put forward the name of a person, to recommend. In M.E. is simply to like or choose one thing rather than another.

prick, (III, I, 217; IV, I, I, 3, 16) (1) to incite or to spur on, (2) to mark down in a list: to indicate by a tick or mark of the pencil.

proceeding, (II III, 103) S.S. a person's advancement or career.

prodigious, (I, III, 77) In S.S. portentous, ominous, or having prophetic significance. In M.E. has lost this sense of pointing to the future, and is simply "tremendous."

prodigy, (I, III, 38; II, I, 198) a phenomenon which presages some future happening. In M.E. an abnormal or unusual happening or object.

proper, (I, I, 29) handsome or well-built. (I, II, 41; V, III, 96) peculiar to, or belonging exclusively to. The original Latin meaning of *proprius* was "one's own," from which the significance of "property" is seen: i.e. "what is one's own."

property, (IV, I, 40) S.S. a tool or implement. The technical term "stage properties" means any article or equipment, etc. which are required for the work of the stage.

protest, (II, I, 239) to assert or announce publicly, S.S. In M.E. the word has come to signify "to lodge an objection or complaint."

purpled, (III, I, 158) poetical for "reddened" *i.e.* with blood.

purpose, (I, III, 35) a noun, = meaning or substance, (III, I, 147) "to the purpose" has the sense of "to the point" *i.e.* in accordance with the matter in hand. (II, II, 27) intended, arranged for the future.

put up, (I, III, 19) describes the action of returning a sword or dagger to its sheath.

quality, (I, III, 64) also (III, I, 41) the nature or character of a person. In M.E. applies to things rather than persons.

quarrel, (II, I, 28) in Shakespeare's days the word had a legal sense, *i.e.* an accusation or charge brought against a person at law. In M.E. has come to mean simply a dispute or difference of opinion which becomes violent.

quick, (I, II, 29: 300) alive, living and active. The old sense of the word had not the M.E. sense of "fast or speedy," but is seen in the words of the Creed, where it is said that Christ will come to judge "the quick and the dead."

range, (II, I, 118; III, I, 271) to roam or rove, to fly about seeking game.

rank, (III, I, 153) overgrown till bad and corrupt: too full. One writer says that it was used by the old-time physicians to describe the conditions of their patients which they diagnosed as over-fulness of blood, and for which they prescribed blood-letting.

rascal, (IV, III, 80) worthless, of little value. In this S.S. the word is an adjective. In M.E. the noun "rascal" denotes a bad fellow. The adjective formed from this would be "rescally."

rebel, (III, I, 40) as an adj. = stubborn, obstinate. In M.E. the noun "rebel", one who revolts against authority, gives the adj. "rebellious."

recover, (I, I, 23) (1) to cure or restore to health; (2) to re-sole shoes.

reek, (III, I, 159) steam, sometimes smoke. Still current in Scotland.

remorse, (II, I, 19) Here S.S. is kindness feelings of pity. But in M.E. the sense is rather feelings of regret for some wrong which one has committed.

repeal, (III, I, 51) here the S.S. is the literal sense of to call back, to re-call. In M.E. it has come to have the special meaning of to withdraw or cancel a law or statute.

replications, (I, II, 50) reply. As used in this S.S. is the reply to a sound, *i.e.* an echo.

repute, (I, II, 173) the S.S. here is "call." In M.E., we do no use it as an active transitive verb, and the usage seems to be limited to the past participles *e.g.* well-reputed; reputed to have said, etc.

resolve, (III, I, 132; III, II, 180; IV, II, 14) to be resolved = to have one's curiosity or doubt settled. This is S.S. and we have no passive usage in M.E. where to resolve is to make up one's mind, to decide.

rheumy, (II, I, 266) S.S. signifies that which causes the flow of rheum, and so causes colds, influenza, rheumatism, etc. Rheumatic diseases were those in which there was a discharge or flow of "the humours" of the body.

rive, (I, III, 6; IV, III, 85) to split or tear. It is still common in Scottish dialect, very uncommon in M.E.

rude, (III, II, 30) here the sense is "rough" or "uncivilised" though it can also mean "ill-mannered."

rumour, (II, IV, 18) the S.S. in this case is "a confused of vague noise." In M.E. it is not applied to sound like this, but means a report or item of news which is unconfirmed.

rote, (IV, III, 98) is always used with the preposition *by,* the meaning of "by rote' being to go over the same thing time and again till it is memorised. Allied to the word "route."

sad, (I, II, 217, 276) this S.S. means "grave or serious," but in M.E. there is the added sense of "grieving."

Save, (III, II, 66; V, V, 69) was commonly used in the sense of "except" in Shakespeare's days. While not obsolete, this usage is now uncommon.

saucy, (I, III, 12; IV, III, 132) in S.S. "insolent" or "insulting." The word, like "naughty" has now become much milder, and denotes playful defiance given by a fried or a child.

scandal, (I, II, 76) Shakespeare uses this as a verb, in the sense of "to slander." There is no such verb in M.E. The noun "scandal" means an affair which is disgraceful and causes comment; something which is shameful and of bad repute. To scandalise a person is to shock his feelings of decency.

scarf, (I, II, 286) probable a ceremonial band placed round the head of an image or person. It now applies to a neck-cloth or muffler.

schedule,	(III, I, 3) any written scroll or paper. Now, in M.E., an official list or catalogue.
secret,	(II, I, 125) able to keep a secret, not likely to reveal confidences. The M.E. sense is that of something hidden or not made known, and the word is not applied to a person.
sennet,	(I, II, 24, 214, Stage Dir.) a flourish of notes from a trumpet, announcing a procession.
senseless,	(I, I, 39) not capable of feeling.
sensible,	(I, III, 18) the opposite of "senseless," *i.e.* "capable of feeling with the physical senses." Now in M.E. we would used the word "conscious," and use "sensible" to describe a stage of intelligence or alertness of the mind.
set upon,	(I, II; V, II, 3) to stake or wager.
several,	(I, II, 318) various, of different kinds. (II, I, 138; V, V, 18) separate, distinct. Shakespeare never seems to use this word in the modern sense of "some" or "a few" with which we are familiar.
several,	(III, II, 10) separately.
shadow,	(I, II, 58) reflection or image.
shrewd,	(II, I, 158) in S.S. keen, deep, or malicious. In M.E. the word means "keen-witted" and usually applies to character or intelligence.
shrewdly,	(III, I, 147) deeply, intensely.
slight off,	(IV, III, 5) to treat with contempt, to put aside as of no importance.
smatch,	(V, V, 46) flavour. In S.S., smack or taste of anything.
soft,	(I, II, 252; III, I, 123) an interjection, meaning "Stop !"
sooth,	(II, IV, 20) S.S. used as a noun, "truth," or as an interjection, Truly." From Old English, *soth,* truth.
sort,	(I, I, 61), class. (I, II, 205), manner, (II, I, 283), in sort = in a way.
speed,	(I, II, 88; II, IV, 40), to make prosper, to send success to. Usually with some appeal to divine guidance, as in "God speed you!" In M.E. the word has come to mean, "to hurry or go fast," though the original meaning is still current.
spleen,	(IV, III, 47) the organ of the body, then supposed to be the seat of bad passions or temper.
spoil,	(III, I, 207) the *Old English Dictionary gives* "the skin of a slaughtered animal." In M.E. has a wider sense, as a noun, of any kind of plunder or booty.
spur,	(V, III, 29) on the spur = at urgent speed, as if spurring on a horse.
spurn at,	(II, I, II) to kick against, to rise up against.

stale,   (I, II, 73; IV, I, 38) to cheapen a thing by making it lose its freshness, to spoil,

stare,   (II, I, 242) to glare at. This is the same as in M.E. But in (IV, III, 278) a special S.S. of "to stand on end" or "to rise up perpendicularly."

stem,   (I, II, 109) to breast, to thrust through anything, as the stem or bow of a ship thrust through the water.

still,   (I, II, 244; III, I, 146) ever, constantly.

stain,   (V, I, 59) stock, family.

submit,   (I, III, 47) to expose one's self.

suburbs,   (II, I, 285) the outskirts or outer fringe of anything. But in M.E. would only mean the outskirts of a city or town. From Latin, *sub,* under; *urbs,* a city.

success,   (II, II, 6; V, III, 65-6) the result of anything, whether good or bad. This Old English usage has become obsolete, and now the word denotes only a good result.

sufferance, (I, III, 84) patience or endurance. (II, I, 115) suffering.

stead,   (V, I, 85) place. This Old English word is now found only in compound forms, as "home-stead," or the word "instead."

sway,   (I, III, 3) government ruling power.

taste,   (IV, I, 34) as a substantive, "in some taste" = to some extent.

tempt,   (I, III, 53; IV, III, 35, 59) to put to the test. (II, I, 266) to risk or venture.

thick,   (V, III, 21) when applied to eyesight, S.S. is "dim." Not so applied in M.E.

thorough, (III, I, 136; V, I, 110) then was use with exactly the same meaning as "through," but has come to be an adjective meaning full or complete in M.E.

tide,   (III, I, 258) the course (of time).

tincture,   (II, II, 89) a colour. This is the technical word used for "colour" in heraldry. Now it means an essence or concentrated liquid, *e.g.* tincture of iodine.

toil,   (II, I, 206) a snare of trap. Becoming obsolete.

trash,   (IV, III, 26, 74) originally bits of broken wood. twigs, etc. found under trees, and this is the S.S. Now has come to mean any waste or useless matter.

tributary, (I, I, 37) a captive or submissive person usually a chief, who has agreed to pay tribute or tax to ruling power.

true-fixed, (III, I, 61) firmly fixed.

turn, (I, II. 56) consider, reflect.

unbraced, (I, III, 48; II, I, 262) with clothes unfastened. (In all proba-bility, Shakespeare was thinking of the "points" by which an Elizabethan doublet was fastened).

undergo, (I, III, 123) to undertake.

unfold, (II, I, 274; 330) In S.S. is usually "reveal" or "disclose."

unmeritable, (IV, I, 12) unworthy, undeserving.

use, (II, II, 25) as a noun, "the natural order of things."

uttermost, (II, I, 213; 214) latest, last.

venture, (IV, III, 222) anything on which something has been staked or risked.

vessel, (V, V, 13) a figurative use, to describe a human being who is the receptacle or container of the soul. In M.E. a vessel is any kind of cup or container.

vouchsafe, (II, I, 313) to deign to accept; to grant an act of grace.

vulgar, (I, I, 74) the literal meaning of the Latin *plebs vulgus* was simply "the common people." The word "vulgar" has come in M.E. to denote rude and disgusting manners.

wafture, (II, I, 246) waving. Obsolete.

warn, (V, I, 5) call to the fight. This in S.S. is little found. In M.E. "to give a caution."

watch, (IV, III, 247) S.S. to keep awake at night. In M.E. to look fixedly at anything.

watchful, (II, I, 98) that which cause loss of sleep. S.S.

weigh, (II, I, 108) to consider, to ponder over.

wind, (IV, I, 32) an intran. vb. meaning to wheel round, to turn.

wit, (I, II, 301) intelligence, understanding, (III, II, 222), inventive power.

while, (I, III, 82) the time, the present. As in the expression, "Woe the while!"

withal, (II, I, 249, 292) besides at the same time.

yearn, (II, II, 129) S.S. to grieve. In M.E. to long for, possibly a misprint for "earn", which is given by some editors in the text.

Classical and Proper Names

Aeneas. Aeneas, the son of Anchises, was member of the royal family
I, II, of Troy. Vergil's *Aeneid* tells how, after the destruction of Troy
112. by the Greeks, Aeneas and his followers settled in Italy and founded the Roman race.

Anchises, When the Greeks burned Troy and Aeneas had to make a hurr-
I, II, ed escape, he carried his aged father, Anchises, on his back out
114. of the burning city.

Ate,
III, I,
270.
the daughter of Zeus, the father of the Gods, who banishe her from Mt. Olympus. In Greek writings, she is the avenger of evil and inflicts punishments on sinners and their posterity.

Brutus.
I, II,
150.
Lucius Brutus, the forefather of the character of the play, belonged to the age of the Tarquin kings. He was himself the son of the sister of King Tarquin the Proud. He led a rising which expelled the kings and set up a Government with himself as the first Consul in Rome. He loved his country so much that he had two of his own sons executed for trying to restore the Tarquin kings. Plutarch says: "the Romans made his statue of brass to be set up in the Capitol along with the images of the kings."

Capitol,
I, III,
136 etc.
one of the finest buildings in Rome, was originally a temple of Jupiter, and stood on the Capitoline hill. Shakespeare is mistaken, however, in thinking that the Senate used to meet there.

Cato.
Marcus Cato, great grandson of Cato the Censor. He stood out as a strong opponent of Caesar, Pompey and Crassus. In B.C. 46 he committed suicide, to prevent himself being taken prisoner by Caesar.

Colossus,
I, II,
185.
the Colossus at Rhodes was described as one of the seven wonders of the world. It was an image of brass, 105 feet in height, with its feet on opposite sides of the harbour entrance. Ships entered between its legs; it was commenced in 300 B.C. and finished after twelve years' work.

Epicurus,
V, I,
76.
a Greek philosopher who founded the Epicurean school of philosophy; B.C. 342-270. He taught that the end of life is happiness or peace of mind resulting from virtue. He held that there were no gods or higher powers who could influence the lives of men. So his followers had no belief in omens and portents, since there were no gods, they thought, to send such warnings.

Erebus,
II, I,
83.
the meaning of the word is "darkness," and it denoted the dark and gloomy region under the earth, through which the spirits of the dead had to pass on their way to Hades after death.

the Fates,
II, III.
14.
the Fates or "Parcae' of the Romans were three women : Clotho, who span the fates of men on her wheel, Lachesis, who assigned her fate to each man, and Atropos, probably the one who terminated the thread.

Forum,
Act III,
II.
the Forum Romanum was a series of buildings round a square enclosure, one of the busiest places in ancient Rome, where most public business was transacted; often spoken of as "the

market place."

Hybla, V, I, 33.	the name of a district containing three towns in Sicily, from one of which was supposed to come a very wonderful kind of honey, often mentioned by classical writers.
Lupercal, III, II, 98.	a cave surrounded by trees on the north side of the Palatine hill in Rome. The name is also used for the festival in honour of the god Lupercus.
Luperci,	priests or devotees performing the rites of the god Lupercus. Originally they formed a College with two classes of priests. Julius Caesar added a third class, and made Antony their high Priest.
Nervii, III, II, 177.	a warlike tribe in that part of Gaul which is now modern Belgium Caesar defeated them in B.C. 58, almost exterminating the whole army of 60,000 armed warriors.
Olympus, III, I, 74.	in Greek mythology, Mount Olympus was the home of the gods, who had their palaces on the summit of its snow-covered heights.
Parthia V, III, 37.	a country to the south-east of the Caspian sea. In B.C. 53 the Romans were defeated at Carrae, and Caesar was making preparations to avenge this defeat, when he was slain.
Philippi,	a city of Macedonia. Here the apostle Paul first preached the Gospel of Christ in A. D. 53.
Plutus, IV, III, 99.	the god of Wealth. It was said that Zeus made him blind, in order that he might bestow his gifts blindly and with no consideration of merit. But Shakespeare may as well be thinking of Pluto, king of Hades.
Pompey,	Pompey, the Triumvir, was brown in 106 B.C. and assassinated at Alexandria after his defeat at Pharsalia. At first an ally of Caesar, he later challenged Julius for supreme power and attached himself to the Senatorial Party. But Caesar "crossed the Rubicon" to accept the challenge, and Pompey had to flee. His sons tried to carry on the struggle against Caesar, but were defeated at Munda just before the action of the play starts.
Sadis, V, I, 79.	capital of Lydia in Asia. In B.C. 42, Plutarch tells us, Brutus and Cassius met at Sardis and united their forces to oppose Caesar.
Stoics, IV, III, 145.	were the followers of Zeno, who set up a school of philosophy at Athens. They taught that true happiness had no connection with external circumstances, but was a state of the inner mind.

Men had to keep free from passion and unaffected by the pleasures of life. They were at the opposite scale from the Epicureans. Mahatma Ghandi was the great modern exponent of the Stoics' creed.

Tarquin,
II, I,
53.
see note on Brutus, Lucius, the last of the legendary kings of Rome, whom the poet Macaulay has celebrated in the episode of Horatius holding the bridge, when Lars Porsena tried to force the Romans to take their king back again.

Thasos,
V, III,
104.
an inland in the Aegean sea, near Philippi.

Troy,
a town in the north-west of Mysia in Asia Minor. The old Greek name of the town was Ilium, and it was the scene of the events in Homers's *Iliad*. After a ten years' siege, it was captured and burned by the Greeks. See Note on Aeneas.

Attention: Students

We request you, for your frank assessment, regarding some of the aspects of the book, given as under:

11 551   **Julius Caesar**
              W. Turner
                                       New Edition 2003

Please fill up the given space in neat capital letters. Add additional sheet(s) if the space provided is not sufficient, and if so required.

(i)   What topic(s) of your syllabus that are important from your examination point of view are not covered in the book ?

....
....
....
....

(ii)   What are the chapters and/or topics, wherein the treatment of the subject-matter is not systematic or organised or updated?

....
....
....

(iii)   Have you come across misprints/mistakes/factual inaccuracies in the book? Please specify the chapters, topics and the page numbers.

....
....
....
....

(iv)   Name top three books on the same subject (in order of your preference - 1, 2, 3) that you have found/heard better than the present book? Please specify in terms of quality (in all aspects).

1 ....
....
2 ....
....
3 ....
....

(v) Further suggestions and comments for the improvement of the book:

....

....

....

....

Other Details:

(i) Who recommended you the book? (Please tick in the box near the option relevant to you.)
     ☐ Teacher   ☐ Friends   ☐ Bookseller

(ii) Name of the recommending teacher, his designation and address:

....

....

....

(iii) Name and address of the bookseller you purchased the book from:

....

....

(iv) Name and address of your institution (Please mention the University or Board, as the case may be)

....

....

(v) Your name and complete postal address:

....

....

....

(vi) Write your preferences of our publications (1, 2, 3) you would like to have ....

....

The best assessment will be awarded half-yearly. The award will be in the form of our publications, as decided by the Editorial Board, amounting to Rs. 300 (total).

Please mail the filled up coupon at your earliest to:
Editorial Department
S. CHAND & COMPANY LTD.,
Post Box No. 5733, Ram Nagar, New Delhi 110 055